COMPLETING YOUR RESEARCH PROJECT

Charlotte Brookfield

Jamie Lewis

COMPLETING YOUR RESEARCH PROJECT

A Guide for the Social Sciences

Sage

1 Oliver's Yard
55 City Road
London EC1Y 1SP

2455 Teller Road
Thousand Oaks
California 91320

Unit No 323-333, Third Floor, F-Block
International Trade Tower,
Nehru Place, New Delhi – 110 019

8 Marina View Suite 43-053
Asia Square Tower 1
Singapore 018960

Editor: Jai Seaman
Assistant editor: Becky Oliver
Production editor: Martin Fox
Marketing manager: Fauzia Eastwood
Cover design: Shaun Mercier
Typeset by: C&M Digitals (P) Ltd, Chennai, India
Printed in the UK

© Charlotte Brookfield and Jamie Lewis 2025

Apart from any fair dealing for the purposes of research, private study, or criticism or review, as permitted under the Copyright, Designs and Patents Act, 1988, this publication may not be reproduced, stored or transmitted in any form, or by any means, without the prior permission in writing of the publisher, or in the case of reprographic reproduction, in accordance with the terms of licences issued by the Copyright Licensing Agency. Enquiries concerning reproduction outside those terms should be sent to the publisher.

Library of Congress Control Number: 2024938667

British Library Cataloguing in Publication data

A catalogue record for this book is available from the British Library.

ISBN 978-1-5296-1710-8
ISBN 978-1-5296-1709-2 (pbk)

Charlotte: For Mum, Dad, Beth and Ben

Jamie: For Rachael, Imogen, Osian, Mum and Dad

CONTENTS

Online Resources — xiii
Acknowledgements — xv
Introduction: Completing Your Social Science Research Project — xvii

    Why have we written this book? — xviii
    What is in a title? — xxii
    Book structure — xxiii
    How to use this book — xxvii

1 What Is Social Science Research and Why Is It Important? — 1

    Introduction — 2
    What is social science research? — 2
    Who does social science research? — 5
    What are the benefits of doing social science research? — 6
    How is social science research conducted? — 8
    Where is social science research undertaken? — 11
    How is social science research presented? — 12
    The importance of developing research questions — 15
    Summary — 20
    What's next? — 22

2 Planning a Social Science Research Project — 25

    Introduction — 26
    Read the module handbook/guide — 27
    Making time — 27
        Producing realistic diaries and timetabling — 27
    Tracking your research trajectory — 28
        Gantt charts — 29
        Kanban boards — 30
    Choosing a topic to research — 32
        Sources of inspiration — 32
        Refining your idea — 33
        Remember you are still learning — 35
    Meeting your supervisor or advisor — 36
    Begin writing — 38
        Producing a research plan — 38

	Summary	44
	What's next?	45
3	**Reviewing Social Science Literature**	**47**
	Introduction	47
	Types of literature review	49
	Why do a literature review?	50
	A different type of essay? Structure and selectivity	52
	Where do you find social science literature?	56
	Effective and active note taking	64
	SQ3R – Survey, question, read, recite, review	66
	How do you write a social science literature review?	67
	Summary	70
	What's next?	72
4	**Being an Ethical Researcher**	**75**
	Introduction	76
	Harmful research	78
	Procedural ethics	80
	Ethics application form	80
	Forward facing documents	90
	Debrief sheets	93
	Personal ethics	93
	Ethics at the edges	95
	The ethics of writing up	96
	Summary	97
	What's next?	98
5	**Methods of Social Science Data Collection**	**101**
	Introduction	102
	Part one: Quantitative methods	102
	Questionnaires	105
	Structured observations	112
	Content analysis	112
	Experiments	115
	Secondary data analysis	116
	Part two: Qualitative methods	118
	Qualitative interviews	119
	Focus groups	122
	Observational techniques	123
	Documents	124
	Social media and online research	125

Creative methods	126
Participatory research	127
Sensory methods	127
Managing the field	128
How much data?	129
Introduction to mixed methods	130
The hybrid methods	130
Part three: Writing your methods chapter	132
Structuring your methods chapter	132
Random sampling techniques	136
Non-random sampling techniques	137
Summary	144
What's next?	146

6 Social Science Data Analysis   149

Introduction	150
Part one: Quantitative data analysis	150
Knowing your data	151
Stage one: Preparing data for analysis	152
Stage two: Descriptive statistics	157
Stage three: Inferential statistics	162
Crosstabulations and chi-square tests	165
Correlation	168
T-Tests and equivalents	169
Quantitative findings summary	170
Part two: Qualitative data analysis	171
So Why Do Qualitative Analysis and Under What Circumstances?	172
General qualitative analysis	173
Creating the research artefact	174
Qualitative data analysis: Some examples	178
Working with text: Thematic analysis of transcripts and fieldnotes	179
Text as stories: Narrative analysis	181
Making sense of documents: Qualitative content analysis (QCA)	182
Making further sense of documents: Documentary analysis	183
Language and order: Conversation analysis	184
Talk matters: Discourse analysis	185
Icons, symbols, signs: Semiotic analysis	186
Mapping the 'situation': Situational analysis	187
Space, time, and everyday life: Rhythmanalysis	187
Interviewing participants about their experiences: Interpretative phenomenological analysis (IPA)	188

Emotions and attitudes: Sentiment analysis		188
Qualitative findings summary		188
Part three: Presenting analysis		189
Dissertation findings and analysis chapters		190
Summary		194
What's next?		195
7	**Presenting Your Social Science Research**	**197**
Introduction		198
Different formats		198
Knowing your audience		199
Compelling oral presentations		201
Structuring a presentation		202
Producing a confident presentation		204
Creating presentation slides		207
Engaging posters		210
Creating a research poster		211
Informative blogposts		214
Promoting your blogpost		215
Captivating podcasts		215
Concise executive summaries		216
Summary		218
What's next?		220
8	**Introducing and Concluding**	**221**
Introduction		221
Part one: The introduction chapter		222
Purpose and presentation		224
What to include?		225
Part two: The conclusion chapter		229
Purpose and presentation		229
What to include?		231
The introduction and conclusion as a couplet		234
Summary		235
What's next?		236
9	**Submitting Your Social Science Research Project**	**237**
Introduction		237
Collating all the chapters		238
Front matter		239

Back matter	243
Revisiting your research questions	244
Checking the requirements	244
Getting feedback from your supervisor	245
Proofreading and editing	245
Plagiarism check	249
Acceptable terminology	250
Dealing with anxiety	250
What will the markers be looking for?	251
Letting go	253
Summary	253
What's next?	254

References	259
Index	285

ONLINE RESOURCES

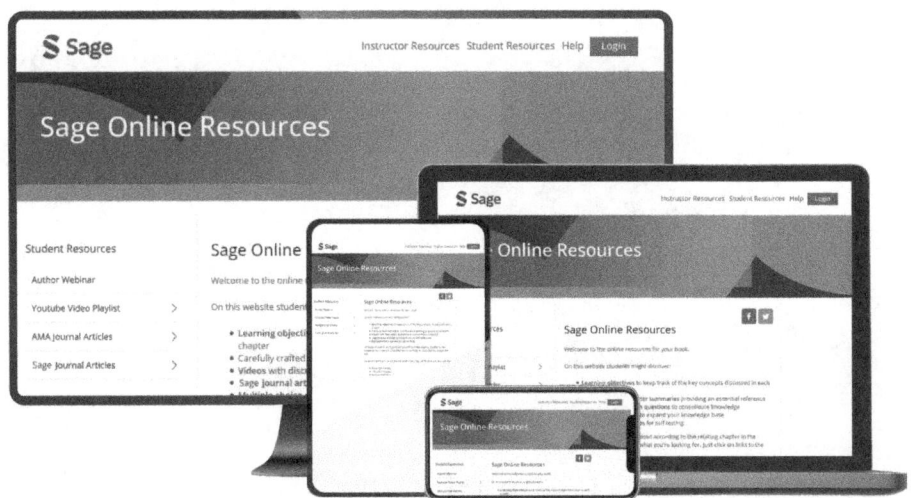

Completing Your Research Project: A Guide for the Social Sciences is supported by a wealth of resources to support teaching, which can be accessed via: **https://study.sagepub.com/brookfieldlewis1e**.

LECTURER RESOURCES

- **PowerPoint decks** to help teach each chapter.
- A **Teaching Guide** with helpful tips on how to explore the content of each chapter.
- **Checklists** to ensure that students have understood the key concepts of each chapter.

ACKNOWLEDGEMENTS

The production of this book has been a shared endeavour. We both took the lead in writing specific chapters before writing over the top and adding to those initial drafts. We were extremely lucky to share draft chapters with generous colleagues who provided invaluable feedback. Our gratitude is extended, in alphabetic order, to Owen Abbott, Charlotte Bates, Roser Beneito-Montagut, Mark Connolly, Rebecca Dimond, Des Fitzgerald, Rod Hick, Jennifer Hoolachan, Kirsty Hudson, Sion Jones, Tomos Jones, Shailen Nandy, Sam Parker, Sioned Pearce, Katherine Quinn, Luke Sloan, Daniel Smith, Victoria Timperley, Gareth Thomas and Malcom Williams for their thoughtful comments and feedback. We are particularly thankful to Victoria Timperley. We would also like to thank the anonymous reviewers and the production team at Sage.

Jamie would also like to thank Paul Atkinson and Sara Delamont for their general kindness and guidance throughout his career.

INTRODUCTION

COMPLETING YOUR SOCIAL SCIENCE RESEARCH PROJECT

If you have chosen to delve into the pages of this book, the chances are that you are either on the verge of beginning a social science research project or you have already taken the initial steps in commencing one. Undertaking a social science research project – often called a dissertation in the United Kingdom (UK) or a capstone or final project in the United States – can be both gratifying and challenging. Whatever your experience, it is often the largest, longest and most demanding assessment that you will have tackled to date, and one in which it is expected that you are self-driven and self-disciplined to complete. The purpose of this book is to serve as your compass, guiding you through the journey of undertaking and writing up your social science research project. We hope that you will find this book, and its accompanying online resources, to be a valuable touchstone to be leant upon alongside the usual sources of institutional support, including supervisors or advisors and module leaders as well as lectures and any accompanying module documentation. Although the book covers the entire journey of conducting a research project, we recognise that some of you may prefer to navigate directly to specific chapters that address certain aspects of the research process or specific questions which you may have. Either approach is perfectly acceptable! It is worth highlighting, though, which there are occasions where we foreshadow a topic before returning to it in more detail in later chapters.

Throughout the book, the terms 'research project', 'dissertation', and 'thesis' are all used interchangeably. However, our preference is to use the term 'dissertation', as it is, in our experience, the most common independent research style assignment undergraduate and master's students are asked to complete. Typically, a dissertation will be the culmination of your degree, bringing together the skills that you have developed in research methods modules with what you have learnt on substantive or conceptual or topic-led modules. This is *your* time to shine! It is your time to formalise a passion that began earlier in your course.

We have written this book with social science students completing a dissertation in mind. However, the messages should be relevant to anybody undertaking a social science research project and may be especially helpful to those with limited experience of carrying out this type of work. Likewise, although this book draws on examples from the social sciences, much of the content, including tips on time management and approaches to editing long documents are relevant to those in other aligned and cognate disciplines.

Principally, the aim of the book is to assist and accompany you in the successful completion of your project. Here, at the beginning of this book, it is important to remind readers that embarking on any type of research project is a significant undertaking. Throughout the book, then, we strongly encourage you to take some basic steps, such as keeping in touch with your supervisor or advisor and allowing yourself sufficient time for editing and formatting as well as other administrative tasks such as creating timetables. This will give you the best chance of enjoying the experience and making the most out of doing a research project whilst minimising stress, especially later down the line. Please do not leave everything to the last minute. Working on your dissertation should be seen as a 'gradual' journey. We wish you the very best of luck and hope you find the world of social science research as rewarding and exciting as we do!

WHY HAVE WE WRITTEN THIS BOOK?

We have co-convened a large social science undergraduate dissertation module for the past five years. This module provides students with the opportunity to explore a social science topic of their choice, in detail, by conducting a small scale but substantial piece of independent research. Running across two semesters, we deliver weekly two-hour lectures, which are supported by fortnightly supervisory meetings. The module assessment is a written dissertation of between 8,000 to 10,000 words, worth 80% of the module mark. Students are also asked to produce a 15-minute presentation, followed by a five-minute question-and-answer session, which is worth the remaining 20% of the module mark. The dissertation module attracts undergraduate students undertaking degree programmes in sociology, social analytics, social science, criminology, social psychology, education and social policy. Additionally, joint honours students studying one of these subjects alongside history, politics, Welsh and journalism can also study the module. Together, we have also produced dissertation resources for postgraduate students on master's programmes in the areas of education, social policy, and criminology. With such an eclectic cohort that have various (though admittedly, connected) disciplinary hinterlands, it might come as little surprise that we read research project proposals covering a broad spectrum of social issues and problems. In that spirit, there is extraordinarily little restriction on the topics that students can research. Indeed, we encourage their social science imagination to run wild. However, of course, there are some restrictions on the way they go about studying the topic and we deal with this specifically in Chapter 4 (*Being an Ethical Researcher*). To take an extreme example, while the topic of female killers' representation in the media is not off limits for criminology students, the approach to studying it might be restricted to the content analysis of newspaper articles or news broadcasts. It would not include interviewing female prisoners to ask them how they feel they have been represented. Such a project would need a much more experienced hand and various levels of (ethical) clearance from both the university and the prison service.

The reason we include this here at the beginning of the book is to stress the elasticity of social science as a broad disciplinary area that has a wide range of substantive topics to offer students, a diversity reflected in the array of methods which can be used to study them. Social science is undeniably promiscuous and this, we maintain, is the reason this book is so important. Equally it is the reason why writing such a book is so challenging. We will pause here to state emphatically that there are already some excellent dissertation and research project books on the market. Our personal favourites include Gary Thomas (2023a) *How to Do Your Research Project: A Guide for Students*, 4th edition and Clark et al. (2019) *How to Do Your Social Research Project or Dissertation*. However, as dissertation module convenors, we constantly field two main questions from students: (1) What stage should I be at in my research project? and (2) What does a completed research dissertation look like? Both questions are reasonable, and understandable, but, as you will learn as you work your way through this book, there is no straightforward answer to either query. That said, these two questions have driven the production of this book, and we hope you find reassurance and guidance in the detail we provide. At its core, then, this book does two things. Chiefly, it functions as your companion and guide suggesting a logical order in which to complete the stages of your research project. Think of it too as a security blanket. Our hope is that it will boost confidence, empower you, and provide you comfort when required. Many students we have taught come away from lectures or supervisory meetings with a purpose and renewed confidence, only to begin to lose that belief after a few days. The intention behind writing this book is that it can act as a stopgap between those teaching activities and therefore help keep your confidence levels high. We also acknowledge and appreciate that when you begin this journey, it can often feel overwhelming. Where do I begin? How do I begin? How can I show progress? Am I on track? How much time should I be dedicating to the project? These questions reverberate across the lecture hall year after year. This book sets you tangible tasks to complete from the outset, enabling you to show supervisors and lecturers your nascent ideas and the processes through which they are maturing and developing coherence. Thinking of your research project as a process or a journey helps you determine where you are in the project, what you have done, and what needs to be done to move forward.

Secondly, and unlike most textbooks of this ilk, it discusses, in detail, how you might go about structuring each chapter of your dissertation. Writing is a significant part of doing social science research, transforming your project from a process you are engaged in to one that you have completed. Converting those thoughts and ideas that you are processing internally into words on the paper or computer screen is the vehicle for sharing your thoughts. The aim is to convince others (including markers) through cogent argumentation and clear presentation. This book, then, helps you complete a *social science* research project by also showing you how to write one.

But just as you will all develop your own style, we have ours too. Others would have written a textbook like this with a different focus, a different argumentation and presented it differently too. However, we feel strongly that the research dissertation or thesis has a general, typical, structure – silhouette, if you will – that students would do well to follow. The various chapters of a research dissertation should act as standalone parts of a coherent whole. Different sections should come together to form a structured and cohesive piece of work that can be read (and marked) by others. That is, a dissertation should have a clear throughline running throughout the document. The order in which this is presented on paper (or on your screen), though, is unlikely to reflect the order in which you complete these tasks. This is another area where we feel this book can help: highlighting how conducting social science research is often circular and not a linear process as is suggested in the finished written product.

The book then is a deep dive into the magic circle of undertaking a social science research project. In the chapters that follow we reveal the tricks social science researchers use to produce a final written product that makes sense to an interested reader, and crucially a reader *not* involved in the undertaking of the research. Alongside these tricks, we also provide tips on how to go about conducting and writing up the research. The book is aimed at final year undergraduate students as well as master's students doing a social science research project. We root the book in our own experiences, from our position as both social science educators and researchers in the field. Consequently, you will see several examples from our own research. Importantly, we also include examples from the projects of students we have supervised through the various chapters as well as questions which they have posed to us, students just like you. We also include sections on both qualitative and quantitative social science projects as well as shorter sections on mixed method approaches.

Jamie is an experienced qualitative researcher, with expertise in observational, documentary, and interview-based research methods. He is a sociologist whose research straddles the relatively porous boundaries between the Sociology of Science or Science and Technology Studies (STS), the Public Understanding of Science (PUS) and the Sociology of Mystery. His interests extend from developments in qualitative research to the boundaries between science, pseudo-science, and non-science. Jamie has also researched and studied the public understanding of risk, science activism, and the practical accomplishment of scientific facts, spending time interviewing scientists and observing their work in laboratories. You will see reference to Jamie's current work examining the community of Bigfooting throughout the book.

Charlotte is an experienced quantitative researcher in the field of education studies. She teaches across social analytics and quantitative methods programmes. Charlotte's specific interest is in the crisis of 'number' in the social sciences. Consequently, her research has explored different approaches to engaging students with quantitative methods. This research informs Charlotte's teaching practice and drives her ambition to develop innovative approaches to inspire interest and engagement in quantitative methodologies amongst students. You will read examples of Charlotte's work on mathematics teaching and learning in various chapters in the book.

Importantly, both of us have been in your position. Both of us have had to undertake a dissertation as part of our degrees. Jamie was a joint honours undergraduate studying psychology and sociology. In his final year he was tasked with producing an 8,000-word dissertation on *empathic accuracy*, also known in some quarters as 'mindreading'. This involved showing participants a set of videos in which couples were talking about their life. Participants were asked to complete a questionnaire, from which, dependent on their responses, they were categorised as either individualistic, pro-social, or competitive. Participants were then asked to infer what each person in the video was thinking. The hypothesis was that pro-social participants would be more empathically accurate than participants categorised as individualistic.

Jamie then went on to do an MSc in Social Science Research Methods where he undertook a 20,000-word dissertation considering the everyday coping strategies that people living with irritable bowel syndrome (IBS) employed. This drew from a qualitative questionnaire that he administered to members of an IBS support group. He produced a temporal analysis of the routines and rituals that people adopted, locating the work in medical sociology but with a strong influence from those theorising about time. Finally, his PhD concerned the ways in which two new scientific disciplines developed and secured coherence. This Science and Technology Studies (STS) project drew from 40 semi-structured interviews mostly with scientists based in the UK working in the nascent academic fields of Bioinformatics and Proteomics.

Charlotte's undergraduate degree was in Education (with psychology). For her final year dissertation, Charlotte facilitated focus groups with parents at two schools and carried out a discourse analysis to explore the ways in which parents used language to justify and explain what they gave their children to eat for lunch. Like Jamie, Charlotte then went on to complete an MSc in Social Science Research Methods. In her dissertation, Charlotte undertook survey research with students studying post-compulsory qualifications in schools and colleges. Specifically, Charlotte was interested in finding out what factors determined students' subject choices. This research involved Charlotte designing and distributing a paper questionnaire and then subsequently inputting the data into a statistical software package to analyse. Finally, her PhD explored sociologists' attitudes toward quantitative research methods. Again, for this research, Charlotte designed a questionnaire. Unlike her MSc research, this questionnaire was distributed online to sociologists working in the UK, the Netherlands and New Zealand. This allowed Charlotte to make international comparisons about the place of quantitative methods in the discipline in different countries.

In this book, we bring together our knowledge of completing social science dissertations, dissertations just like the ones that you are undertaking, with our more recent experience of designing and conducting qualitative and quantitative research projects. We combine our skills in supervising and teaching students to guide you on your research journey. We also share with you examples of well-designed and executed research projects, as well as some of the challenges we have faced as researchers, providing you with practical tips for avoiding or overcoming them. The book unapologetically makes reference to research from our colleagues at the Cardiff University School of Social

Sciences, a department which is home to the longstanding Ethnography, Culture and Interpretative Analysis Group, and the Cardiff Q-Step Centre of Excellence in Quantitative Methods Teaching and Learning, as well as where the journals *Qualitative Research* and the *International Journal of Social Research Methodology* are edited from.

WHAT IS IN A TITLE?

Deciding on a title for a manuscript is a surprisingly challenging task. We know many colleagues who have been kept awake at night, agonising over naming their book. Here, in the UK, there ran, for three decades, a well-known television advertisement for Ronseal – a wood staining preserve used to coat and protect wood from the changeable weather in the UK. The advert is best known for its punchy and direct strapline – 'Ronseal: *does exactly what it says on the tin.*' Today that term forms part of the common vernacular in the UK, stabilising into a common idiom that means an accurate and fair definition of its properties: simple, straightforward, and not masquerading as anything else. In determining the title for this textbook, we too wanted the title to reflect the contents without being too florid or nebulous. We wanted a title that *'does exactly what it says on the paper (or screen)'*. We hope therefore that *Completing Your Research Project* works as an accompanying guide that helps you undertake and finish a piece of social science research.

Crucially, the book is a guide. It does not, and simply cannot, include everything that you need to know to complete your unique and idiosyncratic project. If it did, there would be little, if any, need for supervisors, advisors, and lecturers. For the avoidance of doubt – there absolutely is. Instead, what we have set out to provide in the pages of this book, and through the online resources, is a textbook that functions as a signpost, directing you to the relevant sources of expertise and information available to you. We provide a general template for what a social science research project involves, how you might go about tackling it, and the common conventions for reporting what you have found. We also explore some of the informal aspects of undertaking a social science research project or dissertation such as managing your time, dealing with anxiety, and what you can expect from the supervisory relationship. These aspects might not always be explicitly taught or formalised on your course, but they are crucial for producing a successful project.

However, as nascent social scientists, you should not take our statement at face value or without critical scrutiny. Let us start as we mean to go on by first assessing this claim, by paying closer attention to our title, which is divided here into its four component parts.

Completing: *the act of finishing a task*

Completing is a verb and a method. It is the process of finishing something, of getting to the end. It suggests that the task has a temporal component that begins somewhere and involves effort and perseverance to conclude. This book takes you on a journey from preparing and designing your research project all the way through to data collection, writing up, and submission.

Your: *a form of the possessive case of 'you'*

The word 'your' indicates that the object or subject being discussed belongs to you. Here, the word 'your' recognises that every social science research project is different, if only subtly so. That difference might simply be you, but what a huge and important difference that is. 'Your' also recognises that the project is an independent piece of work which you must undertake and lead on. This textbook will support you in that achievement. It is a useful guide that provides general tips. It recognises that all research journeys differ and so it directs you to the relevant people you can discuss your specific journey and project with.

Research Project: *a systematic study of a topic*

The phrase 'research project' denotes a study where you ask a searching question or set of questions and methodically endeavour to answer the question(s) through a form of systematic evidence-gathering and analysis. This is then detailed and justified during the write-up. Most research projects tend to have both a conceptual – theoretical – and empirical – referring to data collection – strand to them. In this book, we presume you are conducting an empirical piece of work that involves the collection and/or analysis of data with the aim of contributing to a body of academic literature.

Put together, then, *Completing Your Research Project* is a guide that has been written to help you understand what a social science research project looks like, something with a structure suitable for the disciplinary diversity we outline in this chapter. We will walk you through the lifecycle of a project, explaining what you might expect, and, in turn, what is expected of you at each stage of a research project. Throughout, we recognise that each project is as unique as the researcher undertaking it. To achieve this, the textbook is divided into chapters that relate to the key tasks and milestones you will face when undertaking a research project.

BOOK STRUCTURE

Chapter 1 – *What Is Social Science Research and Why Is It Important?* – sets out what we understand by the term *social sciences*, detailing who might most benefit from reading this book. It stresses the importance of social science for our understanding of global contemporary problems and outlines the challenges social science researchers face when studying the complexity involved in these issues. The chapter also acknowledges that a social science research project might have various audiences or publics or counter-publics (Warner 2002, Burawoy 2005, Lewis et al. 2023), e.g., academics, students, policy makers, charities, governmental institutions, 'the general public,' all of whom will receive and digest information differently. The focus of this textbook is to showcase how you, as a student, might undertake and write up a dissertation or research report drawn from your research project. This first chapter also recognises the various forms that the findings of research projects can be disseminated in, from the more traditional journal article or monograph through to more contemporary digital forms such as blogs and podcasts. This is then further developed in Chapter 7 (*Presenting Your Social Science Research*). Crucially, we also dedicate space in Chapter 1 to discuss the importance of developing robust research questions that anchor your project and guide your research journey, before importantly outlining the typical structure of a social science dissertation.

A major thread running through the textbook is the importance of managing your time. We want to help you understand that completing a research project is not something you can leave until the end. It needs to be approached iteratively. Most importantly, it is a craft that you can continue to work on (and improve at). Chapter 2 – *Planning a Social Science Research Project* – specifically focusses on sketching out your research journey. The chapter encourages you, from the outset, to consider where you are on your research journey and where you want to end up. This can then be translated into a series of steps and actions required to achieve this goal, making the process feel more manageable. It will also help you to identify if there are any gaps that need addressing such as training opportunities. As part of this, we discuss designing a 'doable' research project, one which is coherent, feasible, and achievable to study and complete with the resources at hand and time available. This might mean you need to narrow your focus a little, not being overly ambitious and not over-reaching or flying too close to the sun, while still generating interesting and meaningful findings. It is often the case that students come to us with very interesting initial ideas, but they are too grand (and thus unachievable) for a student project. Remember, a good research project is a completed research project. We provide several examples of time management tools, which we encourage you to use such as Gantt charts and Kanban boards and tips for managing your project. We also provide an indicative research plan which we recommend you draft in the early stages of your project.

Chapter 3 – *Reviewing Social Science Literature* – centres on how you might approach finding the academic literature you want to locate your work in. The Literature Review is almost certainly the first substantive chapter of your dissertation that you begin drafting. Chapter 3 presumes you have read the chapter *Planning a Social Science Research Project* and sketched out your research design. The Literature Review chapter is then where you begin to formalise both the topic you want to study and the way you want to research it. The main purpose of reviewing the academic literature is to help you to further narrow the gaze of your knowledge, focussing in on your specific topic and proposed methodology. Reviewing the literature adds robust context to the topic at hand and should help inform your methodological approach (Maggio et al. 2016). The formative intention of a Literature Review is to collect pertinent, timely research on your area of interest and to synthesise it into a coherent summary of the state of the field, identifying gaps and illustrating any (in-)consistencies. As such in the Literature

Review you should develop a line of argument that informs your research questions. Beyond describing the purpose of the Literature Review, Chapter 3 details the numerous ways you can structure this chapter as well as providing tips on how and where to search for literature, highlighting the importance of selectivity and academic scrutiny.

The fourth chapter – *Being an Ethical Researcher* – discusses the necessity for putting ethical concerns front and centre of your project. A doable project is also an ethically sensitive project, one which considers the potential risks for participants in your study, for you as a researcher, and for the university or organisation which you are representing. Here, we discuss both procedural and personal ethics or what might be understood as institutional and *in-situ* ethics. We recognise that being out and about conducting your research can never be fully reflected in an account of the research field on an ethics form. Dynamic situations will always arise. Ethics, then, is better thought of as a mindset (as well as a process to navigate). At the same time, having peers, colleagues, and lecturers look over, assess, and provide comments on the ethics of a research project can only strengthen your work and offer further protection for all involved. After all, peer review is the bread and butter of academic work. Therefore, the chapter functions partly as a practical guide on what to expect when completing an ethics application, and partly as a chapter that discusses the purpose of achieving institutional ethical approval, including some of the current debates on the subject.

After drafting your Literature Review, the next step is typically to begin working on your Methods chapter. Hopefully, you will have already got a clear idea of the most appropriate methods to use to answer your fledgling research questions. You might also have submitted an ethics application to your institution detailing your methodological approach. Chapter 5 – *Methods of Social Science Data Collection* – discusses some of the most popular and pervasive social science research methods that you can employ and the reasons why you might choose them for your own social science research project. The chapter contains a section detailing quantitative methods such as questionnaire design, experiments, and secondary data analysis. It also includes a section on qualitative research methods where both traditional and more contemporary forms, such as observational techniques, interviews, documentary methods, and sensory methods are explained. It also discusses mixed methods projects but cautions that for a student research project, with all its attendant time limitations, there needs to be a compelling reason to combine methodological approaches. To this end, students working on their research design might want to read this chapter out of order and to return to it again when commencing data collection/production. Chapter 5 concludes by suggesting a general structure for writing your Methods chapter, which you can begin drafting before entering the research field.

Following a similar structure to Chapter 5, Chapter 6 on *Social Science Data Analysis* is divided into three sections: quantitative data analysis, qualitative data analysis and presenting your data. The first section draws on data from the UK National Survey of Sexual Attitudes and Lifestyles (2010–2012) to introduce approaches to the statistical analysis of numerical data. Each of the three stages – data preparation, the production of descriptive statistics, and doing inferential statistics is discussed and explained in turn. The second section of the chapter discusses some of the practical concerns that you should consider if you decide to draw on qualitative research methods. We introduce some of the most popular types of qualitative data analysis such as thematic analysis, narrative analysis, documentary analysis, and conversation analysis. We also direct readers to Sage Research Methods Datasets, an international pedagogical data analysis resource, for more step-by-step instructions on how to undertake these analyses, as well as Sage Foundations. Once you have collected and analysed your data, the next step is to present and make sense of your main findings. The final section of this chapter, then, discusses how you might present your findings and analysis in your dissertation.

We anticipate that most of you who are producing a dissertation as part of your research project might also be asked to put together another output such as a short report, a poster, a blog or a presentation too. As such, Chapter 7 called *Presenting Your Social Science Research* is devoted to presenting other types of 'research' outputs. For example, we provide tips and suggestions on how you might deliver a presentation of your project, create a poster, craft a blog entry, produce an executive summary or put together a podcast. While these different formats demand specific styles of presentation, they have more in common than you might first think. The chapter provides some useful generic guidance on how to present your research to different audiences that covers a range of different outputs. As part of this, we also discuss the importance of knowing your audience.

Chapter 8 concerns the topping and tailing of your research project. We present and discuss – *Introducing and Concluding* – as sibling chapters that have a family resemblance to one another. While one is the first substantive chapter that a reader or marker will encounter in your written dissertation and the other the last chapter, they tend to be written in partnership toward the end of the project journey. As before, the sequence in which you draft your thesis does not reflect the order in which those chapters are presented in the finished product. The Introduction and Conclusion chapters should have a symmetry to them: they tend to be of similar word length with the Introduction telling the reader what it is you are going to do and the Conclusion telling the reader what it is you have done. In line with the rest of the textbook, we include sections suggesting what to include when writing these chapters.

The closing chapter – *Submitting Your Social Science Research Project* – details what work is required to get your written dissertation ready for submission. Primarily, it focusses on editing and formatting as well as producing the front matter of your thesis: the content page, abstract, and acknowledgements. We discuss referencing conventions and proofreading before considering other matters such as 'letting go', dealing with anxiety, and writer's block. The key message of this section is that good enough really is good enough. All research projects are open to further tinkering but at some point, the project needs to be submitted to be assessed. A reminder of the maxim that a 'completed project is a submitted one'. So long as you have followed all the steps covered in this book, especially keeping an open channel of communication with your supervisor and giving yourself enough time to edit your final draft, then we expect that you will have completed a well-rounded social science research project. This final chapter includes a checklist to help ensure that you have completed all the sections of your social science research project. You may find it helpful to refer to this checklist as you progress with your project. Alternatively, you may wish to refer to the checklist before submission to check that your research project contains all the necessary elements.

HOW TO USE THIS BOOK

We envisage this book to be relevant to a whole spectrum of disciplines including, but not limited to, anthropology, business studies, communication studies, criminology, cultural studies, development studies, economics, education, history, human geography, linguistics, marketing, organisational studies, psychology, social analytics, social sciences, social policy, social work, sociology, and science and technology studies (STS). We must stress again that this book is not a replacement for the lectures, workshops, and supervisory sessions on your research project module. Rather, it should be used as a reassuring accompaniment to the formal resources provided to you on your university course, which you can digest at your own pace. Your first port of call for any information about completing a social science research project should always be the lecturers and supervisors on your course, and the resources they provide. There will be subtle but important differences in how different institutions and even departments or schools in the same institution expect your research project to be conducted and presented. Always refer to your course convenors and module handbooks as the ultimate authority on these expectations. This book has been written to supplement your university experience and to help you prepare as best you can to ask the right questions of your lecturers. The structure of the book is intended to mirror your research journey. Again, it is important to remind you that this order is different to the order presented in a completed dissertation thesis. However, each chapter works as a freestanding resource, and it is possible to move back and forth and skip chapters that do not reflect the stage of your research project journey you are at. For example, Chapter 1 (*What Is Social Science Research and Why Is It Important?*) considers the importance of research questions, but it would be perfectly acceptable to read Chapter 3 (*Reviewing Social Science Literature*) on reviewing the literature before ruminating over your research questions. Each chapter in the book begins with a set of chapter objectives and concludes with a checklist and reflective task or set of tasks, which we encourage you to complete. This should enable you to demonstrate your understanding of the content included and to think about how that content relates to your own unique research project. We provide a detailed reference list at the end of the book, which includes the location of the Sage Datasets and Sage Foundations entries discussed in Chapter 6 (*Social Science Data Analysis*). There are also accompanying PowerPoint decks available for each chapter which you can access as part of the online resources. In full, the book aims to achieve the following objectives:

- To boost your confidence in completing a social science research project.
- To function as a touchstone to be accessed in the days and/or weeks between formal lectures and supervisory meetings.
- To signpost you to the relevant sources of information and literature.
- To act as a navigational tool through your dissertation journey.
- To help manage the dissertation process by setting realistic and tangible milestones.
- To introduce you to ways to approach and structure your social science research project.
- To describe the various types of data collection tools and analytic techniques available to you.
- To showcase how you might go about writing up a social science research project.
- To talk you through the steps involved in submitting your research project.
- To direct you to the requisite sources of help at your institution.

Good luck and *bon voyage* on wherever your social science research journey takes you.

1
WHAT IS SOCIAL SCIENCE RESEARCH AND WHY IS IT IMPORTANT?

We begin this first chapter by stressing the significance of social science research and outlining what is entailed in undertaking a social science research project. We emphasise the importance of developing clear, crisp, and cogent research questions that both anchor and direct your research project and which can be clearly and directly answered during the lifecycle of your project. We discuss the benefits of undertaking a social science research project to both you and the wider community. Recognising that students will have different interests and varied backgrounds, we illustrate the ways in which a research project might be an attractive proposition to undertake for all manner of reasons. Examples include furthering an interesting module you studied, choosing a research topic that is culturally timely or newsworthy and/or thinking about your hobbies or potential career pathways. Finally, we provide a skeletal structure of what a social science dissertation or thesis should look like, including an outline of the main substantive chapters such as the (i) Introduction, (ii) Literature Review, (iii) Methods, (iv) Findings, (v) Analysis and (vi) Conclusion, as well as detailing the skills that you likely will develop from undertaking a project.

Chapter Objectives

- To understand the broad range of topics that can be explored or examined in a social science research project.
- To recognise and consider the benefits of undertaking a social science research project.
- To consider the different approaches to collecting data for a social science research project.

(Continued)

- To identify potential sources of existing data for a social science research project.
- To understand the main components of a written social science research report or dissertation.
- To begin developing clear, purposeful research questions for a social science research project.

INTRODUCTION

To begin, we ask three questions in this chapter: (i) What is social science research? (ii) Why is it important? and (iii) Who is it for? In doing so, we set out the importance of social science research for all sorts of people and publics and showcase some examples of how social science research can contribute to knowledge as well as influence policy and practice. Almost by definition, the social sciences are plural and diverse, so we also spend time demonstrating the breadth and potential variety of social science research projects on offer for you to undertake and discuss why you might choose them.

Although social science research can be disseminated in many ways and via myriad media depending on the audience, including academic journal articles, books, reports, presentations, and even blog posts and podcasts, there are key components and a generic structure that is generally followed when presenting research both textually and orally (see Chapter 7: *Presenting Your Social Science Research*). In this chapter, then, we also introduce you to the main components that make up a research project and stress the importance of developing clear, robust, and effective research questions, which both firmly ground and direct the research project.

Finally, we discuss the main skills that you will develop while undertaking a social science research project and consider how these skills might be beneficial for your future. Various key terms that appear repeatedly throughout this book are also introduced.

WHAT IS SOCIAL SCIENCE RESEARCH?

The term 'social sciences' is a rather elastic, umbrella category, which includes various disciplines such as sociology, criminology, social analytics, education, human geography, psychology, economics, politics, social policy and communication studies, among many others. While all different, these disciplines share a common focus on studying the social world and the social structures, groups, and individuals within it. Easy to define, then! Well, in truth, it is not so straightforward. If you were to ask 100 'social scientists' to define the term 'social sciences', you would likely receive 100 (slightly) different responses. But despite the likely diversity in definitions, there is a tendency among scholars to consider the roots of social sciences as a unifying factor. The origin story, to use the terminology of Franklin and McNeil (1993), of the social sciences, is characterised by significant societal shifts in the 19th century like the industrial revolution, the scientific revolution, the emergence of capitalism, and the broader transition to modernity. Yet, this 'traditional' narrative, itself a mid-20th century retrospective, has recently faced robust challenges for its perceived bias in favour of the contributions of a specific group of individuals: white, male, European scholars such as Karl Marx, Adam Smith, Georg Simmel, Max Weber, Friedrich Engels, Sigmund Freud, and Émile Durkheim who were all dealing with and trying to understand the social problems of their time. In making this critique, most point to other scholars that have been written out of the social science story, such as Ibn Khaldun, a 14th century North African social philosopher writing several decades before those typically highlighted in the social science tradition (Irwin 2018). Indeed, contemporary voices, including Woodman and Threadgold (2021) and Bhambra and Holmwood (2021), now advocate for a more inclusive and de-colonised approach to the social sciences which recognises and addresses historical omissions in the canon, scholars such as Octavia Hill (Wohl 1971), Harriet Martineau (Hoecker-Drysdale 2011), Jane Addams (Deegan 1988) and W.E.B. Du Bois (Abbott 2023), to pave the way for more productive advancements in the field.

So, if the origin story is not as unifying as was once suggested, what else links the social sciences? Its methods, surely? Again, we would be hard pressed to argue this with any confidence. Within the social sciences, diverse, and often incompatible, positions on theoretical frameworks, research methods, and even the fundamental concept of 'the social' coexist, leading to a variety of different methodological and theoretical perspectives (Lewis et al. 2023). For example, within the United Kingdom (UK), sociology is characterised as a more qualitative discipline (Strong 1988, Williams et al. 2017), whereas, in the United States of America (USA), quantitative research is dominant (Bechhofer 1981, Gartrell and Gartrell 2002, Seale 2008) and, in France, it is often theoretically driven (Lamont 2000). That is, even when examining a single discipline of the social sciences, internal divisions persist, some of which concern what has been termed the **methodological divide**. Qualitative research within the social sciences draws inspiration from a more humanities-oriented perspective, emphasising theory-building and constructivism, as exemplified by works such as Berger and Luckmann (1991), Glaser and Strauss (1967), and Urquhart (2019). In contrast, quantitative research leans towards experimental methodologies characterised by deduction and falsification, akin to approaches found in the natural sciences (Popper 1935).

However, despite all this messiness, the term 'social sciences' does mean something (to universities, to policy makers, to the broader public). Principally, it entails some type of systematic and theoretical approach to exploring the social world so to provide an updated understanding of or insight into society (Grossman 2021). It is a phrase that covers various disciplines that study society, its social institutions and the human relationships within it. It is a term that involves studying the mundane, the typical, the routine as well as the 'carnivalesque' (Bakhtin 1968) – the unusual, the extreme, the colourful. Moreover, despite recent public and political criticisms, it is gaining traction in some quarters. For example, data highlights an increase in the number of students in the UK studying social science at post-compulsory levels (Revise Sociology 2023). Indeed, in the academic year 2000/1, 141,665 students were enrolled on a social science degree in the UK (HESA 2001), but this increased to 286,325 students by the academic year 2021/22 (HESA 2023). Many of these students will have embarked on a social science research project, just like you are doing.

So, why have we begun this book by discussing the various positions, perspectives, and cultural preferences in social science research. Well, the broad scope of the social sciences means that the topics you have on offer to research are rich and diverse, including, for instance, health and wellbeing, education and employment, everyday life, the environment, the family and kinship, access and inequalities, poverty, crime and policing, gender, race, class, science and medicine as well as housing and migration. This can pose a distinct set of challenges for social science researchers. Often social science research will involve examining and exploring parts of the human world which are difficult to measure, such as behaviours, meanings, experiences, attitudes, and feelings. But it also offers huge opportunities since the social is entangled in all our lives, impacting everyone, you, your family, your friends, your peers on your course, your work colleagues.

For example, the aims of social science research can include tracking change over time such as exploring the various stages of fatherhood (Shirani and Henwood 2011), comparing different groups – either explicitly or implicitly – (see Allen et al. 2017), exploring the impacts of a new policy or practice such as welfare changes (Harrison 2014), and making forecasts and predictions (van Creveld 2020; Chen et al. 2021) though Grossman et al. (2023) argue that this is not our strength. Work can be **normative** pertaining to establishing the values that best fit the needs of society (how it should be or how we would like it to be) or **descriptive** pertaining to how it currently is. Social science research is interested in both the big and small questions too, but what connects social scientists is their distinctive way of thinking about the social world – what C. Wright Mills (1959) called the **sociological imagination** and what we refer to in this book as the **social scientific imagination**. This way of thinking involves making connections between what happens in people's everyday life with the broader social context in which we live. For instance, the reason why there is an extended queue in your local foodbank is not something that can be solely understood in isolation; it is very likely to be connected to an increase in inflation and food prices. Likewise, a rise in unemployment should not be attributed to the individuals who find themselves out of work, but instead considered and understood within the context of job market trends and societal factors influencing unemployment rates, including technological advancements, or systemic inequalities that affect job opportunities for certain groups. Wright Mills discussed this connection or relationship in terms of how personal or private troubles – everyday concerns which we all face – are rooted in public issues; that there is a structural basis for people's problems and circumstances. Making sense of this connection – whether you are interested in the minutiae of everyday life (like ethnographers are) or macro, global problems (like quantitative social and public policy scholars) – is then a central task for nascent social scientists like you.

As such, despite the tendency for certain social science disciplines to favour different approaches, and the dramas over its beginnings (Franklin and McNeil 1993, Knorr-Cetina 1999), there are commonalities and crossovers in social science research and a generic structure that is often used in the presentation of research findings that we highlight later in this chapter and throughout the rest of the book (see also Chapter 7: *Presenting Your Social Science Research*). More concretely, in this book, we discuss approaches to research across the social science disciplines and draw on a variety of examples from education, sociology, criminology and social policy as well as other disciplines to help induct you into the variety of questions asked, methods drawn from, forms of analysis, and means of presentation used within the social sciences.

WHO DOES SOCIAL SCIENCE RESEARCH?

Naturally enough, social science research is undertaken by academic researchers working in university social science departments across the globe from Australia to the USA, from the Global South to Europe, from Asia to Africa. However, social science research occurs in other settings too. For example, non-governmental organisations (NGOs), public opinion and data companies, schools, charities, government organisations, independent and private research institutions, trade unions, large businesses, lobby groups and local authorities all conduct a type of social science research to help them identify trends, evaluate practice, and improve provisions. These, of course, are all organisations and places where social science students such as yourself, might look to work in the future.

Yet, there is lively debate and discussion concerning the place of social science research in modern society and who can (or who is best placed to) undertake such research (see Chapter 5: *Methods of Social Science Data Collection*). Concerns about the place for social science have been fuelled by, among other things, the rise of Big Data; colossal amounts of data which are collected and harvested routinely using various algorithms and super computers, including transactional data as well as social media data. For some commentators, data is the new oil (Hirsch 2014). This means that companies, such as Amazon, Google, Tesco, and Walmart, now have stored a wealth of data, which can provide insights into social behaviours, patterns and trends in our society. However, questions have been raised by academics (Bartlett et al. 2018) over the extent to which these organisations can provide the necessary substantive social insights to interpret and understand these data. Data are not only valuable, but they are value-laden too. Such theorists argue that the role of social science researchers is to bring methodological rigour, ethical sensitivity, and a conceptual understanding to research findings, some of which are grounded in relevant literature and lineage. While these arguments are compelling, as are arguments that we need to decolonise as well as internationalise social science research, it is highly likely that continued developments in technology and AI (Artificial Intelligence), in particular, will open further opportunities for the way in which social science data is collected and analysed, both inside and outside universities, providing new and exciting opportunities as well as challenges for those studying the social sciences.

What we strongly believe, though, is that having a grounding in social science research will aid anybody attempting to collect and make sense of social data. We add this here as our job is to demystify the research process, to open the *Blackbox* (Pinch 1992, Latour 1999) of research so to speak, to make it visible, by demonstrating how it is a craft with various skills to be learnt and finessed. Students studying the social sciences have opportunities to undertake their own research during their degree programme to develop these critical and analytic skills. For some students, undertaking a research project or a dissertation is even a compulsory requirement of their degree programme. This can often be the case if the degree is accredited by a professional body. For example, in the UK, psychology and social psychology students must complete an independent research project to fulfil the requirements set out by the British Psychology Society (BPS), which accredits psychology degree programmes in the UK. This accreditation also comes with some limits on what can and cannot be studied and the way in which students go about researching the topic. Other students who are not constrained by a professional body, may be able to choose whether or not they do a dissertation as part of their degree. For these students, it can be helpful to speak with academic staff and to look over examples of dissertations completed in previous years to help you decide whether undertaking a social science research project is for you. Importantly, this book details the importance of being an ethical social scientist, one that locates your work in academic social science literature (see Chapters 3 and 4).

WHAT ARE THE BENEFITS OF DOING SOCIAL SCIENCE RESEARCH?

First and foremost, a social science research project is an accomplishment; it involves work to produce a product. Undertaking and completing something like a dissertation is likely to have several intended as well as unintended impacts for both you and others. Some projects have rich, academic merit and further knowledge in a particular discipline (such as medical sociology or social psychology), while others are more applied having a broader range of beneficiaries, impacting on policy and practice. Social science terminologies have also been assimilated in everyday vernacular (Mandler 2019, Lewis et al. 2023). Terms such as stigma (Goffman 1963), moral panic (Cohen 1973), emotional labour (Hochschild 1983), and to a lesser extent toxic masculinity (origins discussed in Harrington 2021), all rooted in social science research, are now discussed in everyday parlance to describe social processes and events. So, while the social sciences can be agents of change helping to solve social problems, they also provide us with a vocabulary to make sense of the social processes at play.

It is safe to argue, then, that studying the social world and the individuals who occupy it can help us better understand the dynamic society in which we live. This in turn can be a catalyst for change, offering new practices (for example, the ways in which teachers use educational aids to teach) and policies (for instance, Children's Rights). For example, the British Academy (2024: 3) states that social science research 'is helping to solve some of the most complex and pressing problems facing society – whether that is related to health sector, the economy or the environment.' Let us look at five examples in detail that reflect the full spectrum of the social sciences and how research has been used to tackle societal problems across the globe: (i) the Whitehall studies (1967/1985) originally led by Sir Michael Marmot have had a profound effect on our understandings of the social determinants of health, providing evidence that the relationship between health and socioeconomic status is not simply the difference between the poor, marginalised and the rest (see Centre for Social Epidemiology 2011). Instead, there is a social gradient that can be seen across society, including within the categories of 'poor' or 'well-off'; (ii) Abhijit Banerjee, Esther Duflo and Michael Kremer won the Nobel prize in economics in 2019 after introducing a novel approach to garnering reliable answers on the best and most efficient ways to tackle global poverty. They emphasised the use of field experiments in research so to realise the benefits of lab-based trials. As a direct result of their studies, 'more than five million Indian children have benefited from effective programmes of remedial tutoring in schools' (Nobel Prize 2019); (iii) Bystander intervention is primarily associated with the work of social psychologists Bibb Latané and John Darley. Their work in the mid-20th century laid the foundations for what has become known as the bystander effect and bystander apathy. Fundamentally, the theory maintains that people are less likely to help a victim when other people are present (presumably believing that others will step forward and they are not needed). But the research suggests that the more bystanders there are, the less likely anyone will offer help. Greater understanding of bystander theory has led to the development of training programmes and educational campaigns aimed at encouraging people to act in emergencies and to step in when they know someone is being bullied. For example, cardiopulmonary resuscitation (CPR) and first aid training now often include components that address the bystander effect, teaching individuals not only the technical skills required to help but also how to overcome psychological barriers to intervening; (iv) studies led by Donald Hirsch (2011) were drawn upon to craft policy in the UK. The work of Hirsch and others identified budgets called minimum income standards, which were then used as the basis of the UK minimum wage; (v) Research undertaken at Macquarie University into the teaching and learning of mathematics in Australia has had positive impacts on both teachers and children in Australia as well as further afield (Macquarie University 2021). Findings of a 2015 study involving 600 kindergarten and Grade 1 students conducted by researchers at the university led to the development of a new assessment tool used globally to measure 4–8-year-olds' understanding and knowledge of number, pattern, algebra, geometry, and graphical representations.

These examples demonstrate how social research can influence the approaches we use to understand the social world as well as providing new methods and ways of measuring that can be implemented in policy. Now, do not sweat, there is absolutely no expectation that a student research project should have such impact. Frankly, you neither have the resources nor the time. But if you consider undertaking a research project as a form of apprenticeship for wherever life takes you in the future, these published works show how powerful social science work can be and why critically understanding society is so crucial. They also show the diversity of projects on offer.

Box 1.1

Social Science Impact Example

Research into child sexual exploitation (CSE) led by Dr Sophie Hallett at Cardiff University (2016 and 2017, Hallett et al. 2017) is an example of research that has made a difference to society through changes in Wales' safeguarding policy and professional practices. Her research, drawn originally from her doctorate studies and which combined ethnographic, qualitative, and participative interviews, with case file analysis and quantitative methods, examined CSE to consider the ways in which we might better define, understand, and therefore prevent and respond to this issue. As a direct result of the research, changes in policy in Wales mean professionals now direct to a list of signs and indicators of abuse with assessment geared towards care and support requirements. The definition of abuse has also been reworded to include the multiple models of this type of abuse that can occur.

But as well as potentially having benefits for society and particular social groups, undertaking social science research can also enable the development of various key skills that might be useful in your future. For instance, conducting a research project involves being able to manage your time effectively (see Chapter 2: *Planning a Social Science Research Project*) so to submit the project before the deadline, a task that is completed alongside competing workloads and other deadlines. Equally, a research project provides you with the opportunity, among other things, to showcase your ability to search for literature, synthesise arguments, collect and analyse data, problem solve, disseminate findings, work with large documents, and draw conclusions. Data analysis for your research project may also involve using specific computer software, for example, SPSS or NVivo, which are skills that can be listed on your Curriculum Vitae (CV). In some instances, you will be required to work alongside others during a research project, enabling you to develop your team-working skills. Sometimes research involves contacting and working with potential gatekeepers (see Chapter 4: *Being an Ethical Researcher*) and/or presenting research ideas or findings in written and oral forms to various stakeholders or academic audiences (see Chapter 7: *Presenting Your Social Science Research*). These opportunities help finesse your collaboration and communication skills.

HOW IS SOCIAL SCIENCE RESEARCH CONDUCTED?

For simplicity, methods of data collection are often separated into **quantitative and qualitative approaches**. This book has separate chapters on *Methods of Social Science Data Collection* (Chapter 5) and *Social Science Data Analysis* (Chapter 6) dedicated to the collection and analysis of quantitative and qualitative data. Quantitative methods of data collection almost always produce numerical data which can be analysed using statistical approaches. Conversely, qualitative methods of data collection result in non-numerical data such as textual, audio, video, or image-based data. Table 1.1 outlines some of the commonly used quantitative and qualitative methods of data collection in the social sciences.

Table 1.1 Quantitative and qualitative methods of data collection

Quantitative	Qualitative
Questionnaires (online, telephone or in-person)	Focus groups
Experiments	Interviews (semi-structured and unstructured)
Longitudinal analysis	Diary research
Structured interviews	Unstructured observations
Structured observations	Photo elicitation
Content analysis	Drawing and images research
Systematic reviews	Video analysis
	Social media analysis
	Documentary research
	Sensory methods
	Action research/participatory research

There are other approaches, which we might label hybrid or mixed method such as Q methodology and social media or Big Data scraping.

But, as foregrounded, various disciplines in the social sciences tend to favour certain methods and approaches. This can reflect the differing research questions posed and topics explored in these disciplines. For instance, Hudson (2017: 736) differentiated economics from the other social sciences, arguing that 'the quantitative nature of most economics research is in contrast to the qualitative methods that characterize the work of many other social scientists'. But in psychology, where experiments tend to dominate, there have been calls for a greater acceptance of qualitative approaches, particularly to enable researchers to explore individual experiences and subjective understandings better (Madill and Todd 2002, Madill and Gough 2008, Henwood 2014, Gough and Lyons 2015). Meanwhile the UK government has invested in quantitative methods to upskill and reskill social science students in statistical approaches (British Academy 2013, Nuffield Foundation 2022). As before, the use of different research methods is as much a cultural preference as it is an epistemic one and, whilst a caricature has been outlined here, it is important to ensure that the research methods you decide to use are the most appropriate ones to enable you to answer your research questions.

Of course, in some instances, social science researchers may employ a **mixed methods** approach. This often means employing a mixture of quantitative and qualitative approaches to data collection and analysis. It is necessary to be aware that drawing from multiple methods in a social science research project does not make the research inherently better or superior. Employing both quantitative and qualitative methods does not allow the researcher to negate the limitations of each approach. Instead, the use of more than one method has the potential to jeopardise the narrative and flow of a research project unless done well, especially when writing to tight word counts. If you decide to use multiple methods, especially mixing qualitative and quantitative approaches, it is important that the justification for using more than one approach is clear and that the reader can see how the two approaches fit together and complement one another. Being able to conduct a research project that uses both quantitative and qualitative methods can be time consuming, and you should consider the time constraints concerning your social science research project before choosing a mixed methods design that draws from both approaches (see Chapter 2: *Planning a Social Science Research Project*). Alternatively, some approaches inherently bridge the quantitative/qualitative dichotomy, for example, hybrid methods such as Q methodology (Davis and Michelle 2011). This relatively novel approach involves participants sorting a series of subjective statements in an interview setting which the researcher later analyses statistically (Herrington and Coogan 2011).

Social science research projects can also be divided into those that use **primary data** and those which draw from **secondary data**. Projects which use primary data are those where the researcher has collected the data themselves specifically for that piece of research. Secondary data refers to situations where the researcher draws from pre-existing data, which was originally collected for an alternative research project and then analysed in a different way, or for a different purpose (e.g., a newspaper article). It is useful to distinguish between secondary data and **secondary data analysis** here. As explained, secondary data is all

Table 1.2 International sources of secondary data

Sources of secondary data	Web link
UK Data Service	https://www.ukdataservice.ac.uk/
Office of National Statistics	https://www.ons.gov.uk/
Consortium of European Social Science Data Archives	https://www.cessda.eu/
US Government Data	https://www.data.gov/
Australian Data Archive	https://ada.edu.au/
Australian Government Data	https://data.gov.au/
Research Data Australia	https://researchdata.edu.au/
StatsWales	https://statswales.gov.wales/Catalogue
Scotland.gov.scot	https://statistics.gov.scot/home
Northern Ireland Statistics and Research Agency	https://www.nisra.gov.uk/
Eurostat	https://ec.europa.eu/eurostat
World Bank Open Data	https://data.worldbank.org/
United Nations Statistics Division	https://unstats.un.org/home/
UNESCO Institute for Statistics	http://uis.unesco.org/
Sage Research Methods Datasets	https://methods.sagepub.com/Datasets

data that exists independent of the research being undertaken and therefore this will include various documentary sources as well as data deposited in raw form in some of the data banks listed in Table 1.2. Secondary data *analysis,* on the other hand, refers exclusively to the second order analysis of existing data (most likely located in these data banks). That is, one can draw from secondary data such as newspaper articles and be the first to analyse it as social science data, whereas secondary data analysis demands that someone else has previously analysed that same dataset (possibly with a different purpose).

Predominately, banked secondary data sources are numerical datasets which can be quantitatively analysed. However qualitative secondary data is becoming increasingly popular and the main government funder of social science in the UK has made it a requirement of their funding that where (ethically) possible, data, including qualitative data, are banked for researchers to use in the future.

WHERE IS SOCIAL SCIENCE RESEARCH UNDERTAKEN?

Society is everywhere. This given, those researchers doing primary data collection may have a particular site or setting which they need to visit to collect their data. Here, it might be useful to distinguish between what we call a site and a setting. A **setting** refers to the backdrop of the research, e.g., the education setting or the employment setting. The **site** (or field), on the other hand, refers to the particular place where the research is to be conducted, e.g. a primary school or a specific organisation. A pivotal time in some social science research projects is the process of obtaining access to the research site. This may involve speaking to **gatekeepers** who can give you access to potential participants (see Chapter 4: *Being an Ethical Researcher*). For instance, if your research involved teachers, the headteacher of a school would be a gatekeeper in your research. Ultimately, the headteacher would be the person who would give their permission for you to recruit teachers working in their school to take part in your study and determine whether this could be done during work time or not. The time it takes to negotiate access with potential gatekeepers is a crucial factor to be mindful of when planning your research project (see Chapter 2: *Planning a Social Science Research Project*).

When deciding where to undertake social science research, researchers must also consider the practicality and safety of the environment in which they are collecting data, for both themselves and their participants. For example, it would not always be practical to audio record interviews in a busy café where it may be difficult to hear the interviewee and, more importantly, they may not want to disclose personal views in such a public space. In this scenario, you may also pick up sounds from other café visitors who have not given their consent to be recorded. However, the choice of a public space is often a good, safe one too as this could be your first encounter with someone who is a stranger. The principles of picking an appropriate place to undertake social science research will be expanded on in Chapter 4 (*Being an Ethical Researcher*).

On the other hand, researchers undertaking secondary data collection may not need to venture from their desk. In fact, and particularly since the Covid-19 pandemic, there has been an increase in the use of online methods of data collection in social science research. For example, with the rise in, and increased familiarity with, video calling platforms, researchers can now interview participants virtually using generic software programmes such as Zoom or Microsoft Teams. There is also a plethora of online survey software packages such as Qualtrics and Microsoft Forms which allow researchers to make professional questionnaires that can be easily distributed online. This shift to collecting data from the desk is a recognition that data can travel, meaning the researcher does not need to. Now, not all social scientists, particularly those of an ethnographic persuasion would champion this research-from-a-distance approach, maintaining that the researcher needs to immerse themselves in their research site. A more detailed discussion of the advantages and disadvantages of collecting data online can be found in Chapter 5 (*Methods of Social Science Data Collection*). It is hard not to argue, however, that while something is lost using this approach, something is also gained, especially for students working to deadlines. Such an approach reduces the travel costs associated with data collection as well as researchers' carbon footprint, while also allowing researchers to connect with participants across the globe. As well as some more traditional methods of data collection moving online, the Internet and specifically, social media sites are increasingly becoming fertile sites for research in and of themselves. For example, Burnap et al. (2016) used Twitter data to predict the 2015 UK general election results. Here, the setting will be political voting and the site Twitter. Similarly, Brownlie and Shaw (2019) explored empathy exchanges between Twitter users. Indeed, the Internet has been the catalyst for new research fields such as digital sociology and new methodological approaches such as netnography that pre-date the COVID-19 pandemic.

HOW IS SOCIAL SCIENCE RESEARCH PRESENTED?

As students, often your first experience of writing up and presenting findings from social science research is completing a research project or dissertation as part of your degree programme. This is essentially an extended piece of writing reporting on a piece of independent research which you have conducted. Often this sets out to answer a set of research questions through empirical exploration and is usually based on some theoretical or conceptual framework. Typically, an undergraduate social science dissertation will be around 8,000–12,000 words in length, whilst a postgraduate dissertation is often longer, usually ranging between 12,000–20,000 words. It is essential that you check the exact word count of your research project or dissertation with your institution.

The structure of a dissertation or research project will depend on the topic being studied and the approach taken. However, there is a general acceptance of what a dissertation or research project should look like. At the most basic level, a research project should always have a clear beginning, middle, and end. The beginning tells the reader what you are going to do and why, the middle sets out how you undertook the project, and the end tells the reader what it is you found and why it is important to your discipline, for policy and/or practice. These separate parts of a research project are usually divided into distinct and discrete chapters: Introduction, Literature Review, Methods, Findings, Analysis, and Conclusion. These chapters are then topped and tailed with an abstract and an accurate reference list, alphabetically ordered. The purpose of each of these chapters is outlined in Table 1.3. The table also outlines which chapter(s) in this book focus on these specific sections of a research project in more detail, allowing you to skip ahead to read the chapters which are most pertinent to your current needs. Crucially, while each chapter should stand for itself, a dissertation needs to have a throughline or thread that connects each chapter.

Table 1.3 The purpose of each chapter

Chapter	Purpose	Chapter in Book
Front matter	Acknowledges all those that have helped with the dissertation (acknowledgements).	9
	Declares that the work is yours and not submitted elsewhere (declaration).	
	Directs readers to the requisite pages (contents page).	
Introduction	Introduces the topic underscoring the importance of the problem at hand and the need for further research in the area.	8
	Signposts the structure of the rest of the writing.	
Literature Review	Locates the topic in a body of literature, critically reviewing what literature exists and how the project speaks to these works.	3
	The Literature Review can be structured in various ways including thematically and chronologically.	
	The Literature Review should funnel into your research questions and Methods chapter.	
Methods	The Methods chapter should tell the reader how you went about collecting data so that a reader can replicate your project. It should also justify the approach.	5
	The Methods chapter might also contribute to contemporary methodological debates and discussions.	
Findings	The Findings chapter should present the findings of the research in a coherent and comprehensible manner. Data such as tables, graphs, interview extracts or fieldnotes should be displayed.	6 and 7
Analysis	The Analysis chapter should make sense of the findings, returning to the work discussed in the Literature Review.	6
	The analysis should remain within the guard rails of the research questions posed.	
Conclusion	The Conclusion should summarise the main findings and explain what this might mean (for policy or practice).	8
	The chapter should answer the research questions posed earlier in the thesis.	
	The chapter might also critically reflect on the project, outlining any limitations to the study and further work that is required on the topic.	
Back matter	An alphabetic list of all literature cited in the text (reference list).	9
	A list of additional auxiliary information (appendices).	

Important to note here is that the Findings and Analysis chapters might be combined into a larger chapter, perhaps called *Analytic Discussion*. This approach is common in qualitative projects that tend to have a more narrative emphasis to them in which describing and analysing the data tends to collapse into analytic description, whereas quantitative projects tend to separate the Findings and Analysis chapters, dividing descriptive statistics from analytic ones.

If you look closely, most research articles use the same structure to what is outlined here when presenting the results of their social science research project. However, rather than having discrete chapters, authors of these journal articles tend to make use of subheadings to structure their writing into these areas. In many research outputs, including research projects, these substantive chapters or subsections are preceded by a short abstract which provides a succinct overview of the research project (see Chapter 9: *Submitting Your Social Science Research Project*). Following the main body of writing, it is also common to see a reference list and, in some instances, appendices, which contain valuable information not included in the main body of text itself (see Table 1.4). Table 1.4 outlines the structure used in a selection of recent articles in some mainstream social science journals. You will see that the structure mirrors that outlined in Table 1.3. Each article begins with an abstract, before introducing the research problem, discussing the relevant literature, describing the present study, presenting the findings, discussing the results and forming a conclusion. Each article concludes with a reference list, and in some cases an appendix is added containing extra relevant information.

Table 1.4 Structure of mainstream social science journal articles

Paper	Journal	Structure
Police contact and future orientation from adolescence to young adulthood: Findings from the Pathways to Desistance Study (2021)	*Criminology*	Abstract
		Introduction
		Background
		Current study
		Data
		Results
		Discussion
		References
		Appendix
Coloniality of gender and knowledge: Rethinking Russian masculinities in light of postcolonial and decolonial critiques (2022)	*Sociology*	Abstract
		Introduction
		The coloniality of power, knowledge and gender
		Russia in the context of global coloniality
		The study
		Eurocentric Russian masculinities
		Colonial Russian masculinities
		Conclusion
		References

Paper	Journal	Structure
The color of law school: Examining gender and race intersectionality in law school admissions (2022)	*American Journal of Education*	Abstract
		Review of the literature
		Analytic framework: quantitative intersectionality and critical legal studies
		Method
		Findings
		Discussion and implications
		Conclusion
		References
Messages for good practice: Aboriginal hospital liaison officers and hospital social workers (2022)	*Australian Social Work*	Abstract
		Method
		Findings
		Discussion
		Conclusion
		References
(De) legitimisation of single mothers' welfare rights: United States, Britain and Israel (2022)	*Journal of European Social Policy*	Abstract
		Introduction
		Background, objective and methods
		Financial dependence versus autonomy
		The coping versus the selfish mom
		Discussion
		References
Student loneliness through the pandemic: How, why and where? (2021)	*The Geographical Journal*	Abstract
		The loneliness of students
		Loneliness and its geographies
		Co-produced research
		Findings: Spaces of relationships, interactions and loneliness
		Conclusion: Student voices and loneliness strategies
		References
Bringing the problem home: The anti-slavery and anti-trafficking rhetoric of UK non-government organisations (2022)	*Politics*	Abstract
		Introduction
		Rhetoric and the problem of terminology
		Method
		Data analysis and discussion
		Conclusion
		References

THE IMPORTANCE OF DEVELOPING RESEARCH QUESTIONS

Notwithstanding the word 'science' in the term social sciences, to a large degree, the social sciences are influenced by the humanities. For instance, it is extremely unlikely that you will have progressed to the end of your social science degree without having to write several essays. As we know, loosely defined, an essay is a piece of extended writing where the author addresses a question by developing an argument. And this is a good starting point to consider a research project too. Social science research projects offer you the opportunity to bring together the specific knowledge gained in different modules, where you might have completed several of these essays, with the general research methods training which you have learnt, to address a series of specific research questions in an empirical manner. Here, **empirical** refers to the collection and/or analysis of evidence or data to support the claims you make. These research questions should be direct and interconnected, outlining what it is you want to find out through your research and should drive the direction of the project. That is, your research questions should not be able to be answered with a simple 'yes' or 'no' response following a quick Wikipedia search. Instead, they require an in-depth, extended period of study so that they can be answered properly and attentively. Research questions should be clear and concise and capture the focus of the research problem being investigated.

Research questions are often developed and finessed through engagement with relevant academic literature (see Chapter 3: *Reviewing Social Science Literature*), from which data are then collected and analysed to help the researcher answer these questions (see Chapter 5: *Methods of Social Science Data Collection* and Chapter 6: *Social Science Data Analysis*). In this way, research questions anchor your research project, often connecting the top half of a research project, which mostly involves synthesising other people's work into a line of argument and situating the project within a particular corpus of published literature, with the bottom half of a research project which presents and analyses the findings from the present research project. The size of the research project (the word count and length of time you are permitted to complete the project) will often determine the number of research questions a project contains, but around 2 to 4 research questions tend to be the norm for a student project. Importantly, research questions are not fixed, they can be tweaked and tinkered with, and it is often the case that researchers will adapt and revise questions or even add or remove questions as the research process progresses. As an active researcher, you should react to changes you encounter during your study, or information you come across along the way, checking whether the original research questions that you began with are still sufficiently focussed and relevant. While it is not unusual for research questions to develop and deviate in a social science project, this might mean it is necessary to revisit the Literature Review chapter toward the end of the project so to ensure that the literature presented and discussed is still pertinent and that there is a clear, interconnected narrative running through the final project (see Chapter 3: *Reviewing Social Science Literature*).

The type of research questions posed should determine the methods of data collection used. For instance, explanatory questions which are concerned with *why* and *how* are typically associated with qualitative methods of data collection and analysis, whereas descriptive questions which are concerned with *who*, *what* and *when* are more often associated with quantitative methods of data collection. Table 1.5 provides some examples of how research questions may be posed differently depending on the specific focus of a research project exploring mature students and university level study. The examples show the ways in which the different questions tend to lend themselves to the collection of distinct types of data.

Table 1.5 Research questions

	Question type	Quantitative/Qualitative	Example
Who?	Descriptive	Quantitative	Who decides to study at university as a mature student?
What?	Descriptive	Quantitative	What subjects do mature students study at university?
Where?	Descriptive	Quantitative	Where do mature students study degree programmes?
Why?	Explanatory	Qualitative	Why do mature students decide to study at university?
How?	Explanatory	Qualitative	How do mature students decide which university to study at?

The first research question in Table 1.5 asks, *'Who decides to study at university as a mature student?'*. Answering this question means exploring variables associated with entering higher education later in life, including age, household income and whether students have parental or caring responsibilities. These variables could be identified in existing sources of data held by universities, or alternatively relevant data could be collected in a quantitative questionnaire. Similarly, the question *'What subjects do mature students study at university?'* might be answered by engaging with existing university admissions records on degree subject choices, or by distributing a questionnaire to mature students studying in higher education. The 'where' question (*Where do mature students study degree programmes?*) could again be answered by using existing secondary sources of quantitative data. But to understand *why* mature students decide to study at university demands a more qualitative approach. Running focus groups, for example, could elicit their perspectives as to the reasons for pursuing a university degree programme later in life. Likewise, to answer the question *How do mature students decide which university to study at?* qualitative data, drawn from interviews for example, would need to be gathered to understand the decision-making processes of these individuals. This demonstrates how different research questions tend to align themselves to different methods of data collection and analysis. It is important that social science researchers choose the best and most appropriate approach to answer their specific research question(s).

Table 1.6 shows various research questions taken from recent articles published in a selection of mainstream social science journals. The table also highlights whether a quantitative or qualitative approach was used to answer the research questions.

Table 1.6 Research questions in recent social science journal articles

Paper	Journal	Research Question(s)	Quantitative/ Qualitative
Police contact and future orientation from adolescence to young adulthood: Findings from the Pathways to Desistance Study (Testa et al. 2022)	*Criminology*	1. Does exposure to personal and/or vicarious police contact, compared with no exposure to police contact, reduce future orientation over time? 2. Does the association between police contact and future orientation vary by perceptions of procedural justice? 3. Does the association between police contact and future orientation vary by sex and race/ethnicity?	Quantitative
Coloniality of gender and knowledge: Rethinking Russian masculinities in light of postcolonial and decolonial critiques (Yusupova 2023)	*Sociology*	1. Is there such a thing as Russian masculinity? 2. Does immigration and a new social and legal environment change Russian men's ideas about masculinity?	Qualitative
The color of law school: Examining gender and race intersectionality in law school admissions (Fernandez et al. 2022)	*American Journal of Education*	1. Whether and to what extent relationships between race and admission differ by gender 2. Whether and to what extent relationships between an intersected race–gender identity and admission differ by law school ranking.	Quantitative

Paper	Journal	Research Question(s)	Quantitative/ Qualitative
Messages for good practice: Aboriginal hospital liaison officers and hospital social workers (Orr et al. 2022)	*Australian Social Work*	1. What do social workers and Aboriginal hospital liaison officers in Victoria identify as good practice? 2. What are the factors that support good [social work] practice? 3. What are the learnings from the findings of this study that can inform the education and training of Aboriginal hospital liaison officers and training and professional development for social workers?	Qualitative
(De)legitimisation of single mothers' welfare rights: United States, Britain and Israel (Herbst-Debby 2022)	*Journal of European Social Policy*	1. In what ways, over time, has welfare policy affecting single mothers in the US, UK and Israel been associated with changes in discourse?	Qualitative
Student loneliness through the pandemic: How, why and where? (Phillips et al. 2022)	*The Geographical Journal*	1. How and why have students in higher education experienced loneliness in the context of the Covid-19 pandemic? 2. What geographical factors – including material, practical and metaphorical barriers to forming and performing relationships – have led to loneliness in this context? 3. What might be done, practically and feasibly, to reduce students' loneliness? What might be done to remove barriers between students and to support them as they interact and build and maintain relationships?	Qualitative
Bringing the problem home: The anti-slavery and anti-trafficking rhetoric of UK non-government organisations (Turnbull and Broad 2022)	*Politics*	1. What rhetoric is used by contemporary NGOs in their anti-slavery and anti-trafficking campaigns? 2. How are slavery and trafficking problems and solutions framed by this rhetoric? 3. Third, what are the similarities and differences between contemporary and historical anti-slavery rhetoric?	Quantitative and Qualitative

Depending on the size of your project you may, of course, have multiple research questions. Importantly, though, having more research questions does not necessarily make a project superior. In some cases, it can be best to have fewer research questions, which are addressed or answered more comprehensively than to have multiple questions which are not adequately answered because you do not have the space or time to answer them fully. For some people, cultivating these initial research questions is a straightforward task. Others may need more time and space to consider and finesse an appropriate set of research questions. If you are struggling to come up with appropriate research questions, it can be a useful idea to look at previous research projects or dissertations, to speak to academic supervisors, peers or other lecturers, or to draw inspiration from topics which you have previously learnt about, potential career aspirations, hobbies and interests or contemporary social affairs (we discuss this in more detail in Chapter 2 under *Sources of inspiration*). In some cases, your university may have more of a steer on the research topics which they allow you to explore. Once you have chosen a topic, a good starting base is to ask yourself what you would like to know about that subject that you do not already know. Here it is important to be aware of any parameters which may concern the topic of your research project before you begin formulating research questions. For example, asking someone about their (mental) health needs to be considered sensitively and may be beyond the scope of a student research project (see Chapter 4: *Being an Ethical Researcher*).

Some research projects may also have different levels of research questions; for example, you might decide to have two main research questions each with two sub-research questions attached to them. However many research questions you may end up with, it is important to ensure that the final research question(s) are feasible and that you can realistically address them in the allocated time with the resources that you have available. This involves careful planning at the outset of a research project (see Chapter 2: *Planning a Social Science Research Project*), but also a willingness to adapt and react positively as the project progresses, maybe even losing a research question if it feels too much.

SUMMARY

In this chapter, we have outlined the purpose of social science research, setting out the variety of topics on offer and methods used, as well as the potential impacts of this type of research. While this flexibility over topic and method can be a little daunting, we advise students to embrace this choice and consult with lecturers, supervisors and even friends and family to find a project which is a good fit for them. Inspiration can come from modules which you have previously studied, career aspirations or hobbies and interests. Most importantly though, choose a topic which will sustain your interest throughout the lifecycle of the research project (see Chapter 2: *Planning a Social Science Research Project*). Enjoy this opportunity that you have been afforded.

We have also stressed the importance of having clear research questions which guide the project. A social science research project should clearly set out how these questions have been informed by existing literature, perhaps even gaps in the literature, and then progress to answer these research questions using either quantitative or qualitative approaches (or even both). This lends itself to the generic structure often adopted when writing up social science research projects and which can be seen in many journal articles. Often a written student dissertation will begin with an abstract before the main body of the text, followed by an introduction, a summary of the relevant literature, an overview of the methods deployed, a discussion of the main findings, an analysis of the findings and a conclusion. This is followed by a reference list and, in some instances, a set of appendices.

In the next chapter, we focus on how to effectively plan your research project. Some of the ideas introduced in this chapter are important to consider when planning your project. It is also essential for you to clarify some of the issues raised in this chapter, such as word length and parameters or guard rails around topic choice with your institution as you plan out your project. Likewise, to enable you to best answer your research questions and depending on the methods chosen to do this, you may need to build in additional time for further training or to allow you space to negotiate access to specific research sites.

Student Question

A research project is an optional component of my degree programme. I am undecided whether to take this module or not. What would you suggest?

(Carly, Sociology and Journalism student)

Charlotte and Jamie say:

To undertake a social science research project is to formalise a curiosity and passion. For any students considering choosing a dissertation or capstone module, we would first ask you to take some time to consider what topics interest you and to put on paper some nascent research project ideas. Yes, a research project requires methodological skills, and absolutely, we believe students will learn and develop important skills as they go along that will help them in the world of work, but first and foremost students need to show their social scientific imagination; they need to have a passion which they want to formalise. If you can come up with a researchable idea, then you have made a giant leap into the world of social science research, and this is a strong signal that a research project is for you.

WHAT'S NEXT?

Chapter Checklist

Table 1.7 Chapter 1 checklist

	Yes	No
I appreciate the breadth and scope of disciplines which the social sciences encompass.		
I understand the importance of research questions when designing and undertaking social science research.		
I can identify different beneficiaries of social science research.		
I can name different groups who undertake social science research.		
I can list different approaches to collecting social science data.		
I know where to find existing sources of social science data.		
I can describe the main sections of a social science research project.		

Read

Campaign for Social Science. 2015. *10 reasons why we need social sciences*. Available at: www.palgrave.com/gp/campaigns/social-science-matters/10-reasons-for-social-science (accessed 7 July 2022).

- In your opinion, why do we need social science research?
- Can you find examples of how social science research undertaken at your university has benefitted society or informed policy and practice?

Listen To

BBC. 2022. *Thinking Allowed*. Available at: www.bbc.co.uk/programmes/b006qy05/episodes/player (accessed 7 July 2022).

Thinking Allowed is a BBC Radio 4 series hosted by Laurie Taylor, which showcases social science research. Previous episodes are available online on BBC iPlayer.

- What kind of topics are covered in the *Thinking Allowed* series?
- Are there any topics which you could explore in your own social science research project?

Complete

Choose a journal article from your own discipline to read.

- Identify the research questions posed in your paper of choice.
- What methods are used by the author(s) to answer the research questions?
- What are the main subsections used in the paper?

Discuss

Kara, H. 2022. *How different are qualitative and quantitative research?* Available at: www.the-sra.org.uk/SRA/Blog/Howdifferentarequalitativeandquantitativeresearch.aspx (accessed 7 July 2022).

- Qualitative research never involves numbers. True or False?
- Quantitative methods can be good for exploring sensitive issues. True or False?
- There are similarities between quantitative and qualitative research. True or False?

Watch

UKRI. 2022. *What is Social Science?*. Available at: www.ukri.org/about-us/esrc/what-is-social-science/videos-what-is-social-science/#contents-list (accessed 7 October 2022).

2
PLANNING A SOCIAL SCIENCE RESEARCH PROJECT

Here, in Chapter 2, we share top tips for helping you design, develop, and plan a research project by including information on how to track your progress, set informal deadlines, and manage your time. We begin the chapter by asking you what you want to get out of your research project and what skills you want to develop during the research process. We encourage you to identify your own training needs ahead of beginning your research project, as well as providing guidance on how to produce a 'doable' project that is coherent and timely. Ideas for effectively managing your time are shared, such as blocking out days for working on your research project and creating Gantt charts and/or Kanban boards to help you stay on track and manage the workload of completing a social science research project. We finish by encouraging you to produce a research plan, showing what an indicative plan might look like.

Chapter Objectives

- To understand that planning is crucial when undertaking a social science research project.
- To recognise the importance of managing your time and tracking your progress.
- To understand the purpose of timetables, Gantt charts and Kanban boards.
- To recognise that a social science research project is an iterative process, and that writing is a craft that can be worked on and improved over time.
- To realise the necessity of designing a 'doable' project.
- To identify what makes a good research plan.
- To grasp the importance of planning for supervisory meetings and building rapport with your supervisors.

INTRODUCTION

Colin Powell was the first African-American US Secretary of State, serving between 2001 and 2005. As a well-respected politician, diplomat, and former army officer he was internationally renowned for his turns of phrase. Amongst many quotable quips, Powell is reported as saying: *'there are no secrets to success. It is the result of preparation, hard work, and learning from failure'*. This chapter concerns the first of these strategies: preparation and planning. Indeed, in our teaching, we often promote the idea that you get out of your research project what you put in, and that success, however perceived, begins at the planning stage. Part of this planning process should include structuring your own bespoke research journey.

At the beginning of a new research project, enthusiasm, energy levels and anxiety are often high. Ideas are hopefully flowing and there is a general excitement and nervousness of embarking on something new. There is therefore a real temptation to jump in two footed without taking the time to consider what it is you want to do, and, importantly, how you envisage doing it. We would in no way want to dampen this enthusiasm, but it is crucial that you take a considered approach. Taking some time to prepare and plan your project, its research design, and likely trajectory, by thinking through the various stages of a research project and how you might manage them is pivotal to completing a **doable** and timely research project. You will never foresee every eventuality, but this sort of dutiful and diligent work will undoubtedly save you time (and stress!) in the long run (see also Brookfield and Lewis 2021, Williams and Reid 2023).

For others, excitement can sometimes overflow into feelings of being overwhelmed by the research if realistic milestones that help track your progress are not set toward the beginning of the project. Unlike many of your other taught modules, a research project deadline such as the dissertation hand-in date might feel a long way off. For many students, both undergraduates and postgraduates, the submission of the research project could be many months away. It can be equally easy, then, to begin the research journey by putting things off until a later date because you are not sure where, when, and how to begin. In short, the start of the project frequently comes with the feeling that there is *everything* and *nothing* to do, leading some to procrastinate and others to begin their project without due consideration.

While most student research projects will be supplemented and scaffolded by a suite of lectures, seminars and/or workshops concerning the general doing of a research project, there will be an expectation, more so than in other modules, that as an independent piece of research, you will spend time planning out the specifics of your research project including its design and feasibility. Setting realistic milestones, agreed with your allocated supervisor or advisor, that cover the lifecycle of the project can be very helpful in this regard. There are various ways to do this, including creating timetables where you schedule in time to work on your research project, setting time aside in your diary and creating what are known as Gantt charts or Kanban boards. In this chapter, we discuss these techniques and tools in some detail as well as pushing you to think through an initial research project idea that we return to in Chapter 4 (*Being an Ethical Researcher*).

READ THE MODULE HANDBOOK/GUIDE

If you are completing a research project within a module or course as part of your degree programme, it is likely that you will be provided with a module handbook or guide. This document should contain important information about your research project, including deadlines as well as details on how you will be supported during the research process. On the surface, module handbooks or guides can appear overly officious and sometimes redundant as most modules include an introductory lecture where expectations are set, and assessments and their deadlines discussed. However, we want you to think of your module handbook or guide as a friend that helps you in times of need. It is a document that allows you to digest all the relevant information associated with the module at your own pace. Importantly, this handbook/guide is written for you, and it is a document that you can always refer to if you are unsure about any aspect of the module. Here, you should be able to read detail on the content that will be delivered in the module as well as all the associated help available to you and the deadlines for individual tasks. When planning for your research project, you should first spend time reading the module handbook or guide in full and take note of the learning outcomes as well as all relevant assessments, word counts, marking rubrics, and stipulations such as font size and referencing guidelines. Also, record all the relevant deadlines – this is essential preparatory work to track your research journey and something that you will return to when submitting your dissertation (see Chapter 9: *Submitting your Social Science Research Project*).

MAKING TIME

Time management is crucial when undertaking an extended piece of work. Part of the challenge of producing a successful research project is carving out the appropriate time to dedicate working on it. One popular aide is the trusty timetable or diary that you should all be familiar with, perhaps from school days.

Producing Realistic Diaries and Timetabling

At the beginning of an academic year or semester your diary tends to be less populated, making it the opportune time to map out or structure your own bespoke timetable. We would always encourage students to think of their timetable as a **live document**. What we mean by this is producing a document that is open to being changed and updated. Remember, circumstances can change, frankly, most likely will change, with unanticipated and unforeseen events impacting on the best-laid plans. Do not be concerned by this. Instead factor this into any planning and be prepared to update your timetable where necessary.

So, what should a 'live' timetable include? Our firm recommendation is to produce a timetable which talks in direct dialogue with your other commitments, both university commitments and external ones. You might begin by including all the formal lectures, seminars and/or workshops that are associated with your social science research project module and which help scaffold your research journey. You might then add in all the key dates pertinent to the research project, which will likely include the formal hand-in deadline, the date you need to submit a research idea to your department's ethics committee, dates and times of meetings with your supervisor, dates agreed with your supervisor to hand in draft chapters to be looked over, and dates for any other assessments, both formative and summative, which are associated with the research project. Once this is done, populate your timetable document with informal deadlines that you set yourself. For example, if you have agreed to submit a draft chapter on a certain date with your supervisor to be looked over then set yourself an informal deadline several days before, factoring in some time for those unanticipated events. Importantly, set yourself an informal deadline a few weeks before the formal final deadline to submit the written product to allow yourself time to edit, tinker and finesse the written piece (see Chapter 9: *Submitting Your Social Science Research Project*). Use your timetable to also mark out other times when your capacity to work on your research project may be reduced, for example, around other university assignment commitments, birthdays or religious festivals, family visits. Being realistic about what you are going to be able to achieve at different points in the year is important in producing a feasible timetable.

But to timetable properly and to track your research trajectory, it is also necessary to schedule time to work independently on your research project. You can label this work under headings, such as those related to the chapter you are working on, e.g., Literature Review work, writing your Methods chapter, or the task at hand, e.g., read a particular journal article, work on the ethics application, or you could colour code them, for example in the Microsoft Outlook calendar you can label activities by colours. This is where it is important to consider other learning commitments but also your social life, e.g., membership of any societies or clubs, caring responsibilities, or work commitments. Even if you produce a diary that is solely centred on the research project, at the very least include the timetabled lectures and seminars as well as assessment deadlines for other modules too. This prevents any clashes and makes your timetable realistic to the demands you have as a student. Also, and this is critically important, add in periods of rest and recuperation. Your health and wellbeing are paramount; without them you will not complete a research project. For example, if you have lectures that run from 9am through to 1pm, make sure you schedule time to have a break and eat some lunch before embarking on any independent work on your research project. Of course, if you do not have all details readily at hand, for example module deadlines for the second semester, populate the diary as best you can with the knowledge that you will keep making entries as the semester progresses. Remember that this is a live timetable that can be continuously updated. Alternatively, produce weekly diaries that simply plan the next seven days ahead.

TRACKING YOUR RESEARCH TRAJECTORY

Having blocked out time to work on your research project in dialogue with your other commitments, it can be beneficial to create documents that explicitly track your social science research journey. Two time-management tools which help track the development of a project are known as Gantt charts and Kanban boards. We discuss both but would advise that students choose one or the other.

Gantt Charts

Gantt charts are a popular aide for people required to manage a project such as a piece of research. They allow you to detail, in one document, all the activities and tasks that require completing and display them against the timeframe you must complete them within. The chart can be produced using a computer programme such as Microsoft Excel (see Brookfield 2021 and Tom's Planner 2024) in which you outline the tasks in the left-hand bar (the vertical y-axis) and set these against the time you have allocated to complete the research project (the horizontal x-axis). Given Gantt charts are most commonly used for tracking project schedules, some people find it useful to show additional detail about the various phases of the project, for example how the tasks relate to each other, how long each should take, how far each task has progressed, who is involved in each of the tasks, what obstacles need to be overcome and so on and so on. If, let us say, your project begins in October and needs to be submitted in the first week of May, you might include the months on the x-axis, or even distil this down to weeks. On the y-axis, you then might include the various tasks required to complete a research project. These could include completing an ethics application, producing the Literature Review chapter, piloting a data collection tool, writing the Methods chapter, analysing the data, negotiating access to the field, data collection, producing a contents page and so on. It is then important to set yourself an appropriate time to complete each undertaking. If you are unsure what an appropriate length of time is to complete the task, then raise this with your supervisor who should be able to provide guidance. Some aspects of the dissertation will naturally come before others, such as sampling before collecting data; others will be a decision between you and your supervisor and may be project specific. Some tasks will overlap, such as gaining ethics approval and writing your Literature Review or, for some, data collection and data analysis. Importantly, the timings of when you should meet these milestones do not need to be fixed in stone, they should be appropriately spaced with flexibility baked in to cater for those unforeseen circumstances. The ambition is to create a bespoke, visual chart that tracks the progress of your research project, but which is flexible enough for you to pivot if required. An example of a simple Gantt Chart is shown in Figure 2.1.

This is not to say that Gantt charts are for everyone, and that they are imperative for a successful research project. They are not. But whether you wish to visualise your project progress in one document or prefer to make monthly timetables or weekly diaries, we strongly encourage you to lay out all the major milestones involved in completing a research project so to keep track of your progress. Some students will want to add extra detail to their planning activities such as scheduling in their supervision meetings or by including any literature that they have read. Others still will want to situate the completion of their research project alongside other studies, work and social events so to create weekly life timetables or Gantt charts. The extent to which you include the minutiae of the project and its relationship to other life events and other university commitments is a personal choice. What is important though is that whatever you produce works for you and that you recognise that you will not be completing your dissertation in a vacuum, meaning it is crucial to build in extra 'auxiliary' time when planning how long you intend to spend on each aspect of the research project. As much as academic research papers might like to portray otherwise, very few research projects run smoothly. If the Covid-19 pandemic has taught us anything, there will be bumps in the road that are out of our control. That is, there is an array of unexpected and unforeseen delays such as your gatekeeper being unwell or negotiating access taking longer than first thought, or a global pandemic, that will likely need to be overcome. Therefore, factoring additional time for delays into your planning gives you some leeway. In structuring your research project, we also advise that you build in time at the end of your project to edit and fine tune your written research project. Set yourself a deadline of around two to three weeks before the official deadline for your research project to be submitted. Leave it to rest for a week, and then with fresh eyes and renewed energy use whatever time you have left to finesse your writing and iron out any creases. This polished veneer can make a significant difference to your finished product (see Chapter 9: *Submitting Your Social Science Research Project*).

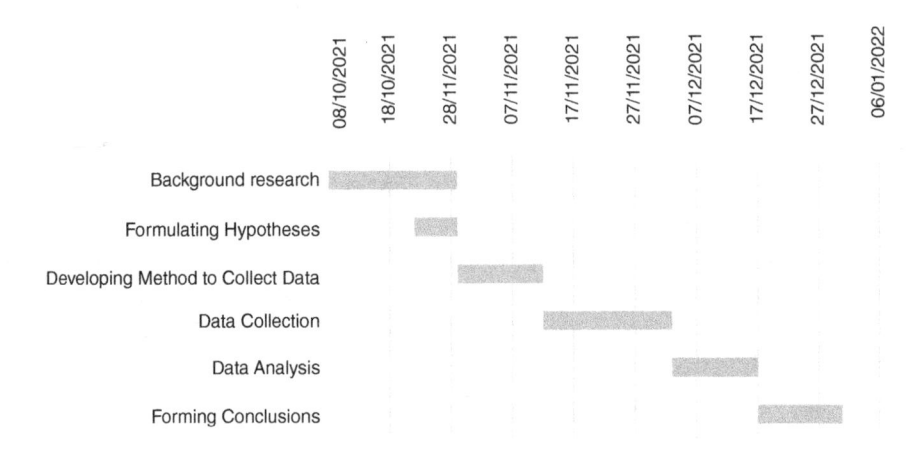

Figure 2.1 An example Gantt chart

Kanban Boards

Kanban is a Japanese word that roughly translates as a 'card that you can see' or a 'visual signal'. Much like a Gantt chart, a **Kanban board** is another organising tool which helps you visualise the tasks at hand. Introduced by the Toyota car company and then refined by David Anderson (2010), it is another visual system which you can use to track the progress of your research project (see example in Figure 2.2). Mostly designed with team or group work in mind, it is also a useful tool to help make a large project more manageable. Here, a research project can be divided into a suite of smaller tasks. A Kanban board is usually presented with three columns, which for the purposes of a research project we might call 'To do', 'In progress', and 'Completed'.

Kanban Board

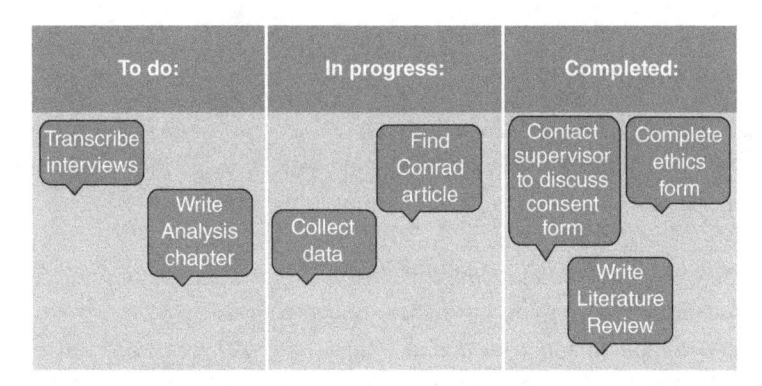

To do:	In progress:	Completed:
Transcribe interviews	Find Conrad article	Contact supervisor to discuss consent form
Write Analysis chapter	Collect data	Complete ethics form
		Write Literature Review

Figure 2.2 An example Kanban board

To begin creating your Kanban board, it is essential to come up with discrete, manageable individual tasks such as (i) draft Literature Review, (ii) produce information sheets and consent forms, (iii) submit ethics application, (iv) prepare methodological materials such as focus groups, interview or observation guides, or questionnaires, (v) contact potential research participants, and so on. Each distinct task is then represented on a card or a post-it-note. Importantly, in stacking the cards or post-it notes, you should order them by priority with the most urgent task being placed at the top of a column. Of course, the order in which you stack the cards or post-it-notes might change as the project progresses, in which case you should move the card or post-it note up or down accordingly. When beginning the research project, you should have no cards or post-it-notes in column 2 (in progress) and column 3 (completed) but a suite of cards or notes stacked on top of one another in column 1 (to do). Once you begin working on the task, you move it from the '*to do*' column to the '*in progress*' column. Include any information that will be helpful to you on the card or note; for example, you might include a description of the task, the deadline for the task to be completed as well as any other pertinent details. Some students might have an accompanying notebook, where they include more detail on the task at hand. Here, if the task is to complete a Literature Review, the notebook might include the various articles and publications that you plan to read. Once the task is completed, you can move the card or note to the '*completed*' column (column 3). This then allows you to begin another task from the '*to do*' column, remembering to always move the card at the top of the column. You can of course make more complex Kanban boards, but the secret is to create an uncluttered workflow chart. As a reminder, set yourself an informal deadline for the completion of the research project, which allows you to let the dissertation 'breathe' for a few days. This provides you the space to make any necessary edits with fresh eyes.

CHOOSING A TOPIC TO RESEARCH

Now that you have blocked out some space or put time aside in your university diary to focus on your research project, it is important to begin thinking about the specifics (if only tentatively) of the research project.

Sources of Inspiration

As touched upon in Chapter 1 (*What Is Social Science Research and Why Is It Important?*), there are various sources you can tap into when seeking inspiration for your social science research project. These include but are not limited to:

i   *Something you have learnt as part of the course* – for example a substantive topic, a social science theory or concept which piqued your interest.
ii   *Current events that are showcased in the media* – here you can scroll through social media or look at the front pages of student, local or national newspapers.
iii   *Life events that you are experiencing or living through* – this might be something specific to you (such as chronic illness) or something that is affecting everyone (the climate emergency or pension provision).
iv   *People you know* – whether family members, friends, or peers who might be experiencing something or working/socialising in an interesting social arena.
v   *Places where you have worked* – even something seemingly as mundane as the ways in which people queue at a pub/bar and what happens when someone disrupts this tacit agreement.
vi   *Career aspirations or plans* – for example, if you hope to be a teacher in the future then maybe researching something in the classroom might help you understand the role further.
vii   *Hobbies and interests* – as far-reaching as baseball (Fine 1987), rowing (King and de Rond 2011), ten-pin bowling (Jackson 2020), outdoor swimming (Scott 2009, Moles 2021), walking football (Thomas and Thurnell-Read 2024), kabaddi (Satwinder 2022), roller derbies (Pavlidis 2012), capoeira (Delamont and Stephens 2021), fishing (Markuksela and Valtonen 2018), surfing (Corte 2022), playing Dungeons and Dragons (Fine 1983), rap music (Riley 2006, Harrison 2008), card games (Punch and Snellgrove 2023), glass-blowing (Atkinson 2013), bonsai pruning (Mansourian 2021), Bingo (Chapple and Nofzinger 2000), cricket (King 2011), or dog training (Gillespie et al. 2010).
viii   *Something you are passionate about* – such as injustice, poverty and homelessness or gender equality. As discussed in more detail later in the book, we strongly encourage you to choose a research topic that you are passionate about since it will need to keep your attention for several months.

Refining Your Idea

Embarking on your research project is to *formalise a curiosity*, to study something you are interested in, and to hopefully provide answers to a set of questions which require answering (see section in Chapter 1: *The importance of developing research questions*). As social scientists, potential research sites are boundless. As described in Chapter 1 (*What Is Social Science Research and Why Is It Important?*), the social is everywhere in society. But while the topics of the research are almost infinite, this provides a challenge, especially for students who have a limited amount of time to conduct their research. A research project without parameters is undefined and likely to become unwieldy and unfocussed. As a social science student, then, your job is to design a meaningful, researchable and manageable research project which can be completed in a timely manner. You need to tame the social. And while research sites are aplenty, there are some settings that *are* off limits, particularly for students. Researching in prisons in most countries is likely a no-go area as are some medical settings. For example, in the United Kingdom (UK), projects recruiting participants through the National Health Service (NHS) nearly always require a favourable NHS ethics decision, a lengthy process that can take many months and which is often incompatible with the timeframes of an undergraduate or master's project. Of course, other social science projects need to be ethically sensitive too, with the decision as to whether they are ethical outsourced to school research ethics committees (and/or other organisations' ethics committees such as charities who might have their own procedures) (see Chapter 4: *Being an Ethical Researcher*). Such considerations may narrow the research project focus and your approach to studying it. Therefore, to design a 'doable' project, it is imperative to discuss your initial ideas with your supervisor so as to produce a researchable study within the timeframe allowed.

Many students have very interesting, and creative, nascent ideas that ask interesting social science questions. However, some of these ideas might be too big, broad enough to fill someone's entire career given the length of time it would require studying everything involved in their outline, or do not work as research projects where the questions can be appropriately addressed. Part of the planning process then is to narrow down the focus of the project into something which can be researched, analysed, and written up in a few months. That is, the task is to design a 'doable' project. Here, thinking through the practicalities of how the research can be undertaken, where and when is vitally important. Building iteratively on other people's work is an effective way to come up with a **doable project**. When reading the literature during the planning stage, do not simply read other people's work for their findings, but also assess how they went about conducting the research and what questions they were asking. Originality comes in multiple forms. It is certainly not expected that a student produces a completely original piece of work that no one has considered before. It is very unlikely that even the most experienced professor can achieve this. Instead, originality comes in many guises, from the approach taken, the sample studied, the data collection tool used, the way the data has been analysed, the context of the study or its theoretical lens or application.

Narrowing the gaze then is a sure sign that the research project is maturing into something *doable*. As you move through your research journey, think small and detailed rather than broad and general.

Box 2.1

A Researchable Idea

Some students might propose research ideas aplenty, others can spend weeks agonising over the issue of what to research. As a reminder, the challenge is to produce a researchable idea, a doable project. That is, not all research ideas are researchable for an assortment of reasons such as access issues, the resources that would be required to do the research, and the amount of time you are permitted to undertake the project within. When initially considering what a researchable idea is then, the acronym SANDS might come in handy.

> **S**pecific: Try not to produce something too broad. A researchable idea is one that is narrow and focussed. It is likely the case that you will continue to distil and refine the research project throughout the first few weeks that you are working on it.
>
> **A**ppropriate: Always consider the appropriateness of the project. Is it ethically sensitive for both the participants and for you? Ask yourself, are the methods I am proposing appropriate to address the research questions I am posing? Does it look like a social science project, and will it contribute to social science thinking on the subject? Does it allow me to demonstrate that I have met the learning objectives of the course/requirements of accrediting bodies?
>
> **N**ovel: A research project should have an element of originality to it. It is worth stating emphatically again that you are not expected to change the world with your research project (as much as you might want to), and equally you are not expected to come up with an idea that no one has ever thought of before. Originality can come in many forms: the perspective you are taking, the methodological approach you are using to address the research questions, the participants you are studying, the site of the research, the subject matter.
>
> **D**oable: Fundamentally, a researchable idea is one that is achievable in the time you have available and the resources you have. Here, it is worth considering what access you have to the site and the sample you wish to study as well as how long you envisage collecting data. Are there any costs involved? How will they be funded? Is travel required?
>
> **S**timulating: Let us not sugar coat this. There will be times during a research project where you will get fed up, even a little stressed. We would always advocate choosing a topic that excites you, that you find interesting, and which will sustain your interest throughout the course of the research journey. This should mean that at those pinch points when the work might feel a little overwhelming you will have the passion and drive to keep moving it forward. For some students choosing a project centred around their hobbies can help maintain their interest. Similarly, doing a project which helps you achieve your future goals or career aspirations can be motivating.

Remember You Are Still Learning

John Eales was a former Australian world cup winning men's rugby union captain who went by the nickname '*Nobody*' amongst his team-mates. Why? Because *nobody* is *perfect*. We will let you in to a secret. No one, including yourself, should expect a research project to be perfect. Examining this unrealistic expectation more closely, what does 'perfect' really mean, and who decides what perfection is? If all the staff from your school or department were to anonymously submit a research project to be marked by other staff, very few would get 100%. The same is true when submitting journal articles, very few submissions to social science journals get an acceptance after the first submission. Most published pieces have gone through several iterations before being submitted and at least one set of revisions set by the reviewers of the paper as needing to be addressed before the paper is deemed suitable for publication. The point we are making here is that we all design and carry out research in a (subtly) unique way, and that any research project is a learning process. Things happen that we have never encountered before, and we must often find workarounds to deal with the issues we are presented with: learnings that we take with us to our next research project; learnings that are often not discussed, save for a few methodological journals and 'confession' pieces/exposés.

For students undertaking a research project as the culmination of their degree or programme, this is an assessed piece of work which should be set against a bespoke marking criteria that sets out what is expected of the project (see Chapter 9: *Submitting your Social Science Research Project*). Ideally, your research project should build upon what you have learnt in previous years, but it is important to remember that the research project is a learning process too. While you might have been taught 'how to do methods', this might be the first time that you are putting what you have learnt into action. While you might have been taught how analysis is done, this might be the first time that you are analysing data collected by yourself or answering research questions which you have developed. It is a mature approach to consider what sorts of deficits you have going into the project and to explore what training workshops are available that might help fill any knowledge lacunas. This training might include learning to use a new analysis or management software package such as SPSS or NVivo, or other computer packages such as Endnote that are designed to help you create your reference list. Other repositories and portals that aim to sharpen your analytical skills are also available such as: Sage Methods Datasets (https://methods.sagepub.com/datasets), which is a pedagogical resource that helps you with qualitative and quantitative analysis, by providing you with some data to practise with; Sage Foundations, which are bite-size introductions to research concepts and methods (https://methods.sagepub.com/foundations); or Sage Campus (https://campus.sagepub.com/), which has online modules dedicated to learning new skills or tools. It is also important to keep a track of when things do not go to plan. This is still data, and you should be assessed not simply on the carrying out of the research but on your final written product. As such, critically reflecting on the 'success' of the research design should be viewed as a strength. We urge you to go into the project with the intention to document aspects of the research project process, recording when things go wrong as well as right, and to keep remembering that you are still learning, so if something does not go to plan in, for example, the first research interview, consider what could be done to make the next one run more smoothly. This is why, as part of any planning, you will often be recommended to conduct a **pilot study** to iron out any creases.

In essence, a pilot study is a microcosm of your project, a smaller scale study of your larger project used to test your research methodology. It is a way to practise and to make sure all is in place before the main research begins. After piloting your project, you might change some of the research tools used, revise some of the questions asked or even alter how a questionnaire is displayed. Pilot studies, then, are a recognition that research projects are a learning process and not everything will work as planned. Above all, remember that while this is an independent piece of work, you are not simply left to your own devices. There will be pillars of support that help scaffold your research project. Your main point of contact will be your supervisor or advisor. We now discuss the role of the supervisor/advisor in more detail.

MEETING YOUR SUPERVISOR OR ADVISOR

When you embark on your research project journey, alongside a suite of lectures, seminars, and workshops that will help centrally scaffold the module, it is very likely you will be allocated a supervisor or advisor (sometimes also called a tutor). Other than yourself, over the course of your project, the supervisor will know your research better than anyone. Above all else, remember that your supervisor will be an experienced researcher and is there to help and guide you throughout the research journey.

It might be the case that you are asked to send an initial brief outline of your research idea before you enrol on the module, allowing your supervisor to be allocated at the beginning of the project, quite possibly matched with you due to their methodological or substantive expertise and interests. That is, if you plan to do an interview-based project researching protest movements, it might be that you are allocated a supervisor or advisor who is interested in or has researched activism, civil action or collective work, or a staff member who has experience conducting interviews with citizens or publics. No matter who you are allocated, your supervisor will have experience of conducting a research project and it is useful to build a strong working relationship with them. Regarding planning, it is crucial to consult the relevant module handbook or guide to understand the expectations placed on both you and your supervisor. As detailed previously, the handbook/guide should include details on the number of meetings you are expected to have with your supervisor as well as the parameters of their role. In most cases, it is worth thinking of your supervisor as a mentor, someone appointed to help advise you on your progress and to discuss and develop ideas with.

We strongly encourage that you are pro-active in supervisory meetings. This form of learning is quite different to large lecture-theatre didactic teaching. While meetings might centre on different pre-defined topics such as Literature Review or Methods, they are not formalised in the same way as structured lectures. There is no lecturer standing at the front of the theatre talking to a series of pre-planned slides. Instead, this form of learning is much more of a partnership, and it is expected in many cases that you dictate the form of, and content discussed in, the meetings. You should first meet your supervisor at the outset of the research project. During this meeting, you should discuss your embryonic ideas. Here, you might send a page or two of your initial idea in advance of the meeting to be discussed. No supervisor will expect your ideas to be refined yet, but they will expect you to have put some thought into what you want to do, why you want to do it and how you imagine doing it. Coming with a proto or primitive plan from which a discussion can unfold will mean this first meeting will be productive. Do not be afraid to ask questions or to seek clarifications. Bring a notepad or laptop to meetings and make detailed notes of what is discussed. Supervisors will be keen to meet enthusiastic, self-driven students who have ideas. Remember, this is *your* project.

At the end of your first supervisory meeting, you should leave with a sharper idea of your research project, and a plan for taking things forward. Here, you might want to discuss timelines, sharing with your supervisor the diary which you have produced or working with them to produce one. As part of this tracking, set a date for your next meeting with your supervisor, and put the date in your diary. Your supervisor may also give you a date by which they want you to submit any work for them to review. It is important to note this date as this will ensure your supervisor has sufficient time to review your work and provide valuable feedback in your next meeting. Add this to your Gantt chart or Kanban board. It might be the case that your supervisor proposes one-to-one meetings or group meetings with the other students they supervise or a combination of both. They may suggest some of the meetings being held online. Whatever the form of the meetings, continue to prepare and plan for these meetings, displaying what it is you have done and asking for advice on aspects that you feel require work or more thought. Also, do not be afraid to make your preference known. For example, if you would rather in-person to online meetings, politely request this.

It is also important to remember that your supervisor is likely to be supervising or mentoring several students. Despite all best intentions, this can mean that they may, on occasion, forget to respond to an email or are late in sending feedback. To avoid such instances that can cause unnecessary delays to your research project, it is a fruitful idea to send a short message after the supervisory meeting confirming actions and, if appropriate, sending calendar invites for the next meeting or to flag a deadline. You may sometimes need to send your supervisor a friendly reminder to complete a task. If this is the case, keep the tone of your correspondence friendly and professional. If you continue to experience delays, it may be a good idea to speak to the course leader or another member of staff in your department, such as your personal tutor.

BEGIN WRITING

Throughout this textbook we endorse the mantra of *get it written first and getting it right after*. You can edit something, but you cannot edit nothing. Start as you mean to go on by writing from the outset. A potentially valuable activity is to develop a nascent research plan.

Producing a Research Plan

Whilst not necessarily a formal requirement, it can be helpful at the beginning of your dissertation journey to produce a nascent **research plan** which should help bring clarity and focus to your project as well as help structure initial supervisory meetings. The plan itself could include as much or as little detail as is useful for you. Importantly, it need not be polished; this is not a research proposal with the purpose of persuading someone else it is a viable project, but a mutable guide which should help you to formalise your idea, one which you can return to routinely to update or edit. This given, it should be a document that you put effort into and that sets out your fledgling thoughts on the project you wish to undertake. It may also be the case that sections of your research plan can be later adapted and pasted into your main research project.

Simply put, your plan should be designed to fit your individual needs and you might want to write it in a conversational style or relaxed manner, adding notes and asking yourself questions that you will hopefully be able to address as your research project progresses. With each iteration, the plan will likely morph into a comprehensive research project compendium. Essentially, a research plan at this stage should be a light touch overview, setting out the general idea, the general direction of the project and including any major milestones and deadlines. Importantly, it also allows you to practise writing from a very early stage in the project.

To get better at running (in terms of speed, endurance, and technique), it is highly likely that you need to train yourself to run, to work at it and to do it regularly, building stamina and confidence. Writing, though not a physical activity in the same way, is also a technique that you can become more proficient at. Writing is a craft, it is an act that you can get better at, become more comfortable with and more confident at doing. Begin as you mean to go on by writing a document, by constructing full sentences and by beginning to build an argument, even if in a conversational style. This will hold you in good stead for the rest of the research project.

There is no correct way to produce a research plan. Instead, as with timetables and Gantt charts, we advocate producing something that works for you. Here, you might embrace the following headings:

1   Title – It is always good to put a name to the project. However, do not feel hamstrung by your initial draft title. As with many aspects of the dissertation, this will likely change. Sometimes data extracts and quotes from the research

project itself end up forming part of the title or subtitle. To begin with though, do not overthink the title, do not try and make it too fancy. Make it direct, punchy and relatable. Make sure it does what it says on the tin (see Chapter 9: *Submitting Your Social Science Research Project* for more on titles).

2   Abstract – Abstract writing is always a useful skill to learn, and we will return to this in Chapter 9 (*Submitting Your Social Science Research Project*). Principally, an abstract is a condensed synopsis of your overall project. You will likely see abstracts in every journal article you read and, while there are some stylistic differences, most abstracts have a consistent internal structure, which is meant to entice the reader into reading the full paper. For the purposes of the research plan, we suggest producing a 150-word abstract that summarises the project that you are about to embark on. Start with the problem, discuss how you will research that problem and how you will likely present the findings. At this stage, of course, you will not have any findings, but you can speculate on the importance of the research and who will likely benefit from it and why.

3   Research Overview – Depending on how it is written, a research overview might look like an abstract so you may decide to include one or the other. But, if you choose to include both, this section allows you to expand on some of your abstract writing, which is supposed to be succinct. Here, you may include the key issues which need researching and argue for their importance and relevance, highlighting how your contribution is original or what you will contribute to the topic. Essentially, a research overview should begin helping you refine what you will do, how you will do it and why you are doing it by clearly documenting the purpose of the project and its significance.

4   Research Context – This section should situate your research within a broader body of literature (see Chapter 3: *Reviewing Social Science Literature*). You might even begin to develop your argument by sketching out what work has already been done in the area and where your project might fit. It is perfectly fine though at this stage to simply produce bullet points summarising work that you think you might lean on in the future, and later return to these ideas and craft them into arguments. However, as we discuss in Chapter 3 (*Reviewing Social Science Literature*), an active writer should always include references and cite properly. In this section of your research plan, you might also want to include details on how you will search for relevant literature, including what databases and key words you will use to carry out these searches.

5   Research Questions – As already discussed in Chapter 1 (*What Is Social Science Research and Why Is It Important?*), research questions help root your research project. They are the questions around which you centre your research. You may even develop your research questions through reading previous work in the area. These questions will then be empirically addressed through the course of your research. As before, it is typical to have somewhere between two to four research questions. This is not to say you could not have more, but for the purposes of a

research plan it will likely be beneficial to come up with a set of approximately three research questions. As with the title, these are not immutable, and it will likely be the case you will still be tinkering with these research questions even after data collection. Here, though, try to produce three different but interconnected research questions that the project will address. By interconnected, we mean research questions which speak to one another, that explore the same substantive topic, often using the same method but having a slightly different focus. For example, you may have three interconnected research questions such as those listed here:

- How do primary school teachers identify anxiety in students?
- What resources do primary school teachers use to support students' wellbeing?
- What challenges do primary school teachers face when talking to their students about their wellbeing?

Here, the three questions cohere around how primary school teachers support students' wellbeing. The topics could all be explored in interviews or focus groups with teachers.

6. Research Methods – How will your objectives be achieved? How will you address your research questions? In this section, begin fleshing out your methodology. What methods will you use to answer your research questions and why? It is also useful to begin thinking about your sample, how you will access your sample and document any initial ethical concerns. Consider the practicalities of the project, for example, how will you gain access, how will you conduct the research, what resources do you need? At this stage, you may also want to consider any training or upskilling which you might need to be able to collect and analyse your data.

7. Significance – At this stage of the project, of course, you have no findings, but what you could begin to formalise is the significance of the project. Why do you think it is important to study your chosen topic or issue? What might it add to the literature? Who might benefit from the findings of the research project? Again, do not overthink this, but it is always useful to keep returning to the reasons why you are doing the research project. What drew you to the subject to begin with and what do you see as its contribution to social science? You may have included some of these contributions in the Research Overview section of your plan too.

8. Reference List – Start as you mean to go on and record the references you are using. Do not leave it to the end of the project to locate references that you have been using. Some students will use a bespoke reference computer programme such as EndNote or Mendeley. Others will prefer to create their own database in Microsoft Word. Check if your university wants the references in a particular style

e.g., Harvard University style, the American Psychological Association (APA) or the Modern Humanities Research Association (MHRA) and practise storing the references against these style guidelines. The earlier you begin doing this, the more comfortable you will become with referencing properly.

9 Gantt Charts and Kanban Boards – Have a go at producing a Gantt chart or a Kanban board described previously in the chapter, which you can update when and where necessary.

It is important to stress though that this plan should not be thought of as the finished article, but more as a conversation piece that you might share with your supervisor for some feedback. It should be thought of as something that will require further tinkering and finessing as your ideas develop and mature. But if you aim to write 200–300 words under each heading, you will have produced a 1,500 to 2,000 word document that sets out your initial thoughts and justification for the research project. Who knows, some of these words may end up in your completed research project too. Significantly, it is a document that demonstrates progress from the beginning, and one that you can revisit, and revise as needed. As such, it is a task that should boost your confidence.

Researcher Reflection

Jamie and his colleague, Andrew Bartlett, are currently conducting an interview project which applies a science and technology studies (STS) approach to understanding the cultures and practices of looking for Bigfoot (or Sasquatch) – commonly referred to as Bigfooting – and how this can tell us something about what it is to do science, about what it is to behave scientifically, and about the boundaries and borders of legitimate scientific practice (see Lewis and Bartlett 2024). It is worth pointing out here that institutional science's position is that there is no evidence that Bigfoot exists or has ever existed as a biological creature, but this has not prevented hundreds upon hundreds of very committed enthusiasts and hobbyists, few with formal scientific training, spending several weeks/months each year looking for Bigfoot. Jamie and Andrew have been interested in what techniques these Bigfooters use to 'capture' Bigfoot? What counts as evidence? How are these techniques and standards taught and shared within and between Bigfooting communities? And what is the relationship between Bigfooting and 'mainstream', institutional science?

But what might a nascent research plan look like for another, similar project about Bigfooting? The type of detail which you might include in a first draft of a research plan follows, You can build upon this initial draft as your project matures.

Title

To what extent is Bigfooting a colonial practice?

Research Overview

Bigfooting can be approached from various analytical perspectives, including as a symbol of colonialism and racialisation (Taussig 1986, Roddy and Castillo 2020). So, as an activity, can Bigfooting be uncritically separated from histories of colonialism and racialisation that have precisely positioned Bigfoot as a monstrous, mysterious creature? What we mean by this is that the name and concept of Bigfoot has an origin story, first appearing in a local Californian newspaper in the Autumn of 1958, when the journalist Andrew Genzoli reported on a footprint cast taken by timber construction worker, Jerry Crew. The term 'Sasquatch' though predates Bigfoot by over three decades. Coined by a schoolteacher and local bureaucrat, J.W. Burns anglicised the name by combining several first nations names such as Sokqueatl, and S'oq'uiam that were used to describe hairy giant-like creatures apparently residing in the Canadian and North American woodlands (Loxton and Prothero 2013; Lewis and Bartlett 2024). Stories of these so-called 'Wildmen' and 'Hairy Giants' have circulated in Indigenous and First Nation cultures for centuries in North America. The project will consider to what extent Bigfooting – the practice of searching for Bigfoot that originated in the 20th century and popularised on television programmes – is simply an appropriation of these First Nations' cultures or whether it is an activity that takes seriously a subject matter that Western science has previously routinely dismissed as fable and folklore.

Research Context

There is a limited but lively body of academic literature on the concept of Bigfoot and the practice of Bigfooting. There are also non-academic books aplenty on the subject, but this present research project will locate itself in the sociology, history, and anthropology of epistemic cultures. It is less concerned with whether Bigfoot is a real biological creature, this is the domain of primatologists and other biologists, but rather it is interested in cultures and sub-cultures, collectives of people who look for and try and make sense of Bigfoot, and the extent to which Bigfoot is a modern-day invention or a 20th century repurposing of an Indigenous object.

Research Questions

1. To what extent is Bigfooting a White, American, male activity and why?
2. How do Bigfooters understand the origins of the Bigfoot story?
3. Is Bigfooting an appropriation of Indigenous culture?

These are three distinct but inter-related research questions which stand alone as questions in their own right, but also work together, to consider whether Bigfooting is a colonial practice.

Research Methods

Living in the UK, we are very unlikely to have the funds and time to go to the Pacific Northwest or other parts of North America to conduct an observational study of Bigfooting. Equally, a survey type approach is unlikely to capture the sensitivity and complexity of the issues at play here. We propose doing an interview study with active Bigfooters, either over the phone or through online video programmes such as Zoom or Microsoft Teams,. We anticipate finding willing participants through social media where there are regularly active Facebook groups and YouTube channels. We will look for public email addresses from these accounts and write to them privately over e-mail using our work e-mail addresses. Some of these individuals have significant followers as well as being authors of their own books and podcasts, so we will need to consider issues such as whether we can offer anonymity and confidentiality or whether they want to be credited for their ideas, and what the repercussions of these choices mean. We will also need to consider the different time zones these participants will likely be in and plan accordingly. For a research project such as this, we propose 30 semi-structured interviews, lasting 45 minutes.

Significance

This is a very under-researched area on a subject matter that is becoming increasingly pervasive in North America. Individuals such as the anthropologist Jane Goodall, novelist Patricia Cornwall and television presenter David Attenborough have all spoken on the subject that is now firmly part of the pop culture in the United States of America (USA) and increasingly worldwide too. As such, I imagine the project will be of interest to cultural sociologists and anthropologists. It will consider how stories travel and the importance of popular television programmes about Bigfooting and the role they have played in refining and repurposing what Bigfoot is and who it belongs to.

Reference List

These are the references used in the Plan:

Buhs, J. 2009. *Bigfoot: The Life and Times of a Legend*. Chicago: Chicago University Press.
Lewis, J. and Bartlett, A. 2024. The Shape of Bigfoot: transmuting absences into credible knowledge claims. *Cultural Sociology*.
Loxton, D. and Prothero, D.R. 2013. *Abominable Science! Origins of the Yeti, Nessie and Other Famous Cryptids*. New York: Columbia University Press.
Regal, B. 2011. *Searching for Sasquatch: Crackpots, Eggheads and Cryptozoology*. New York: Palgrave MacMillan.
Roddy, D. and Castillo, M. 2020. Is Bigfoot racist? *Sh** Gets Weird* [Podcast].
Taussig, M. 1986. *Shamanism, Colonialism and the Wild Man: a Study in Terror and Healing*. Chicago: University of Chicago Press.

SUMMARY

In this chapter, we have focussed on the planning and preparation required to design a feasible social science research project. We recognise that the beginning of the project can be both exciting and slightly overwhelming for students. As such, we encourage you to develop good habits by creating documents that help track your progress and by developing a strong working relationship with your supervisor from the beginning. Such documents and artefacts not only build confidence through the creation of tangible outputs, and help organise and plot the research project journey, but they are also good testbeds to practise writing and develop your writing style. Several tools and techniques such as creating diaries, producing a research plan as well as designing Gantt charts and Kanban boards have been described as aids that should help with both time management and the planning of a research project. These will hopefully make a research project feel more manageable, more doable.

We also emphasised the importance of not delaying when it comes to starting your research project. This is not in any way to suggest you should rush into it, but rather it is to highlight that designing a research project takes both time and consideration and that the more you spend time thinking about the project, the more wriggle room you create yourself to advance your argument. This is where coming prepared to supervisory meetings is essential. Take charge by attending your first supervisory meeting with a *foreshadowed problem* (Malinowski 1935) or nascent idea that you want to discuss and direct the meeting accordingly. Leave the meeting knowing what your next steps are and how you intend to achieve them.

In the next chapter, we consider how to go about writing the Literature Review chapter, locating your research project in a body of work as well as being an active note-taker. Of course, completing the Literature Review might be a discrete task that you include in your Gantt chart or Kanban board with the 'live' research plan document that you have produced also coming in handy.

Student Question

At what point in my research journey do I need to settle on a clear plan of what I want to do?

(Christoph, Anthropology student)

Charlotte and Jamie say:

This is a difficult question to answer and without trying to fudge it – it all depends on the particulars of your project. That said, slightly misapplying Bronislaw Malinowski (1935), we believe that all projects should at least have a 'foreshadowed problem'. You need a direction, and the project requires a purpose. Without it, your draft Literature Review will likely go around in circles. This is why the research questions are so important as they act as the fulcrum point on which the rest of the dissertation hinges. While you need to be adaptable and open to change as your research project progresses, the sooner you can narrow the focus of your project and design robust 'doable' research questions, the sooner you can begin to make real progress. Getting these research questions locked down – but with the knowledge they might be tweaked later – will hopefully mean that the rest of the project falls into place. As such, we would encourage students, in conjunction with their supervisors, to set their own deadline for when to have a research plan formalised.

WHAT'S NEXT?

Chapter Checklist

Table 2.1 Chapter 2 checklist

	Yes	No
I appreciate the importance of planning a research project.		
I understand the purpose of a Gantt Chart and Kanban Board.		
I appreciate the importance of producing realistic deadlines.		
I know where I can find sources of inspiration for picking a topic.		
I recognise that I can get better at writing the more I practise.		
I am aware that I need to design a manageable research project.		
I am cognisant that I need to come prepared to supervisory meetings.		
I acknowledge the usefulness of producing a research plan.		

Read

The module handbook/guide associated with your research project and check the expectations required of both you and your supervisor.

Complete

Fill in the table with the required information.

Table 2.2 Important research project details

Deadline for my research project:
Name of my supervisor/mentor:
Contact details of my supervisor/mentor:
Office hours of my supervisor/mentor:

Complete (at Least One of the Following)

- Your own Gantt Chart.
- Your own Kanban Board.
- Your own nascent Research Plan.

Contact

Unless otherwise instructed by your department, contact your supervisor to schedule your first, initial supervisory meeting. In this email include the following information:

- Your name and the degree programme you are studying.
- The research areas you are considering exploring.
- The research methods you are considering using.
- Your availability for a meeting.
- Attach your Gantt chart/Kanban board and Research plan.

Complete

- Complete the University of Sheffield's online workshop on Supervisor/Supervisee Relationships: https://xerte.shef.ac.uk/play.php?template_id=906#page1
- List the tasks you think your supervisor could help you with during your project. It is a good idea to take this list to your first meeting with your supervisor so that they can confirm what they are able to assist you with.

Read

For more on planning your dissertation please read: Brookfield, C. and Lewis, J. 2021. *Plan Your Dissertation.* London: Sage.

3
REVIEWING SOCIAL SCIENCE LITERATURE

In this chapter, we set out the aims and purpose of a Literature Review chapter, detailing the importance of situating a social science research project in an existing body of academic work. We also discuss how you might structure the chapter, proposing diverse approaches for organising and presenting the pertinent literature associated with your topic. We explain that the Literature Review is the chapter most like an essay, which you will have likely submitted for assessments in the past. However, rather than ending with a conclusion that definitively answers an essay question, your Literature Review chapter should end with a set of (research) questions that you will answer later in the project. Crucially, we include information on how you might effectively search for and critique relevant literature. Practical advice on how to record what you read is also provided. Finally, we discuss the importance of finding your own authentic voice, your own line of argument, when synthesising other people's work.

Chapter Objectives

- To understand the purpose of a Literature Review.
- To identify sources of social science literature.
- To describe and critique existing literature in your field of interest.
- To make effective notes while engaging with literature.
- To acknowledge that the best Literature Review chapters contain a throughline or line of argument that funnels into your research project.
- To understand the various ways a Literature Review chapter can be structured.

INTRODUCTION

Academic writing should always be in conversation with other academic writing that came before. By this, we mean that your research should be set against a backdrop of what is already known about the topic of exploration, what research already exists in the academic field. It is in the Literature Review chapter of a social science research project where you set up your argument and locate your work in dialogue with previous work, showcasing how your work will contribute to current academic conversations and debates on the issue. Presuming you will have already written some social science essays during your degree programme, the Literature Review chapter should have a form that is vaguely familiar to you. It might be a relief to hear, then, that the Literature Review chapter is almost always the first substantive chapter you begin drafting when starting your research journey. This allows you to 'ease' into your project with some degree of familiarity.

As a student, you will also know that you should always read about and around your subject. This is the basis for any academic assignment. In a Literature Review you can build upon this reading to locate your nascent research idea in a 'body of academic literature', whether that is social psychology, urban sociology, organisational studies, environmental planning, medical education, etc. and to underscore why further research on a particular issue or topic is necessary. As Ridley (2012: 6) maintains,

> … your research is a small piece in a complicated jigsaw puzzle; it does not exist in isolation. It is dependent on what others have done before and you will contribute to an ongoing story or debate.

In a Literature Review chapter you may identify inconsistencies or gaps in existing research on the topic of your choosing, always with the purpose of developing a set of research questions to be answered later in your own project. These findings will then hopefully further the knowledge on your chosen issue, adding to the discussions and debates in the literature that you have located your work in.

Crucially, the Literature Review chapter needs to draw out the relevance of the ideas for your project clearly so that the reader can see how the Literature Review provides a foundation for your project. It is also the section of your dissertation where you (implicitly) set out your 'research passion' and your 'research identity', showing enthusiasm, energy, and effervescence. This means it should not simply be a list of previous studies on the topic. Finally, a Literature Review serves to help define key terms which will be used throughout the dissertation and provides a space to set out the theories or concepts that are essential to the project. As Blaxter et al. (2010: 24) state succinctly, the purpose of a Literature Review chapter 'is to locate the research project, to form its context or background, and to provide insights into previous work'.

This chapter can be read as two halves. In the first section, we outline three main principles for you to take away: the importance of (i) drafting an argument, (ii) writing critically, and (iii) being selective. The second half is dedicated more to the practical challenges of writing a Literature Review. Here, we discuss how you can go about finding and choosing appropriate literature and discuss the best ways to structure this chapter, as well as dedicating space championing the importance of active note taking.

More generally, in both sections of the chapter we stress that the Literature Review chapter is a piece of writing that you will need to draft and then return to later to re-draft. While the Literature Review is typically drafted early in the research process, it is almost unavoidable that you will need to revisit it later in the research journey to make edits and revisions or to simply 'tidy up'. This is because, depending on the length of your research project, the field you are studying can move on, resulting in new, important literature being published. Alternatively, as your project develops and matures, your research questions may need to be adapted or modified depending on the access you secured and the findings that you generated. This should mean that you need to rework your Literature Review, if only slightly, to make it clear to the reader where these research questions have stemmed from and to make sure that the Findings chapter of your research project speaks to the definitive version of the Literature Review chapter. It is also important to remember one of the main messages of Chapter 1 (*What Is Social Science Research and Why Is It Important?*) that the research questions are pivotal to the overall narrative of a research project. They should be developed from engagement with existing literature presented in the Literature Review section, and later, should be answered in the Findings section. Also critical to state is that while the Literature Review chapter is often the first substantive piece to be written, it will be preceded in the final written document by an Introduction section or chapter. Indeed, it is often the case that some of the writing of the first draft of the Literature Review will eventually end up being moved into the Introduction chapter as your project progresses and takes shape.

TYPES OF LITERATURE REVIEW

Like your favourite chocolate bar, literature reviews can come in different forms and styles. According to Arshed and Danson (2015) there are at least four types of literature reviews. These include:

i   The *meta-analysis literature review*, which uses statistical procedures to analyse findings from your chosen literature. It is an approach that you typically find in scientific and clinical disciplines.
ii The *meta-synthesis literature review*, which uses *non*-statistical procedures to analyse the findings of qualitative studies. This is a style still in its infancy but one you might come across in medical disciplines.
iii The more common *systematic review*.
iv The pervasive, in the social sciences at least, *narrative review*.

Systematic reviews are used widely in scientific and healthcare research and like the meta-analysis and meta-synthesis reviews require a procedural, structured, approach to exploring the literature. They are also reviews that are proving to be increasingly popular with students working in certain social science disciplines such as medical education and social work, fields that are influenced by the scientific and health model discussed in Chapter 1 *(What Is Social Science Research and Why Is It Important?)*. The 'systematic' approach is argued to be 'rigorous' (Sataloff et al. 2021) and involves setting search terms and pre-determined inclusion and exclusion criteria, meaning selectivity is outsourced to a formula. The authors must then synthesise and present all the literature which the search returns within the parameters set. Additionally, the procedure used to undertake a systematic review should be explained in a way that other researchers are able to replicate unambiguously. Subsequently, systematic reviews are both a type of literature review and a method of 'analysing' secondary data. For more information detailing how to do systematic review, please see Boland et al. (2023).

In rest of this chapter, though, we focus on **narrative literature reviews** since these are what students undertaking empirical research for a social science research project are often expected to complete. Here, we see the influence of the arts and humanities in the social sciences discussed in Chapter 1 (*What Is Social Science Research and Why Is It Important?*). This approach to putting together narrative literature reviews explicitly recognises that the researcher is the instrument of analysis and argumentation. There are no hard and fast parameters set and selectivity is wholly in the hands of the researcher. The best narrative literature reviews have a narrative flow and do not read simply as a list of previous relevant research studies. Rather, the Literature Review should have a sense of direction and purpose in which the arguments made connect to form a *line of argument* that runs through the chapter building toward the research questions. Put differently, narrative literature reviews are building toward something – most typically, your research questions. They are telling a story.

WHY DO A LITERATURE REVIEW?

Literature reviews are crucial chapters in a dissertation or research project. Undertaking a literature review provides you with the opportunity to determine what is already known about your chosen topic of research. Through engaging with literature which you have deemed relevant, it is likely that your own knowledge of your research topic will extend and deepen. By reading about other research projects, you may absorb more substantive knowledge about the research area, as well as ideas about how best to approach studying your chosen topic. For instance, you might access new and different ideas about the methods or approaches to analysis, which will influence the way in which you approach your project. This can be particularly pertinent for quantitative researchers since they may want to use measures which have already been tested and deemed reliable by others and therefore choose to replicate existing questions used in other studies.

Reviewing the literature also affords you the opportunity to set the backdrop and context for your research project. For instance, if your research aims to explore the impacts of the Covid-19 pandemic on loneliness among students studying in New Zealand higher education institutions, you will want to provide some background details on the Covid-19 pandemic and the New Zealand Government's response to the crisis under the leadership of Jacinda Ardern (and how this might have differed from other countries). For instance, what restrictions were put in place in New Zealand and how did they specifically impact students? Likewise, if your research examines the physical education provision available in primary schools in different European countries, you will need to provide some contextual information on the legislation in place around physical education training in each country that you are planning to study. This contextual information can be particularly important if the research topic you are studying is potentially unfamiliar to your reader. Sometimes this means unpicking and explaining ideas or scenarios which may seem very familiar and obvious to you, particularly if you decide to do a research project based on your own interests and hobbies. It is crucial that while you should certainly not dumb down, you should also not assume too much of the reader; you should not make them do too much of the work. Narrative literature reviews should not have gaping holes.

Producing the Literature Review chapter is also an opportunity to define key terms which you intend to use in the dissertation. This is particularly important if you are likely to use concepts or terms which have been defined differently throughout the existing literature or over time or between cultures or disciplines. For example, in Charlotte's research exploring the teaching of quantitative research methods in social science disciplines, it was important that she defined which social sciences disciplines were included and excluded from her research (see the following Researcher Reflection). Providing definitions is not only helpful to the reader, detailing and justifying your approach, but it also allows your research to be replicated more easily in the future. Again, a critical reading of the literature is important here as you may need to make the case for the inclusion criteria that you are using.

Researcher Reflection

Charlotte's research explores the role of quantitative research methods in different social science disciplines. Specifically, Charlotte is interested in the ways in which quantitative research methods are taught across the social sciences as well as initiatives which have been put in place to engage social science students with these methods of data collection and analysis. This interest has stemmed from existing literature suggesting that there are a limited number of social science graduates with the skillsets to analyse and interpret quantitative data. There have been several educational initiatives established in the United Kingdom (UK) in response to this perceived deficit. This has included the implementation of the £19.5 million Q-Step programme funded by the Nuffield Foundation and Economic Social Research Council, launched in 2013.

However, the trend of a deficit in quantitative research methods skills has not been observed uniformly across all the social science disciplines. For example, as discussed in

(Continued)

Chapter 1 (*What Is Social Science Research and Why Is It Important?*), economics and psychology in the UK both have strong quantitative traditions and the mainstream journals for these disciplines contain lots of quantification. With this in mind, Charlotte opted to explore only those social science disciplines listed in the *Aims and Activities of the Q-Step Centres* document produced by the Nuffield Foundation at the beginning of the Q-Step programme. These include: Area Studies, Criminology, Education, Environmental Planning, Human Geography and Demography, Linguistics, Management and Business Studies, Political Studies and International Relations, Social Anthropology, Social Policy, Social Work, Socio-Legal Studies and Sociology.

It was imperative that Charlotte was explicit about the definition that she was using for social science disciplines when writing research papers and reports. This allowed the readers of her work to understand the context in which the findings have been discovered and provided them with the information to either replicate her research later, or to critique it.

A DIFFERENT TYPE OF ESSAY? STRUCTURE AND SELECTIVITY

The Literature Review section of a research project is the one which reflects most closely a standard social science essay that you should have experience of writing for other substantive modules during your time at university. That is, when drafting a Literature Review, much like an essay, you should evidence engagement with relevant academic readings as well as demonstrating your ability to synthesise and critique literature and craft an argument. However, whereas in an essay it is typical to finish with a clear summary that directly addresses the essay question asked, a Literature Review concludes with a set of research questions to examine, which then act as a transition axis into your project. So, how do you go about organising your Literature Review chapter?

When it comes to discussing the content in a Literature Review, we recommend thinking of a Literature Review like a funnel where you begin broader before narrowing into your project. In a way, this tapering and focussing of the gaze mirrors the thought process concerning the research design (see Chapter 2: *Planning a Social Science Research Project*). But where there you are refining your idea, here you are moving the story away from the work of others on the topic and toward your own project. This can be accomplished in various ways, which we illustrate in Table 3.1.

There are several mantras we endorse when putting together a research project (Brookfield and Lewis 2021), one of which is 'say what you are going to do, do it, then say what you have done'. The distillation or funnelling process should mean that the end of the Literature Review chapter acts as a segue between saying what you are going to do, and then doing it (the Methods chapter). For instance, a Literature Review for a project evaluating the effectiveness of initiatives to close the awarding gap between

Table 3.1 Different approaches to organising literature

Approach to organising literature	Definition
Thematically	Group together literature that explore similar or related substantive issues. Here, you might organise and present the literature in a concentric circle technique where you discuss a theme, then another theme, then another theme before concluding on a section where the three themes meet.
Chronologically	Begin by reporting the oldest studies and finish with the most recent material published in the area.
Importance and Relevance	Order the literature in terms of importance with the most relevant studies for your project appearing at the end of the chapter.
Theoretically	Structure the literature by the different theoretical contributions to the subject. This can again follow the concentric circle approach described in the thematic section above.
Specificity	Similar to organising the literature by importance is the idea of moving from the general to specific, funnelling into your project.
Complexity	Order the literature from simple to complex.
Dramatic Ending	Follow the narrative style that you might come across in films, TV series and novels by having a dramatic ending.

students of different ethnicities in Australian higher education institutions may adopt the following structure:

- An introduction setting out what to expect from the chapter

Followed by several subheadings such as:

- What is the awarding gap?
- What are the outcomes of different ethnic groups in Australian higher education?
- What initiatives have been put in place to close the awarding gap?
- Why does the awarding gap still exist?

Then conclude with a summary of the chapter that transitions to the research questions and Methods chapter:

- Summary of the arguments made
- A list of research questions

This example structure gives the reader an overview of the problem being explored and then becomes more focussed. Importantly, though, it does not digress (too much) from the topic under exploration by including, for instance, details on the awarding gap between students from different socioeconomic backgrounds. This indicative structure should be topped and tailed by a punchy introduction to the chapter, foreshadowing what is to come in the Literature Review, and a short conclusion that summarises the main messages of the chapter. This concluding section should lead to the presentation of the research questions as well as transitioning into the Methods chapter.

Some of the journal articles introduced in Chapter 1 (*What Is Social Science Research and Why Is It Important?*) have clear subsections within their reviews of the literature. For example, in Table 3.2, you can see that Testa et al. (2022) organise their Literature Review into three subsections (i) 'Criminological relevance of future orientations', (ii) 'Police contact and adolescent development: A life-course perspective' and (iii) 'Youth police contact and future orientation'. Similarly, Fernandez et al. (2022) and Herbst-Debby (2022) divide their Literature Reviews into two subsections: (i) Access to law schools and (ii) Admissions as enrolment management, and (i) Single motherhood and (ii) Welfare policy directed at single-parent families. The use of subsections or headings can be extremely helpful when organising a Literature Review insofar as they help the author structure the literature which they have engaged with in a meaningful and logical way, making it easier for the reader to digest.

Table 3.2 Literature Reviews in journal articles

Paper	Journal	Literature Review subsections
Testa et al. 2022. Police contact and future orientation from adolescence to young adulthood: Findings from the Pathways to Desistance Study	*Criminology*	2.1 Criminological relevance of future orientations
		2.2 Police contact and adolescent development: A life-course perspective
		2.3 Youth police contact and future orientation
Fernandez et al. 2022. The color of law school: Examining gender and race intersectionality in law school admissions	*American Journal of Education*	Access to law schools
		Admissions as enrolment management
Herbst-Debby 2022. (De)legitimisation of single mothers' welfare rights: United States, Britain, and Israel	*Journal of European Social Policy*	Single motherhood
		Welfare policy directed at single-parent families

Again, much like an essay, it is also essential that the Literature Review not only presents the existing literature pertinent to the issue being explored, but that it also critiques it. At the simplest level, critiquing means not definitively accepting what it is you have read. For example, if we were to tell you that the earth was flat, you would most likely question this statement, arguing that despite the existence of a community of flat-earthers, scientific consensus maintains that the earth is spherical. Or if we were to state that dragons exist as biological creatures, you may respond cautioning that, yes, 'Komodo' dragons and dragonflies exist, but that fire breathing dragons are the domain of television programmes such as *Game of Thrones* and cultural folklore in countries such as Bhutan and Wales. To critique, then, is to think about what you have read, why the author(s) may have come to the conclusion they have, and to possibly question or even endorse their conclusion. Bluntly, to think critically is to consider what persuasive techniques are used to argue a point and what forms of logic and reasoning are drawn from them (see Chatfield 2017 and 2020).

Critiquing can happen outside the written word too. To critique is to also make decisions on what to include in your Literature Review and what to leave out. For instance, you may ask yourself some of the questions listed in Table 3.3 when engaging with and selecting potential literature. Asking yourself these questions will help you highlight some of the parameters of the existing research in the field and, in turn, identify ways in which your research project can fill a gap in the existing knowledge and make an original contribution to the field.

Table 3.3 Questions to ask yourself when reading the literature

Is this literature relevant to the project I am undertaking? If so, why?
Are the research findings relevant to the country and/or context which I am researching? If not, what can I draw from them?
Are the research findings dated, and does that matter? If not, why not?
Has the research topic been over- or under- researched? If it has been over-researched, is there a different approach to exploring it? If it is under-researched, might it prove problematic to study?
Have perspectives or voices been ignored or sidelined? Which ones and in what ways?
Has this topic been pursued through a particular theoretical lens and does that differ from my approach?
What is absent in the literature that I have read? Is there a (compelling) reason it is absent?

As described, a good Literature Review is one which is focussed and contained to the research problem at hand, not meandering off-piste. It needs to be tamed. Of course, this is easier said than done. Selectivity is pivotal to writing a good Literature Review chapter. Importantly, reading a piece of literature does not necessitate that you include it in your chapter. You should only include literature that is pertinent to the argument which you are making. To know what is relevant, though, you will first need to read articles and manuscripts that you decide not to include. None of us has a crystal ball. But if you have read a work, this does not necessarily mean you include it. You may deem it totally irrelevant or not relevant enough to justify inclusion. Part of the skill of writing a Literature Review, then, is deciding which literature to 'exclude' since you cannot include everything. Indeed, selectivity is a key component of any academic piece of writing. It can be a clever idea to be explicit about what is beyond the scope of the current study and some authors like to begin their Literature Reviews with clear statements regarding the inclusion and exclusion criteria employed in their search and subsequent review of the existing literature. But be mindful to keep this relevant.

An alternative way to start your literature search is to begin with a key article that is particularly pertinent to your research topic and then look at who the author(s) has/have referenced as well as who has subsequently cited their work.

Box 3.1

A Golden Thread

Throughout the book we discuss the idea of having a 'golden thread' or throughline that ties the dissertation together. When writing a Literature Review, we sometimes refer to the analogy of a central nervous system as akin to this thread. While there are opportunities to branch off down different routes, always make sure that these are connected to the central spine of your argument. That is, there should be a clear backbone (and purpose) to the Literature Review that connects the various smaller points you make.

WHERE DO YOU FIND SOCIAL SCIENCE LITERATURE?

Relevant literature for your project can be found in journal articles, monographs, textbooks, reports, government documents, websites, newspapers, and even blog posts. For instance, if you were exploring the topic of student loneliness in higher education institutions in the UK you may consider the different sources highlighted in Table 3.4. It is likely that your institution will have access to several databases which you can use to search for literature. These might include databases such as *Scopus* and *Web of Science* which are useful for searching out journal articles. You may also have access to databases such as *LexisNexi*, which allow you to search specifically for newspaper articles or the *OECD iLibrary* which allows you to search for grey literature, documents, and governmental reports. We strongly recommend that you familiarise yourself with what databases your university library subscribes to and to attend any training courses that are offered on searching for literature.

With the onset of multimedia platforms, there are now many new accessible sources of literature compared to previous decades which you can engage with to research your topic. This creates both opportunities and poses challenges. It should be emphasised though that not all these sources are given equal weight in academia. Generally speaking, some sources of literature such as academic books (monographs) and journal articles written by specialists in their field are deemed more appropriate and reliable than others (hence why these sources are listed at the top of Table 3.4). This is because academic books and journal articles will normally be required to undergo a process called **peer-review** before being published. In a similar way to how your lecturers might provide feedback on drafts of work, the peer-review process involves academics submitting work for other academics to review and comment on before it can be accepted for publication. This means that the publications you read in academic books or journal articles have been scrutinised by other scholars researching and writing within the field to ensure they are of a certain quality. Anything that is deemed to fall short of this threshold is often rejected and not published or is sent back to the author to make revisions. Essentially, then, these publications have been given a sort of

Table 3.4 Sources of literature

Type of literature	Source example
Monograph (academic book drawn from research)	Oakley, L. 2020. *Exploring Student Loneliness in Higher Education. A Discursive Approach*. London: Palgrave Macmillan.
Journal article (academic research paper published in a journal)	Vasileiou, K., Barnett, J., Barreto, M., Vines, J., Atkinson, M., Long, K., Bakewell, L., Lawson, S. and Wilson, M. 2019. Coping with loneliness at university: A qualitative interview study with students in the UK. *Mental Health & Prevention*, 13, 21–30.
Online news article (broadsheet, tabloid and TV news websites)	Jeffreys, B. and Clarke, V. 2022. University students are far lonelier than other adults – study. *BBC*, 9 June. Available at: www.bbc.co.uk/news/education-61735272 (accessed 29 July 2022).
Government publication (Working Papers, Policy Documents, White Papers)	Department for Digital, Culture, Media and Sport. 2018. *A connected society: A strategy for tackling loneliness*. Available at: https://assets.publishing.service.gov.uk/government/uploads/system/uploads/attachment_data/file/936725/6.4882_DCMS_Loneliness_Strategy_web_Update_V2.pdf (accessed 29 July 2022).
Blog (author or institutional blogsite)	L. I. 2022. My experience with loneliness. *University of London Student Blog*, 13 May. Available at: www.london.ac.uk/news-events/student-blog/experience-loneliness (accessed 26 March 2024).
Website (general website such as a charity or think tank page)	Mind. 2022. *How to cope with student life*. Available at: www.mind.org.uk/information-support/tips-for-everyday-living/student-life/connecting-with-other-students/ (accessed 29 July 2022).
Report (commissioned reports)	Tinsley, B. 2020. *Coronavirus and the impact on students in higher education in England: September to December 2020*. Office of National Statistics. Available at: www.ons.gov.uk/peoplepopulationandcommunity/educationandchildcare/articles/coronavirusandtheimpactonstudentsinhighereducationinengland septembertodecember2020/2020-12-21 (accessed 29 July 2022).
Radio show (news radio shows, and podcasts)	BBC Radio 4. 2018. *All in the mind*, 14 February. Available at: www.bbc.co.uk/programmes/b09r6fvn (accessed 29 July 2022).
TV programme (documentaries)	*The Age of Loneliness*. (2016). BBC One, 19 October.

endorsement by other members of the academic community. For example, each social science discipline will have various mainstream academic journals that are valued by members of the community. For example, some of the key journals for the discipline sociology include *Sociology, British Journal of Sociology, European Sociological Review, European Journal of Sociology, Journal of Sociology, American Journal of Sociology, Sociological Bulletin, Canadian Journal of Sociology*, and *Social Forces*. As well as having generic journals, some are associated with certain theoretical positions and specific topics. For example, *Gender and Society, Journal of Gender Studies, Indian Journal of Gender Studies*, and *Gender, Work and Organisation* all contain articles concerning the topic of gender. There is also an array of methodological journals such as the *International Journal of Social Research Methodology, Qualitative Research, Qualitative Inquiry, Sociological Methods and Research, International Journal of Qualitative Research*, and *Journal of the European Survey Research Association*, which can be effectively drawn upon for inspiration when undertaking a research project and used to help provide a clear rationale for the chosen methodological approach.

For other outputs such as blogs or even news articles (though there will likely be editorial oversight for the latter), it is not typically the case that the work is peer-reviewed. This is why, of course, although often very useful, your lecturers will caution you about trusting websites such as Wikipedia. Anyone can change a Wikipedia page and while references are often included at the bottom of the page, it can be difficult to determine who authored the piece and whether they are a trusted source with the requisite expertise on the topic.

Generally, then, you want to make sure that you are engaging with literature that has been authored by experts in the field of your research. In most instances, you will be searching for literature which has been written by academics in higher education institutions and research centres. By engaging with literature which has been peer-reviewed, you can be sure that the literature has undergone a thorough review process. It is worth adding here that some organisations such as think tanks may produce literature with an intended purpose or aim in mind and these publications should be approached with caution, critiqued or avoided completely. You want to ensure that the literature you draw from does not provide biased information on a topic. You may also want to check which country the author(s) of a publication is from. While a lot of research may have been undertaken exploring your chosen topic in a different country, the findings may not always be applicable to your own country and its specific policies, regulations or culture.

Beyond the databases which your university subscribes to, there are other places you can use to search for literature. For example, *Google Scholar* is understandably a very popular website tool that allows you to search for scholarly literature. Its strength is in how it constantly updates and trawls the Internet for new research publications. But as previously mentioned, you may also have access, via your institution, to databases of relevant literature which you can search. Other examples include the *International Bibliography of Social Sciences, Applied Social Sciences Index* and *Abstracts (ASSIA), ProQuest* and APA *PsycINFO*. One fast moving development that will likely have at least some impact on the way in which we search for literature is Artificial Intelligence (AI). We would currently caution against using AI to find appropriate literature. At present, Artificial Intelligence tools such as ChatGPT can produce significant inaccuracies as well as fabricated references.

> **Box 3.2**

Generative Artificial Intelligence

A cautionary word on the use of generative Artificial Intelligence (AI) technology and Large Language Models (LLMs) such as ChatGPT, Bard, LLaMA or Quillbot. Generative AI is a tool capable of generating text, images, artificial data, or other media, using predictive and probability models. Generative AI models learn the patterns and structure of their input to generate new 'synthetic' data. Essentially, a programme such as ChatGPT predicts the next word from the previous one. We are writing this at a point at which these technologies are still in their relative infancy and there are no clear rules or use patterns, so our views are necessarily speculative. But there are groups of people forecasting that they will play an ever-increasing role in the write up and structure of research in the future, including the way in which we search for literature. However, we want to remind students that LLMs such as ChatGPT do not have the personal insights, experience, and knowledge that you bring to your work. Likewise, these technologies will not have the familiarity with university formatting and presentational guidance you will have been provided with. In other words, they should not take the place of a module guide or handbook or be relied on more than your supervisor. Your own institution will likely have information on whether you can or cannot use these technologies, and the ways in which you can use them. If you do decide to use these technologies, it is imperative that you ensure citations and the provenance of ideas are correct, and that you are not including false (synthetic) or inaccurate information that you are not able to verify. Some of the writing it produces is not at the level one would want to aspire to either. Be cautious and critical when using these technologies. Indeed, we would strongly encourage you to have confidence in your own abilities to search for relevant literature and in structuring and writing the Literature Review chapter rather than rely on generative AI.

Of course, it can be difficult to know where to begin when searching the literature and putting search terms into a search engine or database without any parameters will likely bring up thousands and thousands of results. For instance, at the time of writing this chapter, the search for 'Student loneliness UK higher education' in *Google Scholar* returned approximately 118,000 results. This is clearly unmanageable for any research project, let alone a student one. Therefore, it can be useful to identify key search terms and parameters to refine your literature search and reduce the number of results returned. **Boolean** search terms are commands which can be used to help limit your online searches. Table 3.5 describes the search terms which you may find helpful when searching for relevant literature for your research project. But a good social science researcher, as we all know, is a cautious and critical social science researcher. Care should be taken when using Boolean search terms, particularly with the NOT search term as it can result in your overlooking important pieces of literature.

Table 3.5 Boolean search terms

Search term	Results	Example	Search result explained
AND	Output must contain both words	Student AND Loneliness	This search would return literature which contains both the word 'student' and the word 'loneliness'
OR	Output must contain either one of the words	Loneliness OR Isolation	This search would return literature which contains either the word 'loneliness' or the word 'isolation'
NOT	Output must not contain the second word	University NOT School	This search would exclude literature which contains the word 'school'
""	Output must contain the exact phrase	"Student loneliness"	This search would return literature which contains only the exact phrase 'student loneliness'

Figure 3.1 shows what happens to our literature search for outputs on student loneliness in higher education institutions in the UK when we introduce parameters and Boolean search terms. To begin, when we refine the search to outputs published between 2020 and 2022, the number of results reduces from 118,000 to approximately 17,000 (better, but still far too many to read though!). But Boolean search terms can help further narrow the number of results. By putting the phrase "student loneliness" in double quotation marks, the search only returns outputs which contain this exact phrase. Suddenly, the results of the literature search decrease to approximately 158 outputs. Once double quotation marks are inserted around "UK higher education" and the AND Boolean search operator is used, the number of results drops to just 3. This means that there are only 3 outputs produced during this 2-year period with both the phrases 'student loneliness' and 'UK higher education'. Here, we might reflect and determine that this is now too few results and subsequently refine our search terms accordingly.

For example, we might consider alternative search terms to help identify more literature. In this example, we decided to swap the phrase 'UK higher education' for 'UK universities'. This then generated 13 publications. Table 3.6 gives some examples of other alternative search terms which can be used in this scenario. Listing the search terms that you have used can be beneficial as you might need to describe your approach for conducting the literature search, while using a thesaurus or looking up synonyms on your computer can help you identify alternative search terms.

As well as searching for literature using key search terms in search engines and databases, you may also come across additional, important sources of literature as you read.

Student loneliness UK higher education **Approx 118,000 results** → Student loneliness UK higher education (between 2020–2022) **Approx 17,000 results** → "Student loneliness" UK higher education (between 2020–2022) **Approx 158 results** → "Student loneliness" AND "UK higher education" (between 2020-2022) **Approx 3 results**

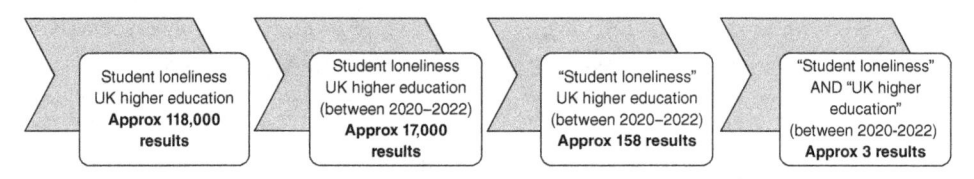

Figure 3.1 A literature search using Boolean search terms

Table 3.6 Alternative search terms

Original search terms	Alternative search terms
Student	Young people
	School leaver
	Undergraduate
	Postgraduate
	Learner
Loneliness	Isolation
	Seclusion
	Remoteness
	Solitude
UK	British Isles
	United Kingdom
	*Depending on geographical scope of the study you could use:
	Great Britain
	Northern Ireland
	Scotland
	Wales
	England
Higher Education Institutions	Universities

Here, it may be apparent that a particular author or a specific paper is referenced on a frequent basis. In these instances, it can be useful to look at the bibliographies and reference lists of the work that you are reading and to access some of these sources of literature for yourself from the university library. This technique is very good for tracking the provenance and lineage of a concept, approach or theoretical standpoint.

Box 3.3

Searching for Literature

A rudimentary but thorough way to search for literature is to thumb through the pages of a text that you have sourced noting down any pertinent citations. This has the added benefit of being able to track the lineage of an idea or a concept because, of course, any references listed will have been published previously. Once you have found an earlier relevant text, you can do the same with that reference list. You can practise this technique when reading Chapters 5 and 6 of this textbook where we have included a bank of references for further reading.

Furthermore, you may want to identify some of the major journals in your discipline to see if there have been any recent publications on your topic of interest. Most online journals have an in-built search tool where you can input key words. Table 3.7 lists some of the main journals in different social science disciplines. The table also shows the impact factor score of these journals. This score reflects the journal's prominence and reputation within its field by indicating the average number of citations an article published in the journal over the past three years has received. You may also want to see if there is an academic journal devoted specifically to your research area. For example, if you are researching 'employment' you may want to consider the following journals:

i   *Work, Employment and Society*
ii *Work and Occupations*
iii *New Technology, Work and Employment.*

Table 3.7 Mainstream journals in different social science disciplines

Journals	Impact factor
General Sociology	
International Sociology	0.741
International Sociology Reviews	2.535
International Journal of Sociology	1.980
International Review of Sociology	1.020
American Sociological Review	6.372
American Journal of Sociology	3.232
Social Forces	3.575
British Journal of Sociology	1.894
Sociology	4.816
Sociological Review	4.258
General Criminology	
Journal of International Criminal Justice	0.753
International Journal of Law, Crime and Justice	0.407
Policing	1.350
Critical Criminology	1.838
American Journal of Criminal Justice	6.037
The British Journal of Criminology	1.818
Criminology and Criminal Justice	2.672
Criminology	3.796

Journals	Impact factor
General Education	
Higher Education	3.000
International Journal of Educational Research	1.976
American Educational Research Journal	4.503
Review of Educational Research	8.241
Comparative Education Review	1.815
Educational Researcher	4.000
Review of Research in Education	1.594
Sociology of Education	3.167
British Educational Research Journal	2.752
British Journal of Educational Studies	2.298
General Psychology	
International Journal of Psychology	1.867
International Journal of Psychology and Psychological Therapy	0.950
Frontiers in Psychology	4.232
International Journal of Psychological Research	0.800
Annual Review of Psychology	27.780
Psychological Bulletin	17.740
Psychological Methods	11.300
The American Journal of Psychology	1.063
Asian American Journal of Psychology	1.547
British Journal of Psychology	3.308
General Social Policy	
Journal of International and Comparative Social Policy	1.340
International Journal of Sociology and Social Policy	1.368
Global Social Policy	0.980
Social Policy & Administration	2.738
International Journal of Public Policy	0.420
Journal of Social Policy	3.063
Social Policy and Society	2.119

Once you have identified sources of literature, it is important to evaluate those sources to ensure that the literature you are presenting is relevant and affords the opportunity to critique what is currently known about the topic. Ask yourself the following questions when reviewing the results of your literature search:

- When was it published?
- Who is the author?
- What was the purpose of the publication?
- Why has it been published?
- Where has it been published?
- Where has it been authored?
- What approaches have the authors employed?
- Who have they cited?
- What discipline is it located in?

Publications which are older may no longer be [as] relevant. Having said this, there may be some historical documents which are essential to include in your research projects as they are understood to be part of the canon. Alternatively, you may note that very little recent research has been undertaken in your research area and this could be the catalyst – and a compelling argument – for undertaking the work. That said, be careful in saying no work has been conducted on this topic. It is very likely that someone has researched the topic, and it only needs the marker to find one piece of work to challenge your statement. Rather than use phrases such as *no work* has been undertaken on this topic, caution with words such as *limited work* has been undertaken on this topic.

Finally, it can be helpful when looking for appropriate literature to seek advice from your librarian. Most universities have department, school, or college level librarians whose speciality will lie in the social sciences and who are more than willing to help with requests concerning finding literature.

EFFECTIVE AND ACTIVE NOTE TAKING

Note taking is an effective strategy when undertaking a successful social science research project. It prevents ideas from being lost as well as keeping a record of where ideas originated and how they have developed. This is particularly pertinent when pulling together a Literature Review. There are various ways in which you can record your developing ideas such as:

i   Traditional note taking by hand in a notebook or online through word-processing software such as Microsoft Word.
ii   Voice recording in which you verbally dictate your thoughts into a Dictaphone or on your mobile phone and upload to a folder.
iii Sketches and mind maps, which help you organise and see your notes visually.
iv   Annotated notes, which often involve more detailed note taking including adding references.

There are various apps available such as Notes, Evernotes, Google Keep, Coggle, Mindly, Sketchbook, Concepts, Day One, Journal It, Voice Recorder, Voice Memos, Easy Voice Recorder, and Notability, which you might find useful to use to record your notes in various forms.

Students can often be tempted to try to write down everything when reading. Again, this is not manageable and is likely to become like the map described by Borges (1988). The mapmaker kept adding more and more detail until the map became the size of the area it was representing rendering it functionally useless. Thus, it is important that your notes are selective and concise and therefore useful. Using bullet points or numbering will help ensure that your notes are succinct and can be revisited easily throughout the research process. Making effective notes whilst reading can not only save you time, but it also allows you to begin to identify patterns present in the literature. For instance, you may notice a particular author is cited frequently across the literature, or you may realise that a considerable number of studies in the research field have explored a certain demographic only. Therefore, it is important that you are active, as opposed to passive, when reading and making notes. Being an **active note taker** invovles identifying patterns, connections, (in-)consistencies, and anomalies in the literature. Active note takers do not simply write down what they have read (taking notes verbatim), but instead write notes in their own words, asking questions about the information they are reading and critically evaluating the source. Writing notes in your own words also helps active note takers to avoid plagiarism. This is because they have already paraphrased the original literature in their own words, even at this early stage of engaging with the literature. An active notetaker should follow two principles:

i   Always record the provenance of ideas and concepts by writing down all the necessary details of the publications you have read.
ii Have a clear system that separates:

    a   verbatim, direct quotes
    b   paraphrasing of someone else's ideas
    c   your own thoughts.

(See *Reading and Making Notes*, University of Reading 2024 for more information on active note taking.)

Table 3.8 Examples of different behaviours of active and passive note takers

Active note takers	Passive note takers
Write notes in their own words	Copy and paste text
Record direct quotes where needed, with all the necessary information to correctly reference the original source including page number	Write direct quotes only
Underline/bold key words in their own notes	Underline/bold in the original text
Are selective about what they write down (notes are concise)	Write down everything they read
Have a consistent approach to making notes, allowing connections to be made more easily	Do not have a logical approach to recording notes
File notes carefully	Do not file notes

Using different colour pens or highlighters can help you distinguish and differentiate key information, direct quotes, and evaluative comments in your notes. Similarly, if you write notes directly on the computer, you can change the colour of the font as well as using the review tab in Microsoft Word to add notes to yourself. If you adopt a consistent approach to recording your notes across all readings it can make it easier to identify patterns and any gaps which exist in the published literature. Another handy tip for note taking is to use abbreviations. For instance, instead of writing the word 'environment' you may simply use 'env'. Similarly, you may decide to use symbols such as an '&' (ampersand) instead of writing 'and' or use three dots to denote 'therefore'. So long as you understand the codes, abbreviations and symbols, this can be an extremely helpful way to speed up your note taking process. We recommend creating a document where you list all the abbreviations and symbols which you use in your note taking – this can be a live document which grows throughout the research process.

SQ3R – Survey, Question, Read, Recite, Review

SQ3R is a specific method for note taking which encourages you to critically think about the literature while you are reading. This method has been shown to improve retention of information and helps readers to think critically (Artis 2008, Carlston 2011). The approach involves five steps: S, Q, R1, R2, and R3.

> **S**urvey: Quickly skim the text paying close attention to headings, subheadings, bolded texts, charts, graphs, and tables. We strongly recommend reading the abstract.
>
> **Q**uestion: Write some questions which you envisage the reading will help you answer.
>
> **R**ead: Read the text looking for answers to your questions.
>
> **R**ecite: Write notes to help you answer your questions.
>
> **R**eview: Review your notes and make sure that you have answered your questions. Add any extra details such as page numbers, bibliographic leads, etc. so that you can return to the ideas later.

Tables can also be an effective way to organise your note taking. For instance, Table 3.9 shows one approach you could use for recording notes when reading empirical studies. The first column in Table 3.9 should be used to record the reference. The second column should summarise the main points or arguments of the paper in three to five bullet points. Forcing yourself to distil the information you have read into a few key points is a neat way to ensure your understanding of the reading and to begin to turn the ideas into your own words. The third column allows you to make notes on the method employed in the study. For example, did the authors use focus groups, interviews, questionnaires, etc? How did they sample the population and recruit participants? How many participants were included in the study? The next two columns encourage you to begin to critically reflect on the literature which you have just read by identifying some of the strengths and limitations of the study. The final column in the table is open for you to record any outstanding or emerging questions which you may have after reading the literature. This should help direct you to your next set of readings.

Table 3.9 Recording notes when reading empirical studies

Reference	Three to five key points	Method	Strengths	Limitations	Outstanding/Emerging questions

Alternatively, you may decide to record your notes using a mind map. Using a more visual approach to organising your notes can make it easier for some students to begin to make connections and synthesise arguments put forward. Drawing images, flowcharts, or even replicating and/or annotating key graphs or charts in a text can be a great way to record what you have read in an accessible and memorable format.

Of course, lots of students like to make notes based on their reading by hand. Nowadays, it is even possible to get notebooks which allow you to handwrite your notes and then scan and save them as PDF documents on your device. But as above, if you prefer to use a computer or laptop when recording notes, you may wish to consider looking at different software packages beyond Microsoft Word. For example, Evernote can be a useful platform to save readings and record notes. You may also be someone who dictates to themselves, and you can record, save, and upload audio recordings to some platforms.

Whichever way you decide to record your notes, we strongly encourage all students to record the bibliographic details of all literature that they engage with as they go along so to speed up both the process of writing and the formatting of a reference list. Therefore, it is a fruitful idea to include the details of the reading in any notes you make.

HOW DO YOU WRITE A SOCIAL SCIENCE LITERATURE REVIEW?

The Literature Review section or chapter of a thesis should bring together and synthesise the literature that you have engaged with. Paraphrasing literature (putting it into your own words) rather than presenting verbatim quotes, can help you develop your own voice and argument in this chapter. That is, despite drawing from others' work, the Literature Review chapter still needs to showcase your ideas and the ways in which you make sense of and interpret published works. When discussing your literature, you should be clear in your own mind how the literature contributes to the argument which you are trying to develop. This may mean that some of the pieces of literature which you have read do not appear in the final revision of your Literature Review. While this can seem frustrating, it is important that the chapter remains focussed and succinct and does not meander off point. A good tip is to begin the opening sentence of a paragraph with the idea, concept, topic, or theme that you want to discuss rather than the authors of a paper you are citing to avoid it sounding too list-like. Let us take the following fictional example about the role influencers play in young peoples' lives. Please note that these are fictional references.

> Brookfield's (2017) questionnaire of 210 undergraduate students demonstrated the ever-increasing role 'influencers' are having on young people's lives. Two years later, Lewis' (2019) work built on this. Drawing from 30 semi-structured, online interviews with marketing experts, he pointed to the way in which new social media sites such as TikTok are now platforming influencers to market certain products. Brookfield and Lewis' (2022) most recent work shows influencers connect with young people in ways that traditional A-list celebrities such as Hollywood stars advertising such products do not.

There is nothing alarmingly wrong with this style of writing but being hypercritical it reads a little list-like and perhaps includes some un-needed methodological information. Compare with the following example that says the same thing but is expressed slightly differently. Again, the references are fictional.

> The role that 'influencers' – young people of the social media age – play in young people's lives is growing (Brookfield 2017). Capitalising on this craze, particular brands are moving away from traditional forms of marketing techniques to now pay influencers to product place on sites such as TikTok (Lewis 2019). The rationale is that social media influencers have a stronger connection with young people, with some maintaining that they can 'imagine them as a friend' and 'they are real people just like us' (Brookfield and Lewis 2022: 9). Seeing an image of themselves in the influencers creates a bond that is not there with A-list celebrities.

Another is to use various verbs (such as those shown in Table 3.10). This enables you to paraphrase and synthesise various pieces of literature without becoming overly repetitive.

As well as describing what is already known in the field and how it might contribute to your project, the Literature Review should also critique existing studies, highlighting limitations in the existing research and gaps in our current understanding of the topic. This requires the use of evaluative language and some examples of useful phrases are outlined in Table 3.11. The inclusion of various perspectives and viewpoints in your Literature Review should help you develop a line of argument and provide a clear narrative for the chapter.

Table 3.10 Some verbs to use when discussing literature

Claims	Argues
Asserts	Questions
Deviates	Challenges
Supports	Debates
Considers	Defends
Analyses	Disagrees
Examines	Counters
Discusses	Deviates
States	Supports
Indicates	Reflects
Implies	Cautions
Recommends	Reveals
Suggests	Repurposes
Explores	Determines
Advises	Proposes
Evaluates	Maintains
Positions	Concludes
Explores	Synthesises

Table 3.11 Evaluative phrases to use in the Literature Review

A strength of this …
A limitation of this …
What is not considered …
What is excluded …
Little attention has been given to …
An oversight in the literature is …
More research is needed on …
Another way of interpreting this …
Despite this work, few studies have …
We can approach this from another perspective …
What is absent from this …

If you do not use in-text citations or include a reference list, you may be accused of plagiarism. **Plagiarism** is when you reproduce the work of someone else without acknowledging the original source. It is also possible to self-plagiarise. An example of self-plagiarism is when a student submits (part of) the same essay for two different assignments. Plagiarism is taken very seriously in higher education institutions and many universities now have software designed to identify cases of plagiarism in students' work. If you are caught plagiarising the consequences can be significant. Therefore, it is important that you put steps in place to minimise this risk. As before, we recommend keeping track of the literature which you engage with throughout the research process and constructing your reference list as you progress. This can save you a lot of time and work trying to relocate sources at the end of your project and should help you avoid the risk of plagiarism. You may decide to use online software such as EndNote to help you organise and store your references, and we return to this later in the book. Of course, work which you have read but decided was not relevant should not be cited. We return to this issue in Chapter 9 (*Submitting your Social Science Research Project*).

In some instances, you may find the original text captures the point perfectly and/or you find it particularly difficult to word things differently. In these cases, where you include selected quotes, you must make sure that you use quotation or speech marks around the inserted sections and properly cite the sources from which they originated to show that you are borrowing others' words. Here, rather than paraphrasing, you are 'copying' the text word-for-word or what is known as **verbatim**. It is paramount that you are familiar with the referencing style that you are required to use in your research project as different universities, and even different academic departments within the same institution, adopt distinctive styles. However, it is typically the case that if you paraphrase by re-purposing ideas and concepts taken from others' work into your own words then you should cite the original text by including the author(s) and the year of publication, whereas if you are inserting a section verbatim, you will need to cite the author(s), date of publication and also the page number of the text. Try not to over-do the latter approach, as markers might maintain that there is limited evidence of your own work and voice (even when properly cited).

All the literature that you decide to use in your thesis needs to be appropriately cited involving in-text citations and included in your reference list which comes at the end of the research project. This enables readers to identify the sources which you have engaged with and drawn from. The reference list should be ordered alphabetically by author's surname and should include all the details needed to make it possible for the reader to locate the literature for themselves (e.g., year of publication, article title, journal name and page numbers). Again, we return to this in Chapter 9 (*Submitting your Social Science Research Project*).

SUMMARY

In this chapter, we have highlighted the importance of writing a Literature Review at the beginning of your research journey. The Literature Review chapter of a research project can be likened to the foundations of a house. The Literature Review forms the groundwork for the research project. And, like the foundations and footings of a house, it supports the development of the research questions which hold the rest of the remaining chapters together. And, just like the builder debating the best approach to building a property from the start of the project (when laying the foundations), as a researcher writing a Literature Review you need to use the process of pulling together a Literature Review as an opportunity to refine your research ideas and consider the best approach to exploring your research problem. Structure is pivotal.

We have provided useful tips for searching and selecting literature as well as sharing ways in which you might organise the presentation of this chapter. But this initial iteration should be seen as a draft. Your Literature Review will require careful editing as your project progresses and, as such, it is a chapter that you will likely need to revisit again toward the end of your dissertation journey.

Student Question

How much editing will my draft Literature Review chapter require after I have collected my data?

(Polly, Criminology Student)

Charlotte and Jamie say:

This is an excellent question, Polly, and the answer depends on two things: firstly, the standard of your original draft, and secondly how far your project has drifted from its original intention as it has progressed. Concerning your initial draft, it is always good to communicate with your supervisor what standard you think it is at before asking them to read it and provide feedback: does it need more work or do you believe it is close to the finished product? This helps your supervisor decide on how they should read it, and what type of feedback they should provide. What we will say is that we expect even the most developed of drafts to be revisited once you have collected (and analysed) your data. Until you submit your dissertation, always think of it as a live document which can be worked on.

You are also sensible to recognise that a Literature Review should speak directly to your Findings and Analysis chapters. It is the case in social science, and especially in qualitative research, that the research can drift into a different direction. This then needs some reconciliation, both in terms of revisiting your research questions that tend to be located at the end of the Literature Review chapter and returning to the Literature Review chapter itself. Make sure that the content you include in this chapter still resonates with the findings you are presenting. If aspects do not, then you may need to be brave and ruthless and take it out and replace it with literature that does. This is why reading around your subject is so important as it might be the case that you now include literature that you had originally disregarded. Finally, make sure you factor in some time to redraft chapters; this is all part of the process of writing.

Tip

Often reading the introduction and conclusion of an article can be a quick trick for identifying whether a piece of literature is relevant to your research area. Often an introduction will set out the context of the research problem or topic under discussion, perhaps even explicitly stating the research question(s). Equally, a conclusion will highlight key findings and often put forward suggestions for future research. If these subsections seem to draw parallels with your own research interests, it is then a fruitful exercise to read the whole paper carefully, making detailed, active notes.

WHAT'S NEXT?

Chapter Checklist

Table 3.12 Chapter 3 checklist

	Yes	No
I understand the purpose of a Literature Review.		
I know how to use Boolean search terms.		
I know where I can find relevant literature.		
I can evaluate different sources of literature.		
I know that there are different ways to organise a Literature Review.		
I know how to find my own voice in a Literature Review and how to paraphrase using my own words.		

Consider

Order the publications in Table 3.4 in terms of how reliable they are.

- Which publication did you place at the top of your list and why?
- Which publication did you place at the bottom of your list and why?

Watch

Watch the video *Read Critically*, Sage Students. Available at: www.youtube.com/watch?v=uV6-BV_gyKs (accessed 6 September 2022).

- What does it mean to be critical when reading?
- How can you read critically? Have a go at writing a 'critical' paragraph.

Write

Thinking about the topic of your research project, write some key search terms. Remember to look for synonyms for the words which you list. But be careful that the replacement verb is an appropriate alternative.

Read

Read Leicester, M. and Taylor, D. 2019. *Take Great Notes*. London: SAGE.

4
BEING AN ETHICAL RESEARCHER

In this chapter, we detail the importance of being an ethical researcher and point to the salience of ethics throughout the duration of a social science research project. We separate **personal ethics** from **procedural ethics** by illustrating that ethics is dynamic and context-specific and by recognising that it should be considered throughout the lifecycle of your research project. That is, while we recognise and spend considerable time discussing the importance of procedural ethics, including practical suggestions on how to go about completing an ethics form for your university's or school's research ethics committee, as well as composing participant information sheets (PIS) and consent forms, we also acknowledge that ethics continues well after any favourable decision to undertake your research from a committee or board. Therefore, as well as discussing what steps you should take to mitigate against ethical concerns, we also stress the necessity for you to be alive to unforeseen or unplanned events, which might require further managing.

In the chapter, we also acknowledge the power dynamics between a researcher and participant and encourage you to consider how your research activities can empower and give voices to marginalised groups. In doing so, we stress that ethics also concerns representation and should also be considered during the write up of your research project.

Chapter Objectives

- To understand the importance of research ethics.
- To distinguish between personal and procedural ethics.
- To complete a research ethics application form.
- To produce a consent sheet and participant information sheet.
- To recognise that ethics extends to include the write-up of your research project.

INTRODUCTION

> Now I am become Death, the destroyer of worlds.

Taken from the Hindu sacred text, *Bhagavad Gita*, this bone-chilling phrase is widely reported to have been re-used by Robert J. Oppenheimer. Oppenheimer was an American theoretical physicist and science administrator at the Manhattan Project who oversaw the separation of uranium-235 from natural uranium during the Second World War. Of course, he was the central character in Christopher Nolan's historical biopic of the same name, winning seven academy awards at the 2024 Oscars. Also known as the splitting of the atom, Oppenheimer's work, with other scientists, resulted in the first nuclear explosion at the Trinity site in New Mexico, United States of America (USA), in 1945. After witnessing the explosion, a physically emotional Oppenheimer recalled the holy Hindu scripture relating what he had created in the name of military duty to the way in which Vishnu (a Hindu God) in the *Bhagavad Gita* took on a multi-armed form to impress the prince. Later that year, two atomic bombs were detonated over the Japanese cities of Hiroshima and Nagasaki, killing approximately 200,000 civilians. Oppenheimer's fears of the possible implications of his work were gruesomely laid bare for all to see. With this phrase – 'Now I am become Death, the destroyer of worlds' – we find ourselves having a window into the mind of a scientific researcher battling with the dilemma between what 'could be done' because of their research, what is possible, and what 'should be done', what is ethical.

In this chapter, we discuss producing an ethically sensitive piece of research. In its simplest form, ethics are a set of moral principles that one should follow in their practice. When one thinks of ethics in research, it is only natural to turn our attention to scientific ethics (see, for example, the Nuremberg Code – *British Medical Journal* 1996) and examples such as the atomic bomb and nuclear power, or more recently developments in biotechnology and 'biomedical ethics', especially research on the body such as bio-medical trials. Indeed, ethical processes as we know them today initially centred on medical malpractice and the potential for concrete physical harms (Connor et al. 2018), which was set against a backdrop of high-profile 'unethical' research and research-related incidents (Capron 2004, Dowsing and Kendall 2007). In such instances, ethics relates to risk and harm, and often concerns weighing up the balance of the worthiness and benefit of the research set against its possible negative effects. Such biomedical research today is highly regulated, entangled in a web of legal, moral, and philosophical frameworks. When research breaches these frameworks, it becomes newsworthy, unethical, and potentially illegal with serious consequences for the participants and biomedical scientists involved as well as the reputation of that area of work. Examples include the Hwang Woo-Suk science misconduct scandal concerning the fabrication of data in his human embryonic stem cell project (Kim 2009), Andrew Wakefield's discredited press conference when he made a completely unsubstantiated connection between the Measles, Mumps, and Rubella (MMR) vaccine and Autism (Collins 2014, Sweet and Giffort 2020) and the He Jiankui affair, when he announced in a conference the unregulated creation of the first genetically edited babies (Dimond et al. 2022). While most social science projects do not include the collection, or tampering, of bodily material or surgical/biomedical intervention, the way in which social science deals with ethical sensitivity tends to follow in the footsteps of the natural sciences. As others have noted (Haggerty 2004), there has been a form of 'ethics creep' in which social science ethics, mirroring biomedical ethics, have become increasingly formalised, institutionalised, and regulated. Where once ethics governance might have been the prerogative of the individual and/or research group, overseen by a professional body such as the British Sociological Association, it is now subject to various levels of scrutiny through institutional review boards (IRBs), school research ethics committees (SRECs) and other regulatory mechanisms (Dingwall 2006). Some, though, have maintained that this form of ethics is too concerned with legal issues and does not take account of some of the more subtle, nuanced ethical issues at play in dynamic social science research settings (Israel and Hay 2006, Leahy 2022). This is not to make a normative point, but it is to recognise that when we discuss ethics, we may wish to separate what we might call *procedural ethics* or *professional ethics* in which the moral framework of the research design has been formalised as part of the professionalisation and audit culture (Strathern 2000) of the discipline and *personal ethics, in situ* or *situational ethics* which recognise that the researcher needs to be alive to the dynamic and contingent nature of the research field and adapt accordingly.

Social scientific ethical codes of practice tend to cover some core domains including:

a   *Informed consent*: providing enough information for participants to make an informed decision on whether they wish to participate in the study or not.
b   *Participation is voluntary*: ensuring that participants do not feel in any way compelled to participate in the study and if they do decide to participate that they do so on voluntary grounds.
c   *Research(er) is alive to potential harms:* the research is designed in a way to prevent and/or minimise any possible harms, physical, social or otherwise (to participants and the researcher).
d   *Transparency:* where possible the research is conducted in a transparent and open manner.
e   *Empowerment*: participants are empowered as much as possible throughout the study.

But ethics covers more than just the doing of the research, it also involves the write up of research findings, including the ways in which participants are represented and credited. UK Research and Innovation (UKRI), which funds most of the social science research conducted in the United Kingdom (UK), maintain that,

> ... researchers, ROs and RECs should consider ethics issues throughout the lifecycle of a research project and promote a culture of ethical reflection, debate and mutual learning. The lifecycle of research includes the planning and

research design stage, the period of funding for the project, and all activities that relate to the project up to, and including, the time when funding has ended. This includes knowledge exchange and impact activities, the dissemination process – including reporting and publication – and the archiving, future use, sharing and linking of data. (UK Research and Innovation 2024)

They also maintain that social science researchers should always aim to maximise the benefit of the research, all the while minimising the potential for actual harm when designing the research. In this chapter, then, we cover the entirety of the research project when discussing ethics. We provide useful practical tips on how you might complete ethics applications, as well as producing participant information sheets (PIS) and consent forms, but importantly we also engage with some of the scholarly debates and discussions concerning good ethical conduct in social science.

HARMFUL RESEARCH

When we think of the potential to harm in research, we are quite rightly concerned with protecting our participants. On the surface, some participants might be seen to be more 'vulnerable' than others, such as young people, the unemployed, the homeless, or patients. But as social scientists, you will also be aware that vulnerability is socially situated. For example, if you were to interview your lecturer, you might think they are relatively empowered. In most situations they wield more power than you. However, if you were to ask them questions about their place of work, and they said something, for instance, which may be viewed as provocative about their employer (and your site of research as well as the place you study), then they are potentially putting themselves in a vulnerable position. Without robust, thoughtful ethical procedures put in place, colleagues, bosses, and even other students in the institution might become alerted to any critical comments, which could have significant consequences. Social science researchers, then, need to be alive to the cultural conditions in which they conduct their research (Brinkmann and Kvale 2004), and we have a duty of care to protect all our participants, whether we believe them to be 'vulnerable' or not, and unquestionably, we should do everything we can to respect their wishes.

But when we are considering minimising risk and harm, our duty of care does not simply stop at our participants. For example, you should also be mindful of who you are representing, namely, your university, your university department and your supervisor. You must do everything in your power not to tarnish the reputation of your department, institution, or supervisors. In the very unlikely event that the research takes a turn that you think might have negative connotations or could potentially damage the reputation of your university, it is pivotal that you speak with your supervisor to discuss how it should be handled moving forward.

Last, but certainly not least, you need to protect yourselves from harm. Research in the social sciences is often undertaken alone, so, with your supervisor, you need to create as safe an environment as possible. This might include setting in motion procedures such as 'buddying up' with someone who you contact when you are out and about collecting data, and then alert them when you are back home safe. However, please remember any promises of confidentiality that you may have made to your research participants. What we mean by this is that you will likely have agreed with your participants not to share their identity, or information which may give away their identity in the research; this can make it very challenging for you to disclose the research site to friends or family. For example, if you are collecting data in a school, you might not be able to tell your 'buddy' the exact location you are travelling to without potentially compromising the anonymity of your participants. That is, unless this is agreed beforehand. In this case a workaround will be needed.

Highlighting the importance of ethics is not to alarm you; most research settings and sites are perfectly safe with no more nor less of a risk than going about your everyday life. But just as you have a responsibility to protect your institution, the university has a clear responsibility to protect you too. Integrating safeguarding measures and procedures is part of that good governance that produces good ethical research.

Box 4.1

Anonymity and Confidentiality

Anonymity and confidentiality are terms that are sometimes conflated and used interchangeably (Kaiser 2009). It is important though, to recognise that these two terms mean slightly different things. For Saunders et al. (2015) anonymity is a branch of confidentiality. That is, anonymity refers specifically to scenarios where the researcher and/or reader is unable to identify participants. This can be the case with online questionnaires which are distributed to large numbers of people and where the researcher has no direct contact with the respondent. Confidentiality, on the other hand, refers to keeping private what was said by participants. Of course, in practice, anonymity and confidentiality cannot always play out in such hard terms, especially in qualitative research. It is folly to suggest that qualitative researchers will not know the identity of their participants particularly if they have undertaken interviews or focus groups or even most observations. Instead, in promising anonymity to participants what researchers are actually committing to is concealing the identity of the participants from potential readers. This is typically done by providing participants with a **pseudonym** - a sort of pen name - as well as obscuring other identifiable information e.g. their home address, place of work, perhaps even the gender by which they identify. True confidentiality is, of course, also unlikely to be workable. We advise caution against making strong promises about something that cannot be guaranteed. For example, if you have organised a focus group, while you might be able to commit to a form of confidentiality in which you do not reveal who said what in any publications and presentations, you cannot be sure that other participants in the focus group will not share this information. An ethical researcher is alive to these intricacies.

PROCEDURAL ETHICS

Importantly, before you proceed with any sort of data collection, you should first receive a favourable decision from your local IRB (institutional review board) or SREC (school research ethics committee) at your university or the requisite department in your university. This might involve completing a research ethics application form to be sent to your university or department and drafting and submitting **forward facing documents** to be checked over and sanctioned. These forward facing documents will be sent to participants when inviting them to take part in your research. Like the rest of your research project, the writing and crafting of the ethics application takes time and it may go through several iterations before you receive a favourable decision.

Ethics Application Form

The Singapore Statement on Research Integrity (Resnik and Shamoo 2011), while acknowledging social, cultural, political, and economic differences across nations that will impact on the ways in which research will be conducted (Resnik 2009), provides a framework for common standards and ethical guidance that crosses national boundaries. As such, most universities around the globe will be alive to ethical sensitivities and will have their own procedures and protocols. Indeed, some countries have even established national frameworks. For example, Australia has developed a National Ethics Application Form (NEAF), which all researchers can use to ensure consistency and quality across and between institutions (O'Leary 2021). On one hand this appears sensible, but this sort of uniformed approach *must* have the flexibility to consider individual research contexts (May and Perry 2022). As Hedgecoe (2020) maintains, ethics committees have a crucial role in shaping the future of disciplines, determining what work can and cannot be conducted and, as such, have significant responsibility for their disciplines.

Let us begin by comforting you. Completing an ethics application form is not something to get overly concerned about, but it is a task to take seriously and to complete thoroughly. The more detail you provide and the more you can show that you have considered all the potential ethical situations in your research and have produced protocols, procedures, and actions to mitigate against those situations, the more likely you will receive a favourable decision to proceed with the research. Here, you can build on the nascent research plan you have already put together (see Chapter 2: *Planning a Social Science Research Project*). While each institution will likely have their own, unique ethics form, these should all have a familiar structure and tend to ask for detail on the following aspects of your study:

1 Provide a general overview of your proposed project.
2 What are the research questions?
3 Provide details of who the participants are.
4 How do you plan to recruit the participants?
5 What data will be collected and how will it be collected?

6   Where do you plan to conduct the research?
7   Are there any acute ethical sensitivities involved in the project?
8   Will people be able to withdraw from the study at their own request, and at what times?
9   Will participants be identifiable, or will they be anonymised, and why?
10 Please detail how you will deal with data security.

Here, we provide some detail on what you could include to address these questions by using the Bigfooting example introduced in Chapter 2 (*Planning a Social Science Research Project*), and by discussing another example concerning research conducted in schools.

Question 1: Please Provide a General Overview of Your Proposed Project

Question 1 concerns the topic of your research project. Here, you can lean heavily on the research overview and context in your nascent research plan. However, it is highly likely that you will have developed your thinking a little since writing your initial research plan, and you can demonstrate this in this section of the ethics application form.

> **General project overview: Bigfooting as a colonial practice**
>
> Stories of so called 'Wildmen' and 'Hairy Giants' have been present in Indigenous and First Nation cultures for centuries in North America. Since the middle of the 20th century, though, groups of mostly white males have been searching for the existence of Bigfoot in the forest slopes of North America. This research sets out to explore the extent to which Bigfoot and Bigfoot research (known as Bigfooting) is an appropriation of indigenous culture. Or conversely, might it be a way of decolonising the subject of Anthropology as some Bigfoot researchers have suggested by taking seriously a subject matter that Western science has routinely dismissed? The project is a sober and serious study of the phenomenon of Bigfooting, considering what has been the catalyst for its rise in popularity and what this means for its history. To achieve its aims, the project has one main methodological strand: 10 online (via Zoom, Skype and Microsoft Teams) or telephone interviews with Bigfoot researchers and academics involved in Bigfoot research. (*Note how this has reduced from the 30 interviews originally suggested in Chapter 2: Planning a Social Science Research Project.*)
>
> **General project overview: Studying mathematics post-compulsory level**
>
> Unlike many other countries, in the UK it is not currently compulsory for students to study mathematics after the age of 16 (Hodgen et al. 2010).

However, the former prime minister for the UK, Rishi Sunak, previously announced that all school-aged children in England (but not Wales, Scotland and Northern Ireland since education is devolved) will be required to study some form of mathematics up until the age of 18 (Lewis and Maisuria 2023). This included learners aged 16–18 studying A-level qualifications who have traditionally had flexibility and choice over the school subjects which they study. The announcement came at a time when the percentage of students choosing to studying mathematics at post-compulsory level was increasing (UK Gov 2022). Indeed, in 2018/19, 83,132 students completed A-level mathematics compared to 88,244 students in 2020/1. This research sets out to explore what motivates students to study specific subjects at post-compulsory A-level and specifically to determine who studies mathematics at post-compulsory level and why. To achieve this aim, the research involves surveying young people currently studying for their A-level qualifications in the UK.

Question 2: What are the Research Questions?

Question 2 concerns the focus of your project. As with Question 1, you can draw from the research questions section of your research plan to address this point.

Research questions: Bigfooting as a colonial practice

In the example here, we have proposed two further questions for the Bigfoot research project from those originally outlined in the research plan in Chapter 2 (*Planning a Social Science Research Project*) to now have four research questions. Equally, we have produced four questions for the school project.

1. To what extent is Bigfooting a white male activity and why?
2. How do Bigfoot researchers understand the origins of the Bigfoot story?
3. In what ways are historical accounts of Bigfoot-like creatures that originated in First Nation and Indigenous people enrolled in or pushed out of contemporary understandings of Bigfoot?
4. How has the Bigfoot story travelled from its original home in the Pacific Northwest to now encompass the whole of mainland North America?

Research questions: Studying mathematics post-compulsory level

1. What school subjects do students study at post-compulsory levels?
2. Who studies mathematics at post-compulsory level?
3. Why do students study mathematics at post-compulsory level?
4. What prevents students from carrying on with mathematics beyond compulsory level?

Question 3: Please Provide Details of Who The Participants Are

This question centres on the sample in your study – who you are going to research. Having worked to develop your draft research plan, you might now have a clearer idea of the demographic and geography of who you plan to study. Again, provide as much detail as is possible, including the number of participants you plan to recruit and any pertinent characteristics, e.g., students, female football players, police workers, fathers over the age of 40. Also, consider your inclusion and exclusion criteria; that is, who is invited to be part of your study and who is precluded from participating and why.

> **Details of participants: Bigfooting as a colonial practice**
>
> Participants for the interviews will be Bigfoot researchers (both archival and field researchers) as well as a smattering of academics such as biological anthropologists and primatologists that work on the subject or an area of research relevant to the subject. All participants will be over the age of 18 and the majority will reside in Canada and the USA. However, researchers may be recruited from anywhere across the world including Australia, Russia and the UK, places that are all said to have their own Bigfoot-like creatures.
>
> **Details of participants: Studying mathematics post-compulsory level**
>
> Participants will be young people aged 16–18 studying A-levels at three different schools based in Northern England. The research aims to recruit a sample of 300 participants (approximately 100 students from each school).

Question 4: How Do You Plan to Recruit the Participants?

Putting thought into how you will contact and recruit individuals is an important ethical consideration, especially if you are concerned with potentially disclosing names publicly (e.g., recruiting through social media), but also in relation to how personal details are gathered and then stored.

It might be the case that you will recruit participants through a single point of contact, known as a **gatekeeper** (see Chapter 1: *What Is Social Science Research and Why Is It Important?*). For example, if you wish to interview teachers, the gatekeeper may be the head of the school or the school's secretary. If you wish to conduct a study of a sports team, the gatekeeper may be the coach. Gatekeepers are then the middle person or conduit between you and access to your potential participants; they open the gate into the research site. If you plan to use a gatekeeper to recruit people into the study then it is vital that this is addressed in any ethics application, along with an explanation of how the recruitment process will work.

Plan to recruit participants: Bigfooting as a colonial practice

Contact will be made through e-mail and via social media. E-mail addresses will be collected from publicly available sources such as Bigfoot websites, academic staff pages, and from books written by authors who include their contact details. Recruitment will also occur through social media sites such as X (formerly Twitter), Facebook, and YouTube, where we will introduce ourselves, explaining the project and ask for an e-mail address to send further information. To prevent personal details being made public, we will ask participants to either e-mail us by providing our institutional e-mail address or ask them to message privately with their details. In addition, we hope that we can use snowballing techniques to recruit further participants (see Chapter 5: *Methods of Social Science Data Collection*). Here, rather than ask for other people's details who might find our contact unwelcome, we will ask for our details to be passed on to relevant people and then they can contact us if interested.

Plan to recruit participants: Studying mathematics post-compulsory level

The headteachers from each of the schools identified will initially be contacted about the potential inclusion of their students in the research. Personal connections exist with two of the schools already through a family friend and through previous work experience. Once permission has been granted, students will be invited to participate in the research. It is envisaged that the students will be given the opportunity to complete the online questionnaire during their registration period. Posters with the QR code to the online questionnaire will also be produced and these will be provided to the school to display in classrooms, study spaces, and common rooms for students studying A-levels. It will be made clear that participation is completely voluntary and while one of the schools was a former place of work experience, staff should feel under no obligation to promote the questionnaire to students on that account.

Question 5: What Data Will Be Collected and How Will It Be Collected

Ethics committees will want to know the data type you are collecting and how you envisage collecting the data because the way in which you gather data concerns the methodological approach you plan to take. Hopefully, this is something you will have already considered in your research plan. But, here, you can expand upon your rationale.

What data will be collected and how: Bigfooting as a colonial practice

Having originally considered doing circa 30 interviews in the nascent research plan in Chapter 2 (*Planning a Social Science Research Project*), as detailed earlier, we decreased this to a more manageable 10 online/telephone interviews given the time constraints of a dissertation. Audio recordings will be created during all interviews. We anticipate a mix of online and telephone data collection tailored to circumstance and the participant's preference. Where online interviews are used, these will be conducted via one of the University-supported platforms (e.g., Zoom, Microsoft Teams).

What data will be collected and how: Studying mathematics at post-compulsory level

Data will be collected from students currently studying A-levels. The questionnaire will consist of closed-ended questions asking students about the subjects which they are currently studying. Participants will also be asked to provide demographic data, including gender and ethnicity. There will be a series of Likert scale statements about their motivations for studying different subjects at post-compulsory level, which students will need to indicate their level of agreement with. These statements will be informed by the existing literature and may replicate existing questions used in previous studies.

Question 6: Where Do You Plan to Conduct the Research?

The setting and site in which you conduct your research needs to be considered sensitively to mitigate against any potential harms that might occur for both you and your participants. Public spaces are often seen as 'safer' spaces, but that needs to be counterbalanced against the possibility of being overheard by others and potentially rubs against any promise of confidentiality you might have included.

Where the research will be conducted: Bigfooting as a colonial practice

Interviews are to be conducted online and/or over the telephone given the presumed geographic distance between researcher and participants and the cost this would incur. Here, it is important to consider differences in time zones and when it is a reasonable and appropriate time to interview someone. For example, Los Angeles is 8 hours behind London, which is itself 9 hours behind Tokyo and 13 hours behind Auckland. Interviews online will be recorded but only the audio recording will be stored with the video recording being deleted immediately at the end of the interview.

Where the research will be conducted: Studying mathematics at post-compulsory level

The questionnaire will be distributed online using Qualtrics Survey Software. Once the data has been collected, it will be downloaded and saved as an SPSS file on the University OneDrive space.

Question 7: Are There Any Acute Ethical Sensitivities Involved in the Project?

Although aspects of your nascent research plan can be used in your ethics form, it must be remembered that an application form is not simply about outlining the detail of the project for others to comment on. Its main function is assessing whether the project adheres to ethical standards. Importantly, the committee will not expect the form to state that there are no ethical issues to consider in the project. Rather, they will want to be convinced that you are cognisant of the potential issues at play and that you have envisaged what procedures might be followed to mitigate against them.

Acute ethical sensitivities: Bigfooting as a colonial practice

While the risks to researchers are minimal as the research will be conducted via the computer or telephone, the online interviews will include cameras. Some participants might find this intrusive given they will likely be at home. In these cases, participants will be given the option to switch off their cameras and simply conduct an audio interview. If they are happy to keep their cameras on, the film recording will be deleted immediately after the interview and only the audio version will be kept.

Given the potential time difference, work will be done to find a mutually convenient time that works for both interviewer and participant. University procedures, best practice guidelines and professional ethical standards will be followed to ensure responsible conduct and prevent harms to the researcher and the participants. Given the nature of the project, the following documents will be particularly relevant: the British Sociological Association (BSA) statement on ethical practice, including specific guidance on digital methods and researching online.

Acute ethical sensitivities: Studying mathematics at post-compulsory level

This research involves young people studying at school. Subsequently, additional forms of consent may need to be obtained. In the first instance, the headteacher – the gatekeeper – at each school will need to provide consent. Given the age of the students – 16 to 18-year olds – they are legally deemed sufficiently old enough to provide informed consent, meaning parental consent will not be required. However, an information sheet will be sent to all parents outlining the aims of the research and the contact details of the researcher should they have any follow-up questions. If the research were to involve younger children (possibly those deciding what to study at post-compulsory level), parental consent would also be legally required.

Students may be concerned that their responses will be viewed by teachers and that, if they report a negative attitude toward a subject, a teacher may hold this against them. The start of the questionnaire will clearly state that the responses are anonymous and that no individual level responses will be shared with school staff or published in the final research project. Moreover, whilst students will be given time and an opportunity to complete the questionnaire during a registration period or tutorial, it will be clearly explained that the questionnaire is optional and that students can simply scan the QR code and complete the questionniare during their own time if they prefer or not respond at all.

The topic of the research could make some students anxious or concerned about their current studies, exams and/or future plans. As such, at the end of the questionnaire, the students will be signposted to relevant online resources as well as a key contact in their school.

Question 8: Will People Be Able to Withdraw From the Study at Their Own Request?

It is always important to remember that participants are volunteering to be part of the study, and as such they should have the opportunity to withdraw if they are feeling in any way uncomfortable. It is usually the case that you will have a question on the ethics form stating something like '*Will you tell participants that they may withdraw from the research at any time and for any reasons?*'. Given the above, it seems obvious to simply state 'yes'. However, what if they want to withdraw after you have submitted your written work or presented your findings at conference? It is vital that you are clear from the outset what rights participants have and what can reasonably be done to withdraw them from the project. For example, when administering an anonymous questionnaire, how might you remove someone who no longer wants to participate? How will you find the correct data if it is anonymous? Some foresight needs to be considered here in which you might ask participants to record the date and time at the beginning of an online questionnaire so you can match them up later, or you set up the questionnaire so that it generates a unique ID number for both the researcher and participant. Alternatively, you may decide to make it explicit to participants that the anonymous nature of the research means that they will not be able to withdraw their data.

> **Withdrawing from the study: Bigfooting as a colonial practice**
>
> In the consent form that will accompany an information sheet about the Bigfooting project, the following line might be included:
>
> I understand that my participation is voluntary and that I am free to withdraw at any time up until three weeks before the submission deadline of the research project (DD/MM/YYYY), without giving any reason, and without any adverse consequences or penalty.

Withdrawing from the study: Studying mathematics at post-compulsory level

At the start of the questionnaire for the project about studying mathematics at post-compulsory levels, the following check boxes will be included:

I understand that my participation is voluntary and that I can stop completing in the questionnaire at any point.

I understand that I do not need to answer any questions which I do not feel comfortable answering.

I understand that the questionnaire is anonymous, and I will not be identifiable. This means that I am unable to withdraw from the study after starting the questionnaire.

Question 9: Will Participants Be Identifiable, or Will They Be Anonymised, and Why?

This question concerns the ways in which you might protect the identity of participants. It is often the case that participants are anonymised with a pseudonym – a fictitious name that conceals the identity of the participants – and for good reason. In many cases this is to protect the individual (from potential harm). It may be the case that you need to conceal additional pieces of information about your participants too. For example, participants may disclose details such as their place of study, where they work, and the place they live. These details, especially in combination, may make the participants identifiable. However, the blanket assumption that this should be default is itself not ethical (Lewis and Atkinson, in press). Instead, as a critical scholar you should be thinking about the ethical reasons to or not to anonymise.

Identifiable information: Bigfooting as a colonial practice

While risks to participants are minimal, the subject matter and activity itself might come in for ridicule and criticism. Thus, participants will be able to determine whether they want to remain anonymous or have their names attributed to any quotes and extracts. For some researchers, Bigfoot research is an intellectual agenda and their ideas about Bigfoot techniques as well as the natural world are their cache and, as such, in a similar way to how academics might cite the provenance of an idea, they may want to be attributed to a quote. On these occasions, the participant will be named. This will be done on an individual basis and will be discussed at the beginning and end of the interview. If there is anything that might present the participant in a negative light, they will be asked to confirm that they are comfortable being named in the research. Equally, if by naming the participants, it runs the risk of revealing another individual then we will anonymise the named individual or participant accordingly. If there is any doubt or hesitation, we will suggest to participants that they should choose to be anonymised.

Identifiable information: Studying mathematics at post-compulsory levels

The questionnaire will be anonymous. Only aggregate level data will be reported and shared. No individual data will be available.

Question 10: Please Detail How You Will Deal with Data Security

Data storage and security is a pivotal aspect of any research project, and you will want to mitigate against any breaches. Data, of course, may be stored online and/or in physical copy. Regarding online data, the ethics committee or board do not expect you to be an IT genius, and so, if in doubt, please ask for help from your supervisors or department. That said, using university programmes and platforms is a safe(r) bet.

For physical copies of transcripts or documents, make sure that they are stored in a locked cabinet, and do not travel around with them where they may be misplaced. Also check with your university and department as it might be the case that data needs to be stored for a certain period in line with your local or national governmental regulations.

Data security: Bigfooting as a colonial practice

The online (Zoom/Microsoft Teams) and telephone interviews will be recorded and then stored on the University's network such as the password protected OneDrive and in accordance with good practice. Access to data will be via networked computers or encrypted laptop computers.

Data security: Studying mathematics at post-compulsory levels

The data will be downloaded and saved on the University's password protected network (OneDrive) in accordance with good practice. Access to the data will be via networked computers or encrypted laptop computers.

Once you have submitted your ethics form to the relevant committee, they will spend time assessing the ethical sensitivity of your project. It is not atypical for them to come back to you to ask you to clarify points or to provide a pending decision dependent on your addressing some outstanding concerns. Do not get concerned about this. Just as ethics is a process so is completing the ethical application. Please also note here that there has been a recent trend of students using various programmes to transcribe their data. Be very careful that this does not contravene what you promised in your ethics application. Some of these sites have in their small print that they can share this data. Others do not store data securely. For more on this, please see Chapter 5 (*Methods of Social Science Data Collection*).

Forward Facing Documents

Typically, there are two forward facing documents which you should share with your participants: (i) **the participant information sheet** (PIS) and (ii) the **consent form**. Depending on the method of data collection which you are using, you will either send these to your participants in advance (e.g. for interviews, focus groups) or provide them at the time of data collection, for instance, the first page of an online questionnaire is often a condensed version of these two documents. These documents should talk to one another so that participants are properly informed about the project. The participant information sheet (PIS) is a document that participants should read prior to the study so that they can decide whether they wish to take part or not. A balance needs to be struck here. It is vital that you provide enough detail about the project written in straightforward language so that a participant gets a good grasp of what the project entails, whilst also being mindful to not make it unwieldy. Make it easy to read and do not meander off point. You do not want to put participants off the study. For qualitative research projects, participants should also be provided with ample time to read, digest, and potentially ask any questions before deciding whether they want to get involved in the research. There is no fixed, standard timeframe, but where possible, it is generally good etiquette to give participants at least a week to decide whether they want to participate in an interview or focus group, for example. For survey research, the information sheet is usually found at the beginning of the questionnaire. Here, you could suggest to participants that they take some time reading and re-reading information about the project before proceeding. As with other documents, the information you provide will be bespoke to your research project, but PISs do tend to have a certain form and grammar. For example, begin your PIS by including your research title followed by a brief introduction as to what is contained in the document. Finish the document by including your contact details so that potential participants know who to contact if they have any questions or wish to withdraw. Here we provide an example PIS template (Box 4.2).

Box 4.2

An Example PIS Template

Begin the information sheet by explaining why your potential participants are being invited to take part in a research project. Make it clear that before they decide whether to take part, it is important that they understand why the research is being undertaken and what their participation will involve. Impress on them to take their time to read the following information carefully and state that they should not hesitate to contact you and/or your supervisor (if necessary) if they have any outstanding queries.

1   What is the purpose of this research project?

Insert basic background information on the research project, its aims and explain it is a student project and what the potential outputs might include. Keep this paragraph short, punchy, and write it in a language that your participants will likely understand. Do not use technical terms, and do not be afraid to be encouraging.

2   Why have I been invited to take part?

Explain your selection criteria and why you have invited them to participate in the study. Again, make them feel welcomed.

3   Do I have to take part?

Make it crystal clear that participation is voluntary and explain what steps participants can take if they decide to participate but later want to withdraw from the research. Perhaps provide them with a time up to which point they can withdraw. You do not want participants asking to withdraw at the point of or after submission of your research project.

4   What does participation entail?

Put yourself in your participants' shoes and make sure that they are aware what involvement in the project entails, including what level of time commitment is required. For example, if they are to be interviewed, state roughly for how long the interview will last and whether and how it will be recorded. If it is a questionnaire, outline roughly how long the questionnaire will take to complete.

5   What are the possible risks of taking part?

Any foreseeable discomforts or risks should be described to potential participants, including the likelihood of them occurring. Explain how you will mitigate against those risks. You clearly need not scaremonger here, but it is important that they have considered all possible consequences to be truly 'informed'.

6   Will my taking part in this research project be kept confidential?

State what you will do with identifying information. Explain whether you plan to offer your participants the protection of anonymity and how this will be done. Be sure to consider whether there may be exceptional circumstances when confidentiality should be over-ridden such as a medical issue or alerting a buddy.

7   What will happen to my personal information?

Detail clearly how data will be saved and stored, and who will have access to this data. Explain how electronic data will be stored and how any paper copies may be stored. Be sure to comply with any data regulations in your country/region in terms of how long the data will be stored, for example General Data Protection Regulation (GDPR), which is applicable across the European Union.

8   What will happen to the results of the research project?

Inform the participants when the results of the research are likely to be published, and in what form, e.g. dissertation, poster, presentation (see Chapter 7: *Presenting Your Social Science Research*).

(Continued)

9   What if there is a problem?

Set out how complaints will be handled and what redress may be available (i.e., describe the process and who should be contacted - this is likely to be your supervisor and/or ethics committee).

10   Who has reviewed this research project?

If the research project has been reviewed by the requisite department or school at your university, explain that the research has been given a favourable decision to proceed.

11   Further information and contact details

Provide your contact details including name and university contact email. Should the participant have any questions pertaining to the research project, state that they may contact you during normal working hours. You should include the contact details of your supervisor too. Make sure that you provide institutional details and not your own private (email) address.

Finish by thanking them for considering taking part in this research project.

Related to the PIS is the research consent form. This document formalises the tacit agreement between the researcher and the research participant, outlining the roles and responsibilities of each individual and how they should relate to one another throughout the research process. Again, we include an exemplar consent form here (Box 4.3). For survey research, the consent form would likely appear as the first set of questions viewed by the participants. If participants do not check all the boxes, they will be diverted to the end of the questionnaire. For other types of research, it will likely be a standalone document.

Box 4.3

An Example Consent Form

Please read the statements below. Checking or ticking the requisite boxes will be considered to constitute giving your consent to participate in this research.

If you have any questions about the research or the statements below, please do not hesitate to contact me.

Name/Signature... ....

I confirm that I have read and understood the information sheet for the study *INSERT NAME OF STUDY* ☐

I understand that my participation is voluntary and that I am free to withdraw before (DD/MM/YYYY), without giving any reason ☐

I understand what will happen to my data (please see participant information sheet) ☐

I give the researcher permission to audio/video (delete as appropriate) record my interview ☐

I give permission for the researcher to quote me directly using my real name ☐ or anonymously via a pseudonym ☐ in their dissertation and any associated presentations

If appropriate, I give permission for the researcher to re-contact me to clarify information ☐

I am happy to take part in the research ☐

DEBRIEF SHEETS

In some disciplines such as psychology it is typical to conduct a **debrief** at the end of the data collection process. A debrief is where the researcher outlines the intentions of the research and what will happen next. It is a process that is carried out, often as a default, if there has been any form of deception in the research project; that is, if the project was conducted covertly, or if an experiment included something that was not originally disclosed because it was pivotal to the research design. Of course, any use of deception should be clearly justified when submitting the ethics application to the IRB, alongside a clear process of how the participant will be informed about the deception later. A typical debrief sheet that has involved deception will include at least the following sections:

Research project title

An explanation of how the participants were deceived or details on what information was omitted or withheld.

A clear rationale of why the deception was necessary for the project.

A section providing participants with the further opportunity to withdraw from the study given the deception.

The name and contact details of the researcher if the participant has any further follow-up questions.

In other studies which cover sensitive topics such as mental health, a debrief sheet may be provided to participants so to signpost them to relevant sources of support, for example, the mental health charity, Mind.

PERSONAL ETHICS

For most of this chapter, we have focussed on the practical components involved in getting ethical approval from your institution to undertake your research. However, the formalisation of ethics as a form-filling exercise has not been immune from critique from social science scholars. Criticisms of the bureaucratisation of social science research ethics centres on two main aspects: (i) the erosion of the autonomy and expertise of individual researchers who know their setting best (Whiteman 2018), and (ii) the dynamic processual nature of ethics in practice (Baarts 2009). Both points acknowledge that ethical issues are constantly in flux, being continually negotiated and re-negotiated between researcher and researched. That is, ethics are not simply something to consider at a discrete period in a research project. Rather, social science researchers should be ethically adept researchers and should be alive to the ethical sensitivities present in their project throughout its lifecycle. This includes the journey from designing the project through to the collection and analysis of data, all the way through to the written output and the ways in which data are presented and participants represented. Moreover, it is pivotal that as a social science researcher, you reflect on your ethical positioning and value judgements *in situ*. No two research sites will be the same and most are continually evolving. This might lead to new and unforeseen issues for you to consider. Even the best laid plans need to be adaptable. Ultimately, ethical research is a process, and every new encounter requires a renegotiation of what was agreed – a renewal of that tacit contract between researcher and researched. That is, the prescriptive nature of professional ethics does not work for all situations, all of the time, and equally can be out of step with some methodological approaches (e.g., ethnographic observations). Moreover, once you have hopefully received a favourable decision from an ethics committee, this, of course, does not necessarily mean you are doing ethical research. It is in the act of doing, and not the application form, that determines whether researchers adhere to ethics. Finally, although very unlikely, on occasions, it might be the case that you need to suspend the research if you feel there is an issue that needs dealing with or if you feel it is moving in a direction that has meant either you or your participant(s) have become uncomfortable. The decision to halt the work and reassess reflects a thoughtful, ethical researcher.

Box 4.4

Being Ethical

Who determines what is ethical and what is not is open to debate. For example, there may be equally weighted arguments for and against bringing back extinct animals, what is known as *de-extinction*. For some, it is reversing the actions of humans that played a part in making the species extinct in the first place. For others, to do so would be to explicitly play God, potentially impacting habitats and environments (see Kasperbauer 2017). As another example, there is a live debate as to the virtues of paying participants for their time. Again, for some, it is simply giving back to the participant who is giving up their time (and data): a form of paid labour. For others, it can feel like pressuring participants into participating, especially those in need of money. To see more on this debate, please see Head (2009) and Surmiak (2020).

ETHICS AT THE EDGES

Some research projects are off limits to students. These might include research in prisons, in hospitals, in laboratories, etc. although on rare occasions these locations are possible to study. One mitigation, of course, would be to study the subject, whether that is researching women in prisons or assessing whether Accident and Emergency wards are overwhelmed, via a different approach such as through the collection and/or analysis of existing secondary data.

There are also research projects which are permissible but require further consideration, form filling, and sometimes, accreditation. Researching in schools and with young people is often a popular choice among those studying for education degrees or for those who wish to pursue a career in teaching. In most cases, researching schools and/or young people is acceptable. However, it comes with an additional duty of care before one can proceed with research. For example, in the UK, researchers may require security checks such as Disclosure and Barring (DBS). Here, of course, depending on the ages of the young people you are researching you will need to think seriously and possibly creatively about how you will obtain informed consent; for example, you may not be confident about young children's ability to give informed consent.

Other research projects that might require further ethical scrutiny include **covert research**. As above, this is concealed research – research which is done without informing the participants that you are doing it. It is fair to say that covert research has a mixed reception in social science (Marzano 2022); some maintain it is ethically deceptive while others argue forcefully it is the only way to study certain subjects and communities. What we can state confidently is that it is certainly not a new form of research and not a new debate either. Laud Humphreys' (1970) *Tearoom Trade: Impersonal Sex in Public Spaces*, which involved researching homosexual activity amongst men in public toilets has been both celebrated as part of social science and ethnography's canon and criticised as an exemplar of bad practice. A common misconception concerning this research is that Humphreys did not reveal his intentions to participants. This is not strictly true. He did reveal his identity to some participants, but later decided to conceal what he was doing to prevent response bias. In so doing, he made aspects of the research covert. There are often competing tensions in research, and this is a good example.

An area of research that is relatively new and which has brought with it new ethical issues is online research including social media research. Here, disciplinary standards are still stabilising, and we need to remain flexible to new and exciting challenges. For example, Williams et al. (2017) trouble the assumed consent of public Twitter (now X) posters. They maintain that while users were not overly concerned with Twitter being used as a site and source of research, their survey suggested that users wanted to be asked for their consent for their tweets to be used in research projects and the right to remain anonymous in research projects. Both these issues cause challenges, especially for qualitative researchers, who will likely find it difficult to keep tweets anonymised. For example, verbatim tweets can be googled and the source of those tweets discovered by their twitter handle. With regards to other social media platforms such as Facebook it is generally accepted practice that a researcher gets permission from the moderator of the group before advertising their project.

THE ETHICS OF WRITING UP

To a large degree, the term ethics is associated with responsibility. As we have been at pains to stress, this responsibility does not begin and end solely with the research collection stage of the project, though this is clearly a pivotal period. But moments of ethical discomfort can also extend to the writing up process where some people may 'suffer from publication' (Whyte 1955: 342). Here, there might be issues related to the presentation of the work such as **voice**, **representation**, **authenticity**, and **anonymity** to consider. For example, if you have promised anonymity then it is very likely that you will need to provide your participants with a pseudonym especially if you have undertaken qualitative research. Pseudonyms can be as plain as participant 1, participant 2, etc., etc., or in keeping with a more narrative style might involve a 'pen' name. For example, if you interviewed a participant called Ryan, you might change the name to Robin. Providing anonymity in research sites that are large such as attendees at a Soccer stadium or people shopping in the high street can be relatively easy. For more closed and smaller sites, though, such as places of work, this can be much more difficult. Indeed, there will be certain research settings where if you decide not to name participants, you should stress during the recruitment stage that while you will make every best effort to anonymise individuals, you cannot promise full anonymisation. Let us take the example of doing some research in a small school that contains 10 teachers, four teaching assistants, three cooks and a caretaker. Simply changing someone's name will very likely not anonymise the person (especially from other individuals in the same school). In this case, you will likely need to delete or conceal other identifying attributes. Some tricks that researchers use to do this are to change the gender of which the participant identifies in the write up so long as gender was not deemed important to the overall aim of project. But even this might not completely anonymise an individual in a small research setting. Therefore, be very careful what you promise during recruitment. Of course, some of the same ethical issues concerning the identification of individuals are at play when you are writing about communities and places too. Thomas (2023b: 81) discusses the dilemma he felt when naming the town in his work, asking 'how could I talk about the stigmatisation of Merthyr and its residents without attending to and amplifying the toxic, unfair and abject external portrayal/s of them?'. But, to eradicate these issues would be a sort of betrayal itself since the project was about poverty and impoverished communities.

As spiderman says 'with great power, comes great responsibility' and the pen can wield surprisingly great power. It is a privileged position to be able to write and speak for your participants. Certain marginalised groups and communities struggle to have a voice and, in putting their words on paper, you become their voice. Therefore, an ethical mindset also concerns the way in which you represent your participants and the places they inhabit. Finally, it is also an ethical duty to consider the limitations and constraints of what you can and should say. The following are a set of rules that you should follow.

- Clearly do not fabricate data, though this needs to be weighed up against the need to storify and conceal identities (as an example, see the controversy around Alice Goffman's 2014, On the Run).
- Make sure that you do not over-reach, over-claim or over-emphasise.
- As much as possible try to produce as faithful a description as possible.
- Include much needed context, especially if data might be seen to shock or could potentially be read in various ways.

SUMMARY

In this chapter, we have discussed the vital role of research ethics in your social science research project. We began by defining what research ethics are and then considered their prominence in doing a good social science research project (Birnbacher 1999). Against this backdrop, we separated ethical issues that surface *in situ* from the need to carefully design a research project that is ethically sensitive, and which has considered the best way to reduce any ethical concerns that might surface in the project. Here, we show that the groundwork done on your nascent research plan can be built upon to complete a research ethics application. Alongside this, we included a draft participant information sheet (PIS) template to help prompt your thoughts, along with a putative informed consent script. Of course, receiving a favourable decision from an IRB or SREC does not automatically mean you are conducting ethical research, and it is important to remain alive to any potential ethical issues throughout the lifecycle of the project, including the way in which you present findings and represent participants. That is, ethics does not correlate to a discrete period in the research project but rather should be always considered throughout the entirety of the project, including the final write up and the ways in which you represent individuals, places and their opinions.

Student Question

If I am using secondary data and not collecting data, do I need ethical approval?
(Shane, Criminology Student)

Charlotte and Jamie say:

This is an interesting question, Shane. You will need to check with your institution's guidelines, but it may be the case that you do not need to go through the same process as those collecting primary data to receive ethical approval. This is because it would be assumed that the data you are using has already received ethical approval (e.g., data stored in a data bank) or is in the public domain and therefore freely available (e.g., newspapers). If you are analysing documents which are not publicly available, then we would imagine your institution will expect you to apply for ethical approval in the same way to those collecting primary data. This, of course, does not mean that you should not be sensitive to ethical concerns though. There are still concerns, such as 'representation', 'credit', and 'anonymisation' to consider. Remember, ethics is as much a mindset as anything else.

WHAT'S NEXT?

Chapter Checklist

Table 4.1 Chapter 4 checklist

	Yes	No
I appreciate the importance of research ethics.		
I understand the difference between personal and professional ethics.		
I am confident I can complete a research ethics application.		
I can produce a participant information sheet.		
I can produce an informed consent script.		

Read

Bryne, D. 2017. *Research Ethics*. Available at: https://methods.sagepub.com/project-planner/research-ethics (accessed 5 April 2024).

Watch

Sage Research Methods. *Top Tips: Ethics*. Available at: https://methods.sagepub.com/video/top-tips-ethics (accessed 5 April 2024).

- What are your university/department's procedures for obtaining ethical approval?

Reflect

SAGE Ocean. (2019). *Top 10 Big Data and social science innovations*. Available at: https://ocean.sagepub.com/blog/top-10-big-data-and-social-science-innovations (accessed 7 July 2022).

- Consider and reflect on the number of times you produce possible data daily, such as buying habits, transactional data, posting on social media, leaving reviews, signing up to e-newsletters, etc. Is it ethical for social science researchers to use this data in their research? What might they do with it? Why might you feel concerned?

Complete

- Your own Participant Information Sheet.
- Your own Consent Form.
- Your university's research ethics application form (if applicable).

5
METHODS OF SOCIAL SCIENCE DATA COLLECTION

In this chapter, we outline various approaches to collecting data in the social sciences and the strengths and limitations of these approaches in different contexts. We stress the importance of using the most appropriate method[s] to address the research questions being asked. We also detail some of the practical constraints which you may encounter when collecting data and some of the steps which can be used to minimise these and make accessing and exiting the 'field' as smooth as possible. Notably, we discuss online methods, which have become increasingly popular since the Covid-19 pandemic. Other sections include secondary data analysis, which is proving increasingly popular, ethnographic methods, interview-based methods, documentary methods, creative methods, and questionnaires. We also address mixed methods or hybrid research. Students often think that choosing this option will allow them to bring together the best attributes of both qualitative and quantitative research. While we do not dissuade you from undertaking a mixed methods approach, we explain that a research project that is solely qualitative or solely quantitative is more than acceptable and quite often the preferred option within the parameters of a student project. The final part of the chapter is dedicated to the way in which you might approach writing up your Methods chapter, whether quantitative, qualitative or mixed methods.

Chapter Objectives

- To differentiate between quantitative and qualitative methods of data collection.
- To compare different methodological approaches to collecting social science data.
- To distinguish between primary and secondary forms of data collection and analysis.
- To consider the possibilities and challenges of researching online/virtually.
- To understand that you should only combine methods if there is a compelling reason that it will help answer the research questions.
- To recognise how a typical Methods chapter might be structured.

INTRODUCTION

Look around the room you are currently in and study it for around 30 seconds. What do you notice? What stands out to you? Some of you will observe the number of people in the room or count the different items of furniture sited in the space. Others might combine their senses and listen to the sounds people are making in the room or observe the way in which the furniture is laid out in the space and the types of furniture on show. This thought experiment, originally put forward by Karl Popper (1963), rather crudely showcases the differences between quantitative and qualitative approaches to social science research. In social science research, research methods are often categorised into quantitative approaches – those dealing with quantity such as counting how many pieces of furniture are in a room – and qualitative approaches – those dealing with quality such as the way in which the furniture is positioned in the room. On occasions this can be a rather hard division. At other times, the boundary is softened with some researchers combining both approaches in their research project, often called a mixed methods project, and some methods such as Q methodology drawing from both positions.

For ease, we divide this lengthy chapter into three sections. We begin by focussing on quantitative research methods. We then move on to discuss qualitative methods, and then finally we consider how you might write up a Methods chapter in a research project or dissertation. Principally, we describe some of the more commonplace methods of data collection used in the social science disciplines and the advantages and disadvantages of these approaches, as well as the most appropriate times to use them. We also include some practical tips that should help you decide which method of data collection is most appropriate for your research project and therefore enable you to begin designing data collection tools including questionnaires, observation schedules, and coding frames. The final section on how to *write your Methods chapter* is relevant for students who have chosen either qualitative or quantitative research methods and includes topics such as sampling, piloting and negotiating access to the field. We begin by discussing quantitative methods.

PART ONE: QUANTITATIVE METHODS

Quantitative methods of data collection produce numerical data, which can be analysed using statistical approaches. Typically, quantitative methods of data collection are used when researchers want to measure the prevalence of a social phenomenon, i.e. they have questions concerning the frequency of certain social events, attitudes, beliefs, opinions, or behaviours. As well as exploring the frequency of these concerns, quantitative social science researchers may also be interested in exploring whether membership of certain demographic groups is associated with holding certain attitudes, beliefs, opinions, or exhibiting particular behaviours. Typically, quantitative researchers have a **deductive** view of the relationship between theory and research. This means that they set out with a theory that they wish to test empirically. These researchers will develop hypotheses – statements which outline what they expect to observe based on existing theory – and then test these using structured approaches to see if they hold true. Based on their research findings, researchers will then refine the theory. This is in contrast with qualitative researchers who are more preoccupied with theory building as opposed to theory testing, often called **inductive** reasoning (see Part Two).

Box 5.1

Quantitative Methods at a Glance

Collecting numerical data for statistical analysis.

Data presented in graphs, charts, and tables.

Theory testing (deductive).

Aim to generalise findings to the wider population.

A structured approach to research which can be more easily replicated than qualitative research.

Common approaches include questionnaires, structured observations, experiments, content analysis, and secondary data analysis.

Quantitative researchers utilise methods or approaches endeavouring to objectively measure the social world and social reality. Despite this, quantitative researchers are still required to make several subjective decisions when designing, collecting, and analysing data. For example, they will need to decide on the response options for questions as well as determine how to deal with missing data. Some of the most typical and popular approaches to collecting quantitative data in the social sciences are detailed in Table 5.1. These methods are also explored in more detail throughout the rest of this chapter.

Table 5.1 Approaches to collecting quantitative data

Quantitative methods of data collection	Definition	Example from a Sage article
Questionnaires	Questionnaires are used to pose a series of questions. These may include demographic questions such as gender, age, or ethnicity as well as attitudinal questions. Questionnaires can be distributed online using software programmes such as Qualtrics or SurveyMonkey, administered via post, over e-mail or even asked in-person such as on the street or by knocking on doors.	Asif, M. 2022. Police legitimacy and approval of vigilante violence: The significance of anger. *Theoretical Criminology*, 19(2), 163–182.

(Continued)

Table 5.1 (Continued)

Quantitative methods of data collection	Definition	Example from a Sage article
Structured observations	Structured observations are used to measure the frequency and/or the timing and ordering of certain events such as the example of counting furniture described previously. The researcher observes and systematically records occurrences unfolding for analysis.	Wilde, E.M. and Welch, G.F. 2022. Attention deficit hyperactivity disorder (ADHD) and musical behaviour: The significance of context. *Psychology of Music*, 50(6), 1942–1960.
Quantitative content analysis	Content analysis is less a tool and more an analytic technique used to make sense of documents. Specifically, it is used to analyse the frequency of items (including text and visuals) in already published material such as websites, social media posts, and newspapers. The researcher systematically records all occurrences of a particular item for analysis. For example, a researcher might count the frequency with which newspapers discuss how the climate is impacted by fossil fuels.	Noetzel, S., Mussalem Gentile, M.F., Lowery, G., Zemanova, S., Lecheler, S. and Peter, C. 2022. Social campaigns to social change? Sexual violence framing in US news before and after #metoo. *Journalism*, 24(6).
Experiments	Experiments, perhaps most commonplace in psychology, are used to explore the impact of changing one variable on another. Laboratory experiments take place in a controlled environment, whereas field experiments or quasi-experiments take place in a real-world context such as a school. Real-world experiments may be followed by interventions to consider what has changed.	Jonathan-Zamir, T., Litmanovitz, Y. and Haviv, N. 2023. What works in police training? Applying an evidence-informed, general, ecological model of police training. *Police Quarterly*, 23(2), 279–306.
Secondary data analysis	Secondary data analysis involves the analysis of existing data which has already been collected by others. This typically includes quantitative data such as questionnaire data collected by other researchers as well as governmental data, including census data. Traditionally, secondary data analysis has been associated with quantitative approaches to analysis; however, increasingly, there are also qualitative sources of secondary data which can be analysed such as interview data.	Zhang, J. 2020. Influence of parenting costs on second-child fertility anxiety among adults of childbearing age in China: The moderating role of gender. *Sage Open*, 10(2). https://doi.org/10.1177/2158244020920657

The numerical data, which is collected through these quantitative approaches is used to undertake analysis using statistical software packages such as Stata, Microsoft Excel, and SPSS. Often the findings of quantitative data collection are visually displayed in bar charts and graphs. Quantitative data analysis and its visualisation is discussed further in Chapter 6 (*Social Science Data Analysis*). Here, we discuss each of the approaches listed in Table 5.1 in more detail.

Questionnaires

Questionnaires are used frequently by quantitative social scientists to elicit responses from participants. Questionnaires are designed to ask participants (sometimes called respondents) a series of questions. These questions tend to be closed-end questions meaning participants must select the most appropriate answer to the question from a list of pre-determined options. For example, *How old are you?*: (18–25), (26–35), (36–50), (51–65), (66+).

These options are then assigned numerical values to enable statistical analysis. Questionnaires can be distributed in-person, via the post, on the telephone, or online. Due to its many advantages, increasingly, researchers are utilising online survey software such as SurveyMonkey, Qualtrics or Microsoft Forms to design and distribute their questionnaires (Callegaro et al. 2015). Callegaro et al. (2015: 6) describe how a 'general development of ICT, widespread adoption of the Internet, the continuous decline in ICT-related costs and the increasing speed of the Internet' are some of the possible explanations for the rise in the number of online questionnaires distributed. A major advantage of distributing a questionnaire online is that the data are automatically coded and can be downloaded into a spreadsheet for analysis immediately. However, there may be very good reasons why you wish to administer a questionnaire in person or on the telephone. Table 5.2 considers the advantages and disadvantages of the different distribution modes and explains scenarios when researchers may choose to use them.

Researcher Reflection

Charlotte was involved in a research project exploring the research methods most frequently used by sociologists working in higher education institutions in New Zealand, the Netherlands and the United Kingdom (UK) (Brookfield 2017). To do this in the most efficient way, Charlotte chose to design and distribute an online questionnaire. Most academics are office workers and so Charlotte was confident that they would have access to the Internet and use a computer regularly. This enabled her to conduct the research in a time-efficient manner, across three countries without incurring any travel costs or the inconvenience of having to undertake telephone questionnaire data collection across different time zones.

While we have discussed issues of efficiency and speed in administering questionnaires and collecting data, time is also needed to be spent designing a robust questionnaire. The more thought put into this process, the more time is saved in the long run. It is very likely that any questionnaires which you design will go through several iterations and extensive **piloting** (discussed further later in this chapter) in which you send the questionnaire out to friends and colleagues to check its design and the question clarity before you settle on a final version. This is perfectly normal and is in fact encouraged. However, there are some rules which you should consider when you begin designing questions that might help you save additional time. These rules are discussed here.

- **Avoid using technical terms:** Questionnaires should be accessible to all participants. This means it is essential to use simple, everyday language which

Table 5.2 Different modes of questionnaire distribution

Distribution mode	Advantages	Disadvantages	Scenario	Example of Sage article
In-person/ Face-to-face	The researcher can provide clarification or answer questions that participants may have concerning the questionnaire. Questionnaires are administered and completed in real time. That is, individual participants complete and return their questionnaire straight away. High response rates. Appropriate method if participants do not have access to the Internet or a phone line.	Time-consuming for the researcher as, while individuals might return questionnaires quickly, the researcher needs to spend time contacting each participant and wait as participants complete the questionnaire. May involve travel costs. Respondents may feel obliged to participate or to provide certain answers if completing the questionnaire in front of the researcher – this is known as the **researcher effect** or **Hawthorne effect** in which the responses are influenced by the researcher's presence. Data needs to be coded and manually inputted for analysis.	A researcher is interested in who goes shopping on a Sunday afternoon. For this reason, they decide to stand on high streets on Sunday afternoons and collect their data face-to-face.	Eskiler, E. and Altunışık, R. 2021. The moderating effect of involvement in the relationship between customer behavioral intentions and its antecedents. *Sage Open*, 11(2). doi:10.1177/215824 40211014495
Post	Respondents can complete the questionnaire at their leisure and away from the gaze of the researcher. Appropriate method if participants do not have access to the Internet or a phone line. Appropriate method if wanting to survey a locale.	Slow return (it can take several weeks for respondents to post back their responses). Costs involved with postage and printing. Unable to provide respondents with any clarification or address any outstanding questions which participants may have concerning the questionnaire. Data needs to be coded and manually inputted for analysis.	A researcher is interested in exploring the mental health of older people. Given the sensitive nature of this topic a face-to-face questionnaire is deemed unsuitable. In addition, the researcher decides that the population (older people) may have difficulties completing a questionnaire online and therefore chooses a postal distribution approach.	Eerola, P., Lammi-Taskula, J., O'Brien, M., Hietamäki, J. and Räikkönen, E. 2019. Fathers' leave take-up in Finland: Motivations and barriers in a complex Nordic leave scheme. *Sage Open*, 9(4). doi:10.1177/215824 4019885389

Distribution mode	Advantages	Disadvantages	Scenario	Example of Sage article
Telephone	Quick return. The researcher can provide clarification or address questions, which participants may have concerning the questionnaire. The researcher can administer the questionnaire from the comfort of their desk.	Costs involved with telephone calls. Difficulties identifying appropriate times to contact respondents. Respondents may feel obliged to participate or to provide certain answers if completing the questionnaire in front of the researcher – what is known as the **researcher effect** or **Hawthorne effect** in which the responses are influenced by the researcher's presence. Data needs to be coded and manually inputted for analysis. Time consuming for the researcher.	A researcher is interested in exploring headteachers' views on initiatives to support teachers' wellbeing. Headteachers' email addresses are not readily available, but school telephone details are. The researcher, then, decides to call each School and ask to speak to the headteacher to conduct the questionnaire over the telephone instead.	Borz, G., Brandenburg, H. and Mendez, C. 2022. The impact of EU Cohesion Policy on European identity: A comparative analysis of EU regions. *European Union Politics*, 23(2), 259–281. doi:10.1177/14651 65221076444
Online	Quick return (participants often complete online questionnaires very quickly after receiving them). Participants can complete the questionnaire at a time which is convenient for them. Participants can complete the questionnaire on-the-go (e.g. on a mobile device). Cheap/free to design and distribute. Less time consuming for the researcher who does not need to be present for the completion of the questionnaire and who can send multiple emails with links to the questionnaire at the same time. Can use skip/branching logic to enable respondents to only see questions which are relevant to them based on their answers to previous questions. Can use a variety of question types easily. For instance, videos/images can be incorporated easily. Can send questionnaire to a broader geographical range. Data are coded and ready to analyse straight away. Participants can complete the questionnaire anonymously and without the researcher being around.	Unable to provide participants with any clarification or address any outstanding questions which they may have concerning the questionnaire. Sometimes there are low response rates as it lacks a personal touch. Risk of participants completing the questionnaire multiple times. May lose particular demographics who do not have access to the Internet.	A researcher is interested in comparing the working conditions of a large, international tech organisation with offices in Sweden, the United States of America (USA) and China. Given the geographical spread of the employees and the familiarity they are likely to have with navigating online platforms, the researcher chooses an online questionnaire. There will also be several time zones to contend with, so an asynchronous online questionnaire enables participants to respond at a time that suits them.	James, E., Robertshaw, T.L., Pascoe, M.J. et al. 2021. Online survey into developing a model for a legal cannabis market in the United Kingdom. *Drug Science, Policy and Law*, 7. doi:10.1177/2050 3245211034931

can be easily understood. Therefore, try to avoid jargon and terms or phrases that participants are unlikely to understand or be familiar with. For instance, a question such as 'To what extent do you agree with the following statement? *The GUI used on Apple products is easy to navigate*' might not be readily understood by everyone. Although the technology company Apple might be a rather pervasive term today and unlikely to be confused for the fruit, acronyms such as GUI (which stands for graphical user interface) require insider knowledge.

A better, alternative question which is getting at the same issue might be phrased as:

To what extent do you agree with the following statement? *The interface on Apple products is easy to navigate*.

> Strongly Agree
> Agree
> Neither Agree nor Disagree
> Disagree
> Strongly Disagree
> Not Applicable

Here, while the participant still needs some knowledge of Apple products, the knowledge required is ubiquitous and not specialist (Collins and Evans 2002). Note also how the categories are pre-determined, with the participant given the choice of five scaled categories, ranging from strongly agree to strongly disagree, plus a not applicable category (presumably the choice they would select if they have never owned or used an Apple product).

- **Avoid overlapping response categories:** Participants need to be able to easily select the response option which best applies to them. Therefore, it is important to avoid overlapping response categories, e.g. 'On average, how many hours of independent study do you typically complete in a week?' 0-4, 4-6, 7–10, or more than 10. In this example, it is unclear whether a participant who spends 4 hours undertaking independent study in a week selects the category '0-4' or the category '4-6'.

  A better, alternative question would be:

  On average, how many hours of independent study do you typically complete in a week?

  > 0–4
  > 5–6
  > 7–10
  > More than 10

Note also how these are listed vertically rather than horizontally so it is easier for the reader to distinguish between the categories.

- **Avoid leading questions:** Questions should be as neutral and value-free as possible. This means that the researcher should avoid conveying personal beliefs or attitudes in the questions which they pose, even inadvertently. For example, it would be inappropriate for a researcher to ask, *'Do you agree that hunting is wrong and should be banned?'* Yes or No. No matter how passionate you are about the topic which you are researching, it is important that your own values and beliefs are not reflected in your questions. Using neutral, value-free language can help participants feel more comfortable providing their honest opinions. This is particularly important when researching topics which are potentially controversial or have a moral component.

  A better, alternative question would be:

  To what extent do you agree with the following statement? *Hunting should be banned.*

  > Strongly agree
  > Agree
  > Neither agree nor disagree
  > Disagree
  > Strongly disagree

- **Avoid asking multiple questions in one:** Questions should be succinct and only ask participants about one issue at a time. For instance, if you asked participants to share their level of agreement with the following statement: *'The school day should be made longer and homework completely scrapped'*, they may struggle to respond if they agree with the first part of the statement that the school day should be made longer, but disagree with the second part of the statement that homework should be dipsensed with.

  A better alternative is to divide the question into two such as:

  To what extent do you agree with the following statements?

  The school day should be made longer.

  > Strongly agree
  > Agree
  > Neither agree nor disagree
  > Disagree
  > Strongly disagree

  Homework should be completely scrapped.

  > Strongly agree
  > Agree
  > Neither agree nor disagree
  > Disagree
  > Strongly disagree

- **Avoid questions which rely on participants' memory:** Questions should be easy for participants to answer. If questions require too much memory recall, participants are likely to skip questions, leading to missing data or withdrawal from the research altogether. For example, if you ask people for the exact date that they last visited the optician they may struggle to recall this precise information accurately. Can you remember the exact date you last visited one?

A better, alternative question would be:

When was the last time you visited the optician?

> Within the last month
> Within the last 6 months
> Within the last year
> Over a year ago

There are also several different biases which may impact on the quality of participants' responses. For instance, **acquiescence bias** is the term used to describe the tendency for participants to agree with statements regardless of their content (Converse and Presser 1986, Callegaro et al. 2015, Tourangeau et al. 2000). It is the idea that participants are inclined to agree with statements to help speed up the process of completing the questionnaire and/or in some instances to help portray themselves as agreeable to the researcher. To help detect acquiescence response bias and to engage respondents with a questionnaire, researchers sometimes use a mixture of positive and negative statements to help them tap into the same underlying construct. For instance, if a researcher is interested in beliefs concerning the amount of music taught in the school curriculum, they may include the two following statements in a questionnaire:

To what extent do you agree with the following statements?

It is important for children to learn music at school.

> Strongly agree
> Agree
> Neither agree nor disagree
> Disagree
> Strongly disagree

Less time should be devoted to music lessons in school.

> Strongly agree
> Agree
> Neither agree nor disagree
> Disagree
> Strongly disagree

In this example, we would anticipate that a participant who agreed that it was important for children to learn music at school would disagree with the statement 'less time should be devoted to music lessons in school'. The same would be true about a question on banning hunting. Again, in this scenario, a researcher may pose two statements which would likely receive opposing responses from participants, such as '*Hunting is cruel*' and '*Hunting is an enjoyable sport*'. If a participant did not select opposing answers, it may suggest that they were not engaging with the questionnaire in the way you hoped. With this in mind, the researcher should consider deleting this participant from the dataset as their answers may introduce bias.

Inspiration for questions can be taken from previous studies. This should not be seen as cheating or plagiarism! In fact, replicating questions which have been used in previous questionnaires is good practice. These questions will have likely been through extensive piloting and testing. By replicating existing questions, you can draw comparisons between your own findings and those of other researchers. Existing questions can be found by looking at secondary sources of data (see Table 1.2). However, even if a question has been used previously in a questionnaire, it does not guarantee it is the best measure or ideal for the population you are studying. It is important to think critically about questions and whether they are appropriate for your study and your sample. Here, **piloting** and **cognitive interviewing** can help.

> ***Piloting*** involves testing or undertaking practice runs of your questionnaire with a small group of your population. The process of piloting allows researchers to identify any further potential issues with question clarity and helps them to gain an insight into how easy or difficult their questionnaire is for participants to navigate. That is, a pilot is used to test the design or delivery of the method used. As such, piloting is not simply limited to questionnaire construction but is often done in interview and focus group research too.

> ***Cognitive interviewing*** can also be used in the process of questionnaire refinement to help researchers understand how participants interpret questions and go about answering them (Willis 2004, Ryan et al. 2012, Collins 2015). Cognitive interviewing involves the researcher asking a series of questions to ascertain more information on how a participant understood a question and reached an eventual response. The cognitive interview allows the researcher to assess whether questions are comprehensible to participants and whether answering the questions poses the respondents any challenges, for instance, in their ability to recall information accurately and to choose an appropriate response option. Cognitive interviewing demonstrates how quantitative and qualitative approaches can be combined in a research project. Here, qualitative interviews are integral to helping the researcher develop and refine their quantitative questionnaire. More information about qualitative approaches to data collection can be found in Part Two of this chapter.

Structured Observations

Another approach to collecting quantitative data is using structured observations. Although observations are mostly associated with qualitative research (see Part Two: *Qualitative methods*), some researchers use this technique to systematically observe behaviours and events and record what is happening in numerical form (Phellas et al. 2012). In comparison to questionnaire data, structured observations can provide researchers with more accurate and detailed accounts of participants' behaviours. This is because the researcher is observing events unfolding first hand and recording the exact order and timing in which they take place. This is particularly the case if the participants are unaware of the researcher observing them – known as a **covert observation**. There are ethical concerns with covert observations and researchers need to be able to provide a clear rationale to their institutional ethics committee for not disclosing their identity to participants and for not using the more pervasive **overt** approach instead (see Chapter 4: *Being an Ethical Researcher*).

Often quantitative researchers will create observation schedules to help them keep track of behaviours which they observe. The observation schedule should contain pre-determined actions, behaviours, or activities which a researcher is hoping to identify and record. Researchers may also include timings on their observation schedule to allow them to capture additional temporal information. Time should be dedicated to produce the pre-determined categories, and we encourage you to read relevant literature and look at previous studies to help you create these categories. It is important to note too, that in the same way as you may find it helpful to replicate questions from existing studies in a questionnaire, it is also perfectly acceptable to use the same categories in your observation schedule as those used by previous researchers.

However, as with face-to-face questionnaires, it can be the case with overt observations that participants adapt or change their behaviour in the presence of a researcher. Participants may alter their behaviour, perhaps even unconsciously, to portray themselves in what they believe the researcher will deem a favourable or positive light.

Content Analysis

As discussed above, quantitative content is more a type of analysis than method. It involves counting and recording the frequency of items, phrases, or words (Gummer et al. 2019). As such, it concerns textual artefacts such as policy papers, newspapers, or posters. For example, you may decide to undertake a quantitative content analysis of newspapers and websites and their portrayal of knife crime in the UK, specifically exploring whether there is a difference in the portrayal of such events in different news outlets with differing political perspectives. To do this, you could count the prevalence of knife crime stories featured in different newspapers published in the UK over a fixed period. Or you might decide to do something more detailed and count the number of articles which include a description or photograph of the victim as well as whether it was a pre-determined attack or not. To assist with this type of research, quantitative researchers will make a coding sheet or manual. An example of a coding manual containing fictitious data can be seen in Table 5.3. Here, the researcher has coded whether each of the news articles read contained a description of the victim, a picture of the victim, a description of the perpetrator, and a picture of the perpetrator. The 'Yes' and 'No' responses can be assigned numerical values to enable further statistical data analysis e.g. if a description of the victim was included then a '1' would be assigned. However, if the article did not include a description of the victim a '0' would be assigned.

Table 5.3 A fictitious example of a coding manual

Newspaper and websites	Date	Description of victim	Picture of victim	Description of perpetrator	Picture of perpetrator
BBC	26 Jan 2023	Yes	Yes	No	No
Guardian	26 Jan 2023	Yes	Yes	Yes	No
Telegraph	26 Jan 2023	No	No	Yes	No
Daily Mail	27 Jan 2023	Yes	No	Yes	Yes
Telegraph	27 Jan 2023	No	No	Yes	No

In some instances, researchers may even quantify the length/number of words dedicated to a particular topic. For instance, in Table 5.4, an additional column has been added to the coding schedule to contain data on the number of words per article. This allows the researcher to explore whether certain news outlets dedicated statistically significantly more words to stories relating to knife crime compared to others.

Other materials which you might consider using for a quantitative content analysis include blog posts, social media posts, TV programmes, radio shows, podcasts, magazines/brochures, prospectuses, posters, and promotional materials.

It is extremely important when undertaking quantitative content analysis to consider the parameters around your study. In the example above, you would not be able to read and analyse all newspapers and websites over an extended period as this would

Table 5.4 An example coding manual

Newspaper and websites	Date	Description of victim	Picture of victim	Description of perpetrator	Picture of perpetrator	Number of words
BBC	26 Jan 23	Yes	Yes	No	No	750
Guardian	26 Jan 23	Yes	Yes	Yes	No	600
Telegraph	26 Jan 23	No	No	Yes	No	1400
Daily Mail	27 Jan 23	Yes	No	Yes	Yes	450
Telegraph	27 Jan 23	No	No	Yes	No	1350

not be feasible within the time constraints of a large, funded research project, let alone a student one. Therefore, you might consider limiting your project to a set of newspapers and websites over a shorter period, such as one month, or you might explore an even narrower selection of news outlets over a longer period. These decisions should be informed by the aims of your research and the research questions posed.

Content analysis has several advantages over other modes of quantitative data collection. The first, and perhaps most salient benefit for student researchers, is that it allows for the exploration of topics which are typically off-limits (especially for students). For instance, undergraduate and postgraduate students are extremely unlikely to be granted ethical approval to design and distribute their own questionnaire exploring sexual harassment among student cohorts (See Chapter 4: Being an Ethical Researcher). However, you could undertake a content analysis of student newspapers to explore the prevalence of these instances and make your own coding manual recording demographic details on victims and perpetrators. The unobtrusiveness of content analysis means that there are fewer ethical concerns associated with this type of research since you are using **found data** – data that exists independently of the current research (Coffey 2014). Indeed, in many cases the approach itself is already a mitigation against any ethical concerns. Content analysis also offers students the possibility to undertake research on sensitive topics and hard-to-reach groups. For example, although you are very unlikely to be able to get access to research high-ranking politicians, you could undertake a content analysis of politicians' speeches. Similarly, instead of collecting data directly from celebrities or influencers, you may decide to conduct a content analysis of celebrities' or influencers' social media posts. You could focus on one celebrity over a set period or choose a topic such as fast fashion and explore social media posts from several celebrities relating to this chosen topic. The ability to track change over time is an important feature of quantitative content analysis. You would struggle to design and distribute two or more questionnaires in the time available for your research project (usually only one or two semesters). However, content analysis enables you to track change over time in a more manageable and less time-consuming way. Using a coding manual makes content analysis a transparent approach to quantifying data from existing sources. This transparency can increase the reliability of research findings.

However, quantitative content analysis is not without its challenges. The coding of data might not always be straightforward or clear cut. Sometimes the researcher needs to make subjective decisions about how to code items. This can be particularly problematic in large-scale projects where there are multiple coders. For this reason, it can be helpful to devise a coding schedule or manual with a list of rules and criteria to follow when coding the data.

Researcher Reflection

Working on your own on a research project is different to working in a group. In a recent research project, Charlotte, alongside two other researchers, undertook a content analysis of research methods used in articles published in the journal *Sociology*. Articles were coded as reporting quantitative or qualitative findings or being non-empirical. Significant time was spent discussing how to code certain articles. These decisions were recorded in the coding manual meaning that future researchers can understand how the researchers decided to code different articles. For example, there was some discussion about how best to code articles which drew on interview data, but also presented demographic data on the sample in tabular form and, in some cases, reported percentages. Similarly, decisions needed to be made about what content to code, for instance, whether the researchers should include other types of academic outputs such as forewords, research notes, book reviews, etc. in their analysis. It was integral that the multiple coders involved in the project were using the same criteria to make uniform subjective decisions when coding the articles to ensure that the research findings were reliable. The coders worked together during the coding process to facilitate easy discussions and developed the coding manual with their decisions as they progressed with their coding.

Experiments

Experiments are a staple in psychological projects (Colman 2004). Experiments aim to test an idea in a controlled environment, enabling the researcher to be confident in their claims of causality, and improving the internal validity of the findings. Typically, we differentiate between experiments which take place in a laboratory and field experiments. Field experiments (sometimes called quasi experiments) are more common in the broader social sciences and involve the researcher studying groups in real, pre-existing settings such as a school or work organisations. Quasi experiments also exist in qualitative work. For example, ethnomethodologists are known to conduct **breaching experiments**, which seek to capture people's reactions to breaches or violations of social norms like jumping queues or standing facing people in an elevator (Rafalovich 2006). Here, the experiment is testing people's reactions to transgressions of social etiquette.

At their heart, quantitative experiments are about comparisons, though, so lab-type experiments are also designed. In a typical experiment, the researcher will divide participants into two groups: the control group and an experimental group. The composition of these two groups should be as identical as possible. The only difference between the control group and the experimental group should be that those in the latter group receive a treatment or intervention, whilst those in the control group do not. By keeping the two groups as similar as possible, the researcher can be more confident that the treatment or intervention has caused any subsequent change observed in the experimental group.

As such, when using experimental research designs, researchers will usually administer some sort of assessment, survey, or test to measure the construct being explored before the treatment or intervention, known as **pre-testing**. The researcher will then administer the same assessment at the end of the experimental period, known as **post-testing**, to allow them to observe and measure any changes that may have occurred because of the treatment or intervention.

The experiment is probably most typically associated in medical disciplines where they are used to measure the effectiveness of new drugs and other therapies. For example, those with high blood pressure may be divided into two groups. These two groups will be matched in terms of other demographic variables as closely as possible, for instance, they will contain the same proportion of people of different ages and ethnicities. The blood pressure of all participants will be taken at the beginning of the experiment. Half of the participants will be given a new drug to try, and the other half will be given a placebo (e.g., a sugar pill) – this is the **variable**. Crucially in this example, participants will not know which group they belong to – the experimental group receiving the new drug or the control group receiving the placebo. After some time, the blood pressure of all the participants will be measured again and the researchers will analyse the data to ascertain whether there has been a statistically significant decrease in the blood pressure levels of those in the experimental group compared to those in the control group. They are then in a position to deduce whether the new drug played a role or not.

In the social sciences, it can be harder to match participants based on demographics and divide them into two identical groups because the variable which we are interested in testing tends to be a social one. Instead, researchers often look for naturally occurring groups. For example, an educational researcher may be interested in exploring the impacts of a new initiative to improve average reading scores among 5-year-olds. In this example, they may take two classes containing students of the appropriate age group and measure their reading ages. They would then introduce the initiative to one class only – the experimental group. The class which does not receive the initiative are the control group and they continue their learning as planned. Once the initiative has finished, the reading ages of all the children would be measured again, and the researcher would explore the impact of the initiative on the reading age of the children in the one class (the experimental group) compared to those in the other class who did not receive the treatment (the control group).

Being able to plan and undertake field experiments can be challenging, especially as a student researcher. A key feature of the experimental design is pre- and post-testing, and this can be extremely time consuming. Further, it can be hard to access participants who are willing to be involved in experimental research. Participants will want assurance that their involvement in the experimental group (and sometimes the control group will not result in adverse or negative effects (see Chapter 4: *Being an Ethical Researcher*).

Secondary Data Analysis

Quantitative secondary data analysis involves the analysis of existing numerical data which has been collected for the purposes of research by other people (MacInnes 2016). However, the researcher explores the data in a different way to the original work to explore new patterns or relationships. For example, a previous dissertation student we supervised used data collected in the British Social Attitudes Survey (2024) to explore how attitudes toward immigration had changed in the UK before and after the referendum to leave the European Union. Examples of secondary datasets which you might like to explore and analyse include the European Social Survey (2024), the World Values Survey (2020) and the US General Social Survey (2022). These datasets contain survey data which can be downloaded from online data archives where researchers deposit their data after completion of their project. Examples of some different online data archives are listed in Table 5.5. National governments also collate and share some data, which is then made available to the broader public. Table 5.6 directs you toward webpages containing governmental statistics for different regions across the globe.

Table 5.5 Examples of online data archives

Data depository	Website
UK Data Service	https://ukdataservice.ac.uk/
The Australian Data Archive	https://ada.edu.au/
Canadian Opinion Research Archive	www.queensu.ca/cora/
Irish Social Science Data Archive	www.ucd.ie/issda/
Data Cymru	www.data.cymru/data

Table 5.6 Sources of governmental data

Governmental data	Country
Data.gov	USA
Data.gov.uk	UK
Data.gov.au	Australia
Data.gov.sg	Singapore
Data.gov.in	India
Data.govt.nz	New Zealand

There are various advantages to analysing secondary data in a research project. Most notably, by not collecting primary data, researchers have significantly more time to be become familiar with the data and undertake analysis. Moreover, it is likely that existing sources of data are from large, funded projects and, therefore, the data quality is often detailed, comprehensive and covers more ground. It can be super difficult for students to collect an equivalent amount of primary data in the short space of time allocated to their research project. Consequently, using secondary sources of data from repositories such as those listed above provides you the opportunity to access datasets which usually have much bigger and more representative samples. It can also enable longitudinal research, meaning that you can consider trends and patterns in the data over time. Again, there is unlikely to be the time to collect your own data at two or more time points, meaning that secondary data analysis can be a particularly valuable approach if you are interested in exploring change over time. By analysing existing datasets, it is also possible to research topics which students are typically unable to collect data on. For example, a university's ethics committee would be unlikely to permit students to collect primary data on participants' experiences of serious crime. However, datasets including the Crime Survey for England and Wales (2024) can be used to effectively explore these issues.

Despite the advantages in saving time collecting data, it is vital not to underestimate the time needed to familiarise yourself with existing sources of data. When downloading datasets from the Internet, always check for accompanying documentation, including the provenance of the data – please check the source and where it came from. This information – sometimes called meta data – should explain how the data was originally collected and should provide details on how the variables were coded and why. Of course, with secondary data analysis you do not have control over the data being collected. This means that, inevitably, you will find some datasets that, on the surface, look as if they are appropriate for your study but do not contain key or important variables that are required to address your research questions. In these instances, you may need to consider altering the focus of your research and tinkering with your research questions or, alternatively, collecting primary data instead.

PART TWO: QUALITATIVE METHODS

The term '**qualitative research methods**' is used to describe a bank of approaches that collect non-numerical data such as audio, text, visual, or video, producing rich, detailed material. Typically, qualitative methods are drawn on when you want to ask 'how' or 'why' questions, especially when you wish to find out the ways in which people understand and experience social situations and social reality. Qualitative research is usually aligned with **inductive reasoning** where the researcher is led by the data collected, gathering evidence through observation, talking methodologies, or experiments, and then draws general conclusions from this collected data. They are approaches commonly used in the social sciences and humanities and increasingly so in certain parts of health research, such as epidemiology, and in projects concerned with lived experience. There are a variety of different qualitative methods, arguably many more than quantitative, ranging from the more traditional to the novel and experimental. Within this section of the chapter, we discuss some of the main qualitative approaches which students might use in their own research projects such as interviews, focus groups, observational techniques, documentary analysis, social media analysis, and creative methods. It is important to stress here that these methodological approaches could be cut up and categorised in multiple ways as there are often overlaps between them and some approaches fit into more than one category. What they all have in common, though, and unlike quantitative approaches, is that while they use various tools to access the social world, it is the researcher who is the instrument of data analysis. That is, qualitative research might be understood to involve an **interpretivist** approach to making sense of data with the interpreter being the researcher who is embedded fully in the entirety of the project from research design to the write up of the analysis.

Box 5.2

Qualitative Methods at a Glance

The collection of non-numerical data such as audio, textual, and visual.

Data usually presented in text or visual form.

Theory more likely to be inductive (bottom up) but, on occasions, can also be deductive (top down).

More interested in representation than generalisation.

The researcher is the instrument of analysis.

Common methods include interviews, focus groups, observational techniques, and creative methods.

Qualitative Interviews

Atkinson and Silverman (1997) maintain that we now live in an 'interview society'. While not endorsing the interview approach as the qualitative research method par excellence, they recognise 'the interview' has stabilised to become a pervasive phenomenon in society (you only need to think of the various types of interviews we encounter in everyday life: sports interviews, political interviews, welfare interviews, job interviews, police interviews, and subsequently in research too). There is little doubt too that interviews are a popular choice amongst students doing social science research. Indeed, they are the most widely employed method in qualitative research (Alamri 2019), used to elicit experiences, opinions, biographies, values, knowledges, attitudes and perspectives, feelings and alternative voices. Qualitative interviews often produce storified retrospectives and accounts. But the interview itself is not one thing and can be dressed up in various ways. We have already discussed a quantitative approach to 'structured' interviews (a face-to-face questionnaire). Conversely, qualitative interviews might be understood to be either unstructured (free from restraint) or semi-structured (flexible but within parameters). Contrast the structured interview with the unstructured interview. Here, rather than a uniform interview schedule, the researcher may simply have an *aide memoire*, a prompt sheet as their guide. The **unstructured interview** is an open-ended interview and might be understood as a *recorded conversation* in which the interviewer takes a steer from the participant, listening as well as asking questions. The interviewer may only come prepared with a set of topics to discuss or a couple of questions to direct the general conversation. Simply put, the approach is interested in the

Table 5.7 Approaches to collecting qualitative data

Qualitative methods of data collection	Definition	Example from Sage Article
Qualitative interviews	A method that elicits data through talk. Interviews involve at least two people: the researcher and the participant(s). Interviews come in many forms and types. Some are individual interviews, others are group interviews, some are structured (may also be considered a type of face-to-face survey) and uniform, whilst others are unstructured and open. Interviews can be conducted in person, over the phone, via online platforms, and even on e-mail. It is the most pervasive qualitative method drawn on by a range of social science disciplines.	Miczo, N. 2003. Beyond the 'Fetishism of Words': Consideration on the use of the interview to gather chronic illness narrative. *Qualitative Health Research*, 13(4), 469–490.
Focus groups	A method in which the researcher facilitates and moderates a conversation between a small group of chosen participants. The focus group is often hand-picked with members chosen due to pre-determined demographic traits. The researcher often attempts to steer the conversation towards a particular topic or issue, such as individuals' views on incarceration, and might bring with them a prompt to help elicit responses. The prompt might include an image or a newspaper article. It is a method commonly used in the fields of marketing and journalism.	Richard, B. et al. 2021. A guide to conducting online focus groups via Reddit. *International Journal of Qualitative Research*, 20.
Observational	A central method employed in ethnographic research where the researcher attempts to spend some time in the shoes of the participant, immersing themselves in their world. Those that advocate observational research are interested in what people do as well as what they say. The general is often extrapolated from the specific with ethnographers spending lengthy intervals with the people they are studying, observing them in their natural setting. It is an approach that is popular in anthropology and strands of sociology such ethnomethodology.	Stephens, N. and Lewis, J. 2017. Doing laboratory ethnography: Reflections on methods in scientific workplaces. *Qualitative Research*, 17(2), 202–216.
Documents	Document research is a rather fuzzy term that includes the analysis of a range of human produced artefacts. In essence though, document research refers to the analysis and categorisation of physical objects, most commonly in text form that exist in the social and online worlds. These can be official documents such as policy and governmental papers, personal documents such as diaries and prescriptions, and public documents such as newspapers. Document research can also extend to the analysis of images and videos in the shape of posters, graphic novels, vlogs, etc.	Ball, M. 2011. Images, language and numbers in company reports: A study of documents that are occasioned by a legal requirement for financial disclosure. *Qualitative Research*, 11(2), 115–139.

Qualitative methods of data collection	Definition	Example from Sage Article
Social media/ Online research	Social media and Online research refer to the collection and analysis of information produced for or created on the Internet. This can involve **asynchronous** communication or information – that is, not occurring in real time – such as a blog, a support group bulletin board, an email. Or it can be **synchronous** – occurring in real time – such as content created in online worlds, through social media chat or through online gaming. Examples of online research methods include netnography, social network analysis and online content analysis.	Bleakley, P. 2021. Panic, pizza and mainstreaming the Alt Right: A social media analysis of Pizzagate and the rise of the QAnon conspiracy. *Current Sociology*, 71(3), 509–525.
Creative methods	Over the past two decades there has surfaced a plethora of novel and experimental methods that might be coined creative methods. This has involved the fusing together of traditional social science methods with methods used in the arts and humanities. Creative methods have been particularly popular when engaging specific publics and groups such as very young people, people diagnosed with dementia, or people whose first language is different to the researcher. Examples of creative methods include arts-based projects, photography and poetry. Creative methods can also include creativity from the researcher, such as drawing, graphic novels, poetry, and creative non-fiction approaches.	Cuthbert, K. 2022. Researching 'non sexualities' via creative notebooks: Epistemology, embodiment and empowerment. *Qualitative Research*, 22(6), 897–915.
Participatory research	Participatory research is more of a mindset than a distinct research category. It involves the active intention to involve the participant in the research process, in the research design, and even in the direction the project takes. The idea here is that data and knowledge is co-constructed. Specific examples of participatory research include Action Research where the researcher and participant are in active dialogue with one another to diagnose, research, and solve an issue, and community-based projects such as Community Science programmes where researchers and the community members collect data such as environmental traces to challenge local policy decisions.	Van de Riet, M. 2008. Participatory research and the philosophy of social science: Beyond the moral imperative. *Qualitative Inquiry*, 14(4), 546–565.
Sensory methods	The term sensory methods captures those research approaches that prioritise the multisensoriality of experience and perception. This might involve research that focusses on participants' olfactory, gustatory, auditory, and tactile experiences. Often sensory methodologists are creative in the ways in which they (re-)present the sensory experience using images, audio recordings, and drawings.	Mason, J. and Davies, K. 2009. Coming to our senses? A critical approach to sensory methodology. *Qualitative Research*, 9(5), 587–603.

participants' perspective much more than the interviewer's concerns. In essence, an unstructured interview attempts to make an artificial situation (the manufactured interview) as close to a natural conversation as possible.

Sitting somewhere between structured and unstructured interviews is what is commonly called the **semi-structured interview**. These interviews often begin with a small pool of pre-determined questions, which are intertwined with other unscripted questions taking a steer from the participants' answers *in situ*. The researcher often comes prepared with an interview schedule but has the freedom to go beyond these questions to probe interesting responses. That is, semi-structured interviews provide the freedom for participants to answer more on their own terms than the structured interview permits and yet provide a greater structure for comparability between interviews than the unstructured. Rather than a completely natural conversation, this style of interview has been described as a 'guided conversation' (Rubin and Rubin 1995) steered by the interviewer.

There are, of course, other ways in which we might understand interviews beyond their structure. For example, there are: elite interviews, that is, interviews with experts, people with detailed knowledge of the topic being studied, and other participants with a certain status and gravitas (Stephens 2007, Harvey 2011); focussed interviews that centre on people who have been in a certain situation (Merton and Kendall 1946); life history interviews that are bibliographic in nature (Walmsley 1997, Adriansen 2012, Blakely and Moles 2017); online interviews which are mediated by the Internet (Deakin and Wakefield 2014, Howlett 2022); and photo elicitation that uses photographs and objects to prompt discussion (Allen 2011, Kyololo et al. 2023).

Focus Groups

The focus group is a popular method employed in disciplines such as media studies, business and marketing, and communication studies. It might be understood as a form of 'group interview' (though strictly speaking, the term 'group interview' is used to describe a distinct and different approach to collecting data) in which the participants will be asked to respond to a series of questions in a mediated setting. A focus group usually consists of more than four people and less than ten, ensuring that the group is not too small so as to stymy interaction and not too large meaning not everyone has the opportunity to participate. The methodological tool uses the interaction between participants as its pivotal component (Kitzinger 1995). Thus, unlike a standard group interview where the researcher asks a suite of question to various participants, the researcher here actively encourages participants to talk to one another whilst they take a more backseat role. Focus groups typically centre on a specific topic which is discussed amongst participants of the group, such as their thoughts on nuclear power, genetically modified crops or ethical shopping. The focus group technique requires the researcher to have skills in steering the direction of the conversation but without curtailing ideas and enthusiasm. They may even use prompts to direct the conversation such as a newspaper article or a photograph that represents the issue at hand. The group of participants are usually chosen due to some pre-determined characteristics or criteria. In some cases, this will mean members will already know one another. This might lead to more natural conversations, but the researcher should be cognisant of existing dynamics which may affect how people present themselves or discuss issues. In other cases, members will be meeting for the first time. Here, it may be the case that participants need 'warming up' and it is useful to prepare ice-breaker sessions before the formal focus group begins. The method is particularly useful for eliciting opinions, experiences and attitudes but is also interesting in revealing how group dynamics work, how dissenting voices are managed, how consensus is formed or not, and whether people are willing to change their opinions. There are marketing and public opinion pollsters such as Ipsos Mori and YouGov that specialise in focus groups.

Observational Techniques

To truly understand a setting, ethnographers such as Hammersley and Atkinson (2007) tend to maintain that you need to immerse yourself in the field site. What better way to do that than being physically there observing the phenomenon at hand? Observational techniques demand that the researcher spends a significant period doing fieldwork, building rapport with those they are studying by securing and maintaining relationships throughout the course of the study as well as observing and documenting the day-to-day practices of their work. This approach is a particularly powerful method to employ when you wish to make sense of and analyse people's behaviours, their practices, their routines and rituals, and how they go about accomplishing those acts in their everyday natural settings. Whereas interviews might be understood to capture how people 'talk the walk', observational techniques capture how people 'walk the walk', and importantly people who employ this method recognise that what people say and what people do might be different (Atkinson and Silverman 1997, Jerolmack and Khan 2014, Small and Cook 2023).

Basically, there are two types of observation: **participant observation** and **non-participant observation**. The first term is said to describe an approach where the researcher becomes an active member of the group, participating in their acts, while the second captures an approach where the researcher, whilst still spending a great deal of time with those they are studying, does so from a distance – is simply an observer and not a participant. In practice, this dichotomy is more of a spectrum with the degree of participation often dependent on a mixture of your approach, the topic at hand, your expertise, and the access you have negotiated. For example, rarely will a sociologist interested in how scientific laboratories work be able to participate in the laboratory setting in the same way as the scientists they are studying given the strict protocols and regulations associated with scientific work. But someone conducting **action research** in the community that seeks transformative change will be doing a sort of participation observation.

All observers capture their data by making detailed notes, in what might be called *thick description* – detailed vignettes that not only describe but also help readers understand the phenomenon being studied. Here, writing is understood as a craft, one that can be worked on and polished. In many cases, observers will first have to make headnotes (Jackson 1990), perhaps with little more than jotting down ideas, prompts, and key 'take homes' from their day in the field. When back home or at the office, it is best practice to turn these into detailed narratives employing the thick description approach. Most observational work is captured under the broader methodological approach called **ethnography**, meaning writing about people or folk. For ethnographers, writing is both a form of data and analysis, while the ethnography, which combines observational work with interviews, is both the approach to researching the setting and the finished product. Most observational work these days is **overt**, meaning the participants are aware that the researcher is there observing their lives. However, certain topics such as white-collar crime might demand **covert** techniques in which the researcher does not disclose their position and intention (see Chapter 4: *Being an Ethical Researcher*).

Documents

From Cave paintings to vlogs, from archaic scripts to tweets, from tapestries to infographics, from newspapers to graphic novels, humans have documented their lives through artefacts since time immemorial. The stuff we create matters. It matters at an individual level, and at an organisational level. It is hard to imagine a modern institution, whether a hospital, school, prison, or university without recourse to its routine documentary procedures (Coffey 2014). As such, the documents we produce shape and are shaped by the cultures we inhabit. Indeed, some of the pre-eminent classical works in social science used documents as forms of empirical data. In writing *Das Kapital,* Karl Marx (1867) used reports from factory workers, in producing *The Protestant Ethic and the Spirit of Capitalism,* Max Weber (1905[2001]) analysed historical documents, Émile Durkheim (1897[1952]) used public records on his work on *Suicide,* and Michael Foucault (1976[1979]) examined historical public documents for *History of Sexuality.*

Documentary research might be understood to come in two forms: the use of **found documents** and **crafted documents**. Found documents are artefacts which exist independently of the intent and design of a research project. That is, they were not created by the social science researcher nor the participants in the researcher's project. Popular documents of this type include newspapers, policy reports, and historical letters. Crafted documents, on the other hand, are documents which are made as part of the research itself. That is, they are produced explicitly for the research at hand. For example, a researcher might ask a participant to keep a diary as part of the study. When we discuss documentary research, we are usually referring to found documents insofar as crafted documents are usually produced as part of a broader methodological approach, e.g., diaries to go alongside interviews.

Importantly, found documents do not exist outside of their context; they are literally 'products' of their environment. They are resources which can tell us something of an institution, of an event, of a site. They are physical traces or residues of a setting, socially accomplished through social interaction. They are not always static artefacts, though; they are often fluid and regularly updated. Moreover, they are often not produced in isolation and, as such, often 'speak' to other documents and artefacts. The connection between various types of documents is known as **intertextuality**.

Scott (1990) challenges documentary researchers to check the authenticity, credibility, and representativeness of the documents that they are analysing. He asks you, for example, to consider whether the artefact is of unquestionable origin, whether the people who produced the document are reliable, and whether the document is typical of its kind? Once you have ascertained what documents to use, it is imperative that you read the documents and then re-read them as a social science researcher being mindful that you are the instrument of analysis. Consider the purpose of the document, who is the author, who is the intended audience? Consider too what is absent, what is being said by being unsaid, how does the document link to other documents, what is the artefact accomplishing and why?

For more on documents research, please see Grant (2022) and Prior (2003).

Social Media and Online Research

While there are significant overlaps, we have included social media alongside online research, as a category distinct from documents. In simple terms, online research refers to the collection of data from the Internet. For some, the Internet is simply an extension or a reflection of the social world. As such, it is often the case that documentary researchers will include social media as a form of document. Social media in essence is a form of new media (Beer 2013), explaining why we have grouped newspaper and tweets as documents above. For others, the Internet demands different and subtle ways to understanding the world and how people interact (Beneito-Montagut et al. 2018, Beneito-Montagut 2022). While in this chapter we discuss social media and online research as a hybrid method, it is important to also recognise that the Internet has given birth to new forms of methods such as netnography – an adaption of the more traditional ethnographic approach to studying social interaction on the Internet (Kozinets 2015) – as well as various forms of social media scraping and social network analysis.

As we describe in the section on Big Data, the Internet creates huge amounts of potential data and stores it there for posterity. This is both a challenge and an opportunity for social science researchers. The online world and the various ways of accessing and encountering it not only change the way in which data are produced (e.g., video content) and then collected and stored, but also raises different and new ethical and methodological issues not present in in-person research (e.g., issues of disclosure and anonymity). Online research, of course, ranges from asynchronous interaction (and research) such as email, WhatsApp, websites, blogs, or online support groups, to social media research on platforms such as Facebook, X (formerly Twitter), WeChat, TikTok, YouTube, SnapChat, Instagram, to synchronous virtual worlds such as Second Life and IMVU, to online games such as Minecraft and PUB to other web applications such as dating apps (Tinder), health apps (Sweatcoin) and education apps (Duolingo) (see Lupton 2016, Thomas et al. 2018). This covers a broad range of technological and social types in which people live, interact, and generate content together and therefore demands various approaches to collecting that content (see Lindgren 2017, Lindgren and Krutrök 2024).

Creative Methods

As with most of these categories, creative methods is an elastic grouping that covers several types of methods that probably deserve their own entry. They are methods that have their influence in both the social sciences, and the arts and humanities. Here, we are including: drawing research (Quinn 2023) and observational sketching (Heath et al. 2018); graphic storytelling (Bates et al. 2023, Scavarda and Moretti 2024); live methods that recognise the artfulness of social science (Back and Puwar 2012); photo elicitation (Mannay 2013, Glaw et al. 2017); participant photography (Harper 2002, Boch 2023, O'Hara and Higgins 2019); storytelling (Carter et al. 2014, Davey and Benjaminsen 2021); art-based and performative methods (Bagley 2008, Lyon and Carabelli 2016); walking methodologies (Kusenbach 2003, Moles 2008, Ross et al. 2009, Bates and Rhys-Taylor 2017, Springgay and Truman 2018, Adekoya and Guse 2020) and more broadly mobile methods (Urry 2010, Buscher et al. 2011, Denton et al. 2021) as well as film-making (Lydall 1992, MacDougall 2001) and fiction writing (see Sociological Review Fiction 2024).

Whether we understand these methods as something different to some of the traditional methods discussed above and part of a broader shift to innovative social science research methods (Wiles et al. 2011) or an extension of 'traditional' visual anthropology (Pink 2021), there is a little doubt they are becoming increasingly more pervasive and mainstream. That is, such methodological creativity is increasingly acknowledged as 'enabling more nuanced perspectives, different modalities of knowledge, engagement with affective, multisensory and more participatory approaches' (Gorman et al. 2022: 1738). Creative methods are often used when the issue at hand is complex and nuanced or is esoteric or speculative (such as the fears and expectations of a future technology). They are also used to engage certain types of research participants. For example, Fleetwood-Smith et al. (2022) employed creative, sensory and embodied methods to work with people with dementia, Vacchelli (2018) used collage making to discuss mental health service provision with refugee and asylum-seeking women, and

Lyon and Carabelli (2016) discuss the challenges of using arts practice to reveal young people's future aspirations. Most recently, with the advent of online research journals, social science journals are now more willing to publish data and artefacts in other forms than simply words, with some giving up pages for images and even videos, therefore enabling researchers to be more creative not just with their methods but with how they present their findings. For more on visual methodologies, we recommend you read Mannay et al. (2019) and Rose (2022).

Participatory Research

Participatory research is another loose term that covers research in which researchers *work with* participants and not *on them*. Participatory research prioritises co-construction in which the researcher works in collaboration with a community or participants with lived experience or local knowledge (Jagosh et al. 2015). To use the language of those involved in science public engagement programmes, the idea with participatory research is to move the involvement of participants upstream (Rogers-Hayden and Pidgeon 2007), to allow 'local' participants to have a say in the design of the project, what issues should be examined as well as how they are explored (Cornwall and Jewkes 1995). In essence, it is a form of methodological democratisation which enables new perspectives and voices to be heard. In some senses, then, in participatory research, the weight of balance leans more toward the emic than the etic. Here, **emic** refers to the insider point of view and what makes sense to that particular collective. Its antithesis, **etic** is more discriminatory and judgemental in which researchers apply their beliefs, theories, and approaches to a group or collective. Working in partnership with your participants enables researchers to step back from their normal ways of doing research and to reflect on their approach, and to learn from those they usually study. Of course, there are varying degrees of participation and initial discussions need to happen about who controls the research at the various stages of the research cycle. This in itself creates an inherent tension between, on the one hand, the importance of social science expertise and the lived experience and voice of the participant. Today, the term participatory action research (or PAR) has surfaced within projects focussed on civil society to 'indicate research that pursues social change as a major aim of knowledge production and that occurs in co-production with participants from the field under study' (Ponzoni 2016: 557). The ethos behind participatory methods has also been the catalyst for approaches such as Sista Circles, focus group type methods which aim to remove power dynamics and prioritise shared experience between the researcher and the researched (Johnson 2015).

Sensory Methods

Sensory methods is a catch-all phrase that describes a group of methods that disrupt and dislodge the traditional primacy of the visual or the enunciative in social science research to draw in modalities such as: sound (Mody 2005, Rice 2013, Gallagher 2014);

smell (Riach and Warren 2015, Dowling et al. 2018, Clark 2022); taste (Stoller 1989 and 1997, Rhys-Taylor 2018); touch (Classen 2012, O'Connor 2017); as well as Indigenous ways of sensing (Schneider and Kayseas 2018, Dell 2021) as sources of information to access the social world. It is the view that simply focussing on the visual misses something about how we, as social beings, navigate the world and stresses that an understanding of our multisensorial experience is essential to understanding aspects of society and culture (Pink 2009 and 2021, Vannini et al. 2011, Vannini 2023). Such a view has seen (i) new methods such as *smellwalks* (Henshaw 2014, McLean 2020, Allen 2023) which focus on information received by the nose as one travels; (ii) the reimagination and repurposing of the voice memo as something more than an artefact needing to be transcribed but data in its own right (Gallagher 2020); and (iii) a primary concern with multimodality which understands communication, interaction, and representation to be more than simply language and action (Dicks et al. 2006). For an excellent book that covers several creative and sensory methods, please see Holmes and Hall (2020).

Managing the Field

We now move on to briefly discuss the importance of effectively managing the field site to support the production of high-quality research artefacts. An interview transcript tends to be only as good as the relationship harnessed between the interviewer (researcher) and interviewee (participant) with the optimum result turning the interview into a type of free-flowing conversation. A fieldnote tends to be only as good as the access negotiated and the relationship you have to the objects, phenomena, and people under study. The quality of a focus group transcript tends to reflect how well you have managed the focus group discussion. It is part of the researcher's responsibility, then, to create the conditions, as best as they can, that will allow them to elicit as good data as possible. Such management of the research setting might include building rapport with participants (Pitts and Miller-Day 2007), negotiating appropriate access, and finding good places to take fieldnotes. None of this is particularly easy and, in some settings, there are conditions and variables you cannot legislate for.

For example, conducting an interview over Zoom or Microsoft Teams can be a quite dissimilar experience to conducting an interview in person. It is unlikely you will have the opportunity for small talk, to break the ice when interviewing over an electronic platform. Whereas in in-person interviews there is often an opportunity to introduce yourself less formally or maybe buy your participant a cup of tea or coffee – what might be called a *research bargain* (Rantatalo et al. 2018) – thank you for participating. It is also possible when interviewing online that the connection buffers or the technology fails. In other settings, the space and layout of the place might determine how and where you conduct your research, especially when conducting observational, interview, or focus group research. That is, no two research sites are the same and you will need to be prepared to adapt to situations quickly.

Researcher Reflection

One of Jamie's research projects concerned undertaking observational work in a stem cell laboratory. After negotiating access, he turned up one day to be confronted with a long table where laboratory members would eat lunch and have coffee, and a panoply of bookcases and frosted office doors which you can see out of but not into. Finding himself the centre of attention, not too dissimilar to a Foucauldian panopticon, Jamie felt deeply uncomfortable taking notes as it felt like he was observing members of the lab in an equivalent way to how these scientists might observe an experimental rodent. He therefore made the decision to only make notes in the toilet, mostly prompts written in shorthand that he wrote up in much more detail in the evenings. For the rest of the time, he took headnotes, which again he wrote up when home. There is no one way to manage a research field, it often depends on the setting itself. The secret is to be willing to be flexible, and to adapt to the situation you find yourself in. While no doubt members of the lab were questioning the frequency in which Jamie used the bathroom, it felt like the best way to control a situation he felt had no control over.

How Much Data?

One of the other frequently asked questions we receive is how many interviews is enough or how many observations should I undertake? There is simply no fixed answer here. Standard responses might include you know when you are finished when you have reached a point of 'data saturation' and are no longer learning anything new about the setting, or that you have enough to address your research questions confidently. These are sensible pieces of advice. But for those of you conducting a research project as part of your degree course, for example undertaking an undergraduate dissertation module, there also needs to be an awareness that: (i) you are still learning so may not know when you have enough to address your research questions, and (ii) the project is time-sensitive so you are unlikely to research data saturation point.

Some convenors and/or supervisors, therefore, might suggest an appropriate range of interviews to be conducted or a fixed number of participants to include, for example six to ten for an undergraduate project and ten to twenty for a postgraduate project. Again, we have no quibble with this, but we want to re-emphasise that every project is different, every setting is different, and every community is studied differently. There will be nowhere near the same amount of Wicca witches as soccer fans, for example. Equally, not all interviews or observational fieldwork, or diary entries are the same. We have already discussed the differences between unstructured, semi-structured, and structured interviews. But, of course, a 10-minute vox pop type interview will collect quite different data to a 75-minute life history interview. Equally, a full day's observation is quite different to short 1-hour observational events and a governmental policy document is likely to be much meatier than a poster. What is non-negotiable, though, when you are doing qualitative research is that you make sure that the data you collect is qualitative. You want to focus on dialogue, on conversation, on action, on practice, on text, on imagery, on behaviour, and on other senses. You want to look for meaning in your data – to consider the whys and hows, much more than whats. This involves an element of skill; it also requires detailed data or what is commonly called *thick description*, providing a thorough and detailed account of a setting and accurately describing the phenomena at hand (see Lincoln and Guba 1985, Younas et al. 2023).

Introduction to Mixed Methods

To be true to the term, mixed methods is a term that denotes the use of more than one method. Traditionally, this might have included two quantitative methods such as questionnaires and secondary data analysis or two qualitative methods such as diaries and interviews. More recently, this type of fusing of methods from within either the qualitative or quantitative category is typically called **multi-method** research. The term **mixed methods**, on the other hand, has secured coherence to have a more specific meaning in which a researcher combines a qualitative method with a quantitative method such as interviews with questionnaires (Tashakkori and Teddlie 1998). That is, mixed methods are the mixing of both qualitative and quantitative approaches.

Now, as a student, it might be appealing to combine qualitative and quantitative methods as a form of safety blanket, believing you are incorporating approaches from both worlds. However, as with the single methods approach, your research questions and what it is you want to address should determine your methodological approach. For us, mixed methods should only be used if what it is you are trying to research justifies such an approach and not as a 'vulgar' form of **triangulation** through methodological pluralism in which you combine methods just for the sake of it (Coffey and Atkinson 1996, Atkinson 2005). If you do decide to employ a mixed methods approach, it is important to consider how the two approaches work together to help you answer your research questions. For instance, you might choose to initiate qualitative interviews with a limited number of participants, subsequently leveraging insights from these interviews to craft a questionnaire tailored for a broader participant pool. Alternatively, your approach could involve commencing with an analysis of an existing quantitative dataset, followed by focus group sessions. Irrespective of your chosen strategy, a well-defined rationale for the sequence of data collection methods is essential. Brannen (2005) discusses the different rationales frequently advanced for using a mixed methods approach and gives examples of how more than one method can be used in a research project.

The Hybrid Methods

As above, a mixed methods approach is most often described as – and achieved when – the researcher combines methods which are qualitative and quantitative. But increasingly, though not pervasively, we are seeing the emergence of methodological approaches that are inherently *mixed* themselves combining qualitative and quantitative components in a single procedure.

This is true of, for example, **Q methodology**, developed by the psychologist–physician William Stephenson in the first half of the 20th century. The approach attempts to bridge the methodological divide described in Chapter 1 (*What Is Social Science Research and Why Is It Important?*). Researchers produce a set of statements which cover the depth and breadth of a topic. These statements might have been produced from responses in interviews, from the literature, or from the news. These are then called the Q set. Participants are asked to sort these statements into a grid depending on how much they agree or disagree with each statement. This sorting is done to create a 'forced distribution', meaning participants have pre-defined categories such as strongly agree, agree, neutral, disagree, and strongly disagree, as well as a finite number of slots on the grid. This then creates a ranked order of statements. The set is then subjected to a by-person factor analysis to help understand how these rankings reflect a particular perspective on a topic (Watts and Stenner 2012). Q methodology has found traction in social psychology projects.

But perhaps one of the most significant changes in social science over the past decade or so has been access to what is often termed *Big Data*. While social science has a long quantitative history with 'big' datasets dating back to Émile Durkheim (1897 [1952]) and before, Metzler (2016) quotes Clive Humby, the man responsible for Tesco's Clubcard scheme, that data in the 21st century is like the new oil. In this statement, Metzler is arguing that data are not simply *a* resource that can be extracted, but '*the*' resource of the 21st century, and those who control data will have tremendous economic, social, and political power (Bartlett et al. 2018). Specifically, what Metzler is referring to here is the rise of what is now called Big Data, with computationally intensive social science undeniably a 21st century phenomenon. These are data and datasets which are routinely collected as we go about our everyday lives, often without our noticing. Examples of Big Data include: transactional data, purchases from Amazon, Walmart, or Humby's Tesco for example; data from wearable devices such as Fitbits or Apple watches (Lupton 2016 and 2017); social media data such as the use of Instagram, Facebook or WeChat; and search engine trend data from using applications such as Google. These data can be analysed by social researchers, academic and otherwise, to explore patterns and trends. For instance, Brewer et al. (2023) analysed loyalty card data to track the purchases of pain and indigestion medication among UK women. These authors found that the purchasing patterns of their sample could be used to help with the early detection of ovarian cancer. This is a novel example of how data which is collected by retailers on a regular basis can be used to help improve society. However, as alluded to in Chapter 1 (*What Is Social Science Research and Why Is It Important?*), there are (justifiable) concerns by social scientists as to how these algorithms are targeting individuals. One only needs to consider the Cambridge Analytica exposé in the UK to understand how these types of data are being used for political ends too. Depending on your disposition, Big Data is both a threat to and the making of social science. *Big Data pessimists* are concerned that it might mean the end for nuance, intricacy, and meaning, and even the need for academic social scientists (Savage and Burrows 2007). The argument here is that if this data exists out there, it is governments, big technology, and pharmaceutical companies that have access to it and will use it for their own gain. For *Big Data optimists* though it is an opportunity to collect social data on a scale never before possible and we should embrace this. Indeed, some academic social scientists have developed tools to harvest and analyse Big Data, for example, Williams et al. (2023) are conducting work to identify cyber hate crimes on Twitter.

Now, this might all seem very quantitative in nature. But one recent book on Big Data considers the opportunities, challenges, and constraints of working with Big Qualitative Data. Weller et al. (2023) maintain that Big Data can challenge the simple quantitative–qualitative dichotomy by discussing how Big Data can be qualitative as well as quantitative. Proposing a breadth-and-depth analysis of large datasets, this hybrid approach might be viewed as a new form of mixed methods. As the authors maintain themselves,

> the breadth-and-depth approach allows researchers to manage and analyse a large volume of qualitative secondary data yet retain the distinctive order of knowledge about social processes, context and detail that is the hallmark of rigorous qualitative research. (Edwards et al. 2021: 1276)

PART THREE: WRITING YOUR METHODS CHAPTER

Structuring Your Methods Chapter

Now that we have introduced you to some of the core methods in qualitative and quantitative research, it is important to consider how you might go about structuring the Methods chapter of a dissertation or research report. While sitting as the third substantive chapter of your dissertation, the Methods chapter tends to be the second chapter that you begin drafting after the Literature Review. In line with this thinking, we have positioned this section here and before we consider data analysis. Indeed, work on writing this chapter can begin even before you have gone out into the field, so long as you have agreed a solid research design with your supervisor and recognise that you will need to revisit the chapter after you have collected data. Importantly, you will need to engage with primary source published literature such as some of the examples we included in Tables 5.2 and 5.7, as well as textbooks on research methods. That is, the stronger Methods chapters tend to be located in current methodological discussions and debates building on work published in bespoke methods journals such as the *International Journal of Social Research Methodology*, *Survey Research Methods*, and *Qualitative Health Research*, but applied to your research project.

Fundamentally, the Methods chapter is the section in your research project where you tell the reader how you went about doing the study as well as explaining why you chose to do it in that particular way. Principally, the central thrust of the chapter is to provide enough detail so that the reader of the chapter could go about replicating the study by following the information you provide (almost like a recipe) and justifying the reason for the approach. First and foremost, then, make sure you tell the reader *what you did*. However, Methods chapters can and should do more than this. They can also engage with live methodological discussions and debates meaning your research project can make methodological contributions as well as substantive ones. As is the case with every chapter in your research project, there is no fixed way to write this chapter and it is imperative to discuss the layout with your supervisor. However, there is a generic set of issues which you should consider including, no matter how much space you wish to give over in your thesis to considering methods. Next we outline a general structure of how you *might* write your Methods chapter. This structure is also summarised in Table 5.8. Of course, you may decide on a more narrative style with fewer subheadings, but these are the general topics one might expect to see in this chapter.

Table 5.8 Indicative structure of a Methods chapter

Introduction
Methodological positioning
Sampling and recruitment
Negotiating access to the field
Methods and data collection
Piloting
Data analysis
Ethical sensitivities
Methodological reflections
Conclusion

Introduction

As with the other chapters in your research project, you should begin the Methods chapter with a short introductory section telling the reader what they should expect to read in this chapter. This may also briefly recap the main gaps in the existing literature so to create synergy between this chapter and the previous one (Literature Review), and you may even (re)specify your research question(s) if you have included them in the Literature Review chapter or introduce them for the first time here. It should finish by including an overview of what you are going to discuss in the rest of the chapter.

Methodological Positioning

Methodology, as something distinct to methods, refers to your overarching strategy and rationale for research. This is then much broader than the specific methods deployed in the research to also concern the specific procedures used to identify, choose, select, and analyse data and information about a topic. Why did you choose the particular sample? Why have you analysed the data in that way? Here, you might consider discussing your epistemological and ontological standpoint that justifies your methodological positioning and your approach to studying the setting. **Ontology** concerns the study of the fundamental nature and essence of our being. Relating this to social research, ontological beliefs are often discussed in terms of a dichotomy between, on the one hand, an objective reality which exists independent of the observer and, on the other, reality as it appears subjectively or, more commonly, as negotiated within social groups (Bryman 2001). Often coupled with ontology is **epistemology** which refers to a branch of methodological philosophy that pertains to how we go about determining what we know – or the process of knowledge acquisition. In simple terms it is the relationship between how we know things and our route to that knowledge. Goode (2012) gives the example of a theologian attempting to prove, or an atheist attempting to disprove, the existence of God as an example of an ontological enterprise. In contrast, the epistemologist would be interested not in whether God exists, but rather the ways in which certain people believe that God is or is not real and what sorts of arguments, traces, and evidence would satisfy them of its existence. Different epistemological perspectives can lead to varying ideas about the nature of knowledge and how it is best acquired, evaluated, and used. In social science, as touched on already, you might have come across the broad distinction between **interpretivism**, which focusses on how social actors – your participants – interpret meanings and events which often directs you to ethnographic and interviewing approaches, and **positivism** that begins from the premise that there is an objective reality out there that can be accessed, but that the researcher needs to remain distant from the objects or subjects under study, often leading the researcher to choosing an experimental approach. Both approaches demand empirical work. But positivism maintains that empirical methods, often associated with the natural sciences, can be extended to the study of human mental and social life. However, this approach has been criticised for oversimplifying complex social realities and neglecting the role of subjectivity in understanding the social world. Other researchers adopt a **realist approach**. This stance does not advocate a particular method, but it does support the use of quantitative approaches, including questionnaires to help understand the social world. But unlike positivists, realists believe that unobservable aspects of society such as beliefs, attitudes, and opinions can be measured in an objective and systematic manner (Williams 2000). There are other approaches that circumnavigate *a priori* debates around epistemology such as **pragmatism** that prioritises practical applications over abstract principles or theoretical considerations or tensions. Pragmatism suggests that one's epistemology is, even if only implicitly, embedded in one's set of research questions and that the choice of methods are the practical decisions to answer these questions (Morgan 2014).

Your methodological positioning will likely affect your thoughts on what your data reveals. A further discussion on this can be seen in the section *Creating the research artefact* in Chapter 6 (*Social Science Data Analysis*) where we discuss the methodological positioning of Conversation Analysts.

Sampling and Recruitment

It is possible that you might include a section called *research* design, but in this book we cover the design of the research across various other subheadings. As part of the research design, you need to be clear on who (or what) it is you are going to study. There are very few cases where, as social scientists, we can study all the relevant members of a group or community (what is known as the **population**). For example, realistically, you would not study all the supporters at the Cricket World Cup in India, the Olympics in Paris or at the Australian Open tennis championships in Melbourne, nor all the students in a local authority. Similarly, we are unlikely to be able to access or analyse the full corpus of documents concerning the topic we are researching. For example, it would be almost impossible to collect and store all the newspaper articles that have discussed the climate emergency globally, or even nationally, especially for an undergraduate dissertation. To overcome these issues, we tend to research or choose a sample of the wider population; a smaller, sometimes representative, subset of the broader community.

In everyday life, you may be given a free sample of a new product or item. For instance, sometimes in the supermarket you may be given a small sample of a new food item to try. This free sample is often smaller in size, but allows you, as a potential customer, to gain an insight into whether you would like to buy the product in full in the future. It is assumed that the small sample of the new product which you are enticed to try reflects the full product being promoted. The idea here is that from that taster we make a generalisation about the taste, quality, appearance, etc. of the new product and then decide whether we would like to purchase it. Similarly, in research, social science researchers want their samples to give them an insight into the wider population they wish to study. To do this, they aim to make sure that their smaller sample is representative of the entire population. In other words, they must ensure that the characteristics of the participants in the sample reflect the characteristics of the wider population. If the participants in the sample do not share the characteristics of the wider population, the researcher is unable to make generalisations. For example, if you decided to do a research project including all school aged children in India, it would be both expensive and time intensive to survey everyone (the population). India is home to 250 million students (Rathore 2023). Instead, you might decide to distribute your questionnaire to a sample of school-aged children in both urban and rural areas of the country and then generalise your findings to all school-aged children in India.

A sampling frame is a list of the entire population. Using the school-aged children in India example, the sampling frame would be a list of all school-aged children in India. The sampling frame should be comprehensive and include everyone in the population, whilst excluding those who do not fit in the population. So, you would need to consider both urban and rural schools as well as private and state funded schools. Researchers use sampling frames to draw samples of participants to include in their research. In situations where sampling frames do not exist, as can often be the case with online research, researchers are unable to confidently generalise their findings of their study to the wider population, though of course that would not be the (primary) aim for (many) qualitative research projects. That said, there are degrees of generalisability, and it would be remiss of researchers to claim a hard divide between projects that are generalisable and others that are not (see Payne and Williams 2005 for a discussion on generalisation in qualitative research).

Taking random samples from a sampling frame means that all participants have a known chance of being selected to be included in a study. Whereas, taking non-random samples means that participants have unequal and unknown chances of being selected to be included in a study. In situations where a sampling frame does not exist, researchers must employ non-random sampling techniques. There are different approaches to taking random and non-random samples which are outlined in Table 5.9. These approaches can be used in isolation or may be used in conjunction. Next, each of these approaches is discussed further.

Table 5.9 Different approaches to sampling

Random sampling	Non-random sampling
Simple random sampling	Convenience sampling
Systematic sampling	Purposive sampling
Stratified sampling	Snowball sampling
Clustered sampling	Quota sampling

Random Sampling Techniques

Where possible, quantitative researchers aim to use random sampling techniques. These include simple random sampling, systematic sampling, stratified sampling, and clustered sampling. This is because these approaches allow the researcher to make generalisations more confidently from the sample studied to the broader population. However, a sampling frame must exist for researchers to be able to deploy any of these approaches. In what follows, the different random sampling techniques are described using an example of a researcher aiming to recruit a sample of 100 students from a school home to 1,000 pupils, organised into five year groups.

- *Simple random sampling* means that everyone in the sampling frame has a known and equal probability of being selected to participate in the research. Typically, numbers are assigned to participants listed in the sampling frame and then a random number generator is used to identify the sample. For example, if you wanted to take a simple random sample of 100 students studying in one school with 1,000 pupils, you would assign all the students in that school with a numerical value. Then you would use a random number generator to return 100 unique numbers. These unique numbers would correspond to 100 of the numerical values assigned to students in the sampling frame – these would be the students in your sample.

- *Systematic sampling* is like simple random sampling. However, instead of using a random number generator to identify the sample, researchers use a 'rule' to select who to include in their sample. For instance, if you wanted a systematic sample of 100 students studying in one school with 1,000 pupils, you could order the names of the pupils alphabetically by their surname and select every tenth pupil for your sample.
- *Stratified sampling* is done in combination with one of the previous types of sampling described and involves taking random samples from different groups which exist in the population. As an example, if you wanted to take a stratified sample of 100 students studying in one school with 1,000 pupils, you might take 20 students from each of the five year groups in the school. Once you have identified the different groups, you should use simple random or systematic sampling techniques to draw the final sample.
- *Clustered sampling* involves the researcher grouping the population into clusters which share similar characteristics. The researcher then takes a random sample from each cluster. So, if you wanted to take a cluster sample of 100 students studying in one school with 1,000 pupils, you would sort each of the classes or forms into year groups and then use simple random or systematic sampling techniques to choose which classes or forms participate in the research.

Non-Random Sampling Techniques

Whilst non-random sampling approaches are more commonly associated with qualitative research, they can be a time and cost-effective way to recruit participants in quantitative projects too. Equally, in some instances, it is simply not feasible for a sampling frame to be created. For example, if a researcher is exploring experiences of homelessness, they will most likely not be able to access an accurate, up-to-date list of all the homeless in a specific area. Therefore, both qualitative and quantitative researchers would need to use non-random approaches to sampling. These can include convenience sampling, purposive sampling, snowball sampling, and quota sampling. Next, the different non-random sampling techniques are described, again using an example of a researcher aiming to recruit a sample of 100 students from a school with 1,000 pupils, organised into five year groups.

- *Convenience sampling* involves recruiting participants who are easier or more convenient to access. For example, if you wanted to take a convenience sample of 100 students studying in one school with 1,000 pupils, you might decide to include just those students who happen to be on a lunchbreak or have a free period when you arrive at the school.
- *Purposive sampling* – also known as judgemental sampling – is another non-random sampling technique. It involves the researcher 'purposively' selecting respondents to participate in the research as the researcher believes that they have a certain characteristic or quality, which will enable the researcher to

successfully answer the research question. For instance, if you wanted to take a purposive sample of 100 students studying in one school with 1,000 pupils, the researcher may purposively seek to recruit participants of different ages to gather potentially different opinions.
- *Quota sampling*, like stratified sampling, requires the researcher to divide the population into subgroups. However, rather than taking a random sample of each subgroup, the researcher continues to recruit participants until they reach the desired number for each group under exploration. For instance, if you wanted to take a quota sample of 100 students studying in one school with 1,000 pupils, you might divide the population into five subgroups based on year group and then collect 20 responses from students in each year group. Data collection with a certain year group would continue until you reached 20 responses for that particular year group.
- *Snowball sampling* involves research participants recommending other potential respondents to take part in the research in such a way that if you wanted to recruit a snowball sample of 100 students studying in one school with 1,000 pupils, you might ask someone you know at that school who has already participated in your research to recommend other students who may be interested in participating. Equally if you interview or survey that student, you then ask them to suggest another potential participant, in doing so you create a snowball effect.

Box 5.3

National Census Surveys

If all members of a population are included in the research, a census procedure is adopted. In many countries, including the UK and Australia, national census surveys are periodically distributed to all adults living in those nations. Residents in these countries have a legal responsibility to complete the census survey and those who do not complete it can face fines and/or prosecution. However, it can be almost impossible for researchers to reach entire populations. National censuses come with a significant cost and take time to design and distribute. For instance, in the UK, the modernisation of the 2021 census cost approximately £900 million over an 11-year period. As a result of these potential huge costs, social science researchers often collect data on samples (small [hopefully representative] subsets of the population) as opposed to the entire population. This makes the project doable.

Walking through your decisions and justifications of who or what were included in your sample should be set out in the Methods chapter. This allows the reader to judge the appropriateness of who or what you are studying. **Sampling** is then a pivotal part of research design, and your inclusion criteria will likely be determined by your access to the field and the resources that you have available to you. Once you have chosen your sample, for example 15 cricket cup fans or articles in the UK broadsheet newspapers which discussed the climate emergency between 1 May 2023 and 7 May 2023, you will then need to recruit the relevant participants or collate the pertinent documents.

Recruitment and **collection** not only needs to be ethically sensitive (see Chapter 4: *Being an Ethical Researcher*), for example not publicly enrolling participants who do not want to be named, e.g. writing a Facebook post asking them directly to be involved in the project, or not putting yourself or your participants at risk by revealing personal information such as your address, but also needs to be effective. You need to give yourself the best chance of reaching your potential participants and getting them to engage with your request. Here, a strong, punchy and professional letter, email, or message to go alongside an information sheet is a good strategy. Chapter 4 (*Being an Ethical Researcher*) provides an example participant information sheet. Do not make these documents too long and make sure they are as relevant as possible to the person it is addressed to. Both aspects of sampling and recruitment should have already been detailed in your ethics application so you can use these sections as a springboard to describe what you did in this section of your Methods chapter. Importantly, describe what you did to recruit your participants and explain why you did it that way. You should also mention here whether you incentivised participation in any way. This section should conclude with a summary of how many participants were included in your research project and, if appropriate, some demographic information relating to the participants.

Negotiating Access to the Field

The data you collect tends to be only as good as the data that you can access. Negotiating access to your research site then is another essential stage in your research journey. It is not as simple as just turning up to a site to observe a group of people or asking them to be interviewed or be surveyed. Groundwork needs to be done to introduce yourself, to let potential participants know what your work is about, and to get across the value of it. Such work will hopefully help convince them to be involved. Gaining access to a field might be mediated by what is often termed a **gatekeeper** – someone who can unlock entry to a setting or group of people. As before, examples of gatekeepers might be community spokespeople or leaders if you are trying to work with local communities, headteachers if you are trying to access a school, moderators of online groups if you are trying to recruit participants from a social media community or university department managers if you are trying to administer questionnaires to students. In your Methods chapter, you should differentiate between formal and informal gatekeepers. Formal gatekeepers are the people from whom you must obtain permission or consent before proceeding with your data collection. Informal gatekeepers are the people you may call upon to initially connect with to access the formal gatekeeper. For example, if your research involves staff in finance companies it would be unlikely that you could simply pick up the phone and speak to CEOs directly about your study and gain access to their staff. Instead, you may need to speak to a personal assistant or reception staff to initiate contact. In this example, the CEO would be the formal gatekeeper and the personal assistant the informal gatekeeper.

Note the term *negotiating* in this heading. This is not always a straightforward task, and some research fields are more difficult to access than others. Settings which are highly regulated (military settings), fields that involve several levels of permission to access (political actors), groups who are wary of being studied (e.g., vulnerable groups including the homeless) and participants who have little free time and space to spend being studied (such as the CEO of the finance company) will invariably require more convincing. Other examples include biomedical and political organisations, individuals with a public profile, and young people. Again, explaining the process and how you needed to adapt to situations to recruit people is an important part of any Methods chapter. In some cases, you might need a 'research bargain' (Hughes 1971, Becker 1974) to get people involved in research. It is commonplace in psychology, for example, to pay people to participate. On one hand, this seems an appropriate gesture, paying people for their time. On the other hand, as detailed previously, some researchers are uncomfortable paying people to participate insofar as it is viewed as a form of consent coercion (MacKay and Walker 2021). This is a live debate which you might want to reflect upon in your Methods chapter.

Methods and Data Collection

As already detailed, the principal purpose of the Methods chapter is to tell the reader what you did. Clearly, as part of this, you need to describe what methods you used and how you went about data collection. For example, if you undertook interviews, here is the place where you would describe: (i) the type of interview you conducted, e.g. semi-structured or life story interviews; (ii) how and where they were conducted, e.g. in person in public spaces, online over Zoom, via the telephone; (iii) how many were undertaken, e.g. six with students and four with university staff; and (iv) the justification for using the method, and how long each interview lasted e.g. between 40 and 75 minutes. If you administered an online questionnaire using Qualtrics' survey software, for example, you should explain who and how many completed the questionnaire. You will probably state how many questions were included in the questionnaire and summarise the topics covered. You might refer specifically to the questionnaire and include a copy in the appendix. Please note that if you include material in the appendices then they need to be directly referred to in the main body of the dissertation and labelled accordingly. Alternatively, if your project involved smellwalks, you might situate this method in relation to broader arguments of using sensory, multimodal, and walking methods. Again, you will detail how many walks were undertaken and with whom, the length of them as well as a description of the terrain (and possibly weather). Here, you might need to decide whether you reveal the place of the walk or not. It is essential that you engage with literature on your method or methods of choice in this section of the chapter.

Piloting

Best practice demands that you pilot your research. This involves a small-scale preliminary study in which you test the robustness of your research instruments, such as your interview schedule or questionnaire to check for any issues before deploying it more broadly when undertaking your fieldwork. For those undertaking observations, this might involve testing where best to situate yourself in a location; for those asking participants to keep diaries it might involve asking them to send you the diary back after two days to make sure all is in order. From this pilot, a decision must be made as to whether to tinker with your approach and instruments and whether some changes are required before you conduct your research proper or whether you are good to go. In your Methods chapter, it is useful to dedicate a short section under the heading Methods and Data Collection detailing how you piloted your project and whether you decided to make any alterations and, if so, why. If changes were made, these should also be discussed. If you are designing and distributing a questionnaire as part of your research project, you may also decide to conduct *cognitive interviews* (see the questionnaire section of this chapter) to explore the suitability of the questions posed. Again, the findings from these cognitive interviews and any subsequent changes made to the question wording need to be explained in your Methods chapter.

Data Analysis

The data analysis section is a vital section in your Methods chapter but is sometimes not given the attention it deserves by students. As a reminder, the Methods section or chapter needs to let the reader know what it is you did and why the approach is the most appropriate. Analysis is a principal component to that. As a qualifier, it is important to recognise that analysis does not simply occur at a discrete moment in time. Analysis begins with the research design and often does not conclude until the findings are presented. That said, there is a part of the research cycle where analysis is more intense and is the dominant component of the research. In this section of the chapter, it is expected that you describe the analytic approach taken and that you can demonstrate that you understand what it is and why you have used it. For quantitative research this might include detailing the statistical tests used, e.g. ANOVAs or Chi-Square as well as the computer programme used, e.g. SPSS. Similarly for qualitative research, this might include the analytic approach used, e.g. discourse analysis, narrative analysis, or reflexive thematic analysis, and if any qualitative data storage packages were used such as NVivo. Sometimes students struggle to write this section of their Methods chapter until they have completed their analysis. This is *perfectly normal* and if you are grappling with this issue, leave this section blank in your first draft and return to it later. Either way, as with all the chapters in the dissertation, it is likely that you will revisit and refine this chapter, perhaps giving particular attention to the analysis section once you have a full draft written (see Chapter 6: *Social Science Data Analysis* for more discussion).

Tip: if your word count permits, show an example of how you analysed data in the Methods chapter.

Ethical Sensitivities

The stronger Methods chapters display a deeper engagement with the ethical sensitivity of the project than simply including bland statements pertaining to the process of receiving a favourable decision from your School Research Ethics Committee or Institutional Review Board. The ethical social scientist recognises that ethics is a process and is alive to any ethical concerns throughout the lifecycle of the project (see Chapter 4: *Being an Ethical Researcher*). So long as it was not assessed formally, the writing you crafted as part of your ethics application can be developed upon and slotted into this section with a little editing to fit with your narrative. This, of course, might also be a section where you develop further on paying for participants if this formed part of your project.

Methodological Reflections

Reading a Methods chapter can make it sound like social science research is straightforward, neat, and tidy. In reality, social science research is messy, and you should not shy away from revealing this in your Methods chapter. For **qualitative researchers**, the researcher is part of the field that they are studying, and they influence the setting, as well as the setting influencing them. This is sometimes discussed in terms of the Hawthorne effect. This is also increasingly recognised in **quantitative research** too (Ryan and Golden 2006). The stronger Methods chapters reflect on the role of the researcher by inserting yourself at the heart of the writing process. Aspects that you could include here include:

- *Fighting familiarity*. For qualitative researchers, in particular, there is a balance to be struck between being too familiar or too strange to a setting (Delamont et al. 2010, Delamont and Atkinson 2021). There is a history of work that demands of us to develop unique adequacy (Garfinkel 2002) or interactional expertise (Collins and Evans 2002) of the field which we are studying, to have knowledge of the subject and setting which we are studying. And yet, equally we do not want to be too close (see Latour and Woolgar 1986). We still want the distance to be able to see things (as social scientists). These debates are also often discussed in the role of **insiders** – those with inside knowledge of the community and **outsiders** – those that sit outside the community (Rabe 2003, Coloma 2008) or in terms of **emic** and **etic** research.
- *Building rapport*. Rapport building is central to good research. Here, you might want to describe your relationship with your participants (King and Horrocks 2010). For example, interviewing elites and those with specialist expertise of the topic that you are studying (Stephens 2007, Mikecz 2012) is a very different experience to holding focus groups with young people (Bagnoli and Clark 2010). Decisions might need to be made on relatively mundane issues such as how you present yourself, the way in which you talk and possibly even how you dress. Such decisions are all part of making a connection with those that you are researching. You might also want to acknowledge the emotional labour (Hochschild 1983) and performance that goes into rapport building. Not everyone will enter the field confidently, which should not preclude you from having insightful interactions (see Scott et al. 2012). Whether you are a

gregarious type or relatively timorous, try not to 'shy away' from writing about the researcher–participant relationship in the Methods section as it may be important for others to learn from.
- *Knowing your participants.* Regarding your relationship to your participants, you might be studying a site you know well and people you know well. To what extent does that change the dynamics of the research? Might your participants feel obliged to participate? Might they not want to reveal certain attitudes or opinions to someone they know? What about participants who know other participants in a focus group, for example? Again, you can reflect on these challenges in this section of your Methods chapter by discussing the researcher–participant dynamic.
- *Inserting yourself in the chapter.* To what extent do you want to insert yourself in this chapter? To what extent does your own positionality impact the data collected? For reflexive researchers, it is important to reflect on your role in the project. Indeed, in qualitative research, you are the instrument of data collection and data analysis and as such there is a strong rationale to write (the Methods chapter, at least) in the first person. Aspects of how you represent yourself also extend to how you **represent your participants.** Again, this section demands that you do not simply describe your choice, but also explain it.

The stronger reflective chapters engage with conceptual debates concerning practical challenges. On the surface, these challenges might appear to be relatively mundane and uninteresting, similar to what clothes you wore, but they are necessary for the smooth running of research, and as such should be of interest to readers.

Researcher Reflection

Let us take Jamie's Bigfoot project as an example. Interviews were conducted online or over the phone to overcome the geographical challenges of someone in the UK interviewing mostly North Americans. However, this meant he was often between five to eight hours ahead and therefore, often scheduling interviews at night and/or over the weekend. A further challenge to overcome was the fact that as a non-believer in Bigfoot as an extant anomalous ape (his ontological position), for the most part, he was interviewing Bigfoot believers. He never shied away from this situation and would often say that it would not be for him to say whether Bigfoot exists as a biological creature or not as he is neither a primatologist nor a biological anthropologist. Save for a few individuals, scientific consensus maintains there is no convincing evidence that it exists, and he has no evidence to dispute this. As a sociologist of science, he understands that science is a consensus-driven culture and so this was his position. But he also recognises that his view should have no more or no less merit than any other citizen. What does exist, though, is Bigfooting or Bigfoot research and that is what he is interested in as a sociologist and that is a topic he feels he has something to contribute to. Finding this common ground proved fruitful insofar as participants

(Continued)

understood further the aims of the project and its boundaries and felt comfortable discussing the subject. Jamie was not there to judge but to understand the world of Bigfooting. In a Methods chapter, then, he could write about this experience in relation to ideas of credulity and incredulity, building rapport and even actors' (participants') and analysts' (researchers') different ontological positions, especially given that some believed that Bigfoot was an uncatalogued ape, and some believed it was of extra-terrestrial origin and/or had supernatural powers. Here, he could even discuss the status of the interview as an instrument that gets at authentic 'truth'.

Conclusion

The conclusion section of the Methods chapter should provide a brief and compact summary of the main take home points discussed in the chapter before transitioning smoothly to the next chapter on *Findings*.

As you will have read, these sections of the Methods chapter have overlaps. Aspects of building rapport speaks to fighting familiarity. Discussing the virtues of paying participants for their time, is as much an ethical consideration as a financial one. As such, you might want to structure your Methods chapter differently to how we have set it up here, but hopefully the general topics discussed give you a good flavour of what to include and how to write your Methods chapter. In what section of the Methods chapter you include this detail is a discussion to have with your supervisor. Importantly, though, a Methods chapter should not shy away from highlighting the limitations and challenges of your chosen approach to collecting and analysing the data as well as describing its strengths. A marker/reader will be mindful of the limitations both in terms of time and money which concern your project and, therefore, they will not be expecting your research project to be completely polished and without any flaws. Indeed, all research projects, including those undertaken by your lecturers, will have limitations and shortcomings. Share details of the compromises which you will likely have had to make when designing the research project. The reader/marker will be impressed that you are not only able to describe what you have done but that you are also able to evaluate and critique your chosen approach. Again, this is all part of reflecting on your methodological approach. For those wanting a meaty Methods chapter, there are other aspects that you might focus on, such as leaving the field (Smith and Delamont 2023). For those that want a thinner chapter then decisions need to be made on what to include and what to leave out to make space for your Findings chapter.

SUMMARY

Divided into three parts, this chapter has concerned itself with the doing of a social science research project. We introduced you to a bank of methods – both quantitative and qualitative – which are routinely used by social science researchers and explored why and in what situations they are deployed. We also discussed the merits and challenges of doing mixed methods or hybrid research. Part Three of the chapter discussed the purpose of the Methods chapter in a dissertation and provided an indicative way to structure one. Notable sections on sampling, negotiating access to the field and methodological positioning are included, as well as a recognition that students are increasingly doing research online. The chapter concluded by discussing how you can locate your Methods chapter in the methodological debates and discussions concerning the messiness of social science research. In the next chapter, we will discuss ways in which to analyse the data you have collected.

Student Question

Surely a mixed methods approach draws from the best of both worlds. Shouldn't I combine a quantitative method with a qualitative one?

(Raj, Social Psychology Student)

Charlotte and Jamie say:

Thanks for the question, Raj. That is one way of looking at the benefits of combining methods, particularly qualitative and quantitative methods. Another, of course, is to recognise that each method has a rich lineage. Just like the tools in your toolbox have different purposes – for example a hammer is designed to knock nails in to wood, a spanner is often used to tighten or loosen nuts and pliers are useful for removing Rawlplugs from walls – each research method also has a different purpose. As we have explained in the book, interviews are good for eliciting accounts, questionnaires are administered to collect responses and opinions, and fieldnotes are used to produce rich descriptions of sites. There are sound methodological reasons we choose methods, not simply because we feel more comfortable using one over the other. So, when determining which method(s) to use, you need to choose the most appropriate one. For instance, if you were to combine a mallet, which could be used to hammer a Rawlplug into a wall, with a set of pliers it may not initially make much sense: one is designed to put the Rawlplug in the wall and the other to take it out. There is an inherent tension there. This might be the case if you are trying to combine a qualitative method with a quantitative method too. However, sometimes a set of pliers and a mallet will work in harmony. For example, you might use the pliers to hold the Rawlplug in position so you can hammer it into the wall with the mallet in your other hand. Methods, like tools, can also work together but only if it is an appropriate task with one often being used more dominantly than the other. That is, it does not make the project any superior *per se* to combine methods; you need a valid rationale to combine methods. You should certainly not get marked down for using *just* one approach (unless it is an inappropriate one such as choosing the mallet to remove a Rawlplug – while this might just work, it is possible that you bring the whole wall down too).

WHAT'S NEXT?

Chapter Checklist

Table 5.10 Chapter 5 checklist

	Yes	No
I am aware of and can describe various approaches to quantitative data collection.		
I am aware of and can describe various approaches to qualitative data collection.		
I understand when researchers may choose to use quantitative methods of data collection.		
I can assess the particular strengths and weaknesses of different approaches to quantitative data collection and choose accordingly.		
I understand when researchers may choose to use qualitative methods of data collection.		
I can assess the particular strengths and weaknesses of different approaches to qualitative data collection and choose accordingly.		
I know when it is appropriate to mix methods.		
I am aware of the different approaches to sampling.		
I know what to include in a draft Methods chapter.		
I recognise that I should not shy away from justifying and critiquing the approach I am using in my project.		
I understand that the stronger Methods chapters engage with current methodological debates and discussion beyond textbook knowledge and can apply this appropriately to my current project.		

Read

Quantitative

Burrell, N.A and Gross, C. 2017. Quantitative research, purpose of. In M. Allen (ed.), *The Sage Encyclopaedia of Communication Research Methods*. London: Sage. Available at: https://methods.sagepub.com/reference/the-sage-encyclopedia-of-communication-research-methods/i11671.xml (accessed 15 February 2023).

Qualitative

Silverman, D. 2022. What you can (and can't) do with qualitative research. In D. Silverman (ed.), *Doing Qualitative Research*, 6th edn. London: Sage. Ch. 2.

Write

Quantitative

Write some questions which could be used in a questionnaire as part of your research project. Remember the rules for writing good questions shared in this chapter.

Qualitative

Write some interview or focus group questions or consider the challenges of doing observational fieldwork or undertaking creative methods. How might you overcome these challenges?

Complete

This activity encourages you to consider the details that should be included in your Methods chapter. Answer the following questions.

- What are your research questions?
- Who are your participants? How and why have you chosen these participants?
- How will you collect your data? Why is this method appropriate? Are there limitations to this approach?
- For secondary data analysis projects: What dataset are you using? Who were the participants and how were they initially recruited? How was the data collected? Is the dataset still relevant?
- How will you analyse your data? And why have you chosen this approach?
- Have you obtained a favourable decision from the ethics committee to proceed with your research? What ethical concerns are associated with your project? How will you store your data and when will you delete it?
- How does your approach to researching this topic differ to others working in the field? How does your approach to researching this topic mirror or build upon the work of others in the field?
- How have your own experiences and beliefs influenced the way in which you have undertaken your research? Would others have approached the research problem differently, and if so, how and why?

The answers provided to these questions should appear in your Methods chapter. You will also notice that the list of questions follows the same order as we suggest you should organise the write-up of your Methods chapter, starting with your research questions, moving on to data collection and data analysis to finishing with researcher reflections. Take your answers to these questions to your next supervisory meeting to discuss further.

6
SOCIAL SCIENCE DATA ANALYSIS

In this chapter, we provide guidance on how to begin analysing social science data. As with Chapter 5 (*Methods of Social Science Data Collection*), this chapter is divided into three parts. The first is dedicated to quantitative data analysis, the second focusses on qualitative data analysis and the third concerns tips on how to present findings and analysis of your research in your written dissertation. We also explain that your analytic approach should align well with your philosophical approach or theoretical lens. In Part One, we discuss various statistical tests drawing from the *National Survey of Sexual Attitudes and Lifestyles 2010–2012* as an example dataset. We also direct you to relevant statistical software packages such as SPSS. In Part Two, on qualitative data analysis, we stress that the researcher is the 'instrument' of analysis. We signpost you to relevant software packages such as NVivo but explain that these programmes should be seen as data storage and sorting databases which can help you 'see' your data in various ways rather than data analysis packages. This section of the chapter also links to Sage Datasets and Sage Foundations housed on the Sage Methods Research Platform. Here, you can find a suite of pedagogical resources which discuss data analysis from various methodological artefacts, such as an interview transcript, a newspaper article, a questionnaire, or an ethnographic fieldnote. In Part Three, we consider the ways in which you might present your analysis in a dissertation, discussing tables, graphs, and data extracts.

Chapter Objectives

- To recognise the various steps involved in doing quantitative data analysis.
- To be able to choose the best statistical test to analyse your dataset.
- To understand that qualitative and quantitative analysis is very different.
- To be able to choose which qualitative data analysis approach is most relevant for your project.
- To be able to navigate to the Sage Research Methods Platform.
- To understand the role of the Findings and Analysis chapter(s) in your dissertation and know how to present them.
- To grasp the ways in which you could present data in a dissertation chapter.

INTRODUCTION

As outlined in Chapter 1 (*What Is Social Science Research and Why Is It Important?*), the findings and interpretation of the data you have collected can be presented across two chapters such as (i) a Findings or Results chapter and then (ii) an Analysis chapter, or, collapsed into one larger chapter called the Discussion or Analytic Discussion chapter. The first is more typical in quantitative research and the latter much more typical in qualitative research. Whether you decide on one or two chapters, this section of the dissertation should highlight the key findings of your research and try to make sense of them. Principally, the chapter(s) should present the data you have collected, alongside your analytic interpretation of what this means to ultimately answer the research questions which you have set up in the earlier sections of your dissertation or research report.

As with Chapter 5 (*Methods of Social Science Data Collection*), we have divided this chapter into three parts. The first concerns the analysis and reporting of quantitative data and uses the *National Survey of Sexual Attitudes and Lifestyles, 2010–2012: Open Access Teaching Dataset* to demonstrate the key information which should be included in a quantitative Findings chapter. The second section is more discursive and discusses both the nature of analysis in qualitative research as well as detailing some of the more popular analytic approaches which may be used to analyse qualitative data. Here, we direct you to Sage Datasets and Sage Foundations, both housed on the Sage Research Methods Platform. The third part concerns how to present data and its analysis in a written dissertation or thesis. Here, we discuss both qualitative and quantitative data.

PART ONE: QUANTITATIVE DATA ANALYSIS

Quantitative data analysis typically involves undertaking statistical tests and creating charts, graphs, and tables to visualise data. Given quantitative social science researchers are dealing with data in 'quantity', they will use statistical software packages such as IBM SPSS, Stata, R, and Microsoft Excel to analyse their quantitative data. It is a good idea to check which software your university or organisation has access to, and to undertake any necessary training to familiarise yourself with that software prior to starting your own research project. There are also useful textbooks which you can read that walk you through how these programmes work (for example, Field 2018 and Pallant 2020 on SPSS; Kohler and Kreuter 2005 and Pevalin and Robson 2009 on Stata; Field et al. 2012 on R; and Brookfield 2021 on Microsoft Excel). It is also worth being aware that many online survey platforms such as Qualtrics Survey Platform, Microsoft Forms, and SurveyMonkey have built-in tools for analysis and visualisation, so it is plausible, depending on your project, that you will not need to use a specialist package to analyse your data at all. Again, it is a good idea at the outset of your project to see which, if any, of these online survey platforms your institution has access to.

The quantitative data analysis process can be broken down into three main stages. Stage one involves *preparing the data*, stage two is best described as *descriptive statistics* and stage three involves *inferential statistics*. These stages are sequential, meaning that you must prepare the data before being able to calculate descriptive statistics and that you should calculate descriptive statistics before calculating inferential statistics. Similarly, when you are reporting your findings in your written dissertation, you should begin by discussing steps taken to prepare the data, then report descriptive statistics, before moving on to report inferential statistics. In this section of the chapter, each of these stages is described in the order in which you will be working on them.

Knowing Your Data

But first we must understand what type of data we have collected, which involves going further than simply stating it is data from a questionnaire or a content analysis of a newspaper. This is because the type of data collected, what is often referred to as the level of data or level of measurement, determines which statistical tests you can run and the most appropriate statistics for you to report. In quantitative research, we often differentiate between **categorical** and **continuous** variables. Categorical variables are more commonplace in social science research and describe the responses which participants give to closed-ended questions with predetermined textual response options. For example, levels of agreement from 'Strongly disagree' to 'Strongly agree' in a **Likert** scale questionnaire or ethnicity categories such as Caribbean, Roma, or Chinese that you might come across on a census. Researchers assign numerical values to these textual response options to enable the data to be analysed statistically. For example, the response option 'Strongly disagree' may be assigned the numerical code '0', whilst 'Disagree' is assigned a '1', 'Neither agree nor disagree' a '2', 'Agree' a '3' and 'Strongly agree' a '4'. Alternatively, continuous variables are those which already have a numerical value such as a salary or age. These variables are measured on a continuous scale where the difference between responses is known, constant, and can be easily measured. For example, the difference between age 14 and age 16 is two years, and similarly the difference between 42 years old and 44 years old is also two years. However, the difference between Roma and Chinese cannot of course be measured numerically.

These two groups, categorical and continuous, can be further sub-divided (see Table 6.1). Continuous level variables can contain either interval or ratio data. The key difference between interval and ratio data is that ratio data has a true zero value. This means that ratio variables do not have negative values. Examples of **ratio variables** include weight and height. A person cannot have a negative weight or height. Salaries are also examples of a ratio variable; it is not possible to earn a negative salary. On the other hand, interval variables can have negative values. Examples of **interval** variables include your bank balance (unfortunately you can become overdrawn despite your salary income), temperature (which can drop below zero degrees Celsius or Fahrenheit), and polls on the popularity ratings of politicians (see YouGov 2023). We summarise the levels of data generated in quantitative research in Table 6.1.

Categorical variables can contain either ordinal or nominal data. **Ordinal** data refers to instances where the response options can be organised into some sort of hierarchy or order. For example, a 'Strongly agree' response is more favourable than an 'Agree' response, and an 'Agree' response is more favourable than a 'Neither agree nor disagree' response and so on. There is a logical, inherent order to these response options. Likewise, educational attainment is an example of an ordinal variable. Here, participants may be asked to select their highest level of qualification from the following options: 'No qualifications', 'School level qualifications', 'Undergraduate degree' or 'Postgraduate degree'. In this example, an undergraduate degree is a higher level of qualification than school qualifications, but it is not as high as a postgraduate degree. Although there is an inherent order to the response options, the difference between the response options cannot be measured and is not necessarily constant. For instance, is the difference between 'No qualifications' and 'School level qualifications' the same as the difference between an 'Undergraduate degree' and a 'Postgraduate degree'? We cannot make this claim in the same way as we can with continuous variables such as age where the differences between responses are constant and measurable. On the other hand, **nominal** data refers to instances where the response options cannot be ordered or organised into a hierarchy. Typical examples of nominal variables used in social science research include gender, sexuality, religion, and ethnicity.

Knowing the level of data (ordinal, nominal, ratio, or interval) which each of your variables contains should help you to select the most appropriate statistical tests. Table 6.1 shows the level of data of some of the key variables in *The National Survey of Sexual Attitudes and Lifestyles, 2010–2012: Open Access Teaching Dataset*. This is a free, open access teaching dataset which you can download from the UK Data service. We use this dataset to illustrate different statistical tests throughout this chapter, so you may wish to download it to help you follow the content discussed. Whilst a secondary source of data is being used to help explain key ideas in this chapter, the same processes described are also applicable if you have collected your own primary data (questionnaire data or data which you have coded as part of a content analysis or structured observation). Most online survey software packages now allow automatically coded responses and enable you to download the coded data directly into the statistical software package, saving significant time. But, as before, depending on the online survey platform you are using and the complexity of the analysis you are planning to undertake, you may even be able to complete your analysis on the online survey platform itself and not need to download your data. Let us now move on to preparing and cleaning your data for analysis.

Stage One: Preparing Data for Analysis

As much as preparation can sound less exciting than analysing, it is crucial that this stage is treated with the care it deserves before moving on to data analysis. Preparation

Table 6.1 Levels of data

Level of data		Description	Examples	Examples from teaching dataset
Categorical	Ordinal	The response options can be organised into an order or a hierarchy	Level of agreement	**snpres** (people are under pressure to have sex)
				Agree strongly
			Educational level	Neither agree nor disagree
				Disagree
				Disagree strongly
				Don't know
	Nominal	The response options cannot be organised into an order or hierarchy	Gender	**ethnicgrpr** (ethnic group-recoded)
			Ethnicity	White
			Religion	Non-White*
			Sexuality	
Continuous	Ratio	There is a true zero value meaning it is not possible to have negative values	Height	**dage1ch** (age of respondent at birth of first child)
			Weight	
			Salary	
	Interval	It is possible to have negative values as well as positive ones	Bank balance	**attconservative** (sexually conservative attitudes scale, higher score = more conservative attitudes)
			Temperature	

*this variable has been crudely divided into two categories. The grouping together of all those who are not white means that important nuances and differences in ethnic groups may be unclear. For more discussion, see Stage one: Preparing data for analysis.

begins by familiarising yourself with the dataset and the way in which it is coded. Statistical software programmes will assign numerical values to different response options. For example, in the *UK National Survey of Sexual Attitudes and Lifestyles, 2010–2012: Open Access Teaching Dataset*, the variable **sexidr** has been assigned the following numerical values; 1 = 'Heterosexual/straight', 2 = 'Not Heterosexual/straight' and 9 = 'Not answered'. Alternatively, if you are inputting your own data, for example if you have undertaken a content analysis or distributed paper questionnaires, you will need to devise your own coding system for your variables. For instance, if you had a variable measuring level of agreement with the statement, 'The school day should be made longer', you could assign the following numerical codes; 0 = 'Strongly disagree', 1 = 'Disagree', 2 = 'Neither agree nor disagree', 3 = 'Agree' and 4 = 'Strongly agree'. By assigning numerical codes to these textual responses, you can analyse the data statistically.

Importantly, if you are undertaking a secondary data analysis of an existing dataset, a crucial step in familiarising yourself with the data is downloading and reading any accompanying documentation. Such **meta data**, as they are called, may include guidance notes with details on the recruitment strategy and final sample, as well as a copy of the original questionnaire. For the *National Survey of Sexual Attitudes and Lifestyles, 2010–2012: Open Access Teaching Dataset*, the accompanying documentation includes the original questionnaire which was administered to participants, a data dictionary which details how the variables are coded, information on how to reference the dataset, and a user guide. The user guide is especially helpful. It provides more detail on the study population, sample, and recruitment process. It also contains information on how some of the variables were measured and recorded. Crucially, this document also explains that a weighting variable (**Total_wt**) has been created and advises using it when analysing the whole sample. **Weighting variables** are used to help make the sample more representative of the population.

Box 6.1

Weighting Variables

Survey weights ensure that the findings derived from a sample accurately reflect the characteristics of the population from which the sample was drawn. The need for weights arises when certain segments of the population are underrepresented or overrepresented in the sample, which can potentially introduce biases to the results.

By applying weights, researchers can account for these discrepancies and adjust the impact of each observation based on its likelihood of being included in the sample. This adjustment helps to create a more balanced and representative picture of the entire population, improving the generalisability of the results.

These weights can be easily applied through statistical software packages such as SPSS.

Another useful step to complete at this preliminary stage is to understand how many respondents provided different responses to each variable. This is known as **running frequencies**. For instance, in the *National Survey of Sexual Attitudes and Lifestyles, 2010–2012: Open Access Teaching Dataset*, there is a variable called '**snpres**'. This variable measures participants' attitudes to the statement *'People are under pressure to have sex'*. Running a frequency on this variable (with the weighting variable applied) shows that there are 3,755 valid answers to this question and nine participants did not answer the question. Of those 3,755 participants, 25.2% of the sample agreed strongly with the statement, 43.6% agreed with the statement, 17.8% neither agreed nor disagreed with the statement, 10.3% disagreed with statement, 1.5% strongly disagreed with the statement, and 1.7% answered 'Don't Know'. The process of running frequencies can also reveal variables which have elevated levels of non-response. High levels of non-response to a particular variable could be a signal that the original question was difficult for participants to answer. This could be because it was unclear, or perhaps because it was asking something deemed too sensitive or personal to answer. This is further evidence for the need to pilot your questionnaires (see Chapter 5: *Methods of Social Science Data Collection*).

You will also notice that the *National Survey of Sexual Attitudes and Lifestyles, 2010–2012: Open Access Teaching Dataset* has some data coded as 'missing'. Importantly, this does not mean that the researcher was unable to locate the data. Instead, it refers to instances where a participant did not provide an answer to a particular question and/or the question was not applicable to them. In the *National Survey of Sexual Attitudes and Lifestyles, 2010–2012: Open Access Teaching Dataset*, the values -9, -8, -1, 9 and 99 are all used to denote missing data. Typically, the values used to denote **missing data** are those which are not plausible response options. As an example, if you had a variable measuring height, you might decide to use the value of -9 to demonstrate that a respondent had not answered this question as this would not be a plausible height since, as before, height does not come in minus numbers (and subsequently is a ratio variable). Using a number unlikely to be mistaken with a genuine response helps to avoid any confusion. In some scenarios, you may also decide to recode data as missing. For example, again using the *National Survey of Sexual Attitudes and Lifestyles, 2010–2012: Open Access Teaching Dataset*, the variable '**snpres**' has a value of 8 which denotes 'Don't Know' responses. You may decide that these responses are not particularly helpful to your analysis and, therefore, add an '8' as a value denoting missing data. This would mean that all participants who responded 'Don't Know' would then be excluded from your analysis of this variable.

Recoding is another form of data preparation that is required in the preparatory stage of data analysis. In instances where you have collected your own data, you may not have achieved a sufficiently large sample size to justify retaining all the original response options to questions for all the variables in your dataset. This can be particularly the case if you have a sample which is fairly similar and who have responded to the questions in a similar way. To combat this, you may decide to recode some variables to reduce the number of response options. For example, you may have initially asked participants to select their highest level of qualification out of the following options: 'No qualifications', 'School level qualifications', 'Undergraduate degree' or 'Postgraduate degree'. However, for the purposes of analysis, you might determine that the numbers of participants ticking undergraduate and postgraduate degree were too low (and, thus, unusable) and so recode this variable into: 'No qualifications', 'School level qualifications', or 'University level qualifications'. This, of course, is not without its problems. For example, when familiarising yourself with an existing dataset, you may realise that some of the response options are not as nuanced or detailed as you would like them to be. In the *National Survey of Sexual Attitudes and Lifestyles, 2010–2012: Open Access Teaching Dataset*, the variable **ethnicgrpr**, which records participants' ethnicity, is a **dichotomous variable** (see Table 6.1). This means that it only has two possible response options 'White' and 'Non-White'. As nascent social scientists, we could critique this dataset for combining all respondents who identify as non-White together, essentially privileging White as a category and grouping all other ethnicities as Other. When interpreting the findings, it is important that we are critical of this crude, unsophisticated approach to measuring an important demographic variable. Collapsing categories and lumping participants together can obscure important differences within groups, in this case, differences within the non-White participants category. Therefore, category generation decisions (a form of interpretation, of course) need to be made by all quantitative researchers.

When writing up these preliminary steps, it can be helpful to present a table containing the key variables of interest and outlining how these are coded, for example, see Table 6.2. Other important information to include is whether any weights have been applied and if any recoding has taken place. You will notice from Table 6.2 that it is not necessary to report frequencies for continuous level variables.

Table 6.2 Frequencies for key variables

Variable name	Level of data	Missing data	Frequencies: Valid %	Original/ recoded
snpres	Ordinal	Not answered (9) = 0.2%	Agree strongly (1) = 25.2% Agree (2) = 43.6% Neither agree nor disagree (3) = 17.8% Disagree (4) = 10.3% Disagree strongly (5) = 1.5% Don't know (8) = 1.7%	Original
snpresRECODE	Ordinal	Don't know (8) = 1.7% Not answered (9) = 0.2%	Agree strongly (1) = 25.1% Agree (2) = 44.4% Neither agree nor disagree (3) = 18.1% Disagree (4) = 10.4% Disagree strongly (5) = 1.5%	Recoded from snpres to make 'Don't know' a missing value
ethnicgrpr	Nominal	Not answered (9) = 0.3%	White (1) = 87.6% Non-White (2) = 12.4%	Original
dage1ch	Ratio	Not applicable (-1) = 38.7% Not answered (9) = 3.7%		Original
attconservative	Interval	None		Original

Now, you have prepared and sorted your data, the next stage is to run some descriptive statistics.

Stage Two: Descriptive Statistics

Descriptive statistics can be divided into measures of **central tendency** and **measures of spread**. Measures of central tendency help you describe the responses of a typical respondent, an ideal type if you like. The three most common measures of central tendency are the mean, median, and mode. The **mode** refers to the value which appears most frequently in the data. If you generated the following set of values (1, 1, 2, 3, 3, 3, 3, 4, 4, 4, 5) then the mode would be 3 as it occurs four times, one more than the value 4 and at least two more than the other values. In contrast, the **median** refers to the value which appears in the middle when the values are ordered from smallest to largest. Using the same set of values, the median would again be 3 as there are eleven different values ordered from 1 to 5, and the sixth and centre value is 3. Finally, the **mean** refers to the arithmetic average. This is calculated by adding together all the values provided and dividing them by the number of respondents. If we add all those values together, we get 33. Divide that by the eleven entries (33/11) and, again, the mean is 3. The types of variables you have will determine which measures of central tendency you should calculate. The mean is only calculated for continuous level variables, whereas the median can be calculated for both continuous and ordinal level variables, and the mode can be calculated for continuous, ordinal, and nominal level variables. Of note, while in this example, the mean, median and mode are all 3, it is perfectly possible that the mean, median, and mode of a dataset are all different. For example, if the last digit was 11 and not 5, then the mode would still be 3, the median would remain 3 but the mean would change to (39/11) = 3.55

While certain measures of central tendency can be used for continuous, ordinal, and nominal variables, measures of spread are only calculated when analysing continuous variables. Measures of spread include the range and the standard deviation. The **range** refers to the difference between the smallest (minimum) and largest (maximum) value in the dataset. Using the initial example, the range is 4 (5-1). A large range may indicate the presence of outliers in the data. Therefore, if we had the same set of results plus the number 25 in our dataset, our range would be altered dramatically (25-1 = 24). These extreme values (either low or high) might prompt you to consider whether there is a data input error and/or an invalid response. In these circumstances, you might decide to recode the data by excluding these extreme values from your analysis. This is because outliers can skew your results and impact on your interpretation of the data. Again, this is another example of decisions quantitative researchers must make which influence their research findings.

The **standard deviation**, meanwhile, is a measure of how dispersed the data is from the mean. Using the same original example, the standard deviation would be 1.3. The sample standard deviation is calculated using the formula shown on the next page; however, statistical software packages will calculate this value for you, so you do not need to memorise or learn this. That said, it is important to understand as best you can what this means.

$$\text{Standard Deviation} = \sqrt{\frac{\sum_{i}^{n}=1(xi-\bar{x})^2}{n-1}}$$

$$S_x = \sqrt{\frac{\sum_{i=1}^{n}(x_i-\bar{x})^2}{n-1}}$$

A large standard deviation is another signal that there may be outliers in the data and that the mean value is not a very accurate representation of the typical respondent. In contrast, a small standard deviation suggests that there are no outliers in the data and that the data is clustered close to the mean. As such, the mean value is an accurate representation of a typical respondent. The smallest possible value for both the range and the standard deviation is 0. However, this is an extremely unlikely value as it would indicate that all participants in the dataset gave the same response.

Table 6.3 outlines these different measures as well as the formula or syntax needed to calculate these measures in Microsoft Excel, SPSS, and Stata.

In a quantitative or mixed method social science research report, you could display information relating to the measures of central tendency and measures of spread in a table (such as the example in Table 6.4). Table 6.4 shows that the median value for the variable **snpresRECODE** is 2. Looking back to Table 6.2, we can see that a value of 2 corresponds to the textual label Agree. Similarly, Table 6.4 shows that the modal value for the variable **ethnicgrpr** is 1. Again, Table 6.2 tells us that a value of 1 corresponds to the textual label White. In relation to measures of spread, Table 6.4 reveals that for the variable **dage1ch**, there was a 25-year range between the ages that participants reported having their first child. The youngest age reported was 15 while the oldest age reported was 40. The standard deviation of 5.33 years is still fairly low, indicating that the mean is a good indicator of the responses of a typical respondent in the data and that the data points are not too dispersed from the mean.

The mean, median, and mode values for this variable are all quite similar (25.7 years old, 25 years old and 24 years old respectively). This suggests that these data are likely to have a **normal distribution**, meaning that when plotted on a graph, the data points *tend* to cluster around the central value and taper out in a downward slope on each side in much the shape of a bell. For the variable **attconservative**, the guidance documents (which accompany the dataset) explain that a high value on the scale indicates a more conservative attitude. Again, the mean, median, and modal scores for this variable are all very closely clustered together around the value of 0 (0.02, 0.06, and 0.11 respectively), indicating that the data are equally normally distributed. Table 6.4 shows that the standard deviation for this variable is 1.00. Even though this value is close to zero, it is greater than the mean (0.02), suggesting that the data points are relatively dispersed.

Table 6.3 Calculating measures of central tendency in Microsoft Excel, SPSS, and Stata

	Definition	Level of data	Microsoft Excel	SPSS	Stata
Mode	Most frequently occurring	Nominal, Ordinal and Continuous	=MODE(Column of interest)	FREQUENCIES VARIABLES=Variable Name /STATISTICS=MODE /ORDER=ANALYSIS.	Codebook Variable name (report the response option with the highest frequency)
Median	Central value when ordered from smallest to largest	Ordinal and Continuous	=MEDIAN(Column of interest)	FREQUENCIES VARIABLES=Variable Name /STATISTICS=MEDIAN /ORDER=ANALYSIS.	Sum Variable name, d
Mean	Arithmetic average	Continuous	=AVERAGE(Column of interest)	FREQUENCIES VARIABLES=Variable Name /STATISTICS=MEAN /ORDER=ANALYSIS.	Sum Variable name
Range	The difference between the highest and lowest reported value	Continuous	Subtract MIN value from MAX value (see below)	FREQUENCIES VARIABLES=Variable Name /STATISTICS=RANGE /ORDER=ANALYSIS.	Codebook Variable name
Standard Deviation	A measure of how spread out from the mean the data is	Continuous	=STDEV(Column of interest)	FREQUENCIES VARIABLES=Variable Name /STATISTICS=STDDEV /ORDER=ANALYSIS.	Sum Variable name
Maximum	The highest value reported	Continuous	=MAX(Column of interest)	FREQUENCIES VARIABLES=Variable Name /STATISTICS=MAXIMUM /ORDER=ANALYSIS.	Sum Variable name
Minimum	The lowest value reported	Continuous	=MIN(Column of interest)	FREQUENCIES VARIABLES=Variable Name /STATISTICS=MINIMUM /ORDER=ANALYSIS.	Sum Variable name

Table 6.4 Univariate analysis

Variable name	Level of data	Measure of central tendency	Measure of spread
snpresRECODE	Ordinal	Median = 2 (Agree)	
		Mode = 2 (Agree)	
ethnicgrpr	Nominal	Mode = 1 (White)	
dage1ch	Ratio	Mean = 25.69	Range = 25.00
		Median = 25.00	Max = 40.00
		Mode = 24.00	Min = 15.00
			Standard Deviation = 5.33
attconservative	Interval	Mean = 0.02	Range = 6.48
		Median = 0.06	Max = 2.60
		Mode = 0.11	Min = −3.89
			Standard Deviation = 1.00

Box 6.2

Normal Distribution

A normal distribution describes a situation where your continuous level data adopts a bell-shaped curve when plotted on a **histogram** which is a graph that shows the frequency of numerical data in tall rectangular boxes that are said to resemble the Manhattan skyline. An example histogram showing a normal distribution can be seen in Figure 6.1.

Positive Skew | No Skew (Normal Distribution) | Negative Skew

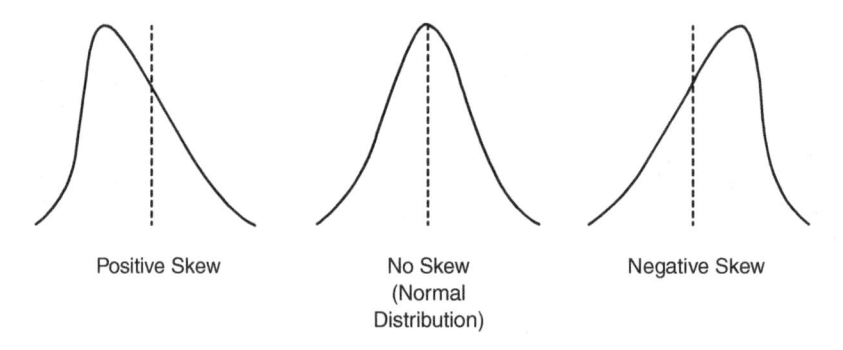

Figure 6.1 Histograms showing skew

The curve of this graph peaks in the centre and tapers out in a downward slope on each side in the shape of a bell. The peak shows the mean, median, and modal value. The curve is symmetrical, meaning that the values to the left and right of the mean, median, and mode mirror each other. This means that you are likely to see a similar distribution to the right of the mean, median, and mode, as you are on the left.

When data are normally distributed, the empirical rule applies. This rule states that 68% of the observed data falls within one standard deviation of the mean, 95% of the data will fall within two standard deviations of the mean and 99.7% of the data fall within three standard deviations of the mean. By this, we mean that 68% of the data will fall between the value of the mean minus the standard deviation and the mean plus the standard deviation. 95% of the data will fall between the value of the mean minus the standard deviation twice and the mean plus the standard deviation twice. 99.7% of the data will fall between the value of the mean minus the standard deviation threefold and the mean plus the standard deviation threefold. The 0.3% outside of this range will be outliers.

68% of the data falls between: (Mean - Standard Deviation) and (Mean + Standard Deviation)

95% of the data falls between: (Mean - Standard Deviation - Standard Deviation) and (Mean + Standard Deviation + Standard Deviation)

99.7% of the data falls between: (Mean - Standard Deviation - Standard Deviation - Standard Deviation) and (Mean + Standard Deviation + Standard Deviation + Standard Deviation)

When the data are normally distributed, almost all of the data falls within three standard deviations either side of the mean value. This can be particularly helpful when generalising data from the sample to the wider population. This is because, assuming that the sample is representative of the wider population, the empirical rule enables some important insights and generalisations about the population to be made. The normal distribution is the underlying assumption of many of the statistical tests used in the social sciences which are discussed throughout the rest of this chapter.

Being able to plot a bell-shaped curve (see Figure 6.1) and having similar mean, median, and mode values are all indicators that your continuous level variables are normally distributed. It is easy to create histograms and check the distribution of your data using statistical software packages. The syntax provided should allow you to create a histogram of the variable **dage1ch** in SPSS and Stata.

Syntax for creating a histogram displaying the variable **dage1ch** in SPSS:

GRAPH/HISTOGRAM(NORMAL)=dage1ch.

Syntax for creating a histogram displaying the variable **dage1ch** in Stata:

Histogram dage1ch, normal

In some cases, histograms will reveal that the distribution of variables is not normally distributed but instead **skewed**. Essentially, this means that there is a greater frequency of data points toward one side of the histogram than the other. For example, if you are researching the ages at which people die, you might reasonably expect more observations toward the right-hand side of your graph (lots of people dying at older ages) and a long tail on the left (very few people dying

(Continued)

at younger ages). This is known as negative skew. Conversely, if you are researching the number of pets people own, you might reasonably expect more observations toward the left-hand side of your graph (lots of people owning no pets or one or two pets) and a long tail on the right (very few people owning lots of pets). This is known as a positive skew. When data are negatively skewed, the mode is greater than the median and the median is greater than the mean. When data are positively skewed, the mean is greater than the median and the median is greater than the mode.

We now ready to move on to the final and third stage of analysing quantitative data.

Stage Three: Inferential Statistics

Whereas descriptive statistics allow you to describe the data in your sample, inferential statistics enable you to make inferences or claims about the population. Importantly, when calculating inferential statistics, there is an underlying assumption that the data from your sample are representative of your population (see Chapter 5: *Methods of Social Science Data Collection*). If your data are not representative, **bias** may be introduced. Bias may be understood as a statistical distortion. Therefore, it is important in the writing up of your findings that you discuss the representativeness of your sample and caveat any findings based on data which may not be representative of the wider population.

The first stage of calculating inferential statistics is to formulate hypotheses. **Hypotheses** are testable statements outlining the relationship or association between two or more variables in the dataset, known as an **independent** variable which you manipulate and the **dependent variable** which should tell you the effect of that change. In quantitative social science research, we speak of the alternative hypothesis and the null hypotheses. The **alternative hypothesis** states that there is a relationship between two or more variables. The **null hypothesis**, on the other hand, states that there is no relationship or association between the variables. The alternative hypothesis will be informed by the literature that you draw from during the Literature Review phase of your research project and outlines what you expect to see occur. The null hypothesis, colloquially known as the devil's advocate hypothesis, is the alter ego of the alternative hypothesis and states the opposite to what you expect to happen: the Yin to the Yang so to speak. For example, we may hypothesise that there is an association between ethnic group (**ethnicgrpr**) and level of agreement with the statement '*People are under pressure to have sex*' (**snpres**). In this example, the alternative hypothesis would be: there **is** an association between ethnicity and level of agreement with the statement '*People are under pressure to have sex*'. The null hypothesis would be: There is **no** association between ethnicity and level of agreement with the statement '*People are under pressure to have sex*'.

The hypothesis formalises the relationship between the independent variable(s) and the dependent variable. In this example, the independent variable – the one we are manipulating – is **ethnicgrpr** and the dependent variable is **snpres** since we are interested to find out whether different ethnic groups are more or less likely to agree with the statement *'People are under pressure to have sex'*.

Inferential statistics are used to test the null hypothesis (that there is no relationship or association between the variables). The evidence is tested against the null hypothesis because it is often quicker and easier to disprove the absence of a relationship (and prove that there is a relationship or association) than it is to disprove the existence of a relationship (and prove that there is not a relationship or association). The annotation H0 or Hn is sometimes used to denote the null hypothesis. Conversely, the annotation H1 or Ha is used to denote the alternative hypothesis.

Another decision you need to make before calculating inferential statistics is whether you are looking for differences in one specific direction or not. For instance, if you were comparing the mean score from the **attconservative** scale for different ethnic groups, your null hypothesis and alternative hypothesis may read as follows:

H0: There is no difference in mean scores on the **attconservative** scale between different ethnic groups (null hypothesis)

H1: There is a difference in mean scores on the **attconservative** scale between different ethnic groups (alternative hypothesis)

Here, we have specified in the alternative hypothesis that there is a difference. However, we have not stated in which direction we expect this difference will point. We have not hypothesised specifically about which ethnic groups will have higher or lower scores on the **attconservative** scale. Therefore, in this example, we would use and report the **two-tailed solution**. This is because two-tailed tests look for differences in both directions. In other words, the two-tailed solution would tell us whether the average score on the **attconservative** scale was statistically significantly *higher or lower* for the White group compared to the non-White group in the data.

A one-tailed solution, on the other hand, considers difference in one direction only. When words or phrases such as 'less than' or 'more than' are used in the alternative hypothesis, it indicates that a one-tailed test should be used and reported. The example provided is a hypothesis you would use a one-tailed test for:

H0: The mean score on the **attconservative** scale for the White group will be equal to the mean score on the **attconservative** scale for the non-White group

H1: The mean score on the **attconservative** scale for the White group will be more than the mean score **attconservative** scale for the non-White group

One-tailed tests have more statistical power. This means that you are more likely to get a statistically significant result with a one-tailed test if your groups are truly different. However, two-tailed tests are typically used more in social science projects because they tend to be more insightful and useful. Take the example above, the one-tailed test would not tell us whether there is a statistically significant difference between the two ethnic groups if the mean score for the non-White group was higher than the White group. One-tailed tests are sometimes called directional, whilst two-tailed tests are sometimes called non-directional.

Box 6.3

P-Values

An example here is illustrative. Imagine we are sat in a room with no one else but you. We open a box of chocolates, Ferrero Rocher perhaps, and you explain that you are hungry and you particularly like nutty, extravagant chocolate that melts in your mouth. We then leave the room and stand outside the door leaving you with the opened box of chocolates. When we return, all the chocolates have mysteriously disappeared. In this scenario, we can be fairly confident that you took or consumed the chocolate. It is very unlikely that there is an alternative explanation for the disappearance of the chocolates. However, without further evidence such as video footage or your sworn testimony (though even then we know both humans and the camera lie), we can never be 100% sure of alternative possibilities. For example, unknown to us, there could be a secret passage in and out of the room which a chocolate thief could navigate. But, in all probability, you are the culprit. That is our working assumption.

When we carry out statistical analysis and calculate test statistics, we calculate what is known as a **p-value** or probability value. P-values vary from 0 to 1, with smaller values indicating greater evidence to reject the null hypothesis – that there is not a relationship or association between the independent and dependent variable – and larger values indicating there is less evidence to reject the null hypothesis. In the fictitious example above, the null hypothesis would state that there was not an association between your being left in the room alone and the chocolates disappearing. In this scenario, there seem to be very few other plausible explanations for the disappearance of the chocolates, so we would anticipate a very low p-value. A low p-value tells us that it is very unlikely that the data we observed (the disappearance of the chocolates) happened by random chance. The p-value tells us the likelihood or probability of seeing the relationship if the null hypothesis was true. In this example, a p-value would tell us how probable it was there was no association between your being left in the room alone and the chocolates disappearing.

In the social sciences, we typically use the threshold of **0.05** as a cut off to determine statistical significance. This means that if the resultant p-value is 0.05 or less, social science researchers deem this sufficient evidence to reject the null hypothesis and accept the alternative hypothesis. A p-value of 0.05 means that there is less than a 5% chance of the null hypothesis being true. In other scenarios, for instance, when conducting potentially risky experiments such as testing the efficiency of new drugs or designing new brakes for cars, researchers would set the threshold for their p-value even lower (e.g. 0.01). This would mean that there was less than 1% chance of the null hypothesis being true. Lowering the p-value is lowering the risk of something unpredictable occurring.

The p-value is impacted by a range of factors including sample size. Therefore, it is important that you provide this information when reporting the findings of your research in your Findings chapter. Equally, for this reason, many researchers advocate explicitly referring to the effect size as well as the p-value when reporting the results of statistical analysis.

Crosstabulations and Chi-Square Tests

Crosstabulations are a way of visualising two categorical variables at the same time. Given the prevalence of categorical variables in social science research, crosstabulations are used frequently. The syntax provided shows you how to create a crosstabulation in different statistical software packages:

Syntax for creating a crosstabulation in SPSS:

CROSSTABS

/TABLES=**ethnicgrpr** BY **snpresRECODE**

/FORMAT=AVALUE TABLES

/CELLS=COUNT

/COUNT ROUND CELL.

Syntax for creating a crosstabulation in Stata:

tabulate **ethnicgrpr snpresRECODE**

PivotTables can be used in Microsoft Excel to create crosstabulations.

In this example, a **crosstabulation** has been made between the two variables **ethnicgrpr** and **snpresRECODE**. Table 6.5 shows how the findings of a crosstabulation can be displayed in a written report. It shows that 45.3% (n=1472) of White respondents agreed with the statement *'People are under pressure to have sex'*. Similarly, the majority or 37.2% (n=163) of non-White respondents agreed with the statement *'People are under pressure to have sex'*. However, non-White respondents were more likely to disagree (14.8%) or strongly disagree (3.7%) with the statement compared to White respondents (9.8% and 1.2% respectively).

Table 6.5 Crosstabulation

		snpresRECODE: People are under pressure to have sex (recoded)				
		Disagree strongly	Disagree	Neither agree nor disagree	Agree	Agree strongly
ethnicgrpr (Ethnic group)	White	39	318	586	1472	832
		(1.2%)	(9.8%)	(18.0%)	(45.3%)	(25.6%)
	Non-White	16	65	81	163	113
		(3.7%)	(14.8%)	(18.5%)	(37.2%)	(25.8%)

In Table 6.5, the number of observations as well as the row percentages have been included. The row percentages tell you the proportion of people in that row who gave different response options. Therefore, for each ethnic group, Table 6.5 tells us what proportion of participants disagreed strongly, disagreed, neither agreed nor disagreed, agreed or agreed strongly with the statement. Reading the first row of Table 6.5, we can see that 1.2% of White respondents disagreed strongly with the statement that *'People are under pressure to have sex'*, 9.8% disagreed, 18% neither agreed nor disagreed, 45.3% agreed and the remaining 25.6% agreed strongly. These percentages correctly add to 100%. If the row percentages do not, then it is a sure sign something has gone awry, or you may be reporting column percentages instead. It is important to compare the row percentages as opposed to the number of responses when interpreting the data. This is because if we only included the number of responses, we may think that the White group were more likely to disagree with the statement than the non-White group (318 compared to 65). However, the row percentages tell us the proportion of participants, allowing us to make meaningful comparisons. This ultimately tells us that whilst more White people selected the option disagree compared to non-White people, as a proportion of the number of respondents, non-White people selected disagree more frequently than White people. Note, however, that the differences may have been more (or less) pronounced if more nuanced ethnic groups were used instead of crudely comparing White and non-White people.

If we had used column percentages instead of row percentages, Table 6.5 would tell us for each level of agreement, what percentage of the participants were White and what percentage were non-White (i.e. what proportion of those participants who disagreed strongly with the statement were White and what proportion were non-White).

Syntax for creating a crosstabulation with row percentages in SPSS:

CROSSTABS

/TABLES=**ethnicgrpr** BY **snpresRECODE**

/FORMAT=AVALUE TABLES

/CELLS=COUNT ROW

/COUNT ROUND CELL.

Syntax for creating a crosstabulation with row percentages in Stata:

tabulate ethnicgrpr snpresRECODE, row

Syntax for creating a crosstabulation with column percentages in SPSS:

CROSSTABS

/TABLES=**ethnicgrpr** BY **snpresRECODE**

/FORMAT=AVALUE TABLES

/CELLS=COUNT COLUMN

/COUNT ROUND CELL.

Syntax for creating a crosstabulation with column percentages in Stata:

tabulate ethnicgrpr snpresRECODE, column

As well as creating a crosstabulation to explore the relationship between two categorical variables, you can also calculate a **chi-square** statistic. The chi-square statistic tells you whether there is a statistically significant difference between the observed and the expected counts in the crosstabulation. The observed counts refer to the actual data collected – what you see in your crosstabulation – whereas the expected counts refer to the number of responses you would expect to see in each cell of your crosstabulation if your null hypothesis was true (there was no difference in level of agreement with the statement 'People are under pressure to have sex' between different ethnic groups). If the observed and expected counts were equal, the chi-square statistic would equal 0.

Syntax for calculating a chi-square statistic in SPSS:

CROSSTABS

/TABLES=**ethnicgrpr** BY **snpresRECODE**

/STATISTICS=CHISQ.

Syntax for calculating a chi-square statistic in Stata:

tabulate ethnicgrpr snpresRECODE, chi2

The results of the chi-square test should be reported as follows:

A chi-square test revealed a statistically significant association between ethnicity and level of agreement with the statement 'People feel under pressure to have sex' (x^2=30.78, 4d.f. $p<0.05$).

In this example, the chi-square statistic is 30.78. The p-value or significance value is less than 0.05. We can therefore conclude that there is a statistically significant association between the independent variable (ethnicity) and dependent variable (agreement with the statement). The 'd.f.' value refers to the **degrees of freedom**. This is a measure of the size of the crosstabulation. The higher this value, the more cells in the crosstabulation. The degrees of freedom can be calculated by hand by multiplying the number of rows in a crosstabulation minus 1, by the number of columns in a crosstabulation minus 1. In this example, there were two rows in the crosstabulation (White and non-White) and five columns (Disagree strongly, Disagree, Neither agree nor disagree, Agree, Agree strongly). This means we need to complete the following sum to calculate the degrees of freedom:

(2–1)*(5–1)

1*4

= 4

Correlation

Correlation coefficients can vary between −1 and +1. They tell us two things: first and foremost, they tell us the direction of the relationship between two variables (positive or negative) and secondly, they tell us something of the strength of a relationship between two variables. A correlation coefficient of −1 indicates a perfect negative relationship, meaning that as the value of one variable increases, the value of the other variable decreases. A good example of a negative relationship which we see in everyday life is the relationship between the number of years someone has owned a car and the value of that car. It is a fair statement to make that the longer someone has owned a car, the less money the car is worth. The car loses value almost as soon as it is driven off the forecourt and then through additional wear and tear, especially the more miles it has clocked up. A correlation coefficient of +1 indicates a perfect positive relationship, meaning that as the value of one variable increases, the value of the other variable also increases. A good example of a positive relationship we may see in everyday life is the relationship between the number of hours spent revising and scores in a test . The longer someone spends revising, the higher they score in a test (see Barbarick and Ippolito 2003; Baliyan and Khama 2020). Correlation coefficients close to 0 denote weak relationships.

There are two types of correlation coefficients known as **Pearson's Correlation Coefficient** and **Spearman's Rho Correlation Coefficient**. Pearson's Correlation Coefficient is used in situations where you are exploring the relationship between two continuous level variables. Pearson's – for short – is also based on the assumption that there is a linear or straight-line relationship between the two variables, with no extreme outliers in the data. These assumptions mean that, often, social science researchers need to use Spearman's Rho Correlation Coefficient. Spearman's – for short – can be used with either continuous or ordinal level variables. The syntax/formulae provided show how to calculate both Pearson's and Spearman's correlation coefficients in SPSS or Stata:

Syntax for calculating a Pearson's correlation coefficient in SPSS:

> CORRELATIONS
>
> /VARIABLES=**attconservative dage1ch**
>
> /PRINT=TWOTAIL NOSIG FULL
>
> /MISSING=PAIRWISE.

(N.B. a two tailed test has been selected here)

Syntax for calculating a Pearson's correlation coefficient in Stata:

> pwcorr attconservative dage1ch, sig star (.05)

Syntax for calculating a Spearman's correlation coefficient in SPSS:

> NONPAR CORR
>
> /VARIABLES=**attconservative dage1ch**

/PRINT=SPEARMAN TWOTAIL NOSIG FULL

/MISSING=PAIRWISE.

Syntax for calculating a Spearman's correlation coefficient in Stata:

spearman attconservative dage1ch

Microsoft Excel can also be used to calculate correlation coefficients. The formula '=correl(array1, array 2)' would return a Pearson's r correlation coefficient. Here, you need to select all the data belonging to the first variable (attconservative) for array 1 and select all the data belonging to the second variable (dacge1ch) for array 2. If you wanted to calculate a Spearman's rank correlation coefficient, you would need to rank the raw data from lowest to highest for each variable before using the formula. This is because Spearman's correlation coefficient demands you use rank data (first, second, third, and so on) as opposed to the raw data. For example, if you are exploring the correlation coefficient between time spent revising and exam marks, a Pearson's correlation coefficient would be calculated using the number of minutes someone spent revising and their exam mark, whereas for a Spearman's correlation coefficient, the times which the respondents spent revising would be ranked from shortest to longest and likewise the exam marks from lowest to highest and then the correlation coefficient calculated.

The results of the correlation coefficient should be reported as follows:

> A Pearson's correlation coefficient ($r=-0.14$, $p<0.05$) revealed a statistically significant negative, weak association between the age at which a respondent had their first child and their score on the conservative attitude scale. The direction of the relationship was negative, meaning that as the age at which participants had their first child increased, participants' scores on the conservative attitude scale decreased. This suggests that older first-time parents have fewer conservative attitudes. The correlation coefficient was close to 0 suggesting a weak relationship between the two variables.

When reporting the correlation coefficient between two variables, you need to interpret both the direction and the strength of the relationship.

T-Tests and Equivalents

T-tests measure and compare the mean – the arithmetic average – score of a continuous variable for two groups of respondents. For instance, T-tests might be used to compare the average pay gap between different groups of employees in the same, large organisation.

Syntax for calculating a T-test statistic in SPSS:

T-TEST GROUPS=ethnicgrpr(1 2)

MISSING=ANALYSIS

/VARIABLES=attconservative

/ES DISPLAY(TRUE)

/CRITERIA=CI(.95).

Syntax for calculating a T-test statistic in Stata:

ttest attconservative, by(ethnicgrpr)

The syntax shown here uses the *National Survey of Sexual Attitudes and Lifestyles, 2010–2012: Open Access Teaching Dataset* to explore differences in the mean scores for the variable **attconservative** between White and non-White participants. In the SPSS syntax above, the (1 2) in the first line refers to the numerical codes which have been assigned to the two groups under exploration. In this example, White participants have been assigned the numerical code '1', and non-White participants have been assigned the numerical code '2'. The results of the T-test should be reported as follows:

The mean score on the conservative attitude scale for White participants was -0.03(+/-0.99) compared to 0.43(+/-0.99) for the non-White participants. A T-test revealed that this difference was statistically significant (t=-8.81, 3471d.f., p<0.05).

The results here show that there is a statistically significant difference in the average scores on the conservative attitude scale between White and non-White participants. The mean score for the White participants is lower (-0.03) than the mean score for the non-White participants (0.43). For both groups, the standard deviation is +/-0.99, suggesting that the spread of scores from the mean value is remarkably similar.

An assumption of the T-test is that the continuous level variable under exploration is normally distributed for each group. If this assumption is not met, an alternative test, known as the **Mann-Whitney U** test, should be used. Moreover, if you are comparing the mean scores of a continuous level variable for more than two groups, there are alternative tests which you can use. For example, if we had a more nuanced variable with more response options to measure ethnicity rather than simply non-White, we could use either an Analysis of Variance or **ANOVA** (when data is normally distributed) or the **Kruskal Wallis** test (when data is not normally distributed) to explore the differences in conservative attitudes between the ethnic groups. For a more detailed text on the distinct types of quantitative tests that exist and the theory behind them, we recommend reading the textbooks written by Field (2018) or Pallant (2020). The findings of these tests would be reported in the same way as the findings of a T-test.

Quantitative Findings Summary

This section has introduced you to diverse ways to analyse quantitative data in your social science project. The summary provided here is not comprehensive and we advise students to use the information provided in this chapter as a jumping-off point for wider reading about the different statistical tests and their assumptions. Indeed, some of you may want to further your analysis by exploring three or more variables at the same time (called **multivariate analysis**). However, this section provides a clear structure and plan for both undertaking your analysis and presenting it in your written research project.

As a final note to conclude this section on quantitative data analysis, we urge you to remember that statistical significance and substantive significance are two different things. Often students can be disheartened to find that their results are not statistically significant and worry that this may negatively impact their project and subsequent mark. This is certainly not the case! In some scenarios, a result which is not statistically significant can be as insightful and interesting as a statistically significant one. We encourage students not to get too fixated on p-values and instead focus on the potential real-world implications of their data: what is the practical importance or meaningfulness of the observed associations? Moreover, markers will be looking for whether you understood the data that you collected and/or analysed, and what inferences you can (and cannot) make from your findings. There is no such thing as bad data, if you understand what it means.

PART TWO: QUALITATIVE DATA ANALYSIS

In this section of the chapter, we turn our attention to the qualitative analysis of social science data. The way in which qualitative social scientists approach data is quite different to quantitative social scientists. We are on safe ground by stating it is less formulaic, and the rules to be followed are less strict. For example, there are not really the same sort of formulae and statistical tests to follow as in quantitative approaches. Instead, qualitative research is open to the various ways in which people see and make sense of the world (Patton 2002). To this end, qualitative social scientists recognise the impact and influence they have on their setting and often embrace it by writing themselves into their Methods chapter. Let us demystify a myth here – qualitative research *is not* easier than quantitative research. While quantitative social scientists collect data, clean data, and determine what variables they want to compare before choosing the appropriate statistical tests such as ANOVAs, T-tests and Chi Square tests, they essentially outsource the analysis to these tests. Qualitative researchers have no such help. Though there are qualitative software packages such as NVivo and even MyRA, these are principally data storage and sorting platforms providing you with the ability to move data around to see it in different ways and to help you make connections (visually). But importantly, they do not do the analysis of the data for you. There are of course recent developments in generative AI technologies such as ChatGPT that supposedly can perform a kind of analysis of data. But this is an artifice based on word association and pattern recognition prediction. The result is that this type of 'analysis' tends to be simply surface level and is nowhere near as insightful as a person who collected the data analysing the data themselves (see Gibney 2024 for the problems of AI). It cannot be, as generative AI does not do meaning. Think for example of the specialised or localised language, phrases, or expressions that your participants may use. They may make comments in jest or use sarcasm, include acronyms in their speech or abbreviate words – all of these conventions will not necessarily be recognised by generative AI. Instead here the researchers' knowledge of the context is needed. The use of generative AI may even breach various ethical requirements. The first relates to our own ethical commitments to our participants in relation to the storage of the data and possible commercialisation of that data. In uploading data to a generative AI website to be analysed who are we inadvertently giving access to that data, and what is being done with it? The second is in relation to the data that the AI model is trained on and the practices of these AI companies mining and scraping other authors' materials that might be under copyright (Taylor 2023). Finally, and more philosophically, there is a question in terms of the authenticity and integrity of your project and whether 'analysis' generated through AI can be rightly attributed to you. That is, is this still your own work? More broadly, the AI boom has raised real and pressing questions concerning the extraordinary energy demands of their servers. Google recently admitted that 'datacentres, a key piece of AI infrastructure, had helped increase its greenhouse gas emissions by 48% since 2019.' (Milmo et al. 2024). Instead, we strongly believe that qualitative researchers should embrace the fact that they are the instruments of their own analysis and grasp this opportunity. This is not to say there are not different, established forms of analysis with some demanding a more formulaic approach than others. But it is to state that in an analogous way to how quantitative researchers must make subjective decisions when generating categories or determining an entry as 'missing', especially if they decide to collapse or merge values when cleaning data in Stage 1, qualitative researchers need to decide how to code and present their data. For them, 'the objective stance is obsolete' (Hammarberg et al. 2016: 498).

So Why Do Qualitative Analysis and Under What Circumstances?

We, of course, should not be dictated to by our methods. Rather than allowing them to use us, we should use them and therefore we need to choose the most appropriate method to explore the issue at hand and to answer our research questions. Numbers and figures are evidently good at conveying certain issues – showcasing the weight of evidence, for instance – but they are poorer at making sense of other aspects of social life. For example, qualitative research is a much more appropriate approach if you want to make sense of people's belief systems and culture, and how they understand the world. As such, qualitative researchers tend to examine social practices, study behaviours and show how people account for events and issues as well as the ways in which they storify their lives. Before detailing some of the many types of analysis available to qualitative researchers, we first discuss some general tips or flexible rules that should hold you in good stead as you cycle through your data, no matter the specifics of your project.

General Qualitative Analysis

1. **Become familiar with your data**. As the instrument of analysis, you need to know your data in as much detail as possible. No one else (including AI) should know your data as well as you, and you should take advantage of this situation. Become 'the expert' of your data. Listen to your data, read your data, play with your data, think about your data, and then repeat this task. Much in the same way that you can get better at writing with practise, you can get better at reading, at listening, and at thinking. On your second or third repetition, you will likely see or hear things in your data that were not apparent the first time around or which you can connect to other bits of data. Whatever way your data was captured, make sure that you absorb it. This process of familiarisation is pivotal. It is your job as the researcher to know your data then infer and draw out its social significance.

2. **Create categories for comparison**. You will not be able to simply plop your data in your research report, dissertation, or thesis. Your job is not simply to collect data but also to analyse it. Analysis, like writing your Literature Review and presenting your findings, always involves a process of selectivity. You can pare your data down by grouping data into proto-codes and then codes, proto-themes and then themes, especially those data that are reinforced by other data. Consider local issues that are in your dataset (specific to your project) but also think of more generic ideas, issues that might transcend the specifics of your dataset and might be seen in other settings. Social science is inherently comparative – whether implicitly or explicitly – so compare within and between pieces of data. Compare with other research published in the literature. Compare with 'official' sources like documents. Look for consistencies and inconsistencies. Group into categories or along a continuum. Organise your data.

3. **Remember your research questions**. Always keep a laser focus on the purpose of your study or the main thrust of your research design. What are you trying to find out? What are your research questions? Although you might tinker with these questions as the project matures, they should generally keep you on track. They should banister your analysis, guide but not constrain.

4. **Use your social scientific imagination**. Look for patterns in your data. How do your pieces of data sit and fit together? Look at pinch points and pivot points in people's accounts (Denzin 1989); what was important for them could very well be important for your project. Remember that private troubles are best understood as public issues (Wright Mills 1959). What surprises or shocks you in the data? Why does it surprise you? What does this tell you about your own assumptions and positionality? Consider the significance of this. Consider also what participants value and why. What is hidden, what is not so easily visible, what is difficult to articulate? What is conspicuous by its absence in your data? What causes discomfort or disillusionment? What is celebrated and what is criticised, and why? Importantly, you are not looking for generalisability in the same way as quantitative researchers. Specificity and insight are vital in qualitative research but think about how that can be extrapolated, made relevant to broader concerns.

5   **Select appropriate data**. Select the most revealing and impactful bits of data which best illustrate the points you are making and arguing and the grouping work that you have done. These quotes (if it is an interview or focus groups), extracts (if it is from a document or a fieldnote), photographs or drawings (if you are using creative methods) will represent and stand for other data in your write-up. Make sure they stand out as well as stand for the other data.

For more on general qualitative analysis, please see Atkinson (2015) who discusses the importance of identifying 'ideas' in your dataset.

Creating the Research Artefact

What program can I use to transcribe my interview? This is probably the most frequently asked question from students using qualitative data in their research projects. But, as Oliver et al. (2005) maintain, transcription should be thought of as much more than a technical concern. So, let us begin by thinking through what the research artefact is, before discussing how to create it. First, we should remind ourselves of the difference between primary and secondary sources. Primary research artefacts are documents created as part of the research project; they have been produced solely for the purpose of the research project. There are two types of primary research artefacts: (i) those produced by the researcher (in conjunction with the participants[s]), for example, an interview transcript, a fieldnote, a photograph; and (ii) those created by the participant, such as a diary entry or drawings. There are also secondary artefacts (again, not to be mistaken for secondary data analysis), which are documents and materials which exist independently of the research study, but which have been collected by the researcher to be analysed as part of the project. This can include a blog post, a tweet, a Facebook post (semi-public data but which require an account to access) a policy document, or a newspaper article. For this section, we are concerned with primary research artefacts and especially those created by the researcher, often in concert with the participant.

---- Box 6.4 ----

Research Artefacts

Important to note is that research artefacts like documents and interview transcripts are not an exact mirror of social settings. They are representations. They should show, of course, some likeness of a setting, of an interaction, of an event but they are not a carbon copy. There is a process of transmission involved. Consider too the role of the author and/or interviewer; what part did they play in creating the document, and should you write that out of your analysis or not?

Returning to the question about how you can transcribe your interview or focus group and, understanding that transcription is much more than simply a note taking exercise, it is good practice to transcribe the interview yourself. Transcription is part of the analysis process, and it is by listening and re-listening to the recording and then reading and re-reading the transcript that you can become familiar with your data. That said, there may be legitimate reasons why you might need a helping hand. There are various outlets that offer transcription services, some for free and others that cost. For example, if you have research money, you may wish to use some of it on a professional transcription service. This is something that you should signpost prospective participants to in your forward facing documents. Please also check with your university on the process they have in place to do this, as they may have preferred suppliers. There are also free software packages online where you need to upload the recording and it will transcribe the audio for you. You will need to check the small print here and work with your ethics committee to confirm whether this adheres to data storage preferences. A recent example is aTrain that is said to transcribe everything locally on your computer. Be mindful though, some of these tools and websites have clauses stating that they then own or can use the data after you upload it or may not store the data safely, so please be cautious and check whether these programmes rub against ethical procedures (see Chapter 4: *Being an Ethical Researcher*).

Another option is Microsoft Word. As a package that will likely be sanctioned by your university, this will more likely adhere to data storage preferences. Here, you can upload your audio file via a USB stick that forms part of a Dictaphone and then if you press the dictate button on the top right of the screen and follow the instructions to transcribe, it will create a transcript for you. While clearly not as accurate, as comprehensive, nor as well laid out as a professional transcriber, the transcript is useful for searching for key words and then finding out where they are in the audio file. For those of you who have interviewed or conducted focus groups online, platforms like Zoom and Microsoft Teams have a transcription function where you can set the recording to transcribe before it begins and then download the transcription once finished. Again, while extremely useful, a cautionary note that they tend to be culturally biased and do not always pick up accents well. For example, Jamie once said the word medicalisation, admittedly a technical medical sociology term, in his broad Welsh accent and one of these transcription software packages picked it up as fire station! Adhering to good ethical practice, at the beginning of the interview or focus group, please make sure you ask the participants if they are happy for you to switch on the transcription service.

The extent to how faithful you want to be when (re-)producing a transcript or document is often determined by the ontological question of what that artefact means to you. That is, do you view the transcript as a document that should be analysed in its own right? Or do you see the interview or focus group transcript, the diagram or the fieldnote, as something that allows you to get at, analyse, and say something about a setting that you are studying? From one position, we might want to consider conversation analysts (we return to conversation analysis as a data analysis technique later in this chapter). Conversation analysts are very loyal to the text. The clue that talk matters to them is in their title – *conversation analysts (CA)*. In producing a transcript, they tend to follow what is called the *Jefferson Transcription System* (Sacks et al. 1974), which captures not only the content of the interview but also the way in which participants' answers are expressed. They will include all the intricacies of everyday speech in their transcripts: pauses, repeats of words, interruptions, repairs, ummms and ahhhs. An agreed type of shorthand is used to indicate some of these inflections, like brackets, ellipses, and other combinations of keyboard symbols. For other analysts though, their interest is not necessarily concerned with what was said and how it was said, but what they – the analyst – thinks the participant (the actor) was trying to say. For non-CA scholars, stumbles, stutters, and clear errors may be overlooked and cleaned up. They produce what is known as an **orthogonal** transcript. For CA analysts, 'a standard orthographic transcript bleaches out crucial components of how humans perform discursive actions, and how they continuously analyse one another across sequences of talk' (Park and Hepburn 2022: 1.) For non-conversation analysts, these cleaned-up versions make the transcript easier to read and represents better what the participant was trying to say, if not exactly what they said.

Box 6.5

Representations

Important to note is that research artefacts, like documents and interview transcripts, are not an exact mirror of social settings. They are representations. They should show, of course, some likeness of a setting, of an interaction, of an event but they are not a carbon copy. There is a process of transmission involved, for example talk gets transmuted into text.

Researcher Reflection

Here is a short extract from an interview Jamie conducted with a Bigfooter. The first extract, while not presented in Jeffersonian form, is a reproduction of the interview that includes all the various stutters, repeats and informal phrases and breaks as well as the question that prompted the reply. The second is a cleaned-up version with only ellipses recognising a break in the talk.

- **Version one (full reproduction)**

    Question: Given you've done research in both Canada and the US, are there any differences between doing research in Canada and the US? And are there any differences in the ways researchers go about looking for sasquatch in those two countries?

Participant response (Todd Prescott): You know, it's more of a challenge for me to go to the US to do research because the border always wants me to ... to let them know what I'm doing, 'Why are you going to the US?' So, that's the challenge, and I'm ... and I'm ... I'm truthful, I'm honest, I tell them I'm doing Sasquatch Bigfoot research, and sometimes they have to call me into the office to have a discussion about that. So, that's ... that's the big challenge. But no, I wouldn't say there's any distinct difference, it's ... it's more of an individual difference with certain groups that have their own ideas of how you should research. I've found though that certain areas it seems, in my experience, that the sasquatch are different. In British Columbia, they seem to be a lot more curious. I've had so many things happen in British Columbia with multiple witnesses, so it's hard to refute, it's hard to deny. It's ... it's ... I can't deny it because there were other people with me, and we described the same thing happening. Whereas in Ontario, I find they're more aggressive. I've been bluff charged, I've had rocks thrown at me, tree shakes, things of that nature. Pennsylvania and New York, I haven't had anything happen in New York state, I've only followed up on reports, but I can't say I've had anything happen there that I could say, 'Well, that may have been a sasquatch, or it was a sasquatch'. I mean, you never really know. But in Pennsylvania, you know, we've had rocks thrown at us and we've heard wood knocks and things like that. But yeah, I think ... I think there seems to be a difference just in the behaviour of the Sasquatch, not necessarily the researchers, be it Canadian or American, other than the fact that individual researchers have different strategies. [309 words plus 40 words question = 349 words]

- **Version two (cleaned up version)**

Participant response (Todd Prescott): It's more of a challenge for me to go to the US to do research because the border always wants me to let them know what I'm doing, 'Why are you going to the US?' So, that's the challenge, and I'm truthful, I'm honest, I tell them I'm doing Bigfoot research, and sometimes they have to call me into the office to have a discussion about that. So, that's the big challenge. But no, I wouldn't say there's any distinct difference, it's more of an individual difference with certain groups that have their own ideas of how you should research. I've found though that [in] certain areas ... the sasquatch are different. In British Columbia, they seem to be a lot more curious. I've had so many things happen in British Columbia with multiple witnesses, so it's hard to refute, it's hard to deny ... I can't deny it because there were other people with me, and we described the same thing happening. Whereas in Ontario, I find they're more aggressive. I've been bluff charged, I've had rocks thrown at me, tree shakes, things of that nature ... I haven't had anything happen in New York state, I've only followed up on reports, but I can't say I've had anything happen there that I could say, 'Well, that may have been a sasquatch, or it was a sasquatch'. I mean, you never really know. But in Pennsylvania ... we've had rocks thrown at us and we've heard wood knocks and things like that. But yeah, I think there seems to be a difference just in the behaviour of the Sasquatch, not necessarily the researchers, be it Canadian or American, other than the fact that individual researchers have different strategies. [285 words]

(Continued)

For Jamie, the interview in this project was an artifice, a mechanism by which he could understand the community of Bigfooting, and he was keen to reflect what he thought the participant was trying to express. As an already highly contested subject, with many Bigfooters ridiculed for their beliefs, he was aware not to make anyone sound foolish by including all the errors and (needless) pauses that we all make in natural talk but which can look a little odd in text.

Conversation analysts, on the other hand, tend to deal in the detail of natural talk, especially talk that would occur outside of a formal scheduled interview, no matter how unstructured it was (see section *Language and Order: Conversation Analysis*). A simple but preeminent example where conversation analysis comes into its own would be if you were interested in how a set of 12 jurors come to an agreed decision or not. Here, turn taking, interruptions, hesitations, and re-framings would be pivotal signals that reflect not only how a group decision is made but who has more influence over whom and how they enact that. As an analyst, your interest might be in how compromises are achieved or how differences are reconciled. As before, the interest here would not simply be about what is said, but also who says it, how it was said and how others react to it. Other examples where CA comes into its own might include discussions between sporting officials when coming to an agreed decision, discussions between medical practitioners and patients, or the ways in which television presenters manage political debates and programmes.

Qualitative Data Analysis: Some Examples

There is not enough space in a generalist book like this to discuss step-by-step how you might approach the vast array of qualitative analytic techniques on offer. Rather, here, we outline and describe some of the more popular qualitative analytic approaches and, where appropriate, direct you to Sage Methods Datasets and Sage Foundations for further reading. Both Sage Datasets and Sage Foundations are pedagogical resources located on the Sage Research Methods Platform. In Sage Datasets, international scholars generously share some of their anonymised data and detail how you might go about analysing it from a particular perspective or approach. Targeted at students, there is a large bank of both qualitative and quantitative entries that describe the specific analytic technique being used, detail how you might go about analysing some data and conclude with a set of reflective questions for you to consider, including on some occasions extra data for you to work with. Data types range from interview transcripts, ethnographic fieldnotes, audio recordings, diaries, and diagrams. In Sage Foundations, international social scientists write introductory pieces ranging from brief, bite-size entries to lengthier contributions defining and describing methodological concepts and approaches. Let us now discuss some of the more pervasive qualitative analytic techniques.

Working with Text: Thematic Analysis of Transcripts and Fieldnotes

Thematic analysis is the most pervasive qualitative analytic technique and is particularly popular among undergraduate social science students. This is partly the consequence of thematic analysis not being tightly aligned to any epistemological or theoretical standpoint (Braun and Clarke 2006). Let us begin by highlighting a common mistake – themes do not simply 'emerge'. As a reminder, you are the instrument of analysis. You are an active agent in generating them. They do not simply materialise. They are identified, generated, or developed. Thematic analysis, then, is an approach that enables researchers to generate themes and concepts that *they* find embedded throughout their dataset (Rubin and Rubin 1995). A theme is something which you have identified in the data that relates to your research question and represents some patterned meaning. Different people have varying ideas as to what constitutes a theme. They can be broad or specific, e.g., (i) risky individuals, (ii) dealing with precarity, (iii) collaboration as competition, or (iv) emotional labour. Usually, though, it is a fruitful idea to generate local or specific themes (e.g. zero-hour contracts, poor pay, poor working conditions, high turnover of staff, 'dirty' work) before connecting them with more generic, broader themes (such as precarious working conditions). Thematic analysis is commonly associated with the analysis of interview and focus group transcripts but also extends to ethnographic fieldnotes. Researchers highlight themes by recognising patterns and then referring back to academic literature. After identifying themes, they then explore the inter-relations between themes by considering commonalities and differences. Braun and Clarke (2006) initially proposed a six-phase model for doing thematic analysis.

a   Step One involves becoming familiar with your data, both in depth and breadth.
b   Step Two is to generate nascent codes or proto codes. Codes refer to 'the most basic segment, or element, of the raw data or information that can be assessed in a meaningful way regarding the phenomenon' (Boyatzis 1998: 63) that you are studying.
c   Step Three is to search for themes. Themes are more overarching than codes and often require another level of analytic insight or interpretation. Essentially, they are (social scientific) ideas.
d   Step Four is to review these themes to make sure that the data organised within a theme coheres meaningfully.
e   Step Five is to define and refine the themes being careful how you name them. Braun and Clarke (2006: 92) warn that it is not enough to simply think about the story within that theme but to also 'consider how it fits into the broader overall story that you are telling about your data'.
f   Step Six is to begin writing up your Analysis chapter by embedding the chosen extracts in an analytic narrative.

But as Byrne (2022) notes, Braun and Clarke recognised that their original paper outlining the process of doing thematic analysis left several issues unresolved, and others open to broad interpretation. If a theme is so elastic, does it render it meaningless was one criticism. The other was the sense that themes naturally existed in the data. Their later work, often called reflexive thematic analysis (RTA) is more nuanced and more sensitive to debates on positionality (Braun and Clarke 2013, 2019). We might, then, understand thematic analysis as a continuum from semantic to latent interpretivism. To return to Byrne, the reflexive approach to thematic analysis emphasises the active participation of the researcher in the creation of knowledge, in which

> codes are understood to represent the researcher's interpretations of patterns of meaning across the dataset. Reflexive thematic analysis is considered a reflection of the researcher's interpretive analysis of the data conducted at the intersection of: (1) the dataset; (2) the theoretical assumptions of the analysis, and; (3) the analytical skills/resources of the researcher. (2022: 1393)

Pedagogical examples demonstrating how to do thematic analysis can be found in Evans (2018) and Orofino (2021), while you can read more on thematic analysis at Fugard and Potts (2019) as well as Maguire and Delahunt (2017).

Researcher Reflection

Using the same piece of text discussed in earlier chapters where Jamie interviewed Bigfooter, Todd Prescott, we have identified several possible themes worth more exploration. As a reminder of the extract:

> 'It's more of a challenge for me to go to the US to do research because the border always wants me to let them know what I'm doing, 'Why are you going to the US?' So, that's the challenge, and I'm truthful, I'm honest, I tell them I'm doing Bigfoot research, and sometimes **they have to call me into the office to have a discussion about that. So, that's the big challenge.** But no, I wouldn't say there's any distinct difference, it's more of an individual difference with certain groups that have their own ideas of how you should research. I've found though that [in] certain areas ... the sasquatch are different. **In British Columbia, they seem to be a lot more curious. I've had so many things happen in British Columbia with multiple witnesses,** so it's hard to refute, it's hard to deny ... **I can't deny it because there were other people with me, and we described the same thing happening. Whereas in Ontario, I find they're more aggressive.** I've been bluff charged, I've had rocks thrown at me, tree shakes, things of that nature ... I haven't had anything happen in New York state, I've only followed up on reports, but I can't say I've had anything happen there that I could say, 'Well, that may have been a sasquatch, or it was a sasquatch'". I mean, you never really know. But in Pennsylvania ... we've had rocks thrown at us and we've heard wood knocks and things like that. But yeah, I think there seems to be a difference just in the behaviour of the Sasquatch, not necessarily the researchers, be it **Canadian or American, other than the fact that individual researchers have different strategies**.' (Todd Prescott)

Three broad themes that Jamie identified are included.

1. *Bigfoot research as an unserious subject.* The interview participant's experience at the US/Canada border tells us something about how migration and cross-border movement are regulated not simply by security concerns but also by the purpose of travel, which is scrutinised for its legitimacy according to official and societal standards. This example illustrates the ways in which borders function as a mechanism of control, regulating the flow of people, ideas, and knowledge. Travellers need to provide a justifiable reason to cross the North American border, for work, to visit family, for a holiday, etc. Unconventional purposes such as Bigfoot research underscore the challenges faced by those whose activities lie outside societal norms with Todd being called into the 'office' to justify his travel intentions. That is, it was not obviously apparent to border control that this was serious reason to cross into the US.
2. *Witness testimonies as evidence.* There is variation in Bigfoot behaviour reported in different regions in North America with Bigfoot described as curious in British Columbia and aggressive in Ontario. This reflects how anecdotal and experience-based knowledge contribute to the overall picture of what Bigfoot is and does. Witness testimony and accounts play a crucial role in the study and public perception of Bigfoot or Sasquatch sightings as well as other cryptids, operating at the intersection of folklore, science, and societal belief systems. Despite the lack of concrete, scientific evidence to prove the existence of Bigfoot, eyewitness accounts have been a primary source of information and intrigue, fuelling ongoing interest and debate, and holding evidential weight within (some) cryptozoological communities.
3. *No cultural differences in the practice of searching for Bigfoot.* There is a tendency among Bigfoot researchers to adopt similar methodologies, such as using camera traps, collecting physical evidence (like footprints, scat, or hair), recording anomalous sounds and collecting eyewitness accounts, regardless of their geographical location. The use of technology and the influence of traditional media and social media to share findings and strategies further homogenises research practices, even across countries. That is, Bigfooting has stabilised into a shared community of practice with distinctive techniques and emerging standards. This has been fuelled by television documentaries and the ability to share resources and findings on the Internet.

Text as Stories: Narrative Analysis

Narrative analysis is typically associated with the 'narrative turn' in the social sciences. At its centre, it concerns how people storify their lives. It begins from the position that 'storytelling is a uniquely human experience that enables us to convey through the language of words, aspects of ourselves and others, and the worlds, real or imagined that we inhabit' (McDrury and Alterio 2003: 31). Narrative analysis is concerned with authenticity much more than any claims to truth-making – what Denzin (1989) might refer to as verisimilitude. It is a technique which is most commonly used with an extended piece of text (Blakely and Moles 2019). Rather than select shorter sections across the dataset and code them into themes, it enables participants to tell more of the story in their own words. The data presented then tends to be more detailed than other forms of qualitative analysis. Such extended pieces of text might be produced from life story or life history interviews that ask participants to narrate their biography.

Importantly, narrative analysis is not interested simply in the content of the interview but also in the way that the narrator (the participant) positions themselves in the account. What performative acts are present? How is the story told? Who are the main actors and why? How are identities enacted and actions justified? That is, narrative analysis focusses not just on what is said but how it is said, how participants account for things. Medical sociologist Art Frank is a key proponent of the narrative form. He identifies three narrative forms that 'patients' use to make sense of and communicate their experiences of illness (Frank 2009). *Restitution narratives* are centred on the patient expecting to get better. The narrative is characterised by the expectation that the illness is a temporary disruption and can be overcome (possibly with medical intervention). It is predicated on the acceptance that illness is a part of everyday life and that some days you will feel well and others you will not. In the *chaos narrative*, hope and/or expectation is pushed to the sidelines. The illness is the central character in the account, overwhelming the individual who does not imagine any obvious resolution. It is a narrative associated with chronic illnesses. By contrast, the *quest narrative* views the illness as a transformative event and that while no cure maybe in sight, something can be gained from going through the experience, such as finding new meaning in life, spiritual growth, or personal development. Here, the illness is repurposed as a life-changing event but not necessarily a life-limiting one.

Cathy Kohler Riessman is another central figure in the narrative turn in social sciences. As with Frank, she has considered the role that narratives play in individuals' understandings of illness as well as their experiences of healthcare. Her book on doing narrative analysis (2008) is broad in scope, relevant to a wide range of social science disciplines, and discusses various ways to tackle narratives by considering the content and themes of narratives or examining the accounts for form and structure, or focussing on the ways in which the narratives are delivered and performed. Her work also moves narrative analysis beyond simply a reliance on text and words to also incorporate images and other forms of visualisations.

For examples on how to do narrative analysis, please see Holmes (2021), Phillips (2015), Dunkley (2018), Loseke and Beahm (2015), and Mlynář (2017). For a comprehensive introduction to narrative research, please see Squire et al. (2013 and 2014).

Making Sense of Documents: Qualitative Content Analysis (QCA)

Probably the most pervasive approach to analysing documents – whether they are letters, newspapers, posters, prospectuses, diary entries, blogs, vlogs or other sources of digital media – is Qualitative Content Analysis (Silverman 2021). Here, textual and/or visual data is analysed for its content. But unlike quantitative content analysis – which systematically separates the content into predetermined categories and is concerned with frequencies – qualitative content analysis attempts to uncover underlying patterns present in the document. From a qualitative standpoint, there is little difference between QCA and thematic analysis and the difference in names is partly a result of their different epistemic lineages. QCA tends to have a hinterland in media studies and is said to have emerged out of the quantitative content analysis of newspapers (Berelson 1952), while the term thematic analysis is more prevalent in the social sciences. Strictly speaking, though, if you are analysing the contents of documents (printed matter including text, sounds, and images) by looking for patterns and trends, then you are doing a form of QCA. However, this type of analysis has been criticised for doing little more than enumerating the frequency (even research that is supposedly analysing documents qualitatively) with which certain items, words, images, metaphors, or categories appear in a text; the dominant concerns of the document so to speak. There are several 'datasets' entries by Steven Wright discussing content analysis, its development as an approach that has influences from qualitative and quantitative research, as well as how new qualitative software can be used to aid with this type of analysis (Wright 2023). Please also see Schreier (2019) for a thorough discussion of the history of QCA, the various types of QCA that can be undertaken as well as a description of how to undertake it.

Making Further Sense of Documents: Documentary Analysis

There is a wider form of documentary analysis that casts a critical eye over what documents are, how they are produced and to what end. That is, notwithstanding the fact that repetitions indicate something about the work the documents are doing as acts of persuasion, we could take this further than what a QCA approach allows us to do. As Bowen (2009: 33) states:

> Although documents can be a rich source of data, researchers should look at documents with a critical eye and be cautious in using documents in their studies. Documents should not be treated as necessarily precise, accurate, or complete recordings of events that have occurred. Researchers should not simply 'lift' words and passages from available documents to be thrown into their research report. Rather, they should establish the meaning of the document and its contribution to the issues being explored.

Here, we might consider why those repetitions are so potent. So, rather than simply recording how often something appears, it might also be worth considering what work is being done with those repetitions. Here, the structure of the document is important too. How is the document organised? How is it arranged? How does it hang together? Is there a logical relation between things, e.g., the text and the images? How is one category of things opposed to another and a further set allied with others? What underlying rules and principles bind statements together? In documentary analysis, then, you consider the text as a social practice; you may look at, for example, how power and hierarchy play out in text, or how classifications are accomplished. Importantly, documents are rarely produced in isolation, so consider how documents relate to one another, what is known as *intertextuality* (Brazerman 2003). It is also important to consider the relationship between that document and its socio-political context. Who is being represented in the document? How are they being represented or accounting for themselves? What is the document attempting to achieve? How does the document shape the way in which people, practices and policies are presented? This form of analysis involves a close reading and re-reading of the text as well as a good understanding of the status of documents. Liz Stanley's (2015) dataset discusses how documents cannot simply speak for themselves. Rather, they are produced, accomplished, and read. See also Stanley and Sereva (2019) on documents of life.

Language and Order: Conversation Analysis

As already touched upon, conversation analysis or CA is arguably the most formulaic of all qualitative analysis approaches. Grounded in ethnomethodology – the way in which order is produced and reproduced through social interaction – it involves the incredibly detailed analysis of naturally occurring conversation between two or more people. Conversation analysis has its own grammar. For instance, Harvey Sacks et al. (1974) maintained that there are three underlying components to any conversation: (i) the *speaking turn*, (ii) *the adjacency pair*, and (iii) *the sequential implicativeness*. Do not worry, these terms are much less daunting than they first appear. The idea here is that any conversation involves people taking turns, so your lecturer asks you a question (first speaking turn) and you respond (second speaking turn): any conversation, of course, needs at least two turns. These turns are usually structured in pairs – so the question-and-answer format, question followed by answer, or the greeting etiquette, acknowledgement followed by acknowledgement. This is then essentially the adjacency pair where the second utterance bounces off the first. Similarly sequential implicativeness links the first sentence to the next sentence. The idea being that was said in that first sentence has implications for what is said in the next.

Importantly, conversation analysis understands people as active, adaptive actors. There is a sense that, in every response, an individual is digesting what was said and anticipating what will come next, allowing each conversation line to link to the next (see Jefferson 1978). When speakers do not follow the turn taking convention, responding idiosyncratically, or mishear, people tend to use *repair* mechanisms to enable the conversation to continue. As you might expect, then, CA demands researchers produce extremely detailed transcripts, often using the Jefferson (2004) system of transcription notation. Indeed, CA researchers sometimes video record conversations since conversations are much more than what is being said verbally. Given conversation analysts are concerned with how people accomplish order within interaction, physical gestures, facial animations, absences, and pauses as well as the physical arrangement of the conversation are all pivotal. Using the Jeffersonian system of notation, keyboard symbols come to represent certain acts in the conversation (e.g., (.) means slight pause, and [ ] means overlapping talk between two or more persons). As described above, conversation analysis comes into its own when you are interested in aspects of power and categorisation, and is often applied to naturally occurring talk – such as recorded talk between a doctor and patient – rather than in formal research interviews. Sean Rintel's (2015) excellent dataset uses CA to analyse long distance relationship conversations over Skype. There are also entries on conversation analysis (Hutchby 2019) and on ethnomethodology (Sormani 2019) in Sage Foundations. For more on conversation analysis, please see Housley (2012). For ways in which people categorise one another in conversation, please see Smith (2022) and Martikainen (2022).

Talk Matters: Discourse Analysis

Discourse Analysis (DA) is another analytic approach which begins from the premise that talk matters. Simply stated, it stresses the ways in which meaning is derived from, and accomplished by, language. It analyses what people do with their words and how they go about doing it, or to rephrase in qualitative research jargon, it is concerned with the types of discursive practices employed, considering patterns of language across talk and the broader social and cultural contexts in which it is used. Indeed, it might be considered the footloose sibling of conversation analysis (CA). DA is more elastic and less formulaic than CA. That is, DA is not wedded to a particular perspective or hinterland such as ethnomethodology and does not conform to a single approach. However, from a social science perspective, at least, DA is rooted in the work of Michel Foucault, with some other well-known proponents of it including Gilbert and Mulkay (1984), Wetherell and Potter (1992) and Gee (2014).

Importantly DA can be applied to other types of text beyond simply talk, including broadcast material and written documents, and does not follow such a rigid transcription system as CA, arguing that this form of codification is not possible (in all cases). Taylor (2013) admits that defining the term DA is a challenge but argues that 'one starting point is that discourse analysis usually refers to a research approach in which language material, such as talk or written text, and sometimes other material altogether, is examined as evidence of phenomena beyond the individual person' (p. 2). Thus, while it is popular in disciplines such as social psychology, history, cultural studies and linguistics, it follows the Wright Mills mantra that the general is in the particular; that private social issues relate to public social concerns. For example, you could perform discourse analysis on early 20th century case-notes from United Kingdom (UK) asylums. This would not only tell you something about the person that the notes refer to, but also about how society treated mental illness at the time. For example, you could consider what language is used to describe the individual and how it fitted – or otherwise – with the broader discourse of how mental health was discussed at the time. Taylor (2019) has an entry on discourse analysis in Sage Foundations.

Critical Discourse Analysis (or CDA) is a particular and popular form of discourse analysis, more tightly aligned to the work of Foucault. Here, there is a specific consideration of the ways in which power and inequality are played out and reproduced through discourse, both talk and text. Two proponents of critical discourse analysis are Spivak (1988) who has examined the role that academic discourse has played in muting and othering cultures, and van Dijk (1993 and 1995) who has explored the ways in which the media, as a particular type of discourse, reifies and reproduces the values of the elite and powerful. Example datasets on discourse analysis include Harding (2015), while Grant (2017) has an entry specifically on critical discourse analysis in Sage Datasets, and Farrelly (2019) has a Sage Foundation entry.

Icons, Symbols, Signs: Semiotic Analysis

Semiotic Analysis, also known as semiotics, is concerned with signs, metaphors, and symbols. It is an approach that analyses symbols in everyday life, treating all phenomena as language that has meaning. It is particularly popular in linguistics, cultural studies, media studies, and communication studies. To this end, it works well with both textual data and non-textual data such as images and other pictorial representations too (Kress and Van Leeuwen 2006). Its roots are to be found in the works of late 19th century/early 20th century philosophers Ferdinand de Saussure (1916 but also see Boussiac 2006) and Charles Sanders Peirce (1883 and 1977) as well as Roland Barthes (1964), in which they argued that all human communication is a display of signs – something to be deciphered (Cullum-Swan and Manning 1994). Semiotics makes the distinction between the signifier – the physical sign such as an image or a sound – and the signified – -the researcher's interpretation of the sign (Eco 1978). For example, red spots might be the signifier and chicken pox the signified. Brand logos, mascots, and celebrity endorsers are also good examples of signifiers. For example, recently, supermodel Kate Moss partnered with Coca-Cola as their brand ambassador. In publicising the partnership, the Coca-Cola Company (2022) stated 'Kate Moss' timeless yet irreverent aesthetic defies categorisation and transcends boundaries; she has played a pivotal role in leading culture since her career began'. There might then be significant purchase for researchers studying business, advertising, and marketing to conduct a semiotic analysis of celebrity brand ambassadors – why were they chosen? What are they representing? How do they link to the product that they are selling? In this example, Moss might be seen to represent someone who has been at the forefront of fashion and trend for decades, someone who is still relevant today, someone who is able to cross boundaries to be recognised globally and across cultures, someone who is tasteful and not tasteless. Moss, then, is the *sign vehicle* for Coca-Cola – 'sign systems can be loosely or tightly connected or articulated, and the relations within them can be various: homological, analogical, or even metaphorical' (Cullum-Swan and Manning 1994: 446). Other examples of projects that would find purchase in a semiotic analysis might include etiquette at the debutante ball as part of the London season, rituals performed by the Royal Navy, for example lowering ceremonies such as Sunset or Evening Colours, British or American sign language, as well as hand gestures when diving. Have a look at the front cover of this book and consider what is being symbolised by the design. For an example of a cultural and social analysis of drawings that speaks to semiotics, please see the work of Rachel Hurdley (2018) and for symbolic analysis see Maggio (2021). Semiotics is also discussed in Dicks' (2019) entry on multimodal analysis in Sage Foundations and there is a shorter entry on Roland Barthes including semiology by Carrabine (2019).

Mapping the 'Situation': Situational Analysis

Situational analysis is the brainchild of Adele Clarke (Clarke 2005, Clarke et al. 2017). It is a chimera, located within the tradition of Glaser and Strauss' (1967) grounded theory, but which blends it together with discourse analysis while also being influenced by other meta-theorists such as Deleuze, Goffman and Wright Mills. It is an approach that would likely be more productive for master's or PhD students and/or those who have more of a grounding in social science and more time to complete their research project. Unsurprisingly, situational analysis takes 'the situation' as the unit of analysis. But surprisingly, a situation is not simply a single event, activity, footing, or setting; it can be various events and moments braided together. To this end, it is open to interpretation and loosely defined. What Clarke and colleagues endeavour to achieve is to show the ways in which social science researchers can combine datasets from a wide array of data types and for them to show how they relate to one another. To do this, they advocate making complex social issues and the relations between them seeable by producing three types of analytic maps located on different planes. Firstly, situational maps, which sketch out the main human, non-human, discursive and other elements of the situation of inquiry and the homologies between them. Secondly, social worlds and arena maps that lay out the major collective, social, and organisational groups and the alignments between them. Finally, positional maps presenting the major positions taken (or not taken) on critical issues. For more on situational analysis please see Clarke and Charmaz (2019).

Space, Time, and Everyday Life: Rhythmanalysis

Rhythmanalysis stresses the importance of time and temporality in social situations. Developed by the Marxist Henri Lefebvre (2004) and published posthumously, the basic proposition is that rhythms structure all social interactions. Environments including humans are all said to be rhythmical in nature, all said to have patterned movements. Lefebvre never set out a prescriptive way to do rhythmanalysis, but his approach has inspired others such as Coletta and Kitchin (2017). In a comparable way to how semiotics or semiology is described as the science of science, rhythmanalysis is an attempt to do the science of rhythms. Examples of sites to do rhythmanalysis include the city and urban life (street cleaners, gym users, daytime shoppers, the night-time economy), the body and disease (living with chronic illness, good days/bad days, morning sickness), waterscapes (seasonal changes, tidal changes), and music (trends, tempos). Here, we might consider differences between clock time (a social construction), circadian time, environmental time, the body clock, and melodic beats as various types of rhythms. Vigren's (2022) dataset is specifically concerned with rhythmanalysis and discusses it in relation to self-tracking digital devices, and Lewis' (2015) dataset, though not a rhythmanalysis, details how you might approach a temporal analysis of living with a chronic disorder. Lyon (2019) also has a lively entry in Sage Foundations.

Interviewing Participants About Their Experiences: Interpretative Phenomenological Analysis (IPA)

Interpretative Phenomenological Analysis or IPA is a qualitative analytic approach with its roots in (social) psychology. It is an approach used by researchers who are concerned with the ways in which participants make sense of their lived experience (Smith 1996). To this end, like most qualitative analytic techniques, it is a bottom-up, inductive approach. It is typically used to analyse semi-structured interviews which draw out in-depth accounts of people's experiences, especially accounts that discuss living with health conditions or living through life changing events such as disasters or war, but it can be used to analyse other interview types too. The analyst's job – in this case, you - is to **I**nterpret (the I in IPA) the **P**henomena (the P in IPA) as described and experienced by the actor or participant. **Phenomenology** is essentially the philosophy of experience, which privileges the subjective perception and lived experiences of individuals. To do this, researchers draw from hermeneutic – referring to the theory of interpretation (Smith et al. 2002) - techniques. Important to stress is that those drawing on IPA techniques, do not simply document people's experiences but also endeavour to interpret their meanings. To see some examples on how to do IPA, please see Spiers and Smith (2017) and Grantland and Peoples (2021). For a comprehensive overview, please read Spiers and Smith (2019).

Emotions and Attitudes: Sentiment Analysis

Sentiment analysis is the approach of analysing (typically digital) text to ascertain if the tone of the message is positive, neutral, or negative. The idea is to identify hidden human emotions embedded in language. For example, if someone on Snapchat stated: 'I am not a big fan of soccer' you might label this 'negative'. If someone on Instagram wrote: 'I am stoked that *Everything Everywhere All At Once* won the Academy Award for best film' you might label it as 'positive'. If there is a report of poor weather coming in on a newspaper website and someone wrote: 'Great! As if we don't have enough to deal with', you may decide to label this 'sarcastic'. And finally, if someone responded to the question of whether they thought they did well in an exam on X with the shrug emoji, you might label that as 'neutral'. Strictly speaking, sentiment analysis can be both quantitative and qualitative. Important, then, is that the subjectivity of the words used will depend on understanding the broader context of the discussion or dialogue. For example, when someone is being sarcastic or not is context specific and likely requires insider knowledge. For example, in the example above, if that same person had simply put 'Great' without the additional qualifier, would we know enough to determine that they were being sarcastic? Sentiment Analysis is a growing field in linguistics as well as in (social) computing (Maynard and Greenwood 2014, Taboada 2016). For further information on Sentiment Analysis please see Thelwall (2020).

Qualitative Findings Summary

This second section has described and discussed several ways in which you can analyse qualitative data such as text, audio, and visual data. Where possible, it has linked to Sage

Datasets and Sage Foundations so you can learn more about the various analytic techniques discussed in your own time. In Datasets, social scientists have shared some of their research data for you to play around with. Foundations include fuller more descriptive accounts of the analytic technique discussed. As with the quantitative section, the summary provided here is not comprehensive and we would advise students to use the information and references provided in this chapter to learn more about their chosen approach. It is also necessary to stress that in qualitative research separating out analysis from: (i) *epistemology*, e.g., grounded theory (Glaser and Strauss 1967), social constructivism (Vygotsy 1978), and critical realism (Sellars 1939); (ii) *theoretical standpoint or sensibility*, e.g., Marxism (Marx 1867, Adorno 1991), Feminism (Oakley 1972), Actor Network Theory (Callon 1984, Latour 1996, Akrich 2023); and even (iii) meta-*concepts*, e.g., Time (Adam 1994 and 2004), Speed (Virilio 1986) and Space (Livingstone 1995) is not always easy nor productive. They can all inform the way in which you approach and make sense of your data. As such, qualitative analysis is not as formulaic as quantitative analysis, and each project will likely have its own idiosyncrasies including significant researcher interpretation. It is imperative that you spend time discussing with your supervisor your analytic approach, and how it links to your broader methodology.

PART THREE: PRESENTING ANALYSIS

Once you have collected data and begun analysing, it can feel reassuring and quite exciting, but it can also feel slightly overwhelming. It can be difficult to know where to begin when reporting your findings and hard to ascertain the level of detail required. Often students report feeling like they are drowning in data, unable to see, let alone make it to, the shore. The question of how to determine when **data saturation** has been reached is often debated, particularly in relation to knowing when to cease data collection (Fusch and Ness 2015; Braun and Clarke 2021). However, regardless of the amount of data gathered, a process of data distillation and crystallisation remains necessary. We might understand this as a form of analysis or a form of analytical presentation. Continuing the watery terminology, as a social science researcher, one of your pivotal tasks is to wade through your data. You must critically filter out what is most relevant in view of your research questions. This is how you prevent your reader from feeling equally submerged. Another metaphor we have found helpful in relaying this to our students, especially for those that have collected qualitative data, is to think of data as we do photographs. Returning from a holiday, you will very likely discuss your experience with friends and colleagues. As well as summarising your trip verbally, you might show them some snaps that you have taken. Social convention and time, however, will typically prevent you from scrolling through the thousands of holiday photographs. Instead, you will select (or analyse) the photographs before curating a collection of those you feel best represent the experience you had. These are the 'findings' of your holiday experience. You can apply these same principles to the findings you present in your research. You cannot include full transcripts of interviews or focus groups. You cannot simply insert completed questionnaires. Rather, you will need to analyse your data before organising and presenting them as representative of the findings collected, always in relation to your research questions (see Chapter 1: *What Is Social Science Research and Why Is It Important?*). Here, then, is another example of the final written product not reflecting the circularity of doing a research project. To decide what to present analysis must then be performed but the Analysis chapter, when separated from the Findings chapter, will proceed the Findings chapter. Following that logic, we focus the rest of this chapter on providing tips concerning presenting your research findings.

Dissertation Findings and Analysis Chapters

Our starting point has always been to assume that most readers of this book will be preparing a written dissertation, thesis or research project. As we outlined in Chapter 1 (*What Is Social Science Research and Why Is It Important?*), this is an extended piece of writing, typically divided into a series of thematic chapters, much like this book. Every chapter should be able to stand for itself as a coherent standalone piece of writing. However, there should also be a 'golden thread' or throughline which weaves together your narrative across all these chapters. Self-evidently, the back-end chapters of your dissertation report, present and interpret the key findings of your research.

Now, as already discussed (see the Introduction of this chapter), some students prefer to write a longer, integrated Findings and Discussion chapter, while others prefer to write two shorter, separate chapters: the first presenting the findings and the next analysing them. There are disciplinary conventions which may influence these choices. Moreover, your course, your supervisor and your topic all might influence the final compilation of your thesis, therefore you should always defer to the guidance you receive on your course as to how you might structure your thesis.

Generally though, qualitative research projects tend to adopt the approach of weaving together the reporting, analysis and discussion of the findings into one longer chapter, perhaps called *Analytic Discussion* or, simply, *Discussion*. On the other hand, quantitative research projects are more likely to have two separate, but inter-connected chapters, called *Findings* or *Results* and then *Analysis*. Whatever structure is chosen, this section of the written dissertation should explain what you have found through the process of analysing the data. It is the culmination of your hard work, collecting and then making sense of the data. The chapter(s) should showcase your ability to undertake a research project capable of answering the specific research questions that you posed. Though these final chapters cannot be fully written until the end of your project, it is crucial to allow as much time, if not a little more, to write them as your earlier chapters. Findings chapters should be crisp, clear and comprehensive, and analysis chapters informative and thought-provoking. Fortunately, there are some strategies that can help you achieve this.

Use of Subheadings

The inclusion of subheadings can be a useful strategy when organising your Findings chapter. You might begin with a short, mini introduction to the chapter, perhaps reminding the reader of the research questions, the method of data collection and the number of participants in the study. This succinct introductory section might also map the structure of the Findings chapter (the way in which it is organised). The main body of the chapter can then be divided up into subheadings which reflect the research questions or, alternatively, into the central themes which you have identified. Do not underestimate the importance of these subheadings, they help provide clarity to the writing. The chapter should also finish with a short conclusion, summarising the main findings before transitioning into the next chapter. The chapter is typically written in the past or present tense as you are describing what you have found. If you have written two separate chapters, you could mirror this approach when structuring your Analysis chapter.

Extracts and Data Visualisations

For a qualitative dissertation, it is likely that the Findings chapter will contain quotes or extracts from interviews, focus groups, fieldnotes, and/or existing documents or images. These extracts and images should illustrate or illuminate an idea or argument being advanced. In this way, they work as evidence to support the narrative being constructed. By including direct quotes from your participants in your written thesis – what is known as **verbatim** quotes – you are enabling their voices to be heard in the way in which they want to say it. However, striking a balance in relation to the number of participant extracts to include in the Findings section of a dissertation thesis can be challenging. Whilst you want to ensure that you can evidence the points you are making, including quote after quote can make the chapter seem list-like and repetitive and you will eat up a lot of your valuable word count. The same is true for fieldnotes or images. A marker will be interested in your ability to select key extracts, notes, or images and to interpret these. This is your job. Your role as a social science researcher is to selectively choose extracts from across your dataset and bring them together to create a coherent narrative. As above, rather than reproducing the full interview transcripts or dumping large amounts of data in your Findings chapter, you are required to find key phrases and standout extracts, which contribute to your argument. Importantly, whilst it can be tempting to include every last detail of your data, the extracts presented must enable you to answer your research questions. The trick in qualitative research is to organise and give structure to what is essentially unstructured, messy data; the job is to create a story.

Quotes, extracts, fieldnotes, or images should be introduced and interpreted. While the data should always lead your analysis, your Findings chapter is close to completion when your writing outweighs or dominates the data to the extent that you could potentially remove the piece of data (whether an interview extract, diagram, or fieldnote) and the paragraph still makes sense. We call this *'owning the data'*. That is, the data itself simply becomes illustrative of the analytic points and/or narrative that you are making. Or to phrase it in other words, the data should not appear in isolation on a page. They cannot simply speak for themselves. This means that text should appear either side of the data and that extracts should not simply hang there. Before the data, you might provide relevant contextual information. For example, you might include whether the sentiment in the data was commonplace, and/or which participant(s) discussed it. As a reminder, though, to ensure participant confidentiality, you may need to change or conceal identifying information. For example, participants may have disclosed information such as the organisation which they work for, their age and their gender. And of course, you might have to deploy a pseudonym. Therefore, it is important to carefully consider whether extra details need to be obfuscated when reproducing extracts, especially if you have offered anonymity. Make sure you also label each piece of data. If you are using a document extract or photograph, be sure to label the source. If you are using fieldnotes, include the date and fieldnote entry number. If you are drawing from interview or focus group data, label the extract, but if you have promised anonymity, please make sure you provide a pseudonym. Following the extract, you need to interpret and discuss the extract in relation to the wider existing literature and tell the reader what it means, especially if this is a combined chapter.

Another way in which you can *own the data* is by leading with the theme or the concept that you are discussing rather than the individual extract or fieldnote which you have analysed. If you are able to do this, it is a strong signal that you have reached a level of sophistication and maturity in your analysis, and the data then feels like it is seamlessly evidencing the argument you are making. However you present the data, a reminder that if you are doing qualitative research to make sure it is qualitative. Markers will want to see meaty extracts or detailed images. They will not want to see one-off sentences.

For a quantitative dissertation, the Findings chapter will likely contain tables, graphs, or charts. These work to summarise large amounts of data in an accessible manner, which the reader can more easily interpret. In turn, they also help the reader identify patterns and trends and they can be referred to quickly and easily. Regardless, thought and care needs to be given when inserting these data visualisations. Some basic rules or considerations when reporting data through tables, graphs, and charts include:

- Give data visualisations clear, succinct titles.
- Label graph axes and include units of measurements.
- Consider your use of colour and shading carefully. Too many colours or shades can be confusing. Also, consider your colour associations and check whether your dissertation will be printed in colour or greyscale only.
- Present data in a logical order or format: chronological, alphabetical, left to right, etc.
- Start axes at '0'.
- Make sure data visualisations are not too busy nor cluttered. They should be clear and legible.

Typically, tables contain horizontal lines only. An example of a table of descriptive statistics (using fictitious data) is reproduced in Table 6.6. It is organised into two columns. The first column lists the demographic variables of interest, which in this example are Gender and Age Group. The name of the variable is listed in bold to enable readers to quickly and easily find the information relating to the variable they are interested in. Under each variable name, the possible response categories are listed. In the second column, the percentage of participants who gave each response is listed. There is no need to include a percentage sign next to each value as the column heading clearly states that the information displayed in the table is reported in percentages, as opposed to numbers. Including percentage signs for each row of the table would risk making the table appear too cluttered. Much like with qualitative research, crispness but not forgoing detail is the aim. Note, the bottom of the table includes 'N' – this refers to the total number of participants. The table also has a clear label '*Table 4.3 A table showing the demographics of participants*'. Regardless of what you are hoping to show, you should aim to produce clear, uncluttered tables making it easy for the reader to make sense of with a quick look.

Table 6.6 Descriptive statistics

Demographic variables	Percentage
Gender	
Female	54
Male	44
Other	2
Age Group	
18–25	12
26–35	23
36–45	45
46–55	10
56–65	3
66+	7
N=1562	

Table 4.3 A table showing the demographics of participants

Commonly used graphs in social science research reports include bar charts, pie charts, and histograms. Importantly, you need to describe and interpret any data visualisations in your Analysis chapter. Similar to qualitative data, you cannot expect your reader to do the work here. The accompanying narrative in the Findings chapter should clearly tell the reader what is shown in the visualisation and highlight key values. It is only by providing this narrative that you can demonstrate to the reader that you have a strong grasp of the data and what they mean. Any tables, figures, or graphs included in the Findings chapter will need to be recorded in a separate list of tables and figures under the contents page at the start of your thesis (see Chapter 9: *Submitting Your Social Science Research Project*). In the Analysis chapter, your job is then to infer what these statistics mean and how they fit in relation to the existing literature.

Argumentation

There are many ways in which you can develop an argument in your Analysis chapter. The idea of an 'argument' here is both the destination you wish to reach, your answer or conclusion, and the way in which you get there. Argumentation is therefore about positionality and convincing a reader or marker of your interpretation of the data presented. The best Analysis chapters are those where the reader is left thinking that it could not have been interpreted and argued in any other way. Rush (2021) presents three popular approaches to developing an argument which he coins:

a   *Pillars and a roof*, in which you have various lines of connected, but not dependent, propositions (the pillars or columns) which are then brought together at the end by an overall position (the roof). For example, you might have organised your analysis into three or four distinctive 'themes' or 'concepts' that you tie together at the end of the chapter.
b   *The logic chain*, in which there is a straightforward, linear structure where each proposition links to and follows the previous point. Here, you are building a coherent argument, with each point building on the next to form a coherent and heavily supported (and argued) thread.
c   *The dual or straight fight*, in which you set one position off against another counter-position in a punch followed by counter-punch style, before perhaps siding with one of them.

Again, there is no one way to organise your Analysis chapter but these three approaches all have their benefits.

SUMMARY

Analysing the data collected in your social science research project should be an enjoyable and stimulating experience. It presents a chance for your social science imagination to flourish. As with Chapter 5 (*Method of Social Science Data Collection*), this chapter is divided into three component parts: (i) quantitative data analysis, (ii) qualitative data analysis and (iii) writing up your Findings and/or Analysis. Drawing from a freely accessible, online dataset, we have shown how you should go about analysing quantitative data by describing the three sequential steps involved: (i) preparation, (ii) descriptive statistics and (iii) inferential statistics. Directing you to the Sage Research Methods Platform, specifically Sage Datasets and Sage Foundations, in the second section of the chapter we described a wide range of qualitative analytical techniques used in social science research, outlining why and when you would use them. In the final section, we discussed how you might think about your data and provided some tips on the ways in which to organise and present this section of your thesis.

Student Question

I am starting to stress that I am making claims beyond what I can support. How confident should I be in my assertions?

(Giovanni, Communication Studies Student)

Charlotte and Jamie say:

Great question, Giovanni. Firstly, working with the data that you have collected should be the most enjoyable part of your research project, so try not let it overwhelm you. Try and enjoy the experience. Second, it is good that you are thinking about what you can and cannot say with the data that you have collected, and we presume you are querying about over-reaching, or making claims that your data cannot support. The fact that you are thinking about this tells us that you are aware that your research project will not be able to answer every question on the subject that you are examining. At the same time, as social scientists, it is our job to say something, to have some confidence in the data we have collected. The trick is to write up your findings and the analysis of those findings with a critical eye. Discuss nuance and add caveats where appropriate. Show the marker what you can say with your data, and perhaps what you cannot. If you want to gesture to a claim but are less confident that your data supports it then use less bold language, reign it in a little. Remember the marker will likely be looking for evidence of that social scientific imagination but also methodological awareness, which involves evaluating what you know and when you are over-reaching. We endorse a form of *cautious assertiveness*.

WHAT'S NEXT?

Chapter Checklist

Table 6.7 Chapter 6 checklist

	Yes	No
I understand the steps I need to take to analyse quantitative data.		
I can choose the appropriate statistical technique to analyse the data I have collected.		
I can recognise which qualitative analytic technique is most appropriate to answer my research questions.		
I understand the purpose of data and how to present it in a written dissertation.		
I am familiar with a range of ways in which I can present an argument.		

Complete

Quantitative

Complete the table provided to identify what level of data each of the variables in your study contains.

Table 6.8 Identifying levels of data

Variable names	Level of data (tick the box)			
	Ordinal	Nominal	Ratio	Interval

Qualitative

Write a paragraph justifying your choice of analysis. Think about the following questions:

- Which qualitative analytic technique will you use?
- Why is this the most appropriate approach to analyse the data you collected?
- Does this help you to answer your research questions or do your research questions need to be tweaked?

Read

Quantitative

When you know which data analysis software programme you are using, read one of the following:

- UK Data Service. 2014. *What is SPSS 20 for Windows?* Available at: https://ukdataservice.ac.uk/app/uploads/usingspssforwindows.pdf (accessed 5 April 2024).
- UK Data Service. 2014. *What is Stata?* Available at: https://ukdataservice.ac.uk/app/uploads/whatisstata.pdf (accessed 5 April 2024).
- UK Data Service. 2019. *Using R to analyse key UK surveys.* Available at: https://ukdataservice.ac.uk/app/uploads/usingr.pdf (accessed 5 April 2024).

Qualitative

If you have access to Sage Datasets on Sage's Research Methods Platform, choose an appropriate dataset by using the search bar. Then read the information provided and have a go at the reflective questions attached to the dataset.

7
PRESENTING YOUR SOCIAL SCIENCE RESEARCH

Presenting your research is a central expectation of most research projects so that markers, peers, and other audiences can understand your work better, provide you with feedback and suggestions, and for your research to have wider impact. Typically, research findings are presented in written format, for example, a dissertation thesis or capstone project, a journal article, or even an executive report. However, there are other ways in which researchers can share findings and this is often done through presentations, posters, and increasingly via contemporary media such as blogs, vlogs, TED talks, podcasts, and even TikTok videos. In Chapter 7, we discuss the presentation of social science research. We provide practical advice on how to present research, including key findings or results in various formats, but specifically focus on presentations, posters, blogs, podcasts, and executive summaries. We also include tips on presenting research to various audiences and/or publics.

Chapter Objectives

- To recognise the different formats that can be used to present your research.
- To determine what makes a good presentation.
- To understand what makes a good social science research poster.
- To identify what makes a good blog post.
- To understand what makes a good podcast.
- To acknowledge what makes a good executive summary.
- To recognise the importance of knowing your audience.

INTRODUCTION

This chapter follows on from the preceding one on social science data analysis. In Chapter 6 (*Social Science Data Analysis*) we discussed at some length how to report and present quantitative and qualitative research findings. However, the focus of this chapter is different. Here, we aim to discuss the different formats, beyond the traditional written dissertation, thesis, or research report which you might use to share your research, and provide some helpful hints and tips on how to go about doing this successfully. For those completing a research project as part of an assessed university module, the written component might only form part of your final module mark. You might also be asked to present on your research experience and/or to create a conference style poster, or even a podcast. With this in mind, the chapter guides you in exploring five distinct approaches to disseminating your research, including (i) designing engaging posters, (ii) delivering compelling oral presentations, (iii) crafting concise executive summaries, (iv) creating informative blogs, and (v) producing captivating podcasts, with each format offering a unique way to structure and present your findings effectively. The emphasis here, then, shifts from presenting research findings to a more comprehensive exploration of diverse modes for articulating your scholarly work. By unravelling the subtleties of each format, we hope to equip you with a versatile toolkit for effective communication of your social science project.

DIFFERENT FORMATS

Let us begin with an everyday example of the ways in which the presentation of the same material or content can differ but also have some coherence too. For instance, take your favourite book, perhaps Dean Kootz's (1981) thriller *The Eyes of Darkness*. A book like this may be adapted into a film or a stage production. However, these other media, while sharing some similarities, will inevitably look different to the original novel. That is, while the substance of the story or the plot will likely remain the same in the film and stage adaptations, the way in which the story is presented might differ between formats. This is more than simply the difference between the written and spoken word though. It is not simply the case that the film cast read the book verbatim and then reproduce it; rather there is a form of interpretive elasticity on behalf of the director and actors. But the new adaptation might come in for criticism if it is deemed too dissimilar or unrecognisable from the original book. Some of you may be familiar with the film adaptation of Jodi Picoult's 2004 novel *My Sister's Keeper*, which tells the tale of two sisters called Anna and Kate. In the novel, Anna sues her parents for medical emancipation when they demand her to donate a kidney to her older sister, Kate, who has acute leukaemia. Without spoiling the plot of the story entirely, at the end of the book one sister dies. However, in the film adaptation, the other sister dies, leaving some fans confused and critical of the adaptation. In a similar manner to film and stage adaptations of novels, the way in which you present your research will vary depending on the format, e.g., dissertation or thesis, journal article, book chapter, conference presentation, or research poster. However, the key messages or the plot should be consistent across all the different formats to avoid confusing/frustrating your audience, although the emphasis, detail, and length will vary across each.

But the way in which you present information about your research project not only depends on the format or medium being used, but also the audience. For example, the audience(s) who read novels might differ from those that watch a film and therefore they will engage with the story in a different way (for more, see *Knowing your audience* section). Think about, for instance, when you watch a new television series. You will likely form an opinion on this TV series: an opinion on the quality of the programme, an opinion on the acting, an opinion on the setting or backdrop and an opinion on the ending or reveal. What you do with this information (or how you present it) will highly likely depend on the **audience** you are speaking with (friends, parents, colleagues, strangers, lecturers, etc.). To your friends and family in-person, you might discuss your assessment of the series in a more relaxed and open manner, perhaps using informal vernacular. To colleagues and/or over social media you might be more reserved and equivocal in how you present yourself. Similarly, when presenting your research, the way you discuss and report on what you have done will likely vary depending on your audience, e.g., markers, policy makers, practitioners, fellow students, family members.

In this chapter, then, we acknowledge that the way in which you present your research will subtly vary depending on the format and the intended audience. Despite these variations, the core messages of your research project should be consistently identifiable across the various formats. As a result, the advice and guidance we offer have commonalities across all five formats (presentation, poster, blogpost, podcast, and executive summary). Our primary emphasis is on the significance of clarity, selectiveness, and structure when showcasing your research. We explore a range of presentation formats and methods, whether your goal is to meet assessment criteria or to engage a broader audience. Initially, however, we delve into the topic of understanding the diverse audiences which you may encounter when presenting your work.

KNOWING YOUR AUDIENCE

There are several bodies of social science literature that have studied the relationship between communicator or presenter and their audience. One of the most well-known areas of research emerges from media, culture, and communication studies. Back in the first half of the 20th century, social science scholars such as neo-Marxists, Theodor Adorno (see 1991) and Max Horkheimer (see Adorno and Horkheimer 2016), and before them, political scientist, Harold Lasswell (1927), focussed their attention on the ways in which the State or the Government shaped and 'nudged' public opinion. Writing between the First and Second World Wars, they were interested in how and why propaganda material worked (so well), with Adorno and Horkheimer, in particular, making similarities between the propaganda industry in Nazi Germany and the 'culture' or

'Hollywood' industry in the United States of America (USA). Popular culture, they proposed, produced standard content which was lapped up by a mass, singular audience. This perspective was founded on the principles of behaviourism: the belief that behaviours are developed through a type of social conditioning. Notably, the most renowned advocate of behaviourism was the Russian scientist Ivan Pavlov, who famously conditioned dogs to salivate on command. Of course, the conditioning of the public through popular culture did not occur in a laboratory setting or as part of a structured experiment, but through their interactions with the media, such as newspapers, radio, and television.

The classic case they used to support this theory was a dramatic radio broadcast of Orson Welles' *The War of the Worlds* that hit the airwaves on 31 October 1938. Included in the broadcast was an urgent announcement that there was an alien invasion in the US. This led to widespread panic among some of the American public who, believing that this was a factual news story, packed their bags and headed for the road. These early 20th century theories on the ways in which audiences uncritically consume mass culture and the media, accepting what is said to be true and factual, rested on three assumptions:

1   The public are a homogenous blob or unitary group.
2   The public are passive recipients and not active, critical agents.
3   All media work in the same effective manner.

From these premises, the concept known as the Hypodermic syringe or Magic Bullet model of communication was developed. This model suggests that the media directly transmits messages into its audiences who receive them uncritically, explaining why *The War of the Worlds* broadcast led to mass panic. It bears a striking resemblance to another communication theory. Originating from the Public Understanding of Science (PUS), the deficit model of science communication portrays 'the public as blank slates or empty vessels' (Gregory and Miller 1998: 17), suggesting they are receptacles waiting to be filled with information which they accept without question. Here, the idea is that if the public are told that nuclear power is a safe and clean type of energy source by nuclear scientists, they will be accepting of it as a technology. In reality, of course, while there are *some* merits to these theories, if PUS research and most recently social media has taught us anything, it is that audiences do have agency, they have their own preconceived ideas, their own thoughts, and importantly can and do resist. That is, people already have existing likes, dislikes, tastes, distastes, experiential knowledge, and beliefs (see the House of Lords Report 2000). Moreover, as the PUS literature has also shown, it is inaccurate to talk about a singular 'public' since they are not uniform; rather there are various 'publics' with varying invested interests in specific topics (Wynne 1995, Renn 2006). So, just in the way that all students are not the same, neither are the public.

For Burawoy (2005) and others who advocate for a public social science, we should do more to actively engage with our various publics. He lists some American sociologists such as W.E.B. Du Bois (1903), David Riesman (1950), and Gunnar Myrdal (1944) who, through their writing, have transcended the academy, proving popular with a broader American audience. And just like these 'trade' books, success in delivering your presentation, putting together a poster, or producing a podcast is judged by the reader, the audience, or the marker. Therefore, understanding your audience is a critical aspect of considering to whom you are presenting, their pre-existing attitudes and knowledge, and how the chosen medium affects your interaction with them. In contrast to those early 20th century theories, media work in different ways. For example, in-person presentations have a live audience, while the Q&A session fosters a more dialogical exchange. A poster is more of a one-way, deficit communication strategy, but it can be perceived as a conversation starter too – a prompt, especially if you are expected to stand next to your poster and answer questions. A blog is likely to have a broader public including readers who are at some remove from the topic being discussed. Podcasts have an imagined – often loyal – audience, who unlike in real-time presentations, are not physically there but will listen to it asynchronously and will still want to feel as if they are part of the conversation. Executive summaries are more formal than blogs and are usually directed to specific publics such as policy makers or funders and are often written to persuade (if only subtly so). Knowing your audience and understanding the purpose of your presentation as well as the benefits and challenges of using your chosen medium should all be factored into your planning. We now move on to discuss five ways in which you might be asked to present your research, beginning with research presentations.

Box 7.1

The Audience

If you were tasked to prepare a meal for a group of people you would likely ask them about their allergies, intolerances, likes and dislikes e.g. whether or not they eat meat, dairy, and so on. In the same way, when presenting your research project, there is merit to get to know your audience beforehand. In this process, start to ponder what might pique their curiosity, what could hold less importance for them, and what questions they might pose to you.

COMPELLING ORAL PRESENTATIONS

In some instances, you may be invited or asked to present on your research as part of an assessed or non-assessed presentational conference. This presentation could either be in-person or online and you may be asked to present live (synchronously) or to pre-record and submit a presentation (asynchronously). Mirroring academic conferences which your lecturers attend, typically students tend to be allocated around 15 minutes to tell an audience about their research project, which might include a discussion of their main findings. This audience might include markers and peers.

If you are presenting in a student conference, the presentation is typically followed by a Q&A session, usually lasting around five minutes. Normally, presentations are grouped thematically, so it is likely that you will be presenting alongside two or three others whose research falls broadly in the same topic area. This means that the audience attending your presentation is likely to have a genuine interest in the topic that you are presenting on and will likely have some thought-provoking questions, but also some pre-conceived ideas. But presenting your research might extend beyond your university assessment and we have been told by students that they have presented on their dissertation findings at job interviews.

Structuring a Presentation

We are all too aware that the thought of presenting your research to peers and lecturers can be anxiety inducing. But presenting is not all on the day. Preparation is as crucial to a good presentation as it is for a written dissertation. When planning a presentation, it can be useful to begin by identifying the key messages that you wish to convey. While it might sound a long time, trust us when we say 15 minutes goes very quickly, and it is extremely unlikely you will be able to present on every aspect of your research project or include all your findings. Indeed, we go as far as to recommend that you do not do this unless otherwise instructed since your presentation is likely to be rushed if you cram in too much content. Your supervisors or project mentor and other members of academic staff that you interact with will be well versed in doing conference presentations and they too will likely only be allocated 15–20 minutes in which to present on only a small aspect of their research rather than an outline on the whole project they are working on. Therefore, structure and selectivity are paramount to good presentations, just as they are for written documents.

Our first piece of advice when structuring your presentation is not to begin drafting your presentation in a presentation package such as Microsoft PowerPoint or Canva. These programmes often force you into scripting your presentation in a restrictive way making the structure feel staccato and fitful. Instead, we recommend beginning by scripting your presentation in Microsoft Word or another word-processing programme. Once you have come up with a general story, with a clear beginning, middle, and end, and a couple of clear messages, then you can transfer to different mediums such as PowerPoint. For a 15-minute presentation, you should be looking at having about eight to ten slides and dedicating about 90 seconds to 2 minutes per slide. There is nothing more distracting for audiences than having too many slides in which the speaker is constantly moving through their presentational show. On the other hand, if you only use a single slide for the entire presentation, it raises the question of why use slides at all. Importantly, the slides are not the presentation. They are a visual aid which are meant to enhance your presentation. What you say aloud, those thoughts that you have put into Microsoft Word, is the presentation. A suggested structure for a research project presentation is outlined here, though again this will ultimately be dictated by the assessment task.

Introductory slide: Introduce yourself, state the title of your presentation and provide a brief description of your project and why you are undertaking it.

Grab the audience's attention by showing enthusiasm and hooking the listener in. It can be hard to introduce yourself at the beginning of a presentation, especially if you are nervous. However, it is important to clearly and confidently tell the audience who you are and what your project entails so to build a rapport with the audience. This should help you ease into the presentation too.

Outline slide: Outline the focus of the presentation (what you intend to do) and summarise the structure of the presentation. This not only helps you organise the presentation but helps the listener navigate the presentation too. In your outline slide, as well as detailing what you will be discussing, you may want to briefly mention what you will *not* be including in your presentation and invite audience members to pose questions on this aspect of your research project during the Q&A session.

Substantive slides: Keep the audience's attention. Assuming you are using a presentational programme such as Microsoft PowerPoint, Canva or Prezie as a visual aid, then typically you should spend a few minutes discussing the content on each slide. You may therefore decide to have one or two slides summarising the pertinent literature, one slide summarising the method employed, and two or three slides summarising the main findings. Importantly, providing some details of your research in the literature review and the methods slides can help foreground your (nascent) findings. Unless otherwise specified by the assessment task, we advise that you spend most of your presentation discussing your research findings. This is because no one will know your data better than you, but markers will likely know theories or concepts better than you. Your findings are also opportunities to show your original contribution to the field of research.

Alternatively, as your lecturers may sometimes do at conferences, you may decide to present on only one aspect of your research project, e.g. your methods, in which case you will again need to flag this to your audience on the outline slide and then decide how you divide up the main substantive part of the presentation.

For the substantive slides, try to avoid overwhelming the audience with information and stick to one idea or concept per slide and use bullet points to break up text. This helps the audience to easily follow your presentation and prevents information overload.

Conclusion slide: Leave the audience in no doubt about the purpose of your presentation. Summarise what you have discussed in the presentation, and why it is important. Reinforce the key take-home messages so that the listener takes away the main points of the presentation.

Questions slide: Thank the audience for attending the presentation and then invite them to ask questions as well as sharing your contact details for any follow up questions that the audience may think of at a later date.

Reference slide: Some people will also include a reference slide at the end of their presentation that contains references to all the literature (and images) which they have referred to. You might leave this slide up when answering the questions in the Q&A, so please make sure it is tidy and that references are organised accurately in alphabetic order with no mistakes.

The structure provided here is purely indicative and some of you may find it useful to have a few more or fewer slides. However, we caution against using too many slides as this can mean that you are changing slides on a frequent basis meaning it is distracting for both you and the audience and therefore may detract from your presentation. While it can seem frustrating not being able to present on all aspects of your research, this selectivity is critical for ensuring a clear narrative and to help prevent you from speaking too quickly. It also will stop you from over-running and/or, worse still, being asked to stop the presentation as you are out of time.

Producing a Confident Presentation

Presentations may be delivered synchronously meaning they take place 'live', or they may be delivered asynchronously, meaning that they are pre-recorded. Whether your presentation is synchronous or asynchronous, when it comes to presenting your slides, it is important that you come across as confident and as engaged in your research as possible. It is normal to feel nervous when presenting, especially if this is your first time presenting on your research project to an audience. Even the most experienced presenters tend to feel some nerves (ask your lecturers how they first felt standing in front of a lecture theatre!). Indeed, we have often found that students find the experience of presenting rewarding and they can often feel quite elated after a presentation. The trick here, again, is preparation! Practising your presentation in front of friends, classmates, or your family should help you feel more familiar with the content of your presentation and, in turn, more confident. Becker (2014) proposes a six-stage approach to help you become more familiar with the content of your presentation and to deliver a confident presentation. These practise steps help you move from reading your presentation from a script to delivering the presentation with just a few aids or prompts which help remind you what to say:

1   Script for content and timing (as Becker says do not be put off at this stage if you falter on content or timing – this is very much a first draft).
2   Script for timing only (here you are hoping that you have smoothed out most of the creases in the content).
3   Prompts for content and timing (here you have reduced that script down to prompts, you have no visual aids, but you are practising to make sure that the content works as a presentation, and the timing is under the allotted time allowing space to include visual aids).

4   Reduced prompts for presentation aids (at this fourth stage, you are adding visual aids to supplement the presentation. Your prompts should be distilled further).
5   Prompts and aids for impact (here you are practising as if there is an audience in front of you digesting the presentation and the presentation aids. This attempt should be to time).
6   Final rehearsal for confidence (this is your final run-through, and you should now be presenting with confidence, being extremely familiar with both the content and the timings of your presentation).

If your presentation is going to take place live but online, we recommend practising using this format at least once to allow you time to familiarise yourself with the technology. Encourage your peers to provide you with feedback and to ask you questions based on the content of your presentation. This should help you prepare for the real thing! A confident presentation is one where the presenter:

- speaks clearly and audibly
- varies their tone to keep the audience engaged and use pauses effectively to emphasise important points
- uses plain language and clearly explains key terms or concepts
- makes good eye contact with the audience
- uses gestures/hand movements sparingly to underscore key points
- is not overly note bound
- includes engaging, clean, and uncluttered slides that enhance the presentation and do not detract
- includes an appropriate number of slides
- remembers that there is an attentive audience in attendance
- has good flow and pace to their presentation and therefore does not talk too fast nor too slowly
- has timed the presentation to finish on time, but at the same time is not too short
- makes it clear to the listeners what the key messages are of the presentation
- has a conclusion slide that summarises the purpose of the presentation.

We must add here that using notes or reading aloud should certainly not be frowned upon *per se*. In some disciplines, for example anthropology, reading a paper is very much valued in which an argument is crafted and developed and, as already explained, we urge you to first draft your presentation in Microsoft Word. This type of presentation though demands of the presenter other skills. Reading it monotone can lose the attention of the listener, so while the paper has been crafted, delivering the presentation still demands a degree of performance to maintain the audience's engagement. In other cases, where people have memorised a script, the presentation can feel overly rehearsed and a little stilted, forgetting that they are engaging with an audience. In our opinion, the best presentations tend to have a naturalness and flow to them. Therefore, presuming you are not reading a paper such as the anthropology example, but instead presenting on your own research project we suggest that you use your notes as *aide-mémoires* only. In other words, you do not want your notes to be the presentation as you are likely to be marked on your presentational skills as well as any substantive content. It may also be harder to hear a presenter who needs to repeatedly refer to their notes since they are likely to be looking down at their notes and not at the audience. Likewise, if notes are overly long it can be easy for presenters to lose their place, therefore creating confusion during a presentation and sometimes leading to your running out of time.

As Becker (2014) advocates, when practising your presentation, it is important to time yourself. You will often find that you speak a little faster when you have an audience in front of you due to understandable nerves. Again, this is perfectly normal. However, if you notice that you are speaking quickly, use the moment you move to the next slide as a prompt to take a breath, have a sip of water, and then continue with your presentation. Though taking a 5- to 10-second breath might feel like a lifetime to you at the front of the room, trust us when we say that the audience will hardly notice this brief pause. In preparing for your presentation, you may also want to consider whether there are some points which you can expand on in the presentation in case you do find yourself racing through the material quickly, or conversely, even slides from which you can lose some content or skim over if you are running out of time. Again, rehearsing in front of various individuals will assist you in timing your presentation accurately, ensuring you know exactly which slide to be on at any given moment.

Although you can practise the presentation, it can be slightly harder to prepare for the Q&A section of a presentation. However, there are some things that you can do to help you prepare for and navigate this session successfully. First, begin by predicting possible questions which could arise from the content of your presentation. Ensure you are well-prepared and informed about the concepts covered. Also, when a question is asked, pause to fully understand the question before providing a response. You may even find it helpful to repeat or paraphrase the question before answering. The process of restating the question gives you a little extra time to gather your thoughts and formulate a coherent response, as well as ensuring that you have understood the question posed. Moreover, repeating the question from the front of the room ensures that all audience members have heard the question and, in turn, makes for a more inclusive discussion. Alternatively, you may find it helpful to write down the question or key words from the question as it is posed. Again, this can be useful in formulating a focussed, relevant response. It is important in the Q&A session to stay calm and composed, even if you are unsure of an answer to a question. Do not be afraid to tell the audience that you 'do not know' the answer to a question but do it in a way that enrols the questioner and does not feel like you do not know your subject. In these situations, it is important to acknowledge the question and express a willingness to consider it further. For example, you might respond with something like:

that is an extremely interesting question and not something I have considered in too much detail previously. However, I am interested in the work of [insert other names here] who have engaged with a different but similar issue but tying it to this point will be super useful for my research.

Remember that the Q&A session is an opportunity to display your knowledge and communication skills. Embrace the experience, and even if you do not have all the answers, use it as a chance to learn and grow as a presenter.

For those presenting online there are a few additional considerations. As previously stated, it is important that you familiarise yourself with the technology – whether that is Google Meet, Microsoft Teams, Zoom, etc. – being used for the presentation. Make sure that you can access the platform and that your microphone and camera are working properly. If you have prepared slides, ensure you know how to share your screen. Before starting the presentation, we advise closing other windows or documents on your screen to make it quick and easy for you to locate and share your presentation. It is also important that you find a nice quiet space to present with minimum distractions. Try to set yourself up in a space with no potential distractions for you or for your audience. Try to position yourself facing a window so to improve the lighting. If presenting online synchronously, you may receive questions via a chat bar as well as verbally. In circumstances where you receive questions via the chat bar, it is particularly useful if you can repeat the question or paraphrase the question for the whole audience before providing a response. Finally, if you are doing a synchronous presentation online and technical glitches occur, do not panic! This happens to all of us, even in the lecture theatre. This is not your fault. Stay calm and try to resolve the issue. The chair of the session should support you to try to ensure your presentation is able to continue.

Creating Presentation Slides

Firstly, a reminder that the key to an effective presentation is a well put together account of your research project and not a set of flashy slides. That said, typically, people will create presentation slides to support their presentation. Most people use Microsoft PowerPoint to create these slides. But there are other platforms which can be used to make interesting, eye-catching presentation slides such as Prezie or Canva. Regardless of the platform you decide to use to create your slides, there are a few stylistic elements which you should be aware of to ensure that your presentation is both engaging and impactful but equally does not detract from what you say.

When designing your slides, it is crucial to think about their appearance from the perspective of those watching your presentation in the audience. To do this, think carefully about your chosen fonts and the size of the text. You want your slides to aid your presentation and not distract. Therefore, the font size and type need to be legible and easy to read from the back of a large lecture theatre (even if you are presenting in a small room!). They should also be consistent throughout. Critically, your slides should not resemble an information dump. Just as a piece of writing is crafted, slides should be curated. They should simply capture the essence of that part of the presentation rather than reproduce word for word what you say. Otherwise, what function have the slides served other than being your script rendering you – the presenter – redundant?

As others have said before, never make your audience work too hard to understand the crucial points of the presentation (Clark and Sousa 2018, Sousa and Clark 2019). Most presentations contain bullet points or key words which you can then expand upon in your presentation. This is a particularly crucial point for qualitative researchers who will typically want to include some data extracts. Here, ellipses are your friend. While you might decide to use your notes to read a data extract verbatim, you should really only use the most pertinent sentences on the slideshow itself. Alternatively, you may reverse the roles, by including a chunkier extract on the slide, but only read aloud a line or two that you have bolded on screen.

Additionally, you might choose to incorporate visuals like graphs, charts, tables, or images on certain slides to simplify and/or clarify complex information. Have you ever come across the saying 'a picture is worth a thousand words'? This expression is believed to have been first introduced by Fred R. Barnard in 1921 to advertise Printers' Ink, and it succinctly illustrates the effectiveness of visuals in communicating what could be lengthy, descriptive pieces of texts. As with the written research project, it is essential that any figures included are clear and labelled accordingly so that the audience can easily determine what they are looking at. Please also make sure they are easy to understand. Even though the inclusion of visualisations can be attractive to the eye and bring some colour to your presentation, it is important that the visualisations you choose to include are meaningful and contribute to the narrative of your presentation. For example, if your research project is exploring the school subject preferences of children under the age of ten, unless you are discussing the ways in which young people measure their height then a picture of a giraffe may seem a little odd and distracting. You might scoff, but this happens more often than you would expect. Though perhaps not as colourful, an image of a classroom or a pie chart showing reported favourite school subjects from your participants would be more meaningful in this scenario and would add to the overall presentation. Where possible, and making sure that you are adhering with ethical principles, always try to use your own photographs as they are personal, more likely to capture the meaning of the content and, importantly, you own the copyright. If this is not possible, please make sure that the images you use are not copyrighted. There are several sites with stock photographs which are free to use, for example, unplash.com.

As with written findings described in Chapter 6 (*Social Science Data Analysis*), you will need to make sure that any data visualisations included in your presentation are explained and interpreted. A further stylistic consideration when preparing a presentation is whether to use animations. While animations can seem fun and entertaining, they can also be distracting and some can take a few seconds to load, thus eating into your valuable presentation time. We advise that if you are keen to use animations, then do so sparingly and cautiously.

We also often get asked can I use a video in the presentation? Unless the videos are data, you should ask yourself what purpose the video serves other than using up a few minutes of your time? For each second a video plays, that is one less second of you speaking and engaging with your audience.

Finally, when preparing your presentation slides, we strongly recommend that you reflect on what you have liked and not liked about other presentations (including lectures), which you have sat in. Consider what makes an engaging lecture and see if you can replicate this style in your own presentation. In Figures 7.1, 7.2 and 7.3 we have produced example slides which you may see in a presentation. Figure 7.1 shows a clear, uncluttered slide outlining the methodological approach used in the study. From the slide, the audience understands how the presenter collected the data. Importantly, this information is stated in short bullet point format. The slide includes a simple image of two speech bubbles, reflecting the content of the slide.

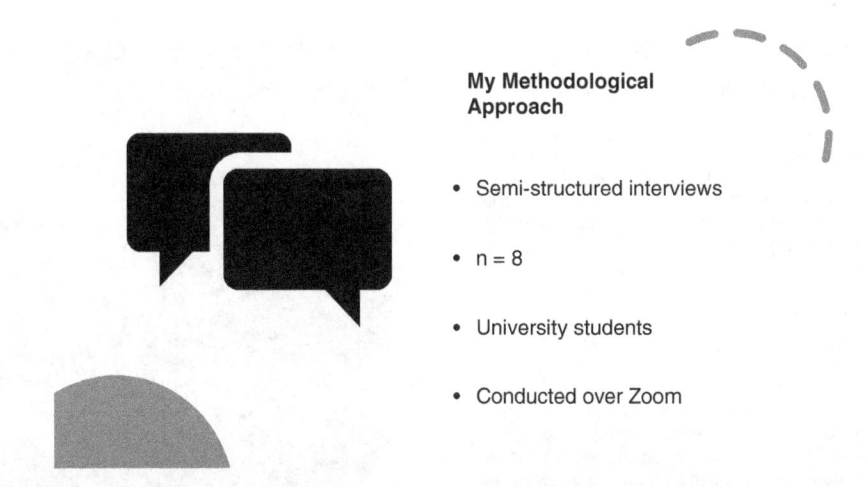

Figure 7.1 An example presentation slide outlining methodological approach

Figure 7.2 shows a slide presenting quantitative findings. Here, the presenter has made a clustered bar chart and has filled the whole slide with this visual making it easy to read and interpret at a glance and visible from the back of a large room. The graph has a clear title and there is a key at the bottom of the slide to help the audience understand what the different colour bars depict.

Finally, Figure 7.3 shows a slide containing qualitative findings. Again, a visual has been used here and you can see that the original creator of the image has been attributed. The data extract has been pasted on to the slide with key segments bolded to help the audience navigate the data without feeling overwhelmed.

Attendance at Different Gyms by Age

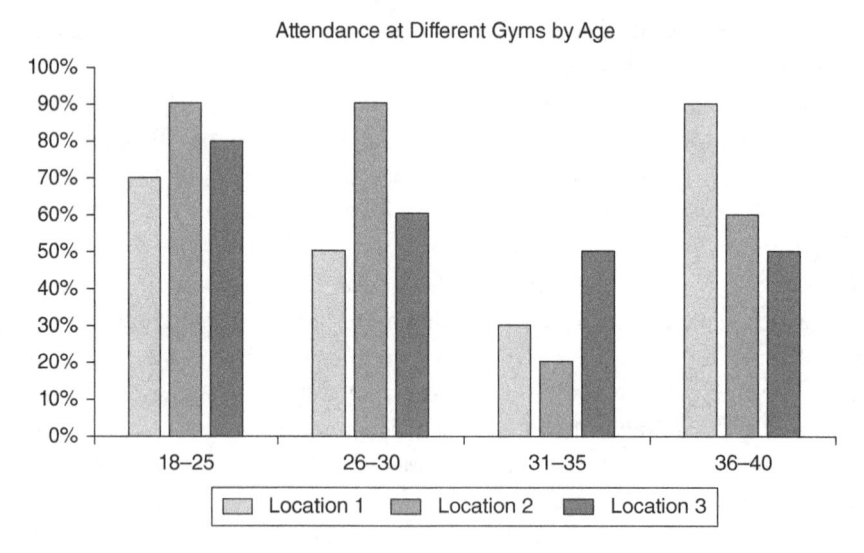

[Bar chart showing attendance percentages across age groups 18–25, 26–30, 31–35, 36–40 for Location 1, Location 2, and Location 3:
- 18–25: Location 1 = 70%, Location 2 = 90%, Location 3 = 80%
- 26–30: Location 1 = 50%, Location 2 = 90%, Location 3 = 60%
- 31–35: Location 1 = 30%, Location 2 = 20%, Location 3 = 50%
- 36–40: Location 1 = 90%, Location 2 = 60%, Location 3 = 50%]

Figure 7.2 An example presentation slide outlining quantitative findings

Photo by Jon Sailer on Unsplash

Qualitative Findings

"It's more of a challenge for me to go to the US to do research because the border always wants me to let them know what I'm doing, **"Why are you going to the US"?** So, that's the challenge, **and I'm truthful, I'm honest, I tell them I'm doing Sasquatch Bigfoot research,** and sometimes they have to call me into the office to have a discussion about that. So, that's the big challenge. But no, I wouldn't say there's any distinct difference [...]

I've found though that in certain areas it seems [...] that the sasquatch are different. **In British Columbia, they seem to be a lot more curious.** I've had so many things happen in British Columbia with multiple witnesses, so it's hard to refute, it's hard to deny [...] because there were other people with me, and we described the same thing happening. **Whereas in Ontario, I find they're more aggressive.** I've been bluff charged, I've had rocks thrown at me, tree shakes, things of that nature" (Todd Prescott)

Figure 7.3 An example presentation slide outlining qualitative findings

ENGAGING POSTERS

In some instances, and again mirroring academic conferences, you may also be asked to create a research poster summarising your research project. This is a presentational tool that originated in the natural and life sciences but is now increasingly commonplace in the social sciences. Social science posters provide a snapshot or summary of your research, and they can be particularly beneficial if you are seeking feedback on initial findings and interpretations. Posters tend to be more concise and focussed than research presentations, and, of course, less interactive. Whereas the slides are simply an aide to a presentation, a poster can be its own form of (one-way) communication. Typically, posters are A1 or even A0 in size and are displayed alongside several other posters in an exhibition space at a conference or event. Normally, the researcher is expected to stand next to their poster to answer any follow-up questions which a conference attendee may have, but this is not always the case. This then repurposes the poster as something of a conversation starter (Rossi et al. 2020), an artefact to attract the attention of a passer-by who will then, mirroring the Q&A presentation format of a presentation, hopefully begin asking you further questions about your research project. Rowe and Ilic (2011) stress that this format means that you need to create a poster which will encourage people to stop, read, and ask further questions. They encourage you to think about what images and messages capture your attention when shopping and to try and incorporate some of these ideas into their own posters.

But how do you make your poster stand out from the crowd and attract someone's attention? For Rossi et al. (2020: 37), a poster should resemble a 'graphical abstract'. Much like creating presentation slides, making an academic poster involves preparation, time, and careful consideration concerning the choice of colour, font, images, and other visualisations. Given the generous size of an academic poster, it can be tempting to fill the space with lots of text detailing your study or several images cluttering the page. However, we strongly advise against this. Again, it is imperative that you are selective when designing and creating your research poster. We recommend that an A1 academic poster contains no more than 500 words and no more than three data visualisations. Remember that others need to be able to identify the key messages quickly and easily on your poster and that you may not be present when they look at your poster. This is one of the key differences between a poster and a research presentation; a research poster requires the audience to make sense of your research and distil the key messages themselves, whereas in a presentation you build a narrative for them. The less cluttered your poster is, the simpler it becomes for your audience to grasp the key messages you are conveying.

Creating a Research Poster

Typically, a research poster will contain the following sections:

> Your name and the title of your research project
>
> Research aims and/or research questions
>
> Key literature
>
> A summary of the methodological approach
>
> Two or three main findings
>
> Limitations of the research
>
> Ideas for future research

We include a template of a typical poster in Figure 7.4.

| LOGO | Title |
| | Name |

Research Question(s)	Main Finding 1	Limitations
•		•
•		•

Key Literature	
•	Main Finding 2
•	

Method		Ideas for Future Research
•		•
•		•

| References: |

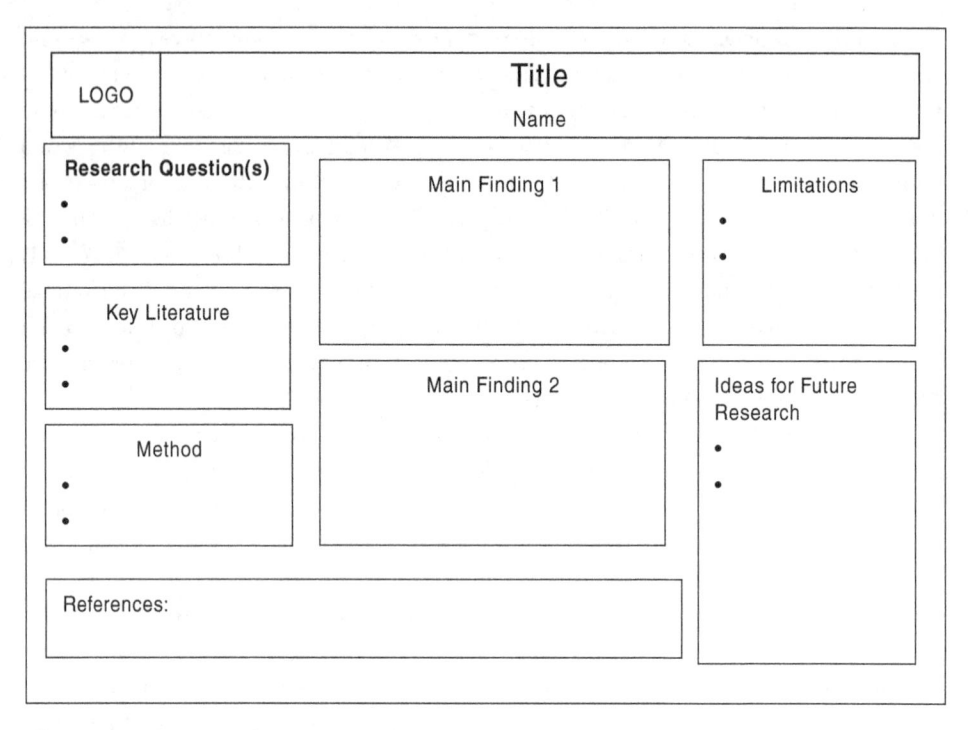

Figure 7.4 Template for an academic poster

Note how the content on the poster resembles some of the sections in a written dissertation. Notice too that Figure 7.4 uses boxes to organise and differentiate the different sections of the research poster. The white space between the boxes is vital; it helps give the poster a clear and uncluttered finish. Likewise, the earlier stages of the research process are described on the left-hand side of the poster, whereas the recommendations for future research appear on the right-hand side of the poster. This creates a coherent structure for the research poster and reflects the fact that in most countries, people read from left to right. You may even want to go further and number the boxes so that the audience knows the intended order that they are to be read in (Rowe and Ilic 2011).

Each box has a short heading which is in bold, making it stand out from the page. The individual boxes also contain bullet points. Like presentation slides, full sentences should mostly be avoided on research posters, and instead, bullet points should be used to summarise key information. Keeping the text concise enables you to ensure that the size of the text is sufficiently large to be read from a distance. We recommend for an A1 size poster that the main body of the text is at least 20 pts in size, the headings are at least 30 pts in size, and the title can be as big as 100 pts. Again, choosing clear fonts which are easy to read is also important here. Crucially, as with presentations, the font used in each of the elements of the research poster should be consistent. In other words, the same font style should be used for all headings, and the same style and size fonts should be used for all bullet points. If you feel it necessary to emphasise a particular point on your poster, it can be helpful to bold the text.

The space on the poster dedicated to findings should be the largest. This is so that you can accommodate any data visualisations you decide to include. As with presentations, these may include charts, graphs, tables, or even quotes. Baker (2021) suggests that 40–50% of a research poster be filled with graphics, 20–25% should contain text and the remainder should be blank space. These are, of course, only rough estimates, guides rather than rules. Like presentation slides, it is necessary to ensure that visuals are clearly labelled and easy for others to interpret. It can also be a useful idea to include a logo on your research poster. This instantly tells delegates or markers where you are from and who your research is funded by (if applicable).

Colour is another key consideration when designing a research poster. Your choice of colour(s) can make a research poster more appealing. However, you need to ensure that the text is still readable and that the colours complement each other. In some instances, it can be effective to use the colours from your university or department's logo to create a colour theme for your poster. This can help avoid the trap of using a large assortment of clashing colours. Crucially, any writing on top of a coloured background needs to be easily read. For the visually impaired, bright colours are best since they reflect light. Equally, to accommodate colour-blind readers, do not combine red with green. Solid colours such as orange and red tend to be easier to be seen than pastel colours. Studies have also shown that the colour green tends to attract the eye too (Jimison 2017).

When it comes to making your research poster, we recommend using a programme such as Microsoft PowerPoint. If you do decide to use Microsoft PowerPoint to create your research poster, you will need to change the size of the default slide (to A1 or A0 depending on the submission guidance provided). However, as with presentational slide shows, there are different software options available such as Canva and Prezzie. Once you have completed your poster, it is a smart move to convert it into a PDF file. This is because this allows you to view the poster as it will appear when printed. This can be particularly useful if someone else is printing your poster on your behalf.

Box 7.2

Things to Consider Before Printing Your Research Poster

Is my poster clear, concise, attractive, and readable?

Are graphs, charts, images, and extracts easy to understand and labelled appropriately?

How does it look from 10 feet away? (Try zooming out and then walking away from your laptop.)

What impression will the reader get if they look at it for just three seconds?

Does the balance of text, graphics, and white space work? (Remember, employing colour thoughtfully can help highlight important areas without overwhelming the reader.)

Does the reader instantly know where to start reading?

Does the poster get across the message(s) you want to convey?

Are the title and your name clearly visible?

INFORMATIVE BLOGPOSTS

Although a blogpost is a piece of writing, and so has arguably more in common with a written dissertation than a presentation or research poster, it tends to be much shorter and more succinct than a written research dissertation or report. Also, blogs – for short – are designed to be read by a much broader group of people than just academics or fellow students (see *Knowing your audience*). It is also important to state emphatically that there are various types of blogs: topic-based blogs, celebrity and gossip blogs, professional blogs, educational blogs (Hookaway 2008), and that a social science blog is almost a genre on its own. Creating a social science blogpost therefore requires a blend of academic rigour and engaging storytelling. We again advise that you first draft your blog in Microsoft Word before transferring it over to a programme such as WordPress. Microsoft's in-built grammar checker is easier to read than most blog programmes, so drafting your blog in Microsoft word makes it easier to spot mistakes such as typographical errors. Most blog posts contain fewer than 1,000 words. As such, the challenge here is conveying what you have done and what you have found in a concise and accessible manner. Therefore, decisions on what to include and exclude in your blog are again paramount.

As blogs are a product of the online world (Rettberg 2014), it can be helpful to devote some time to considering a snappy and enticing title that people can find on search engines. You need to think of a title which captures the essence of the research but at the same time will stand out and appeal to others. The LSE (London School of Economics) impact blog (2024) has become a successful and popular space for academics to share developments in their research fields. The London School of Economics (LSE) blog website offers broad advice on crafting effective blog posts that draw from research. It provides tips on catering to a wide audience by sharing insights into engaging writing, structuring content, and ensuring the relevance and clarity of the information presented. These include:

1 Making sure that your writing is accessible to a more general audience.
2 Avoiding jargon and overly complex terminology.
3 Keeping paragraphs short, succinct, and snappy.
4 Making sure the main point of the article is captured up front to catch the readers' attention (this can be different from other types of writing).
5 Ensuring the blog works as a standalone piece of writing even if it is drawn from a larger piece of writing; that is, include a beginning, middle, and punchy end.

Gardiner et al. (2018) describe different approaches which authors can take to ensure that their blogs are made accessible to wider audiences. These authors found that the use of images could increase the appeal of blogs to readers outside of the author's discipline or direct, close community. They also found that videos improve the appeal of blogs to those inside the field. Beyond following these tips, we recommend trying to use shorter sentences and/or paragraphs to enhance the readability of the piece. Try to make the content engaging and interesting and put thought into the terms that you are using and what readers might search for on the Internet.

Finally, writing to a shorter word count can seem appealing. But writing to a shorter word count can be more challenging than a larger one. Words are at a premium in a blog, meaning that your writing needs to be sharp, crisp, and pithy – unneeded sentences stand out more in shorter pieces of writing.

Promoting Your Blogpost

It can be advantageous to promote your blog on social media. This can help you reach a wider audience (possibly even a global audience) and may lead to more discussion about your research. Indeed, in 2023, it was estimated that just under 5 billion people globally used social media (Wong 2023). Including rhetorical questions or calls-to-action at the conclusion of a blog can be a particularly powerful way to encourage wider discussion and debate about your research on social media (see Carrigan 2016 for more on blogging). Mollett et al. (2017) provide more guidance on blogging, podcasts (see captivating podcasts), and on how to promote these outputs via social media. Here, you might decide to post your blog content or links to your blog on Facebook, X, Instagram, or LinkedIn. This is an effective way of building a community of readers. To keep their attention, you will need to keep posting blogs regularly. Again, understanding your audience, their likes, dislikes, and the way they engage with your content is important. Tools like Google Analytics can provide help too.

CAPTIVATING PODCASTS

Podcasts involve an audio recording of you telling an audience about your research. This may include details of how you came to research your chosen topic, the process of carrying out your research as well as its main findings. It is a medium popular with journalism and science communication students. The absence of video or slides, or even a live audience, can make it difficult to connect with listeners through this format. Typically, podcasts are media which individuals listen to on their own, perhaps whilst completing another task such as driving, exercising, cooking a meal, before falling asleep, etc. Therefore, creating a clear and engaging narrative is key here. Relatedly, you should avoid creating a podcast which is overly long. We recommend that it does not last longer than 30 minutes, and probably much shorter for a student project (10–15 minutes would likely be sufficient). It can be extremely challenging for the audience to stay engaged when there is only audio to rely on and the inability to respond immediately. Like blogs, having a snappy title that entices a listener and including some rhetorical questions for the listener to consider can be a useful technique to keep the audience engaged. Consider, here, who your potential listeners are and tailor the content accordingly. Some of the techniques used for promoting a blog are equally pertinent for promoting a podcast.

It is important to introduce yourself clearly at the beginning of a podcast. This allows your audience to 'get to know you' and picture you whilst listening to you discuss your research project. Of course, unlike the other modes of presenting discussed in this chapter, a podcast may involve other people in its production. It is possible that when you prepare a podcast about your research you enlist the help of a friend or colleague who can take on the role of the 'interviewer'. The interviewer is then a sort of stooge, responsible for asking questions about the research project. In this scenario, the interviewer is representing the audience by asking questions which are likely to be of interest and relevance to listeners. In other circumstances, you may discuss a specific research topic or area of interest with peers to form a podcast. This 'multi-host approach' can be useful to present a diversity of perspectives on one particular issue. It also means that it is a productive idea to discuss with friends and peers your research in advance of putting together the podcast. This should provide you with a good steer as to what aspects they find interesting and the types of questions they would ask. Another technique is discussed by Kinkaid et al. (2021). They explain that podcasts can provide the opportunity to hear from the participants themselves and that in dialogue with the interviewer this produces a more polyvocal product. Of course, you will need to be mindful of this approach that it does not reveal identities if you have promised anonymity. Another approach would be to have people stand in as speakers for your participants. Again, this requires thought and considerations in relation to voice, authenticity, and representation (see Chapter 4: *Being an Ethical Researcher*).

As with online presentations, podcasts involve a technical aspect. A good quality microphone and recording equipment are crucial to produce good audio. It is then important to check that your microphone is working correctly before you begin recording. We recommend that you identify a quiet space where you can record your podcast with few distractions. Brumley (2013) provides more guidance on setting up and recording your podcast.

Editing is another crucial task before posting a podcast. This is not simply a technical accomplishment but also requires a clear sense of the story that you are telling. Editing a podcast might involve cutting up the podcast in a certain way, removing unwanted noises and adding mood music or voiceovers where appropriate.

Before creating your own podcast recording, you may find it helpful to listen to some existing social science podcasts. By listening to these, you will gain further information on the different ways podcasts can be structured and techniques for enrolling the listener. The We Society Podcast or the Social Science Bites Podcast may be of interest to social science students.

CONCISE EXECUTIVE SUMMARIES

An executive summary is a concise, pithy summary of a research project's main findings and recommendations that is aimed at audiences who may not have sufficient time to read an entire report, thesis or dissertation (Vassollo 2003). Given the shorter length of executive summaries, it is possible that your institution may ask you to submit an executive summary as a smaller weighted assessment before the submission of your final written dissertation or even as a formative task which will not contribute to your final mark. Generally, executive summaries are no longer than 10 pages in length and can be as short as just one page. They are usually inserted before the longer, main document and they should follow the same order as the main document – for instance, if the main document presents key literature followed by details on the method used, the executive summary should mirror this and begin with details on key literature and then outline the method employed (Vassollo 2003). By following this structure, interested readers can navigate themselves to sections of the main report which have piqued their interest. Conciseness, clarity, and simplicity are crucial components to produce a good executive summary.

Executive summaries typically begin with some contextual information and then focus on main findings, recommendations, and finish with some ideas for future research. Any unnecessary details are removed to keep the document succinct. Crucially, whilst this is a shorter document, it should still work effectively as a standalone piece from the original research report or thesis. With this in mind, it is important to consider effective approaches to convey lots of information in very few words. As with some of the other formats of presenting discussed in this chapter, bullet points are a useful way to share several ideas without using too many words. Moreover, graphs, charts, tables, images and/or extracts tend to be particularly useful in executive summaries for providing clear overviews of patterns and trends.

Tips for a good executive summary:

1 **Concise and to the point**. An executive summary should be brief and punchy. It should highlight and convey only the most crucial messages of the project.
2 **Be crystal clear.** Make sure that your executive summary is lucid. Use only language that your readers are familiar with.
3 **Have a strong introduction**. Begin with a clear opening that captures the main purpose of the document and orientates the reader. Make sure you capture the reader's attention from the outset. You should include the headline messages here.
4 **Make sure that the key findings and arguments are obvious**. Summarise only the most crucial arguments and key findings. Make these easy to read and easy to locate. Only focus on the most significant data.
5 **Have a strong conclusion**. Finish by clearly stating any recommendations or outcomes, perhaps using bullet points so that a reader can easily scan them.
6 **Structure appropriately**. It can be a sensible idea to structure your executive summary in a way that mirrors the full dissertation or capstone. Or if you are writing the executive summary in advance of writing the full dissertation, use it as a springboard for how you structure the dissertation. Here, the research plan

that was discussed in Chapter 2 (*Planning a Social Science Research Project*) should come in extremely handy.

7 **Spend time editing**. Factor in time to revise and edit your executive summary so to remove any unnecessary waffle, ensuring every sentence contributes to the overall message.

Vassollo (2003) recommends that you begin writing your executive summary by typing out the key message that you wish to convey and then gathering relevant data and evidence from the main document to support this message. As stated earlier in this chapter, Vassollo (2003) also underscores the importance of imagining your audience when writing your executive summary and suggests that you should have a clear idea of who you are writing the summary for and the purpose of writing it. For instance, do you want to put forward a recommendation to change practice or policy, or are you simply providing an overview of the state of the field? Garner's (2013) book suggests some techniques that you can use to write crisply and to a shorter word count such as an executive summary.

Box 7.3

Abstracts Versus Executive Summaries

Executive summaries have some resemblance to abstracts and Introduction chapters. Abstracts (which are discussed in Chapter 9: *Submitting Your Social Science Research Project*) provide a concise overview of a research project. However, these are primarily aimed at academic audiences and tend to be less than 250 words in length. Executive summaries, on the other hand, are primarily of interest to stakeholders, funders, practitioners, and policy makers and could be as long as 10 pages. The external facing nature of executive summaries underscores the necessity for clear, transparent language and the importance of steering clear from jargon or specialised vocabulary. An executive summary is also not an introduction to the main report or written dissertation. Although both an introductory chapter and an executive summary provide contextual information, an introductory chapter is part of a broader and longer document and serves as an important role in signposting or scaffolding the rest of the report or research thesis. Crucially, an introductory chapter or section would not contain findings, whereas these may form a central element of an executive summary. See Vassollo (2003) for a longer discussion on the differences between an abstract and an executive summary.

SUMMARY

At this crucial stage of your research project, having carefully collected and analysed your data, the next step is to effectively share your research and communicate with others about what you have done and what you have found. The emphasis here is on 'effectively'. Your research may hold significant and impactful discoveries, but if you cannot convey them in an appropriate and accessible manner, the essence of your message risks being obscured or overlooked. Whatever way you choose or are asked to share your research, it is important that you clearly and succinctly tell the audience the main messages. As with writing the chapters of your dissertation, selectivity is pivotal to successfully conveying the central messages of your research. By incorporating the principles laid out in this chapter when sharing your research, you should be able to effectively highlight the significance of your research, capture various audiences' attention, and ensure your hard work is not only acknowledged but also understood and appreciated. As such, we emphasised how it is important to consider carefully who your intended audience are and the ways in which the medium you are using impacts the way you engage with them.

In addition to the suggestions and recommendations shared in this chapter about effectively sharing research findings, we encourage all students to carefully proofread any outputs, including presentations, research posters, executive summaries, or blog posts for grammatical and typographical errors. Tips for proofreading and identifying grammatical and typographical errors are shared in Chapter 9 (*Submitting Your Social Science Research Project*).

Student Question

What do I do if I get asked a question at the end of a research presentation that I do not know the answer to?

(Marten, Sociology Student)

Charlotte and Jamie say:

Do not panic! This has happened to us on several occasions. You are not expected to know everything. Instead, it is important that you carefully listen to the question and to show the questioner and audience that you have considered what has been said. This may be done by explaining that whilst you are unfamiliar or uncertain about the specific topic or issue raised in the question, you are keen to find out more. You may also choose to respond by repurposing the question (if only slightly) to something that you are (more) familiar with so displaying your broader knowledge. For example, you might state that while you are unfamiliar with the issue or the work of the author raised, you can expand on a related issue or another author's work that is equally pertinent to your project. We include an example of how to do this in the chapter.

WHAT'S NEXT?

Chapter Checklist

Table 7.1 Chapter 7 checklist

	Yes	No
I see the value in communicating and presenting my research.		
I recognise that audiences are diverse and different.		
I recognise the many ways in which my work can be presented.		
I know what to include in a research presentation.		
I know what to include in a research poster.		
I know what to include in a blogpost.		
I know what to include in a podcast.		
I know what to include in an executive summary.		

Read

Becker, L. 2019. *Give Great Presentations*. London: Sage.

Watch

Sage Students. 2020. *Give great presentations – a super quick skills video*. Available at: www.youtube.com/watch?v=RJ-Py7VzfJ8&list=PLfW3Wp3x6cZRK7PA8gQ3PwJoFvU0kurZf&index=7 (accessed 5 April 2024).

Complete

Complete the poster template provided in Figure 7.4.

8
INTRODUCING AND CONCLUDING

In Chapter 8 we discuss the importance of topping and tailing your research project. The Introduction and Conclusion chapters are often shorter than some of the other substantive chapters in a written research project. But this does not make them any less pivotal. Here, we discuss their necessity in setting up and concluding the narrative being told in your research project. That is, in this chapter, we explain the way in which the Introduction should hook the reader in, setting the context for the research project so that it acts as a signpost for the whole thesis. We also detail how the Conclusion chapter brings together the main findings along with suggestions for further research and identifies potential limitations of the research and the implications of the findings. Finally, we stress that the Conclusion chapter should make it clear how the research questions have been answered.

Chapter Objectives

- To understand the purpose of an Introduction chapter.
- To understand the purpose of a Conclusion chapter.
- To recognise that the order the chapters in a research project appear is not necessarily the order in which they are written.
- To stress the importance of answering the research questions.
- To acknowledge the relationship between the Introduction and Conclusion chapters.

INTRODUCTION

What all pieces of writing have in common is that they have a beginning and an ending that bookend the central section. For example, think of your favourite novel, and then reflect on the ways in which you get drawn in to read more and the impression you are left with on finishing it. Consider your preferred film or television series and how the beginning attracts your attention and how the ending often determines how you felt about the programme or movie. We can all remember a book, film, or television series which has had a disappointing ending and that feeling of discontent that we have subsequently associated with it. What we are expressing here is that the topping and tailing of any narrative is pivotal to any prose. It is no different with academic writing – the Introduction and Conclusion chapters or sections are essential to the overall framing of the writing, providing the backdrop, setting out the problem at hand as well as drawing your arguments together, synthesising those arguments and presenting any policy, practice, methodological, or intellectual implications. If we consider the analogy of the skipping rope, the Introduction and Conclusion chapters of a research project resemble the handles at either end, containing and constraining your writing and preventing it from unfurling into unsettled, undisciplined directions. Pulled tightly they create the impression of a coherent, cogent, and linear document with a clear throughline. Put bluntly, they are pivotal chapters in your research project and can often be the difference between a good piece of work and an excellent piece of work. Psychologists remind us that there is a primacy/recency effect when absorbing and recalling information, meaning that the information presented at the beginning (primacy) and at the end (recency) of a learning session, or in this case in the Introduction or Conclusion of a dissertation or research report tend to be retained better than the information presented in the middle (Sousa 2011). This suggests that these chapters will leave a lasting impression on your readers and markers, thus reinforcing the significance of spending time getting these chapters up to the required standard.

The Introduction and Conclusion are also sibling chapters; there is a relationship between them, a deeper relationship than merely the first and final substantive chapters of the research project. They work together to order and organise the research project, telling us what you will do, and then what was done. In this chapter, we discuss the purpose of both the Introduction and Conclusion chapters as well as providing an outline on how you might structure them. We begin with Part One, focusing on the Introduction chapter.

PART ONE: THE INTRODUCTION CHAPTER

Seven decades ago, in 1964 to be precise, Welsh writer and poet Dylan Thomas published his still in print play set in the fictional seaside village of Llareggub. 'To begin at the beginning', Thomas starts his play *Under Milkwood* before setting the scene through detailing the atmospheric backdrop to the quaint fishing village. Thomas is not alone in using this literary device. A very similar narrative technique is used in other famous works such as 'Let's start at the very beginning, a very good place to start', which Julie Andrews sings in Rogers and Hammerstein's (1965) *The Sound of Music*, or 'Begin at the Beginning', the King says gravely in Lewis Carroll's (1865) *Alice in Wonderland* and 'go on till you come to the end: then stop' when responding to the White Rabbit's question of 'where shall I begin …?'.

There are no hidden subtleties to these opening statements. They are simply reminders that someone must start somewhere, whether travelling on a journey like the White Rabbit or narrating a tale like Dylan Thomas, and what better place to start than at the beginning? And yet the journey one goes on and the recounting of that tale might involve an element of artistic licence. So, where are we going on this literary journey? What is our purpose in setting this out in this chapter? Well, while the first substantive chapter of your research project should begin at the beginning – open with an Introduction chapter – how you arrive at the beginning requires work, needs to be accomplished, and does not always involve a straightforward route. Expressed differently, ask yourself is it possible to write a complete, coherent Introduction chapter to the entire research project without first knowing what the topic and project entails? We argue it is not. Indeed, we might understand this problem as the *social science researcher's regress*. How do you introduce a research project without an Introduction, but how do you write an Introduction without knowing what it is you want to introduce? The truth is that in crafting *Under Milkwood*, it is very unlikely that Dylan Thomas began at the beginning and certainly not without a solid idea where he was travelling with his piece.

The same task faces you when writing about your research project. The good news is that the social science researcher's regress is not insurmountable. It can be overcome with a neat sleight of hand. While the structure of a completed, polished research project suggests a linear, sequential narrative that begins at the beginning with the Introduction chapter and concludes at the end with the Conclusion chapter, the production of the work in practice is much more circular. Crafting and drafting a research project involves interim periods of writing, editing, circling back, and moving around repeatedly until you have produced a logical order to your writing that directs and orients the reader to where you want them to go. And essentially that is the neat trick: order and sequence need to be accomplished. It is the work of the writer to make the reader believe the writing could not have been produced differently. In practice, then, the Introduction chapter should not be written first. It cannot be. Instead, it is highly likely that the Introduction chapter is one of the final sections to be written in your research project and only after you have familiarised yourself with the relevant literature and collected (and analysed) your data; in other words, when you have a firm idea of where you are going. This, of course, is quite different to saying you should not be thinking about what to include in this chapter earlier in the writing up phase, nor to say that you will not have drafted some proto paragraphs that can be dropped into the definitive final version of your Introduction chapter. As discussed in Chapter 3 (*Reviewing Social Science Literature*), we always recommend that students begin near the beginning and draft the Literature Review chapter first. In pulling this Literature Review chapter together, it is our experience, that on reflection, some sections of the initial drafts tend to sit better in the Introduction chapter and end up in there in the definitive version of the final written research report. So, while you are not intentionally writing elements of the Introduction at the beginning, you will likely draft some sections that can be tinkered with later and included in the Introduction.

But the fact that the Introduction chapter is likely one of the final chapters that you dedicate time to write is one of the reasons we have grouped the Introduction and Conclusion chapters together in this book. And the reason why this chapter is positioned toward the end of this book is to reflect the writing process. Indeed, we like to think of these chapters as couplets: firstly, they tend to be the final chapters which you write, topping and tailing the written thesis; and secondly, they tend to be of similar length, often shorter and punchier than the Literature Review, Methods, and (combined) Findings/Analysis chapters. But most importantly, they should speak in dialogue with one another, the Introduction outlining what it is you are going to do and the Conclusion leaving the reader in no doubt about what it is you have done. As such, we want you to think of them as sibling chapters.

Purpose and Presentation

One of the central functions of the Introduction chapter is to grab the reader's attention. After drawing the reader in, you then want to keep hold of them. The Introduction is a shorter chapter compared to others in your dissertation, perhaps only 750–1,000 words depending on the research project word limit set by your institution, and therefore your writing needs to be sharp, punchy, and purposeful. You have limited words to spare and 'waste'. Most importantly, you should be outlining the case for the project so that by the end of the chapter the reader is left in little doubt that the topic, and your approach to researching it, is a worthwhile endeavour. Questions which should frame how you write the Introduction chapter include: What prompted the research? What curiosity do you want to formalise? What is the topic's social science significance? Bringing this energy to this chapter should also enthuse the reader. There are also some standard techniques and tricks which can help you write the Introduction chapter. We include some of these next.

Grab the Reader's Attention

Effective Introductions set the tone, style, and expectations for the entire dissertation, encouraging readers to continue reading with a clear understanding of what is to come in the following chapters. That said, the writing style employed in the Introduction can be a little less formal than in the other chapters and you can draw on resources and literature beyond academic ones – using what is sometimes called grey literature (see Chapter 3: *Reviewing Social Science Literature*). For example, if the topic under study is currently newsworthy, you may wish to situate or frame the topic within current debates or articles and reports published in newspapers or policy documents. This instantly grabs the reader's attention and helps find a common ground between you, them, and the project. By doing this you are also displaying how the project is contemporaneously relevant. This is not to say that you should not include academic literature in this chapter though – the grey literature should complement academic works, not replace them. We would not expect the Introduction to include anywhere near as many references as, let us say, the Literature Review chapter.

Show Enthusiasm

As discussed in Chapter 2 (*Planning a Social Science Research Project*), there are several resources which you can draw from when attempting to choose a topic to study for your dissertation or capstone project. One suggestion we make is to choose a topic of passion, a labour of love, so to speak, and an issue that will hopefully retain your interest. Now, the truth is that there will be some strains during the writing process where this interest wanes and the same is true for a reader reading your research project. Aware of this, we encourage students to make sure the passion for their project comes across strongly at the beginning of their research project in the Introduction chapter. Passion is infectious and so if you can get across to your reader the importance of the project, this affection and animation will hopefully transfer to them too. Write energetically in the Introduction chapter, keep the flow going and direct the reader to the following chapters. Write with purpose, attract their attention and sustain their interest.

Leave the Reader Wanting More

The trick with the Introduction chapter is to provide enough detail to scaffold the rest of the project and orientate the reader, but without giving away too much. The Introduction chapter should act as a signpost for what is to come in the rest of the chapters. Put bluntly, you want the marker or reader to have read the chapter and come away wanting to read the rest of the thesis. You might think of it as doing a similar job to a trailer for a movie in the cinema or on Netflix, with its purpose to sell the rest of the project to the reader.

Play It Straight

The Introduction chapter is the first substantive chapter someone will read. It is therefore pivotal that you leave the reader in no doubt what the research project is about. While we all have our own unique narrative style and writing tongue, we encourage you to include some direct statements. Therefore, in this chapter, pepper a few sentences which read something like: 'This thesis concerns …' or 'This research project considers …' or 'This project examines …' or 'The study is located in the field of …'.

Set the Tone

The Introduction chapter should set the tone for the rest of the dissertation. It should provide readers with a basic understanding of what you are about to examine, setting the context for the argument and narrative to come. Through crisp, punchy, and engaging writing it should let the reader know what is going to be studied and why it matters. It should introduce the reader to the topic in an accessible manner.

What to Include?

As with all social science research chapters there is no one-size-fits-all approach to structuring an Introduction chapter. Each chapter should have your own individual stamp on it, your own individualised touch. But there is a difference between style and structure, and the ambition is to strike a balance between your own personal mark while keeping within the confines of a generic structure that one tends to see in the Introduction chapter. The introduction should state what you are going to do in the Introduction chapter, it should detail the purpose of the project, raise questions, and tease the reader with what is to come in the rest of the project. Subheadings within an Introduction chapter might include:

- introduction
- contextual backdrop
- aim, purpose, and direction of the research
- summary of the chapters to follow.

Remember, this chapter is typically shorter than some of the others in your dissertation.

An Introduction to the Introduction Chapter

Without subscribing to the infinite regress that there are turtles all the way down, the Introduction chapter itself requires a brief introduction. Here, a snappy first line that captures the essence of the 'problem' or 'issue' at hand such as 'classifications have consequences' or 'familiar faces are found in familiar spaces' or 'we all need to eat but do we all need to dine?' can capture the reader's attention from the outset. Too often we have read opening lines to a thesis that are too long, unwieldy, and attempt to cram in too much. You should aim for short, punchy, and to the point. Provoke an interest. Alternatively, you might want to set the scene by introducing an event and/or a public figure such as (i) Venus Williams first won the Wimbledon's Tennis championship in 2000 or (ii) on 9th November 1989, the Berlin Wall came down; six weeks later David Hasselhoff sang *Looking for Freedom* in a cage hovering above the ruins. These newsworthy starters can also be an effective way to engage the reader. Another technique is to use statistics and social facts such as (iii) at the last count just shy of 60,000 people died in the devastating earthquake that hit Turkey and Syria on 6 February 2023, or (iv) in 2021 more than 235,000 people were classified as homeless in Canada with as much as 30,000 experiencing homelessness on any given day. This ploy can quickly emphasise the significance of the topic that you have researched. Such openings, which might be used to discuss social science topics as diverse as the medicalisation of behavioural conditions (classifications have consequences), social class and capital (familiar faces are seen in familiar places), austerity measures and the cost of living crisis (we all need to eat, but do we all need to dine?), equality in sport (Venus Williams first won the Wimbledon's Tennis championship in 2000), the role of politics in music (on 9th November 1989, the Berlin Wall came down, six weeks later David Hasselhoff sang *Looking for Freedom* in a cage hovering above the ruins), the social impacts of 'natural' disasters (60,000 people died in the devastating earthquake that hit Turkey and Syria on 6th February 2023) and homelessness among Indigenous populations (235,000 people were classified as homeless in Canada with as much as 30,000 experiencing homelessness on any given day), tend to quickly attract interest and make clear to the reader the purpose of the project.

The Contextual Backdrop

The Introduction chapter needs to provide the reader with the general information required to understand the project. For some projects, the setting and site of your research project might be commonplace and thus require less explaining. Examples here might include schools, police stations, or medical centres. Most readers will have a general understanding of these institutions and organisations. This is not to say that certain key terms should not be introduced though. Organisations produce their own technical languages and jargon meaning certain phrases and concepts might need to be introduced. Moreover, a school in India might look very different to a school in Sweden, a medical centre in Australia might be regulated differently to one in Peru, and the relationship between the police, the public, and the state will also vary between nations and even regions. So, while you need to be selective as to what information is vital for the reader to know in your project, equally you should not assume too much of the reader. As such, make sure key terms are defined (and applied, if relevant).

Conversely there are other project settings that are less common, known by a much narrower group of people. For example, some social media worlds such as *Second Life*, some gaming communities such as *Fortnite* and *Dungeons and Dragons*, some religious groups such as neo-pagan Wicca witches in South West England or communities of ultra conservative Mennonites in Paraguay and Bolivia, some sub-cultures involving extreme thrill seekers like those that perform Parkour, flipping and tumbling through our cities or those known as 'stalkers', young Ukrainians who enter and spend days in the off-limits Chernobyl exclusion zone and site of the Chernobyl nuclear power station disaster to create and record videos to be posted on social media site such as TikTok, as well as some knowledge-making cultures such as Neuroscientists or Nanotechnologists or the example of Bigfooters discussed throughout the earlier chapters of this book, are much more esoteric and will likely require more explanation to familiarise the reader. Here, you might need to explain who the community is, what they do and set out any general rules which the reader might need to know to understand the setting. The trick is not to assume too much of the reader but at the same time do not oversimplify – it is important that you demonstrate your knowledge of and ability to use key social science concepts.

The Aim, Purpose, and Direction of the Research

The Introduction chapter needs to orientate the reader. Here, you should raise questions (to be clear, not your research questions) outlining what aspect of the setting – whether that is *Second Life*, Wicca Witches, Mennonites or Medical Centres – that you are interested in. For example, you might be interested in how the virtual world *Second Life* allows users to erode or play with gender identities. *Second Life* users are called Residents.

They create virtual representations of themselves called avatars and can interact with other avatars, places, and objects that are in that world. But these virtual representations enable users to also play around with gender roles. Some cis women, for example, re-present themselves as cis men and vice versa. Your interest then might concern to what extent are gender identities fluid online?

Or you might be interested in how modern secular concerns and troubles such as the environment or the climate have led to a shift in modern faith practices. You might question the extent to which people attracted to neo-pagan beliefs such as Wicca Witches or ultra conservative Mennonite beliefs act as avenues to find comfort in an uncertain and troubling world where our relationship to nature, to technology, and to the past is changing. Alternatively, you might be interested in why Peru became the country with the highest mortality rate due to Covid-19 with some sources indicating that as many as 665 per 100,000 of the population died or 5% of all who were infected (Johns Hopkins Coronavirus Resource Center 2023). Unlike some of its neighbouring Latin American countries such as Brazil under the stewardship of Jair Bolsonaro, and Mexico under the leadership of Andres Manuel Lopez Obrador, Peru did not deny the existence of Covid-19. However, the structural weaknesses in the Peruvian health system were aggravated by the pandemic. So, what was it about Peru's health infrastructure that meant it was so vulnerable to a pandemic? Importantly, when setting out the purpose and aim of your project, there may be scope to outline what your research is not about and is not interested in as well as what it is concerned with. Continuing with the previous example, you may set out in your Introduction chapter that your dissertation is concerned with the death toll from Covid-19 infections only and is not interested in the number of infections or hospitalisations. That is, the Introduction chapter should set out and justify the parameters of the research and, in so doing, manage readers' expectations.

A Summary of the Proceeding Chapters

One of the central purposes of the Introduction chapter is to orientate the reader and to signpost and foreshadow what is to come in the rest of the research project. Here, look at your favourite manuscript or academic book and it is likely that they conclude the Introduction chapter with an overview of how the rest of the book is structured and what is to come in the following chapters, saying what they are going to do. This not only directs the reader but helps you structure your overall thesis. The Introduction to this book has a subheading 'Book structure' which directs the reader to relevant chapters. Similarly, in your research project you might include the following signposting:

> In Chapter 2, I review the literature locating my work in the sociology of religion. The Methods chapter discusses the epistemological, ontological, and practical approach to studying the setting and justifies the use of online semi-structured interviews. The Findings chapter presents extracts from 12 interviews with Mennonite farmers from different generations, before the discussion considers the findings in relation to Max Weber's (1905/2001)

protestant ethic and the spirit of capitalism, and the Conclusion chapter determines the significance of this work for understanding peripheral communities, marginal religious practices, and their future in South America.

PART TWO: THE CONCLUSION CHAPTER

It is reported that the Beatles band member, John Lennon said that 'everything will be okay in the end. If it is not okay, it is not the end'. While clearly not a comment about research projects, the sentiment holds true for this setting too. The Conclusion chapter is the final substantive chapter of your research project and, as such, you want to leave the reader with a strong, lasting impression of your overall project. You want the chapter, to misquote Lennon, to be okay. Well, actually, you want the chapter to be more than okay. If you feel it is not okay, and not up to the standard of the rest of the thesis, then it is not doing your thesis justice.

The Conclusion is not simply the last substantive chapter of your research project, it, along with your Introduction chapter, is also likely to be one of the last chapters of your research that you will write. It is understandable then that in reaching this stage of the project you may begin to run out of steam a little. But as a standalone substantive chapter of your research project, the Conclusion chapter is of equal importance to all the other chapters which you have written. Reaching the Conclusion chapter is not the end. It is the beginning of the end. It must be written, and as such it also needs to be written with the same energy and enthusiasm as the other chapters in your research project, even if you are understandably struggling with a little dissertation lethargy.

Writing Conclusions are not always the most pleasant experiences but they are the final act we produce for the reader. A well-crafted Conclusion chapter is crucial for reinforcing your main argument(s), for synthesising your main points and is an opportunity for you to communicate the significance of your research, ensuring that your central points are remembered. Remember, the Conclusion chapter will give your reader and marker a lasting impression about your research.

Purpose and Presentation

It is said that everything that begins must come to an end. The main purpose of the Conclusion chapter is to unequivocally tell the reader what the main messages of the research project were: to summarise the findings and importantly, to answer the research questions which you set out with, and to infer what these results mean for the broader research problem. Fitting with a thesis word count of 8–10,000 words, then, you should aim to dedicate around 1,000–1,250 words to the Conclusion chapter. In this sense, the Conclusion chapter tends to be a little bit longer than the Introduction chapter, but still shorter than some of the other substantive chapters in your research project. But, as with the Introduction, there are some standard techniques and tricks that can help you write a purposeful and decisive Conclusion chapter.

Broaden Out

We might want to think of the write up of a research project as resembling a wave. Remember in Chapter 3 (*Reviewing Social Science Literature*), we discussed how it is often the case when writing the Literature Review chapter that you begin relatively broad before funnelling into your research project by narrowing the focus. Conversely, the Conclusion chapter is an opportunity to ride that wave back out. From the narrow focus of your project, you can begin to extrapolate and aggrandise a little in the Conclusion chapter by situating your research within broader social science debates and discussions. The global is in the local or to use Wright Mills (1959) again, personal, or private troubles are public concerns. So, ask yourself, in what way is your research project a broader, public (or societal) issue? What is its relevance beyond the specific setting you studied? Make these connections in the Conclusion chapter, showcasing its social significance (but without over-selling its importance).

Be Assertive

But while the Conclusion chapter provides the opportunity to broaden out your argument, only conclusions that you can safely and robustly defend should be made. While it is tempting to move beyond or to claim too much, be careful that what you say can be justified and that there is a logical extension from your findings. There is a balance to be struck here, and we suggest a type of 'cautious assertiveness'. Be cautious with what you say but be bold in saying it. That is, too many times we read chapters that are afraid to say anything. Too many times we read Conclusions that use qualifier word after qualifier word. For example: the statement 'this somewhat suggests that class may (or may not) be a factor in the political party young Brazilian students vote for, with perhaps gender being an intervening variable' is clearly too meek, is too diffident. Instead, a more confident and considered sentence would be: 'This suggests that class may be a factor in the political party Brazilian students vote for, with gender potentially being an intervening variable'. Not only does this sentence read more crisply, but it is also more concise, helping save valuable words. Remember, being careful what you say is qualitatively different from being afraid to say anything. But while you should use this cautious assertiveness to clearly stress the importance of your project, equally you can discuss the limitations of the project in your Conclusion. Acknowledging limitations should not be seen as a limitation itself. Rather, it shows that you are a critical, reflective researcher. Recognising your own weaknesses is a sign of a mature social science researcher.

Talk Back to the Literature

It is vital that the Conclusion chapter is the logical conclusion to the whole research project. A good signal that the chapter feels at odds with the preceding chapters is if you introduce a suite of new references in the Conclusion chapter and locate the work in completely different literature. While there is scope to introduce a new piece of work, this should be evidently justified. Realistically, though, this should be the exception and not the rule. The key word here is 'introduce'. This is the Conclusion chapter, and the central texts should have already been introduced and discussed earlier in the research project. Importantly though, the Conclusion should still be situated in a field of research. It is therefore a useful technique to go back (to your previous chapters) to spring forward to the end; to remind readers of the purpose of what has come already before finishing with an emphatic ending.

So What?

The Conclusion chapter is your opportunity to unequivocally tell the reader why the research project was required as well as what original contribution you have made or gap in the literature that you have filled. Include a clear, absolute statement or paragraph that convinces the reader that the research project was valuable. Why did they just read it? What do you want their take home messages to be? Have you been unmistakably clear? In what ways have you added to or challenged the work in the epistemic field which your research is in? What has been your original contribution, no matter how big or small? That is, you have written this project, so what? Tell the reader what the 'so what?' is. Why is it an important contribution to the social science literature you have located your work in?

Provide Closure

Reading a piece of academic work is an investment on the part of the reader, much in the same way as watching a television series or reading a novel. It is an investment in time, energy, focus, and sometimes emotion. Audiences do not like feeling that their investment was unwarranted. They do not like feeling unfulfilled, unsatisfied, and being left with a lot of unanswered questions. Writers need to provide readers and audiences with a sense of closure, that the Is have been dotted and the Ts crossed. Nobody expects you to have all the answers to the setting you have studied; again, even the most experienced professors would struggle to evidence this. But this is where having a tight, coherent structure with well thought out and refined research questions work in your favour. Closure is accomplished in a research project through the write-up. In the Conclusion chapter, answer the research questions you have raised, return to the broader questions which have been discussed in the project, and close off any methodological concerns that the reader might have. Provide that closure while accepting there is always more work to be done (by others). Perhaps finish with a closing thought or reflective comment that underscores the significance of the project. As William Shakespeare (1623) wrote 'All's well that ends well'.

What to Include?

The Conclusion chapter might be divided as follows:

- an introduction to the Conclusion chapter
- a section that deals with the main findings and/or how you have answered the research questions

- implications of findings
- future direction for the research.

Again, this is only a guide and it is vital that you speak with your supervisor or course convenor to discuss the best approach for your research project.

Introduction to Conclusion Chapter

We have threaded some simple, direct messages throughout the book. One of the central ones being to (i) say what you are going to do, (ii) do it, and (iii) say what you have done. While this message is directed at the research project as a whole, meaning you should say what you will do in the opening chapters (Introduction and Literature Review), show how you do it in the Methods chapter, and say what you have done in the final chapters (Findings, Discussion and Conclusion), the maxim works at the individual chapter level too. Each chapter should have an introduction subheading and a summary or conclusion subheading. This sort of signposting work is crucial when working with large documents. Therefore, just in the way that you will highly likely have an introductory section to the Introduction chapter, the same is true with the Conclusion chapter.

Main Findings

The Conclusion chapter provides you with a wonderful opportunity to tell the reader definitively and decisively what the main findings of your research were. Whereas these might have been shared in the Discussion or Findings chapter, here you should be explicit and direct. We are certainly not suggesting you overplay your hand and claim your research shows something it does not or hyperbolise the findings. We are also not suggesting eroding ambiguity and complexity from your project; rarely is the social world not messy. We are though encouraging you to be confident in your work and to make sure you present that accordingly. We also strongly recommend that you directly answer the research questions in the Conclusion chapter. Here, you may wish to create further subheadings sorted by the research questions and then directly respond to them in turn. However, this is not the place to trudge back through what was included in each chapter (see Thomas 2023a). Coalesce these points and synthesise them into a compelling and persuasive narrative. The stronger Conclusion chapters will also show the ways in which the main findings relate to the literature discussed in the Literature Review. The Conclusion chapter should still be situated in academic literature, but as explained previously we would not expect too much (or any) new literature to be introduced in this final chapter. If you find yourself introducing several new references, it is a good signal to stop and to make sure that the research project is hanging together as a coherent document. Ask yourself in this section, how do my findings relate to the research discussed earlier in the research project? Do they challenge or support previous research findings and why? Ask yourself too whether you are directly responding to your research questions. If you are – great. If you are not, then you might want to revisit your research questions and re-purpose them to fit the data you have collected and the conclusions you have drawn. This may also require you to edit or review your Literature Review chapter to ensure that the narrative remains coherent. While this might seem a little frustrating, it is much easier and less time consuming than the alternative, which might be to go and collect new data. All social science research is a process, and this is not atypical.

Implications of Findings

You have now clearly demonstrated your findings. So what? This is not meant to be boorish and impolite. As already explained, it is a question that the Conclusion chapter should acknowledge. Why are your findings important? Who might find them important? How might they be understood? What is your original contribution? You should include a section on why your project matters and to whom. Are there any policy implications? For those of you working in the field of applied social science, social policy for example, this will likely be very pertinent. Or how might your research matter in practice? Those doing education research or communication studies, or social work might want to consider how your work relates to teaching, science communication, or social work *in situ*. If your work is more of an intellectual endeavour, you might draw out the substantive or methodological implications. Has your research furthered the intellectual work in your epistemic field, in psychology, in critical geography, in science and technology studies, in criminology? Does your work have methodological implications – does it raise questions for your analytic approach, for the way in which you collected data, for how you determined your sample? Does this mean you require an extended Methods chapter? Finally, you might wish to discuss the moral justification of your work. We might consider any social science research project to either be a descriptive piece of work or a normative one. As before, descriptive here does not mean it is not analytical. It means you attempt to approach the project from a neutral stance providing an analytic account of the world or community you are studying without judgement. A normative approach, on the other hand, takes the approach of this is how it should be, rather than how it is. Here, there is an evaluative component to your research where you might challenge the status quo and question or critique the setting or problem studied.

Future Direction of Research

The Conclusion chapter tends to end a little differently to other chapters. While we always recommend including a summary sentence or sentences which state the most poignant and pithy points made in the research project, you may decide to forego a formal summary section and conclude with a subheading called something akin to *Future Directions* or *Further Research*. Earlier we stressed the importance of being direct and confident. This does not mean though that you should not be critically reflective, and in this section, you can discuss the shortcomings of your research project. It is not necessarily how the research project is conducted that will determine the strength of your project, but rather it is whether you are able to demonstrate your understanding of what you have done and that you are aware of what you can and cannot say from the data which you collected. All research projects could have been set up differently. All research projects have bumps in the road. Rare is the smooth research project. Understanding, articulating, and critically discussing these obstacles and shortcomings is imperative. It tells the reader that you understand the relationship between method, theory, and findings. It enables you to gesture toward future avenues for research and roads you did not take or were unable to drive. There may have been practical issues, such as the time you had to complete the project, or financial restrictions which prevented you from approaching the project in another way. Tell the reader that you are aware of these other approaches and restate your justification for taking the path you did. It is important not to shy away from any limitations of your research and to use this opportunity to showcase your awareness and understanding of these shortcomings. Highlighting them will not reduce your mark. In fact, quite the opposite. The marker should be impressed that you are aware of these issues and should reward this criticality and reflection. Furthermore, your findings may have opened further questions which you believe need addressing, questions which were beyond the scope of your current research project, but questions others might wish to address in their research or questions which you might examine in future further research.

THE INTRODUCTION AND CONCLUSION AS A COUPLET

Beyond the fact that the Introduction and Conclusion chapters bookend the research project, they also have a deeper relationship. We have already detailed how these chapters tend to be the two shortest substantive chapters in your research project, with the Conclusion chapter tending to be a little longer than the Introduction one. But the content in the Introduction chapter should also speak to the content in the Conclusion. That is, the Introduction raises questions, sets out the problem at hand, and the Conclusion addresses those questions and provides an explanation for – or even proposes a (re)solution to – the problem. Both chapters also provide a summary of the research – the Introduction says what you will do, while the Conclusion says what you have done. The Introduction sets out what original position the research project is taking, and the Conclusion definitively states the original contribution of the research project. Finally, the Introduction lays out the potential importance of the research and the Conclusion stresses the significance of the findings for policy, for practice, in intellectual terms, etc. Good Introductions and Conclusions are inextricably intertwined, which is another good reason they should be written together at the same time toward the end of the research process. For those symmetrically minded, you might even begin with an anecdote or story in the Introduction chapter and then refer to it at the end of the Conclusion chapter to create a satisfying sense of closure and connection.

SUMMARY

It is extremely easy to fall into the trap of focussing all your attention and expending all your energy on the central components of your research project – the Literature Review, the Methods, and the Findings and Discussion chapters – only to feel like you are running out of steam when you arrive at the chapters that bookend your research project. In this chapter, we stressed the importance of the Introduction and Conclusion chapters in your research project and made it clear that they should not be neglected. So, while they are typically written after the other substantive chapters, they should not be treated as an afterthought. Importantly, the reader should be able to read the Introduction and Conclusion chapters and draw from them a very solid, though admittedly short, summary of the purpose, context, and findings of your research. There should therefore be a smooth connection between these chapters so much so that they may be thought of as a couplet or sibling chapters, with one not working very well without the other. Remember the handles of the skipping rope analogy? These chapters provide order to your research project, containing, constraining, directing, and guiding the project. The Introduction chapter should grab the reader's attention and the Conclusion chapter should provide closure to the research project. Therefore, keeping your enthusiasm and energy levels high and writing these chapters with the same gusto with which you wrote the others is crucial.

Student Question

I understand the rationale behind writing these chapters later in the process but at what point in the process should I begin thinking about what content I might use?

(Lily, Urban Studies)

Jamie and Charlotte say:

Earlier in the book, we stressed the importance of active note taking as well as not deleting earlier draft chapters. This is where that work comes into its own. Given that these chapters serve the purpose of opening and closing your dissertation, you should have hopefully noted down ideas concerning the reasons why the project is important as well as the direction you are heading. Moreover, it is highly likely that some of the prose in the initial drafts of the Literature Review chapter will end up in the Introduction chapter, and some of the prose from the initial drafts of the Discussion chapter will end up in the Conclusion chapter. This is why it is pivotal not to delete work, it is not wasted effort. And on occasions the writing can be shuffled around and form parts of other chapters. So, while you may not come to formally write these chapters until the end of your project, nothing prevents you from writing notes earlier on in the process that will eventually form the basis for these chapters. This is another reason why we call completing your social science project a process or journey.

WHAT'S NEXT?

Chapter Checklist

Table 8.1 Chapter 8 checklist

	Yes	No
I understand the purpose of the Introduction chapter to the research project.		
I recognise that the best time to complete the Introduction chapter is after data collection.		
I understand the purpose of the Conclusion chapter to the research project.		
I recognise the importance of directly addressing the research questions.		
I appreciate the relationship between the Introduction and Conclusion chapters.		

Write

Write down three interesting facts about your research project and answer the following questions.

Introduction Chapter

- How is your research distinct from previous research on the subject or related area?
- How does your research relate to, build upon, or challenge previous research?
- Why is it important that we know about this research NOW?

These answers can provide the foundations for your Introduction chapter.

Conclusion Chapter

- Would you approach your research project differently based on what you have learned during the process?
- Would you approach your research project differently if you had more time, and in what way(s)?
- Would you approach your research project differently if you had more money, and in what way(s)?

These answers can provide the foundations for your Conclusion chapter.

9
SUBMITTING YOUR SOCIAL SCIENCE RESEARCH PROJECT

In this final chapter, we discuss the importance of bringing the full document containing your research project together. We ask you to consider whether your research questions have been answered, and if not, whether they need revisiting. We then provide tips on how to edit your draft chapters and provide advice on what to leave in and what to take out, as well as tips on tightening your expression. We stress the necessity of leaving yourself time to read over and then re-read over the final version so as to finesse and polish your dissertation. The chapter also includes some guidance on writing abstracts, as well as other front matter issues for a research project and information on putting together a thorough reference list as well as other back matter. Finally, we conclude the chapter by putting together a checklist of the main sections of a research project so that you can tick them off in the comfort of knowing that you have completed all the main components required of a social science research project.

Chapter Objectives

- To produce and organise the front matter of a completed research project.
- To produce and organise the back matter of a completed research project.
- To understand how a completed research project is formatted/organised.
- To understand the importance of proofreading and editing.
- To manage feelings of anxiety.
- To know when a research project is good enough to be submitted.

INTRODUCTION

Though some self-doubt is common when undertaking a piece of independent research, if you have followed the steps outlined in the previous chapters of this book and feel satisfied with the content, analysis, and overall presentation of your research project, it likely indicates that you have reached the point of completion. However, before you follow Disney's Snow Queen Elsa's advice to 'let it go, let it go ...' (Buck and Lee, 2013), there are a few more delicate steps required to make sure your written social science research report is polished and ready to be submitted. These steps might be thought of as the swirls of icing on top of your chocolate cake. You have mixed all the ingredients together and produced a substantial and solid structure, which is ready to be consumed. But, to attract the eye and to hide any imperfections, some final changes or edits are required. This final chapter outlines the steps that should help you reach this point, as well as providing tips for letting go of your research project. If you have read the previous chapters, especially Chapter 2 (*Planning a Social Science Research Project*), you will know that we have strongly advocated setting yourself an 'artificial' deadline ahead of the official submission date for your dissertation to ensure that you have sufficient time to review the research project in its entirety, seek feedback, and make any necessary changes. You should now be at the point where you can make use of this extra time to edit and finesse your project as well as to tackle the front and back matter that bookend your social science dissertation.

COLLATING ALL THE CHAPTERS

Reaching the stage where you have completed drafts of all the chapters or sections of your dissertation is the clearest indication that you are nearing the point of submission. Until now, you might have simply focussed on reading and reviewing each chapter as standalone sections. Indeed, you will likely have the different chapters on separate documents. This is perfectly sensible. However, as you approach the final stages of your research project, it becomes crucial to pay special attention to the overall flow and cadence of the entire document, to note whether there is too much repetition, and to check whether sections foreground and signpost what is to come. Now is the time to ensure that each chapter seamlessly connects to the next, creating a smooth and coherent narrative. That is, the research project needs to be braided together as tightly as possible. Transitions between chapters or sections play a vital role in maintaining the logical progression of your research and arguments. This will mean first combining all the chapters into one larger document. And then by examining the linkage between chapters, you can strengthen the 'golden thread' that ties the whole project together, ensuring that your central argument and narrative remain clear and consistent throughout.

As well as having all the substantive chapters in place, it is also necessary to have various other elements of the front and back matter in place to top and tail your dissertation. The front matter typically includes essential components of a social science research project such as the (i) title page, (ii) an abstract, (iii) acknowledgments, and (iv) a table of contents. As part of the submission process, you may also be required to include a signed declaration form stating that the research project is your own work.

Conversely, the back matter consists of sections like the (i) reference list and (ii) a set of appendices. We discuss each of these in turn.

FRONT MATTER

At the very beginning of your dissertation, you should have a title page. As the name suggests, this will clearly state the title of your research project. It may also include your name, the date of submission, the name of the degree programme that you are studying as well as your institution's logo. As we have previously alluded to, deciding on a title can itself be a source of anxiety. To stress, it is perfectly fine to have a mundane, *plain* title which reflects the contents of the written project, or which acts as an overarching question that you are answering. However, for others it might be alluring to include some data as part of your title, for example a standout quote from your research project. Others still might prefer a play on words but be a little careful to make sure this neither detracts nor comes across as whimsical. Simply put, make sure the title has some punch and is relevant to the content in the project. It is extremely unlikely that your title will have a significant impact on your overall mark, but it does add important context for what is to come and might also determine who marks the dissertation if the marking is allocated based on the titles of the research.

Some fictional examples of different types of titles are listed here:

Plain (but informative)

- A content analysis of the media's representation of New Zealand's female farmers
- Surveying young people's views on their alcohol consumption
- What coping strategies do students employ during exam periods?

Note how the first two are statements and the third is phrased as a question for the project to answer.

Real example: Li et al. 2023: Can polycentric urban development simultaneously achieve both economic growth and regional equity? A multi-scale analysis of German regions.

Using data (quotes) in the title

- 'It makes me feel as if I am one with nature': An ethnographic study of California's surfers
- 'It is just another version of me': Making sense of online virtual worlds
- 'Cuts have consequences': Perspectives from serving police officers on cuts to public services

Real example: Fercovic 2023: 'He is my refuge': Upward mobility, class dislocation and romantic relationships.

Playing with words

- Who is aFreud of Virginia Woolf: Psychoanalysis and modernism
- Full Marx: Class and educational attainment
- Sham-Pain Supernova: To what extent are faith healers and astrologists simply charlatans?
- Caravandalism: petty crimes at trailer parks

Real example (concerning a project about families setting up gin distilleries): Thurnell-Read 2020: Kindred spirits: Doing family through craft entrepreneurship.

Use of alliteration

- Public perspectives on policing
- Analysing Australian attitudes towards air travel
- 'Becoming' British: Negotiating national identity

Real example: Brundage 2023: Responsibility and recognition. State sovereignty as performative.

When crafting the title for your research project, please keep in mind its potential use on your CV, job applications, or applications for postgraduate study. A clear and informative title is crucial for effectively communicating your research topic, demonstrating your interests, and showcasing your skillset to potential employers or admissions tutors.

The title page of your written research project tends to be followed by an abstract. An abstract performs the function of a concise summary of your research project, typically 150–250 words long. It is usually written as one paragraph, but sometimes extends to two and its purpose is to synthesise the larger document – the whole dissertation – into a smaller, bitesize summary. Importantly, it should not be a catalogue of what is contained in each chapter but rather should be a précis of the overall substance of your study. Though it is positioned at the beginning of the document to help the reader understand the purpose of the project and the contents of the work to follow, given that it is a succinct synopsis of the whole research project, it tends to be written at the end of the writing process when you have a clearer and more complete idea of your findings. You should be used to seeing abstracts at the beginning of the journal articles you have read to compile your Literature Review and Methods chapters. You should also then have your own opinions on the usefulness of abstracts. We like to think of them as doing the work of film-trailers or the blurb of a book, enticing readers to determine whether they want to read the whole thing. A well-crafted abstract should enable readers to swiftly grasp the main objectives of your study, the methods employed as well as the key findings. Additionally, it can include extra details such as the number of participants involved in your research and the implications of your research findings for policy or practice. To this end, an abstract is a synthesis of the Introduction, Methods, and Conclusion chapters. There is no need to cite others' work in an abstract. Indeed, normal etiquette is to write an abstract that does not include other literature. A fictional example of an abstract following this general format is included here:

The Many Faces of Barbie: A content analysis of Barbie Doll advertisements

In 2023, Margot Robbie and Ryan Gosling starred in the award-winning American fantasy comedy movie, *Barbie*. Inspired by the Barbie fashion dolls created by Mattel in the late 1950s, the film re-purposes the original mid-20th century image of Barbie to, among other issues, critically comment on gender, and patriarchal and matriarchal societies in the 21st century. This research project considers the evolution of Barbie over the past six decades to understand changes to the ways in which advertisers market Barbie products and imagine their consumers. It draws from a content analysis of 20 Barbie commercials available on YouTube, including the original Barbie commercial screened in the late 1950s and the latest version, 73 years later. Comparing videos through the decades, the study shows the ways in which the presentation of Barbie has changed dramatically over the years. From the beginnings where Barbie is presented as a white female who is looking for love dressed in a wedding gown and cooing after Ken to the 2023 version that states, 'you can be anything' showcasing Barbie as a multicultural and multiracial figurine who is an independent and active woman, Barbie reflects some of the broader social and cultural shifts in gender and race relations in Western society.

This example succinctly-enough introduces the research area (Barbie and gender roles) and justifies the importance of the topic, it outlines the method used (content analysis of 20 YouTube videos) and shares a key finding (Barbie reflects some of the social and cultural shifts in gender and race relations in Western society). It also situates the research project within a broader social discussion showing how it is socially relevant and newsworthy (the 2023 *Barbie* movie).

The abstract is usually followed by an acknowledgments section on a separate page. This provides you with the opportunity to express gratitude to the individuals who supported your project. This may include thanking family and friends who have provided emotional (and maybe monetary) support, supervisors and lecturers who have provided academic guidance and, significantly, the participants who generously contributed their valuable time to make your research possible, as well as any financial contribution if you have been funded to do your studies. Importantly, the acknowledgements page is not assessed or marked, so it is not necessary to thank everyone (especially, if there are people you are unsure about thanking), nor does this page need to be written in a formal manner. Indeed, it is nice to bring your own flavour or twist to the way in which you acknowledge people, so feel free to use your own style. Please remember though that while it is nice to thank your respondents for their participation you must not forget about any promises of confidentiality made, so be careful not to inadvertently reveal identities (see Chapter 4: *Being an Ethical Researcher*).

Some institutions will also ask for a set of up to six key words which describe your project. When deciding what to choose, consider the types of words that you would put into a search engine to try and find your research project. Using the fictional Barbie project abstract as an exemplar, you might choose the following key words: Barbie, Advertising, Content Analysis, YouTube, Gender, Toys.

As part of the front matter, you should also include a separate page with a table of contents, which lists the pages on which each chapter starts. More detailed tables of contents will be more granular, providing further information such as the page that each subsection within a chapter begins. If your research project includes tables and/or figures you should also include a separate list of tables and figures at the bottom of the contents page. An example of a contents page – which incidentally can run over several pages – is shown in Figure 9.1. A contents page can be made quickly and easily in Microsoft Word if you use the heading styles (Heading 1, Heading 2, etc.) to format titles and subtitles consistently throughout the main body of the text. This will, of course, mean collating all the separate chapters you have drafted into that one large document. When doing this, be careful to make sure that each new chapter begins on a new page. You can do this easily by using the Page Break function in Microsoft Word. The button to create a contents page can then be found under the 'References' tab in Microsoft Word represented by an icon of a page of writing folded in the top right-hand corner. Note how the numbering of the front matter – page of contents, abstract, and acknowledgements – is represented by Roman numerals on the contents page, while the rest of the pages are in the Arabic system. As a tip, we suggest not having more than three levels of headings/subheadings otherwise it becomes very difficult to read.

Page of Contents		
Abstract		i
Acknowledgements		ii
1	**Introduction**	1
	1.1 Background	1
	1.2 Research Objectives	2
2	**Literature Review**	4
	2.1 Theoretical Framework	4
	2.2 Review of Related Studies	6
3	**Methodology**	10
	3.1 Research Design	10
	3.2 Participants	12
	3.3 Data Collection Methods	14
	3.4 Data Analysis	16
4	**Findings**	20
	4.1 Quantitative Findings	20
	4.2 Qualitative Findings	24
5	**Discussion and Analysis**	30
	5.1 Interpretation of Results	30
	5.2 Comparison with Previous Studies	34
6	**Conclusion**	38
	6.1 Summary of Findings	38
	6.2 Implications and Recommendations	40
7	**References**	46
	Appendices	53
	Appendix A: Participant Consent Form	53
	Appendix B: Interview Questions	55
	Appendix C: Statistical Tables	57

Figure 9.1 An example contents page

It is often the case that both the Front and Back matter will not count toward your final word count for your written research project. However, there may be marks available for the presentation of your written thesis and therefore it is essential to format these sections according to your institutional guidelines.

BACK MATTER

Your written research project will also have several pages which appear after the final word of your Conclusion, located in what might be called the back matter. For example, following the substantive chapters, it is typical to have a list of references. This is a compilation of all the texts (journal articles, books, policy papers, websites, newspapers, grey literature, etc.), which you have consulted *and* cited throughout your research project, encompassing both substantive and methodological sources. Of course, it is vital that you reference the provenance of the ideas that you are using, borrowing, and drawing from. Ensure that your reference list is organised alphabetically by the first author's surname and be attentive to the referencing style preferred by your department or institution, as institutions follow distinctive styles such as Harvard Referencing, APA (American Psychological Association), or Chicago. If you cite two or more different publications from the same author, then you will need to order these by date. If you cite two or more publications from the same author published in the same year, then under most citation rules you will need to add a letter after the date in both the main body of text and the reference list to show unequivocally which publication you are referring to. For instance, to use a fictional example, Brookfield and Lewis (2021a) and Brookfield and Lewis (2021b). Correctly referencing the literature that you engaged with during the research process is vital as it allows others to access and validate the texts which you relied on for your research. Software packages such as Endnote and Mendeley have been designed specifically to help you store and organise your references throughout your project and can present them in the referencing style which you request. Microsoft Word also offers a built-in referencing tool. This too allows you to manage and format your citations and and reference list easily. This add-in can be accessed via the 'References' tab in Microsoft Word. Whichever way you decide to reference, as discussed in Chapter 2 (*Planning a Social Science Research Project*), it is crucial that you begin as you mean to go on, inputting or noting down references from the beginning of the project. This will save you valuable time at the end of your project.

Following the reference list, you will typically have a list of appendices, though these are not always necessary. These supplementary materials might include copies of data collection instruments like questionnaires or interview schedules. Additionally, appendices may contain other relevant documents, such as template consent forms used in your research. It is important that if you include appendices they are referred to in the main body of the text. That is, just as references cited in the main text should be included in your reference list, then only appendices referred to in the main text should be included in your list of appendices. These should be listed alphabetically as appendix

A, appendix B etc. with appendix A being the first document referred to in the main body of your written research project, appendix B the second document, and so on. It is also important that appendices are anonymised if you have promised this too. Therefore, if you are including consent forms, you should simply be including a template and no signed forms from individual participants which could identify them. It is almost certainly the case that appendices will not form part of your overall word count.

REVISITING YOUR RESEARCH QUESTIONS

Whilst it may sound obvious, it is important at this final stage of your research project to check that your dissertation directly answers the research questions which you initially posed. As explained throughout this book, it is not uncommon for researchers to begin with a specific set of research questions or objectives but later realise that these may not be entirely feasible, or that the data collected offers valuable insights into a slightly different aspect of the topic to those which they originally set out to explore. As your research progresses, you might become more critical of your original questions and their phrasing, prompting you to refine and adapt them to better align with your findings. This process of fine-tuning the research questions is a natural and necessary part of the social science research journey, ensuring that the data presented in later chapters adequately addresses the final questions listed. However, this adjustment may also require revisiting earlier chapters to maintain a consistent and coherent narrative throughout your dissertation. Although the chapters at the front end of your dissertation should set up the research questions, it is important that the chapters toward the back are the ones that provide answers and insights into the topic being explored. Should you find discrepancies between the research questions set out at the start of your research project and the data presented and analysed toward the end of your research project, it is essential to (re)consider whether the data are the most appropriate for the research objectives or if the research questions need slight modifications to fit with your findings.

Remember: you cannot change the data you have collected without collecting new data – a lengthy process – but you can change your research questions.

CHECKING THE REQUIREMENTS

At this stage of the dissertation journey, it is always productive to revisit the module handbook or guidance provided to ensure compliance with all the requirements and criteria. Pay particular attention to essential aspects such as the word count, making certain to clarify what is and is not included in the final word count. We need to stress that different institutions and even different departments, will have different rules regarding the flexibility of word counts and what they include (e.g., reference lists) when calculating the final word count of an assessment. Additionally, be attentive to the specified formatting guidelines, including whether double spacing and specific margin sizes are necessary. If you are using Microsoft Word to write up your research project, the drop-down menus for indents and spacing can be found by clicking the Home tab followed by the Paragraph tab. Equally important is understanding the prescribed structure for your dissertation.

Furthermore, take this opportunity to review the marking criteria thoroughly. Familiarising yourself with the assessment criteria is always beneficial no matter the assessment, ensuring that your work is aligned with the assessment standards. One aspect of the marking criteria that you can address at this stage concerns the presentation of the research project.

It is also important to double check essential information, such as the submission date and time of your dissertation. Check also whether there is a requirement to complete or attach any other documentation to your submission such as research diaries. After dedicating substantial effort to your work, it would be dispiriting to make a simple error at this stage that could easily have been avoided by (re-)checking the requirements.

If you are unclear or unsure about any of the requirements, it is always worth seeking clarification from your supervisor or course convenor.

GETTING FEEDBACK FROM YOUR SUPERVISOR

Other than yourself, at this stage of the research process, your supervisor will possess the highest degree of familiarity with your project. As discussed in Chapter 2 (*Planning a Social Science Research Project*), it is important to be prepared for supervisory meetings to ensure that you can get the most out of them – this is true even at this late stage of the research journey. As you approach the end of your project, it is crucial that you check your supervisor's availability to review final drafts and the last possible date to ask any outstanding questions. This proactive approach should provide ample time to address any last-minute adjustments and ensures that neither party is under undue pressure.

When you receive feedback and feedforward from your supervisor on a final draft, take time and care to review these comments and seek clarification on any comments which are unclear to you. If you have doubts or concerns, do not hesitate to ask for further examples or for clarification.

PROOFREADING AND EDITING

Proofreading is an important practice of any writing process, but it is essential when compiling a large document such as a dissertation research project. This activity should ensure that your research project attains a polished veneer by identifying and rectifying typographical and grammatical errors, which are an inevitable scourge for all writers. While word processing software's grammar and spelling tools, as well as programmes such as Grammarly, are valuable aids for spotting potential errors, they are not infallible and may not recognise specialised jargon. Equally, they may not always pick up on homophones (words which sound the same but have a different spelling). For example, 'to', 'too' and 'two', or 'there', 'their' and 'they're' all have different meanings and are used in different contexts. Therefore, we really encourage you to employ additional techniques to conduct a thorough proofread. For instance, reading your work aloud can be immensely helpful in identifying errors, as it enables you to notice missing punctuation or misspelled words that may not be apparent when reading silently. This is also an excellent way to sense check your writing. Reading from a hard copy of your work rather than from a screen can also make errors more evident. Printing out a version of your written research project allows you to view the text from a fresh perspective and may highlight errors that were overlooked on the screen and help you identify passages which have not been expressed clearly. Make sure that you print on both sides of the paper and try to use recycled paper. Enlisting the assistance of a friend or family member for proofreading can also be beneficial. They will approach your work with a fresh set of eyes and are therefore more likely to spot errors which you may have become desensitised to after extensive reviewing. As part of the assessment criteria, it is almost certain that there will be a band descriptor called presentation. Here, markers will be assessing the research project on aspects such as writing skills including grammatical and typographical errors. They will value concise, incisive writing with a logical and coherent presentation of the work. They will be keen to see correct use of specialist vocabulary and will expect consistent and accurate referencing with very few mistakes. Aspects of expression and presentation are both tasks that you can revisit during this proofing stage. That said, proofreading extends beyond simply identifying typographical and grammatical errors. In the final proofread of your written research project, you should also be attentive to the following issues:

- Consistency: have you consistently used terminology, capitalisation, and spelling conventions throughout the document? Consistent language and style contribute to a polished and professional presentation of your work. For example, writing *do not* rather than *don't*, or if you have spelt it as *organisation*, make sure there are no rogue *organizations* in the document.
- Reporting: have you double checked that all numbers and/or statistics reported in the main text correspond with the values shown in charts or graphs? Accurate and congruent reporting strengthens the credibility of your research.
- Acronyms: have you written out any acronyms used in full? The first time you use an acronym, it is good practice to spell it out in full, for example the Organization for Economic Cooperation and Development (OECD), and then use the acronym OECD thereafter. An additional extra step which can be helpful for the reader is including a list of acronyms after your contents page.
- Formatting: have you followed the instructions laid out in the module handbook or guide? Make sure you that you use page numbers throughout the document, and that they are consistently positioned on the page. On Microsoft Word, click Insert and this will bring up a row of icons. Under the heading page numbers, you can add page numbers as headers (at the top of the pages) or footers (at the

bottom of the pages). Make sure that all new chapters begin on new pages and insert a page break if necessary. Again, this tab can be found under the Insert button at the top of a Microsoft Word document. Make sure all main headings and subheadings are formatted consistently too.
- Meaning: have you used the correct word? Have you checked the meaning of the word? For example, while the word 'full' is usually used in a positive fashion, fulsome often has pejorative connotations.

Researcher Reflection

In a draft version of a manuscript, Charlotte intended to write about the potential **causal** relationship between two variables. However, she accidentally typed this incorrectly and repeatedly wrote about the potential **casual** relationship between two variables. This typographical error was not detected by a spelling tool as 'casual' is a legitimate word spelt correctly, and to a computer the sentence still made sense. It was only by asking others to proofread her work, that Charlotte became aware of this typographical error.

Editing is the process of revisiting your writing to sharpen the expression and may involve reducing the word count, making sentences more succinct or restructuring sections. The aim of editing is to enhance the clarity and coherence of your writing to improve the overall readability and flow. Specific aspects to consider when editing a document include:

- Presentation: have you correctly titled chapters and labelled all visualisations (images, charts, etc.) as well as any appendices used? Clear and accurate labelling enhances the readability and understanding of your work.
- Formatting: have you adhered to your institutional guidelines in relation to issues such as spacing, margin size, and referencing style? Adherence to formatting guidelines ensures compliance with academic standards.
- Tense: is the tense consistent throughout? If not, is there a valid reason for this? For example, some people write their Methods chapter in the first person so to enrol themselves in the project, recognising their influence. Remember writing in the present tense saves words: 'In this chapter I will examine' is six words but, 'In this Chapter I examine' is five words.

Indeed, editing is one way in which to make your final document as concise as possible. Though a word count of 8,000–10,000 words can feel a little daunting to begin with, you will soon recognise words get eaten up very quickly and we often have students asking us how strict the final word count is and whether they will be marked down for going over the specified word count. Word counts have a function beyond containing your research project, they are also instruments of equity, enabling fair comparison across a cohort. Some institutions may allow students a leeway of plus or minus 10% in relation to final word counts for assessments. But it is important to check whether this is applicable for your course and to remember to confirm with the module convenors or your supervisor exactly what is included in the final word count.

Reducing the word count without losing any content involves careful reading. Here are two paragraphs, one is the original paragraph, and the second is an edited version of the paragraph where we have tried to lose some words without losing any content or meaning:

Original paragraph

This research study will explore the eating habits and dieting behaviours of young females aged 18–25 in the United Kingdom (UK) during the extraordinary context of the Covid-19 pandemic. This research project explores the multifaceted relationship between the pandemic, lifestyle changes, and the impact on dietary choices and habits among this specific demographic. The Covid-19 pandemic has ushered in a new era, altering daily routines, exacerbating stress levels, and influencing societal norms. Against this backdrop, the study employs interview-based research to uncover the intricate interplay of factors such as lockdowns, remote working or studying, social isolation, and heightened health concerns on the eating patterns and dieting motivations of young women. By engaging in intimate conversations with these individuals, the study investigates the ways in which the pandemic has affected their nutritional preferences, meal planning, perceptions of body image, self-esteem, and the role of societal influences in shaping their dietary decisions. Ultimately, this research endeavours to shed light on the complex dynamics of young women's eating behaviours during a period of global upheaval, with the hope of informing strategies to promote healthier and more resilient lifestyles in the face of unprecedented challenges. (192 words)

Rewritten paragraph

This study explores the eating habits and dieting behaviours of females aged 18–25 in the United Kingdom (UK) during the Covid-19 pandemic. The research explores the relationship between the pandemic, lifestyle changes, and the impact on dietary habits among young females. Covid-19 has led to altered routines, heightened stress levels, and has influenced societal norms. Against this backdrop, the study employs interviews to uncover the interplay of factors including lockdowns, remote working or studying, social isolation, and heightened health concerns on the eating patterns and dieting motivations of young women. It considers how the pandemic has affected these women's nutritional preferences, meal planning, perceptions of body image, self-esteem, and the role of societal influences in shaping their dietary decisions. This research sheds light on the complex dynamics of young women's eating behaviours during a period of global upheaval, with the hope of informing strategies to promote healthier and more resilient lifestyles in the face of unprecedented challenges. (158 words)

The fictional examples here show how you can reduce words without having to simply cut content. The original paragraph was cut by 34 words from 192 to 158. While this might not sound like much, modelling this percentage of reduction across a 10,000-word dissertation or research report (excluding references) would see you save 1,770 words, 17.7% of the content, or the size of a chapter.

PLAGIARISM CHECK

Plagiarism is when someone fails to properly attribute words or ideas to the original author and is judged to be presenting the ideas of others as their own. This manifests when in-text citations are omitted or when the proper referencing of authors in the reference list is neglected. Such omissions lead to ambiguity about the rightful source of credit. It is also possible to self-plagiarise – this occurs when you reuse work you have already published (or submitted for assessment elsewhere) and do not properly cite the original source. As before, self plagiarism is a way to prevent you from benefitting from the same work more than once. Being referred for unfair practice and being judged to have plagiarised can be extremely distressing and can have significant consequences for your degree. We do not want to concern you. This is something not to be unduly worried about, but it is something to be aware of and to avoid at all costs.

It is also something universities are acutely aware of, especially with developments in generative AI (Artificial Intelligence) such as ChatGPT and the growth of writing mills or farms (see Chapter 3: *Reviewing Social Science Literature*). Universities typically employ plagiarism detection software to scrutinise written content. This software identifies instances where sources lack proper attribution and produce similarity scores. Similarity scores themselves, of course, do not mean someone is guilty of unfair practice. In many instances, it can mark-up particularly good citing practices as one would expect the references in your reference list to show in a similarity report. It will also show sentences that have been properly cited. This tool should be available to you as a student to scan your research project before submitting it too. Therefore, before submitting your work we strongly encourage you to run your dissertation through a software package such as Turnitin or CrossRef to check that you have not made any inadvertent mistakes. It is a fruitful idea to check with your institution about what plagiarism software is available and whether there is a limit on the number of times you can check one assessment. Putting your work through a plagiarism software programme is also an efficient way to ensure that you are not over relying on other people's words even when properly credited. That is, try not to include too many direct quotations, even when accurately crediting. Direct quotes should only be used when you cannot express the point any other way or when you are stylistically stressing a point. At other times, paraphrase, use your own words to make the point, but of course always cite the provenance of the idea. This shows you understand concepts and ideas and can express arguments. It also helps with the flow of the writing. As discussed in Chapter 3, being an active note taker should help in this regard. Beyond software reliance, we strongly urge you to spend time familiarising yourself with the referencing style used by your department or institution. It is likely that your university library will be able to provide support on how to reference.

ACCEPTABLE TERMINOLOGY

As social science students, you will be aware that words and how they are expressed matter. Writing in gender-neutral vocabulary is an important professional requirement. This, of course, does not refer to the ways in which you introduce research participants who identify as a particular gender; if someone identifies as a cis female then you should introduce them as a cis female. Rather, this concerns the general writing of the thesis. It is comparatively easy to make nouns gender neutral. For example, rather than using 'mankind' you should use another word such as 'humankind' or 'people'; rather than use 'policeman' use 'police officer'; rather than use 'chairman' use 'chair' or 'coordinator'; rather than use 'manning a desk' use 'tending a desk'; and rather than use 'founding fathers', use 'trailblazers' or 'founders' (please note that pioneers has colonial connotations). Pronouns are more difficult because English does not have neutral forms, but the following strategies should work in most situations:

1   The use of plurals is, arguably, the simplest coping strategy. For example, sentences such as: 'When the supporter began swearing at the steward, he was escorted from the premises' could be re-phrased as 'when the supporter began swearing at the steward, **they** were escorted from the premises'.
2   Delete pronouns that are not strictly necessary. For example, rather than 'When the student completes his final year …' use 'When the student completes **their** final year …'.
3   Avoid making sex, gender, race, or class-based assumptions about people and their abilities.
4   Do not specify the sex or ethnicity, etc. of an individual unless it is relevant to the study. If it is not, ask yourself why you are referring to it. Language is always evolving, and it is important to be aware of what is appropriate and what is not. Acceptable terminology also differs between cultures and nations so please check the appropriate sources.

DEALING WITH ANXIETY

If you are apprehensive about submitting your research project, we strongly suggest that you speak with your dissertation supervisor and/or university personal tutor. They will not only be able to reassure you about the submission process but should also be able to provide you with valuable suggestions on how you can improve your work. Considering this, as discussed in Chapter 2 (*Planning a Social Science Research Project*), it is important that you maintain a good relationship with your supervisor throughout your project. To reiterate, if you are unable to meet deadlines or attend meetings for whatever reason, communicate these with your supervisor. If your supervisor is aware of the challenges you are encountering, they will be able to advise and support you through these tricky times.

It is also crucial to remember that most people will feel some stress and anxiety about their dissertation and progress at some point during their research project. Such feelings are common, and it is healthy to share these concerns not only with academic staff, but also with friends and family. What is important is that stress does not turn into distress. Working alongside friends can help ensure that you stay on track, meaning that you are there to support one another if one of you has a difficult day or has writer's block, for example. Plan study dates and organise treats for when you reach certain milestones, e.g., completing a chapter or transcribing your last interview.

Some students find it beneficial to keep a research diary or notes (see Chapter 3: *Reviewing Social Science Literature*) when undertaking their project. This can help you keep track of your project but also serve as an outlet for your thoughts, concerns, and questions. Putting these thoughts on paper can unburden your mind.

While it is natural to feel anxious when not working on your dissertation, strive to maintain your regular routines. Continue spending time with friends and family, pursuing hobbies, engaging in sports, and dedicating time to yourself. These practices provide a much-needed break from your research and can even offer a fresh perspective when you return to it. Sometimes you need to put your writing away for a few days so to return to it with fresh eyes, especially when editing.

Crucially, if feelings of anxiety do overwhelm you, it is important that you seek professional help and support. Your university will likely have a wellbeing and/or counselling team and you can also ask medical professionals for help. Remember, it is essential not to keep these emotions to yourself and to reach out for help when needed. Your health and wellbeing are always the priority, certainly over and above any research project (and its deadline). Please check what avenues and processes are available to you if you are struggling, such as applying for extenuating circumstances to get an extension or an interruption of study if you need an extended break from your studies. Again, proactive communication is essential here.

WHAT WILL THE MARKERS BE LOOKING FOR?

Having finished your research project, it is advisable to review the marking criteria one last time before submitting your dissertation. Keep in mind, though, that every institution has its own, unique set of criteria, so it is essential to consult the specific criteria for your module to ensure compliance. That given, generally speaking, markers typically assess your dissertation against the following kinds of requirements.

Review of appropriate literature

- Can demonstrate knowledge of the principles, key concepts, and theoretical approaches relevant to the subject researched.
- Draws selectively, appropriately, and critically on a range of sources, but primarily research-based social science evidence.
- Shows clear evidence of extensive independent reading.
- Demonstrates understanding of the subject in both breadth and depth.

Research design and execution

- Draws on appropriate methodological literature.
- Critically evaluates the appropriateness and rationale of the method(s) employed.
- Demonstrates an understanding of the ethical sensitivity of the research and outlines steps taken to minimise any concerns.
- Demonstrates a logical, coherent throughline, meaning the dissertation has a clear line of argument.

Presentation of findings and data analysis

- Exhibits an ability to present data in a variety of forms.
- Analyses concepts and theories and applies them to issues of policy and/or practice in a systematic way.
- Displays an ability to interpret or infer the data so to contribute to social science research.
- Draws on a range of knowledge and skills to answer clear, well-articulated research question(s) or equivalent objectives.

Conclusions and recommendations

- Reflects on own value systems and on the limitations of theory and research, putting forward suggestions for future research.
- Displays evidence of clear and critical thinking and clearly summarises what was learnt in the project and its contribution (to policy, practice, and/or to the discipline itself).

Presentation and structure

- Demonstrates confident, accurate, and critical use of specialist vocabulary.
- Produces a connected dissertation with standalone chapters that transition well to the next chapter.
- Provides appropriate signposting and summarising throughout the dissertation.
- Displays authenticity, originality, and independence.
- Produces a dissertation that is:

- free from grammatical errors
- concise, crisp, and sharp
- properly formatted
- logical and coherent
- clear and consistent throughout
- accurately referenced.

LETTING GO

In some cases, submitting your research project or dissertation is a point of celebration, but for others it can be a source of anxiety. Having dedicated considerable time carefully planning, undertaking, and writing up your research project, it can be difficult to let it go. It is no longer yours to tinker with and is now with someone else to assess. To help with this challenge, we recommend that you take a few moments to reflect and take stock of what you have accomplished. Often students surprise themselves at the fact that they have written such a lengthy document and successfully undertaken a research project akin to the ones which they have read about throughout their degree programme in journal articles. As well as taking pride in your accomplishment, you should reflect on the skills which you have developed and how these will surely help you going forward, in either postgraduate level study or in the workplace. As well as undertaking a piece of independent research, you will have developed your report writing skills, analytic skills, communication skills, time management skills, and critical thinking skills (Brookfield and Lewis 2024).

As previously stressed, it is worth reiterating the value of setting an internal deadline a few days or weeks even ahead of the official dissertation submission date. This approach fosters greater confidence in submitting your project on time and letting go of your dissertation.

Lastly, we suggest that you organise a special treat for yourself to celebrate your accomplishment. Submitting a research project which may contribute toward a sizeable proportion of your final degree classification is a big achievement. Take the time to acknowledge this milestone and plan a meaningful reward for yourself. Whether it is enjoying a meal out (or in), spending quality time with loved ones, going to an exercise class or binge watching your favourite TV series, this act of recognition can provide a well-deserved sense of closure and accomplishment. Huge congratulations!

SUMMARY

In this chapter, we focussed on the final touches required before submitting your dissertation. We stressed the importance of completing a draft of your dissertation a couple of weeks before the official deadline. This then allows time to go back and sharpen sentences, check for typographical errors as well as to make sure all references have been included. We discussed what is expected in the front matter of the dissertation as well as providing tips on how to produce these sections. We outlined what back matter material is required for a research project too, such as a reference list and appendices. Crucially, we also discussed other matters such as dealing with anxiety, letting the dissertation go, the use of consistent and acceptable terminology as well as editing and formatting. We feel confident that you are now ready to submit your social science research project. What an amazing achievement – well done!

Student Question

Do I need to get my dissertation printed for submission?

(Fatima, Media Studies Student)

Charlotte and Jamie say:

It is important to check the submission guidelines to see if you are required to get your dissertation printed and bound for submission. Some institutions require students to submit printed copies of their dissertations and, in some cases, students need to print multiple copies to submit to multiple examiners. These might come with strict instructions on margin size and how the thesis is bound. However, increasingly institutions do not require students to print their dissertations but instead submit electronic copies. Make sure you check the guidance from your institution and if you are unsure, please ask your supervisor or course convenor.

WHAT'S NEXT?

Chapter Checklist

Table 9.1 Chapter 9 checklist

	Yes	No
I know how to proofread my social science research project.		
I understand the importance of editing my social science research project.		
I have familiarised myself with the submission guidance for my social science research project.		
I can write an abstract for my social science research project.		
I can create a table of contents for my social science research project.		
I know how to compile a reference list for my social science research project.		

Read

Connolly, L. 2022. *Proofread Your Essay*. London: Sage.
Leicester, M. and Taylor, D. 2017. *Get a Better Grade. Seven Steps to Excellent Essays and Assignments*. London: Sage.
Wilson, C. 2019. *Manage Your Stress*. London: Sage.

Watch

Microsoft Support. 2024. *Insert a table of contents*. Available at: https://support.microsoft.com/en-us/office/insert-a-table-of-contents-882e8564-0edb-435e-84b5-1d8552ccf0c0 (accessed 5 April).

Watch the video on creating and inserting a contents table in Microsoft Word. Once you have watched the video, have a go at making your own contents table. Do not forget to make a separate table listing any figures or tables in your written research project.

Do

Read your research project aloud. You may find it useful to print your research project off before you start reading. Please make sure that you set it to print on both sides of the paper. Use this opportunity to identify typographical and grammatical errors. Alternatively, you can use 'Read Aloud' software and listen to your report being read aloud from your computer or laptop.

- Do you spot any frequent errors? Note these down on the space provided and use the 'Find' function on Microsoft Word to identify all instances of this error.

Complete

Use the checklist provided to help ensure that you are ready to submit your research project. If there are items which you are unable to check off this list, it may indicate that you need to revisit some chapters or aspects of your research project.

Table 9.2 Research project submission checklist

	I have not done this	I could do more on this	I have definitely done this
Front matter			
I have come up with a title, and created a title page.			
I have written an abstract providing a clear summary of my research.			
I have written an acknowledgements page thanking people who supported my research.			
I have created a table of contents (and, if relevant, a table and figures content page).			
Introduction chapter			
In the Introduction, I have clearly stated the importance and relevance of the research and set the scene.			
In the Introduction, I have clearly outlined the structure of the whole research project.			
I have proofread and edited the Introduction.			
Literature Review chapter			
In the Literature Review, I have defined key terms/concepts and ideas used throughout the research project.			
In the Literature Review, I have described and critiqued existing studies noting their relevance for my project.			
In the Literature Review, I have drawn primarily on academic literature (books and journal articles).			
In the Literature Review, I have predominately included contemporary references to ensure the information is up-to-date and relevant.			
In the Literature Review, I have identified gaps in the existing research and have subsequently developed research questions.			
I have proofread and edited the Literature Review chapter.			

	I have not done this	I could do more on this	I have definitely done this
Methods chapter			
In the Methods chapter, I have described the chosen approach to answering the research question(s).			
In the Methods chapter, I have provided a clear rationale for the chosen approach to answering the research question(s).			
In the Methods chapter, I have provided details of the sample used in my research.			
In the Methods chapter, I have outlined the ethical concerns associated with my research and the steps taken to minimise these.			
I have proofread and edited the Methods chapter.			
Findings chapter			
I have structured the chapter so that it flows well as a narrative.			
I have presented key findings which answer my research question(s).			
I have proofread and edited the Findings chapter.			
Discussion chapter			
I have demonstrated how my findings answer the research question(s) I set out with.			
I have interpreted the findings and inferred what they mean (for social science).			
I have discussed my research in relation to the wider literature.			
I have highlighted the policy and/or practice implications of my research findings (this could be part of the Conclusion chapter instead).			
I have proofread and edited the Discussion chapter.			
Conclusion chapter			
I have outlined the main findings from my research and answered the research questions.			
I have highlighted the limitations of my research.			

(Continued)

Table 9.2 (Continued)

	I have not done this	I could do more on this	I have definitely done this
I have suggested ideas for future research.			
I have proofread and edited the Conclusion chapter.			
Back matter			
I have created an alphabetically-ordered reference list.			
I have inserted appendices (where appropriate).			
Other			
I have carefully proofread and edited the whole dissertation.			
I have sought advice and guidance from my supervisor.			
I have asked a friend/family member to review my written work.			
I have checked the submission guidelines and dates for my written work.			

REFERENCES

Abbott, O. 2023. W.E.B. Du Bois's forgotten sociology of morality: Contesting the foundations and informing the future of the sociology of morality. *The Sociological Review*, 71(5): 957–975.

Adam, B.E. 1994. *Time and Social Theory*. Cambridge: Polity Press.

Adam, B.E. 2004. *Time*. Polity Key Concepts Series. Cambridge: Polity Press.

Adekoya, A.A. and Guse, L. 2020. Walking interviews and wandering behavior: Ethical insights and methodological outcomes while exploring the perspectives of older adults living with dementia. *International Journal of Qualitative Methods*, 19. https://doi.org/10.1177/1609406920920135

Adorno, T. 1991. *The Culture Industry: Selected Essays on Mass Culture*. London: Routledge.

Adorno, T. and Horkheimer, M. 2016. The culture industry: Enlightenment as mass deception. In T. Adorno and M. Horkheimer, *Dialectic of Enlightenment*. London: Verso.

Adriansen, H.K. 2012. Timeline interviews: A tool for conducting life history research. *Qualitative Studies*, 3(1): 40–55.

Akrich, M. 2023. Actor Network Theory, Bruno Latour, and the CSI. *Social Studies of Science*, 53(2): 169–173.

Alamri, W.A. 2019. Effectiveness of qualitative research methods: Interviews and diaries. *International Journal of English and Cultural Studies*, 2(1): 65–70.

Allen, J.A., Fisher, C., Chetouani, M., Chiu, M.M., Gunes, H., Mehu, M. and Hung, H. 2017. Comparing social science and computer science workflow processes for studying group interactions. *Small Group Research*, 48(5): 568–590.

Allen, L. 2011. 'Picture this': Using photo-methods in research on sexualities and schooling. *Qualitative Research*, 11(5): 487–504.

Allen, L. 2023. The smell of lockdown: Smellwalks as sensuous methodology. *Qualitative Research*, 23(1): 21–37.

Anderson, D.J. 2010. *Kanban: Successful Evolutionary Change for Your Technology Business*. Bilbao: Blue Hole Press.

Arshed, N. and Danson, M. 2015. The literature review. In R. MacIntosh and K.D. O'Gorman (eds), *Research Methods for Business and Management: A Guide to Writing Your Dissertation*. Oxford: Goodfellow Publishers, pp. 31–49.

Artis, A.B. 2008. Improving marketing students' reading comprehension with the SQR3 method. *Journal of Marketing Education*, 30(2): 130–137.

Asif, M. 2022. Police legitimacy and approval of vigilante violence: The significance of anger. *Theoretical Criminology*, 19(2), 163–182.

Atkinson, P. 2005. Qualitative research: Unity and diversity. *Forum Qualitative Social Research*, 6(3): art 26.

Atkinson, P. 2013. Blowing hot: The ethnography of craft and the craft of ethnography. *Qualitative Inquiry*, 19(5): 397–404.

Atkinson, P. 2015. Working with ethnographic fieldnotes: Learning tango. *Sage Datasets*. https://doi.org/10.4135/9781412962056

Atkinson, P. and Silverman, D. 1997. Kundera's *Immortality*: The interview society and the invention of the self. *Qualitative Inquiry*, 3(3): 304–325.

Baarts, C. 2009. Stuck in the middle: Research ethics caught between science and politics. *Qualitative Research*, 9(4): 423–439.

Back, L. and Puwar, N. 2012. A manifesto for live methods: Provocations and capacities. *The Sociological Review*, 60(1): 6–17.

Bagley, C. 2008. Educational ethnography as performance art: Towards a sensuous feeling and knowing. *Qualitative Research*, 8(1): 53–72.

Bagnoli, A. and Clark, A. 2010. Focus groups with young people: A participatory approach to research planning. *Journal of Youth Studies*, 13(1): 101–119.

Baker, D. 2021. Presentations: Creating conference posters using PowerPoint. In E. Barker and V. Phillips, Creating conference posters: Structure, form and content. *Journal of Perioperative Practice*, 31(7–8): 296–299.

Bakhtin, M. 1968. *Rabelais and His World*. Cambridge, MA: MIT Press.

Baliyan, S.P. and Khama, D. 2020. How distance to school and study hours after school influence students' performance in Mathematics and English: A comparative analysis. *Journal of Education and E-learning Research*, 7(2): 209–217.

Ball, M. 2011. Images, language and numbers in company reports: A study of documents that are occasioned by a legal requirement for financial disclosure. *Qualitative Research*, 11(2), 115–139.

Barbarick, K.A. and Ippolito, J.A. 2003. Does the number of hours studied affect exam performance? *Journal of Natural Resources and Life Sciences Education*, 32(1): 32–35.

Barthes, R. 1964. *Elements of Semiology*. London: Cape.

Bartlett, A., Lewis, J., Reyes-Galindo, L. and Stephens, N. 2018. The locus of legitimate interpretation in Big Data sciences: Lessons for computational social science from -omic biology and high-energy physics. *Big Data & Society*, 5(1). https://doi.org/10.1177/2053951718768831

Bates, C. and Rhys-Taylor, A. (eds) 2017. *Walking Through Social Research*. London: Routledge.

Bates, C., Moles, K. and Kroese, L.M. 2023. Animating sociology. *The Sociological Review*, 71(5): 976–991.

BBC Radio 4. 2018. *All in the mind*, 14 February. Available at: www.bbc.co.uk/programmes/b09r6fvn (accessed 29 July 2022).

Bechhofer, F. 1981. Substantive dogs and methodological tails: A question of fit. *Sociology*, 15(4): 495–505.

Becker, H.S. 1974. Photography and sociology. *Studies in Visual Communication*, 1(1): 3–26.

Becker, L. 2014. Preparing to present. In L. Becker, *Presenting your Research: Conferences, Symposiums, Poster Presentations and Beyond*. London: SAGE Publications, pp. 81–93. https://doi.org/10.4135/9781473919815

Beer, D. 2013. *Popular Culture and New Media: The Politics of Circulation*. London: Palgrave MacMillan.

Beneito-Montagut, R. 2022. Digital and non-digital: Researching digital practices as trans-situated activities in everyday later life. In U. Flick (ed.), *The SAGE Handbook of Qualitative Research Design*. Vol. 2. London: Sage, pp. 835–850.

Beneito-Montagut, R., Cassián, N. and Begueria, A. 2018. What do we know about the relationship between Internet mediated interaction and social isolation and loneliness in later life? *Quality in Ageing and Older Adults*, 19(1): 14–30.

Berelson, B. 1952. *Content Analysis in Communication Research*. Glencoe, IL: Free Press.

Berger, P. and Luckmann, T. 1991. *The Social Construction of Reality*. London: Penguin.

Bhambra, G. and Holmwood, J. 2021. *Colonialism and Modern Social Theory*. Bristol: Polity.

Birnbacher, D. 1999. Ethics and social science: Which kind of co-operation. *Ethical Theory and Moral Practice*, 2: 319–326.

Blakely, H. and Moles, K. 2017. Interviewing in the 'interview society': Making visible the biographical work of producing accounts for interviews. *Qualitative Research*, 17(2): 159–172.

Blakely, H. and Moles, K. 2019. Everyday practices of memory: Authenticity, value and the gift. *The Sociological Review*, 67(3): 621–634.

Blaxter, L., Hughes, C. and Tight, M. 2010. *How to Research*, 4th edn. Buckingham: Open University Press.

Bleakley, P. 2021. Panic, pizza and mainstreaming the Alt Right: A social media analysis of Pizzagate and the rise of the Qanon conspiracy. *Current Sociology*, 71(3): 509–525.

Boch, E. 2023. When respondents become photographers. Participatory photography: Characteristics, implementation, and interest for research in marketing. *Recherche et Applications En Marketing* (English edn), 38(2): 108–132.

Boland, A., Cherry, M.G. and Dickson, R. 2023. *Doing a Systematic Review: A Student's Guide*, 3rd edn. London: Sage.

Borges, J.L. 1988. *Collected Fictions* (trans. A. Hurley). New York: Penguin.

Borz, G., Brandenburg, H. and Mendez, C. 2022. The impact of EU cohesion policy on European identity: A comparative analysis of EU regions. *European Union Politics*, 23(2): 259–281.

Boussiac, P. 2006. Saussure's legacy in semiotics. In C. Sanders, *The Cambridge Companion to Saussure*. Cambridge: Cambridge University Press, pp. 240–260.

Bowen, G.A. 2009. Document analysis as a qualitative research method. *Qualitative Research Journal*, 9(2): 27–40.

Boyatzis, R.E. 1998. *Transforming Qualitative Information: Thematic Analysis and Code*. London: Sage.

Brannen, J. 2005. Mixing methods: The entry of qualitative and quantitative approaches into the research process. *International Journal of Social Research Methodology: Theory & Practice*, 8(3): 173–184.

Braun, V. and Clarke, V. 2006. Using thematic analysis in psychology. *Qualitative Research in Psychology*, 3(2): 77–101.

Braun, V. and Clarke, V. 2013. *Successful Qualitative Research: A Practical Guide for Beginners*. Thousand Oaks: Sage.

Braun, V. and Clarke, V. 2019. Reflecting on reflexive thematic analysis. *Qualitative Research, Sport Exercise and Health*, 11(4): 589–597.

Braun, V. and Clarke, V. 2021. To saturate or not to saturate? Questioning data saturation as a useful concept for thematic analysis and sample-size rationales. *Qualitative Research in Sport, Exercise and Health*, 13(2): 201–216.

Brazerman, C. 2003. Intertextuality: How texts rely on other texts. In C. Brazerman and P. Prior, *What Writing Does and How it Does it: An Introduction to Analyzing Texts and Textual Practices*. New York: Routledge, pp. 83–96.

Brewer, H.R., Hirst, Y., Chadeau-Hyam, M., Johnson, E., Sundarm S. and Flanagan, J.M. 2023. Association between purchase of over-the-counter medications and ovarian cancer diagnosis in the Cancer Loyalty Card Study (CLOCS): Observational case-control study. *JMIR Public Health Surveillance*, 9: e41762

Brinkmann, S. and Kvale, S. 2004. Confronting the ethics of qualitative research. *Journal of Constructivist Psychology*, 18(2): 157–181.

British Academy. 2013. *British Academy welcomes Nuffield Foundation's new Q-Step Programme*. Available at: www.thebritishacademy.ac.uk/news/british-academy-welcomes-nuffield-foundations-new-q-step-programme/ (accessed 27 March 2023).

British Academy. 2024. *The SHAPE of research impact: Key messages*. Available at: www.thebritishacademy.ac.uk/documents/5083/tBA-SHAPE-research-impact-briefing.pdf (accessed 21 February 2024).

British Medical Journal. 1966. Nuremberg Code 1947. *BMJ*, 313: 1448. https://doi.org/10.1136/bmj.313.7070.1448

British Social Attitudes Survey. 2024. *British social attitudes*. Available at: https://natcen.ac.uk/british-social-attitudes (accessed 3 January 2024).

Brookfield, C. 2017. 'Quantification is the root of all evil in sociology'. What does it add up to? The place of quantitative research methods in British sociology, Doctoral dissertation, Cardiff University.

Brookfield, C. 2021. *Using Microsoft Excel for Social Research*. London: Sage.

Brookfield, C. and Lewis, J. 2021. *Plan Your Dissertation*. London: Sage

Brookfield, C. and Lewis, J. 2024. *What skills will I develop from undertaking a social science research project*. Available at: https://www.jsg-studentportal.co.uk/content.asp?categoryid=11&article=what-skills-will-i-develop-from-undertaking-social-science-research-project-281 (accessed 18 October 2024).

Brownlie, J. and Shaw, F. 2019. Empathy rituals: Small conversations about emotional distress on Twitter. *Sociology*, 53(1): 104–122.

Brumley, C. 2013. *The simple guide to academic podcasting: Microphones and recorders*. Available at: https://blogs.lse.ac.uk/impactofsocialsciences/2013/02/21/the-simple-guide-to-academic-podcasting-microphones-and-recorders/ (accessed 26 March 2024).

Brundage, J.S. 2023. Responsibility and recognition. State sovereignty as performative. *American Journal of Sociology*, 128(5): 1335–1380.

Bryman, A. 2001. *Social Research Methods*. Oxford: Oxford University Press.

Bryne, D. 2017. *Research ethics*. Available at: https://methods.sagepub.com/project-planner/research-ethics (accessed 5 April 2024).

Buck, C. and Lee, J. 2013. *Frozen*. Walt Disney Studios Motion Pictures.

Buhs, J. 2009. *Bigfoot: The Life and Times of a Legend*. Chicago: Chicago University Press.

Burawoy, M. 2005. For public sociology. *American Sociological Review*, 70(1): 4–28.

Burnap, P., Gibson, R., Sloan, L., Southern, R. and Williams, M. 2016. 140 characters to victory?: Using Twitter to predict the 2015 general election. *Electoral Studies*, 41: 230–233.

Burrell, N.A and Gross, C. 2017. Quantitative research, purpose of. In M. Allen (ed.), *The SAGE Encyclopaedia of Communication Research Methods*. London: Sage. Available at:

https://methods.sagepub.com/reference/the-sage-encyclopedia-of-communication-research-methods/i11671.xml (accessed 15 February 2023).

Buscher, M., Urry, J. and Witchger, K. (eds) 2011. *Mobile Methods*. London: Routledge.

Byrne, D. 2022. A worked example of Braun and Clarke's approach to reflexive thematic analysis. *Quality and Quantity*, 56: 1391–1412.

Callegaro, M., Manfreda, K.L. and Vehovar, V. 2015. *Web Survey Methodology*, 1st edn. London: Sage.

Callon, M. 1984. Some elements of a sociology of translation: Domestication of the scallops and the fishermen of St Brieuc Bay. *The Sociological Review*, 32(1): 196–233.

Campaign for Social Science. 2015. *10 reasons why we need social sciences* Available at: www.palgrave.com/gp/campaigns/social-science-matters/10-reasons-for-social-science (accessed 7 July 2022).

Capron, A.M. 2004. When experiments go wrong: The US perspective. *The Journal of Clinical Ethics*, 15(1): 22–29.

Carlston, D.L. 2011. Benefits of student-generated note packets: A preliminary investigation of SQ3R implementation. *Teaching of Psychology*, 38(3): 142–146.

Carrabine, E. 2019. Roland Barthes. In P. Atkinson, S. Delamont, A. Cernat, J.W. Sakshaug and R.A. Williams (eds), *Sage Foundations*. Available at: https://methods.sagepub.com/foundations/barthes-roland (accessed 7 October 2024).

Carrigan, M. 2016. *Social Media for Academics*. London: Sage.

Carroll, L. 1865. *Alice's Adventures in Wonderland*. London: MacMillan.

Carter, C., Lapum, J.L., Lavallée, L.F. and Martin, L.S. 2014. Explicating positionality: A journey of dialogical and reflexive storytelling. *International Journal of Qualitative Methods*, 13(1): 362–376.

Centre for Social Epidemiology. 2011. *The Whitehall Study*. Available at: https://unhealthywork.org/classic-studies/the-whitehall-study/ (accessed 5 April 2024).

Chapple, C. and Nofzinger, S. 2000. Bingo! Hints of deviance in the accounts of sociability and profit of Bingo players. *Deviant Behaviour*, 21(6): 489–517.

Chatfield, T. 2017. *Critical Thinking: Your Guide to Effective Argument, Successful Analysis and Independent Study*. London: Sage.

Chatfield, T. 2020. *Think Critically*. Super Skills Series. London: Sage.

Chen, Y., Wu, X., Hu, A., He, G. and Ju, G. 2021. Social prediction: A new research paradigm based on machine learning. *Journal of Chinese Sociology*, 8: 15.

Clark, A.M and Sousa, B.J. 2018. *How to be a Happy Academic*. London: Sage.

Clark, J.N. 2022. Following one's nose: 'Smellwalks' through qualitative data. *Qualitative Research*, 24(2). https://doi.org/10.1177/14687941221128496

Clark, T., Foster, L. and Bryman. A. 2019. *How to do your Social Research Project or Dissertation*. Oxford: Oxford University Press.

Clarke, A. 2005. *Situational Analysis: Grounded Theory after the Postmodern Turn*. London: Sage.

Clarke, A. and Charmaz, K. 2019. Grounded theory and situational analysis. In P. Atkinson, S. Delamont, A. Cernat, J.W. Sakshaug and R.A. Williams (eds), *Sage Foundations*. https://doi.org/10.4135/9781526421036825838

Clarke, A., Friese, C. and Washburn, R.S. 2017. *Situational Analysis: Grounded Theory after the Interpretative Turn*. London: Sage.

Classen, C. 2012. *The Deepest Sense: A Cultural History of Touch*. Champaign, IL: University of Illinois Press.

Coca-Cola Company. 2022. *Diet Coke appoints fashion icon Kate Moss as Creative Director*. Available at: www.coca-cola.com/gb/en/media-center/diet-coke-appoints-fashion-icon-kate-moss-as-creative-director#:~:text=Kate%20Moss'%20timeless%20yet%20irreverent,to%20everyday%20followers%20of%20fashion (accessed 5 April 2024).

Coffey, A. 2014. Analysing documents. In U. Flick (ed.), *The SAGE Handbook of Qualitative Data Analysis*. London: Sage, pp. 367–379.

Coffey, A. and Atkinson, P. 1996. *Making Sense of Qualitative Data: Complementary Strategies*. London: Sage.

Cohen, S. 1973. *Folk Devils and Moral Panics*. St. Albans: Paladin.

Coletta, C. and Kitchin, R. 2017. Algorhythmic governance: Regulating the 'heartbeat' of a city using the internet of things. *Big Data & Society*, 4(2). https://doi.org/10.1177/2053951717742418

Collins, D. 2015. *Cognitive Interviewing Practice*. London: Sage.

Collins, H. 2014. *Are We All Scientific Experts Now?* Bristol: Wiley.

Collins, H.M. and Evans, R.J. 2002. The third wave of science studies: Studies of expertise and experience. *Social Studies of Sciences*, 32(2): 235–296.

Colman, A.M. 2004. Psychology. In A. Kuper and J. Kuper (eds), *The Social Science Encyclopedia*, 3rd edn. London: Routledge, pp. 820–826.

Coloma, R.S. 2008. Border crossing subjectivities and research: Through the prism of feminists of color. *Race Ethnicity and Education*, 11(1): 11–27.

Connolly, L. 2022. *Proofread Your Essay*. London: Sage.

Connor, J., Copeland, S. and Owen, J. 2018. The infantilized researcher and research subject: Ethics, consent and risk. *Qualitative Research*, 18(4): 400–415.

Converse, J.M. and Presser, S. 1986. *Survey Questions. Handcrafting The Standardised Questionnaire*, 1st edn. London: SAGE.

Cornwall, A. and Jewkes, R. 1995. What is participatory research? *Social Science and Medicine*, 41: 1667–1676.

Corte, U. 2022. *Dangerous Fun: The Social Lives of Big Wave Surfers*. Chicago: Chicago University Press.

Crime Survey for England and Wales. 2024. Available at: www.crimesurvey.co.uk/en/index.html (accessed 3 January 2024).

Cullum-Swan, B.E.T.S. and Manning, P. 1994. Narrative, content, and semiotic analysis. In N.K. Denzin and Y.S. Lincoln (eds), *Handbook of Qualitative Research*. London: Sage, pp. 463–477.

Cuthbert, K. 2022. Researching 'non sexualities' via Creative Notebooks: Epistemology, embodiment and empowerment. *Qualitative Research*, 22(6): 897–915.

Davey, N.G. and Benjaminsen, G. 2021. Telling tales: Digital storytelling as a tool for qualitative data interpretation and communication. *International Journal of Qualitative Methods*, 20. https://doi.org/10.1177/16094069211022529

Davis, C.H and Michelle, C. 2011. Q Methodology in audience research: Bridging the qualitative/quantitative 'divide'? *Participations: Journal of Audience and Reception Studies*, 8(2): 527–561.

De Saussure, F. 1916. *Cours de Linguistique Générale*. C. Bally and A. Sechehaye (eds) with the assistance of Albert Riedlinger. Paris: Payot.

Deakin, H. and Wakefield, K. 2014. Skype interviewing: Reflections of two PhD researchers. *Qualitative Research*, 14(5): 603–616.

Deegan, M.J. 1988. *Jane Addams and the Men of the Chicago School, 1892–1918*. New York: Routledge.

Delamont, S. and Atkinson, P. 2021. *Ethnographic Engagements: Encounters with the Familiar and the Strange*. Abingdon on Thames: Routledge.

Delamont, S. and Stephens, N. 2021. The Belts are set out: The batizado as a symbolic welcome to capoeira culture. *Ethnography*, 22(3): 351–371.

Delamont, S., Atkinson, P. and Pugsley, L. 2010. The concept smacks of magic: Fighting familiarity today. *Teaching and Teacher Education*, 26(1): 3–10.

Dell, K. 2021. Rongomātau – 'sensing the knowing': An indigenous methodology utilising sensed knowledge from the researcher. *International Journal of Qualitative Methods*, 20. https://doi.org/10.1177/16094069211062411

Denton, H., Dannreuether, C. and Aranda, K. 2021. Researching at sea: Exploring the 'swim-along' interview method. *Health and Place*, 67(102466): 1–7.

Denzin, N.K. 1989. *Interpretive Interactionism*. Newbury Park, CA: Sage.

Department for Digital, Culture, Media and Sport. 2018. *A connected society: A strategy for tackling loneliness*. Available at: https://assets.publishing.service.gov.uk/government/uploads/system/uploads/attachment_data/file/936725/6.4882_DCMS_Loneliness_Strategy_web_Update_V2.pdf (accessed 29 July 2022).

Dicks, B. 2019. Multimodal analysis. In P. Atkinson, S. Delamont, A. Cernat, J.W. Sakshaug and R.A. Williams (eds), *Sage Foundations*. Available at: https://methods.sagepub.com/foundations/multimodal-analysis (accessed 7 October 2024).

Dicks, B., Soyinka, B. and Coffey, A. 2006. Multimodal ethnography. *Qualitative Research*, 6(1): 77–96.

Dimond, R., Lewis, J. and Sumner, A. 2022. The unexpected and unanticipated announcement of the 'world's first' gene edited babies: Breaching, repairing and strengthening community boundaries. *New Genetics and Society*, 42(1): article number: e2155124.

Dingwall, R. 2006. Confronting the anti-democrats: The unethical nature of ethical regulation in social science. *Medical Sociology Online*, 1: 51–58.

Dowling, R., Lloyd, K. and Suchet-Pearson, S. 2018. Qualitative methods III: Experimenting, picturing, sensing. *Progress in Human Geography*, 42(5): 779–788.

Dowsing, T. and Kendall, M.J. 2007. The Northwick Park Tragedy – protecting volunteers in future first in-man trials. *Journal of Clinical Pharmacy and Therapeutics*, 32(3): 203–207.

Du Bois, W.E.B. 1903. *The Souls of Black Folk*. New York: A.C. McClurg

Dunkley, R. 2018. Narrative analysis: Attending to the poetic structure of interview transcripts to understand the tourist experience. In J. Lewis (ed.), *Sage Datasets*. https://doi.org/10.4135/9781526439307

Durkheim, E. 1897[1952]. *Suicide*. Abingdon-on-Thames: Routledge and Kegan Paul.

Eco, U. 1978. *A Theory of Semiotics*. Bloomington, IN: Indiana University Press.

Edwards, R., Davidson E., Jamieson, L. and Weller, S. 2021. Theory and the breadth-and-depth method of analysing large amounts of qualitative data: A research note. *Quality and Quantity*, 55: 1275–1280.

Eerola, P., Lammi-Taskula, J., O'Brien, M., Hietamäki, J. and Räikkönen, E. 2019. Fathers' leave take-up in Finland: Motivations and barriers in a complex Nordic leave scheme. *SAGE Open*, 9(4). https://doi.org/10.1177/2158244019885389

Eskiler, E. and Altunışık, R. 2021. The moderating effect of involvement in the relationship between customer behavioral intentions and its antecedents. *SAGE Open*, 11(2). https://doi.org/10.1177/21582440211014495

European Social Survey. 2024. *European Social Survey*. Available at: www.europeansocialsurvey.org/ (accessed 28 March 2024).

Evans, C. 2018. Analysing semi-structured interviews using thematic analysis: Exploring voluntary civic participation among young adults. In J. Lewis (ed.), *Sage Datasets*. https://doi.org/10.4135/9781526439284

Farrelly, M. 2019. Critical discourse analysis. In P. Atkinson, S. Delamont, A. Cernat, J.W. Sakshaug and R.A. Williams (eds), *Sage Foundations*. Available at: https://methods.sagepub.com/foundations/critical-discourse-analysis (accessed 7 October 2024).

Fercovic, M. 2023. 'He is my refuge': Upward mobility, class dislocation and romantic relationships. *Sociology*. https://doi.org/10.1177/00380385231189174

Fernandez, F., Ro, H.K. and Wilson, M. 2022. The color of law school: Examining gender and race intersectionality in law school admissions. *American Journal of Education*, 128(3): 455–485.

Field, A. 2018. *Discovering Statistics Using IBM SPSS Statistics*, 5th edn. Newbury Park, CA: Sage.

Field, A., Miles, J. and Field, Z. 2012. *Discovering Statistics Using R*. London: Sage.

Fine, G.A. 1983. *Shared Fantasy: Role Playing Games as Social Worlds*. Chicago: Chicago University Press.

Fine, G.A. 1987. *With the Boys: Little League Baseball and Preadolescent Culture*. Chicago: University of Chicago Press.

Fleetwood-Smith, R., Tischler, V. and Robson, D. 2022. Aesthetics and dementia: Exploring the role of everyday aesthetics in dementia care settings. *Design for Health*, 6(1): 91–113.

Foucault, M. 1976[1979]. *The History of Sexuality, Volume 1: An Introduction*. London: Allen Lane.

Frank, A. 2009. *The Wounded Storyteller: Body, Illness and Ethics*, 2nd edn. Chicago: University of Chicago Press.

Franklin, S. and McNeil, M. 1993. Editorial: Procreation stories. *Science as Culture*, 3(4): 447–482.

Fugard, A. and Potts, H.W.W. 2019. Thematic analysis. In P. Atkinson, S. Delamont, A. Cernat, J.W. Sakshaug and R. A. Williams (eds), *Sage Foundations*. Available at: https://methods.sagepub.com/foundations/download/thematic-analysis (accessed 7 October 2024).

Fusch, P.I. and Ness, L.R. 2015. Are we there yet? Data saturation in qualitative research. *The Qualitative Report*, 20(9): 1408–1416.

Gallagher, M. 2014. Urban listening and the production of space: Reflections on Tuned City Brussels. *Tacet*, 3: 163–185.

Gallagher, M. 2020. Voice audio methods. *Qualitative Research*, 20(4): 449–464.

Gardiner, A., Sullivan, M. and Grand, A. 2018. Who are you writing for? Differences in response to blog design between scientists and nonscientists. *Science Communication*, 40(1): 109–123.

Garfinkel, H. 2002. *Ethnomethodology's Program: Working out Durkheim's Aphorism*. Lanham, MD: Rowman and Littlefield.

Garner, B. 2013. *HBR Guide to Better Business Writing*. Brighton, MA: Harvard Business Review Press.

Gartrell, C.D. and Gartrell, J.W. 2002. Positivism in sociological research: USA and UK (1966–1990). *The British Journal of Sociology*, 53(4): 639–657.

Gee, J.A. 2014. *An Introduction to Discourse Analysis: Theory and Method*, 4th edn. London: Routledge.

Gibney, E. 2024. AI models fed AI-generated data quickly spew nonsense. *Nature*. https://www.nature.com/articles/d41586-024-02420-7 (accessed 24 July 2024).

Gilbert, N. and Mulkay, M. 1984. *Opening Pandora's Box: A Sociological Analysis of Scientists' Discourse*. New York: Cambridge University Press.

Gillespie, D.L., Leffler, A. and Lerner, E. 2010. If it weren't for my hobby, I'd have a life: Dog sports, serious leisure, and boundary negotiations. *Leisure Studies*, 21(3–4): 285–304.

Glaser, A.L. and Strauss, B. 1967. *The Discovery of Grounded Theory: Strategies for Qualitative Research*. Piscataway, NJ: Aldine Transaction.

Glaw, X., Inder, K., Kable, A. and Hazelton, M. 2017. Visual methodologies in qualitative research: Autophotography and photo elicitation applied to mental health research. *International Journal of Qualitative Methods*, 16: 1–8.

Goffman, A. 2014. *On the Run. Fugitive Life in an American City*. Chicago: University of Chicago Press.

Goffman, E. 1963. *Stigma: Notes on the Management of Spoiled Identity*. Englewood Cliffs, NJ: Prentice Hall.

Goode, E. 2012. *The Paranormal: Who Believes, Why they Believe, and Why it Matters*. New York: Prometheus Books.

Gorman, R., Farsides, B. and Gammidge, T. 2022. Stop-motion storytelling: Exploring methods for animating the worlds of rare genetic disease. *Qualitative Research*, 23(6): 1737–1758.

Gough, B. and Lyons, A. 2015. The future of qualitative research in psychology: Accentuating the positive. *Integrative Psychological and Behavorial Science*, 50(2): 234–243.

Grant, A. 2017. Analysing online news comments about public breastfeeding using critical discourse analysis. In J. Lewis (ed.), *Sage Datasets*. https://doi.org/10.4135/9781473999138

Grant, A. 2022. *Doing Your Research Project with Documents: A Step-by-Step Guide to Take you from Start to Finish*. Bristol: Bristol University Press.

Grantland, J. and Peoples, K. 2021. Using interpretive phenomenological analysis to explore rural counselors' use of technology to address professional isolation. *Sage Datasets*. https://doi.org/10.4135/9781529764246

Gregory, J. and Miller, S. 1998. *Science in Public: Communication, Culture and Credibility*. Cambridge: Basic Books.

Grossman, P. 2021. *How Social Science Got Better: Overcoming Bias With More Evidence, Diversity and Self-Reflection*. Oxford: Oxford University Press.

Grossmann, I. et al. 2023. Insights into the accuracy of social scientists' forecasts of societal change. *Nature Human Behaviour*, 7(4): 484–501.

Gummer, T., Blumenberg, M.S. and Roßmann, J. 2019. Learning effects in coders and their implications for managing content analyses. *International Journal of Social Research Methodology*, 22(2): 139–152.

Haggerty, K.D. 2004. Ethics creep: Governing social science research in the name of ethics. *Qualitative Sociology*, 27: 391–404.

Hallett, S. 2016. 'An uncomfortable comfortableness': 'Care', child protection and child sexual exploitation. *British Journal of Social Work*, 46(7): 2137–2152.

Hallett, S. 2017. *Making Sense of Child Sexual Exploitation: Exchange, Abuse and Young People*. Bristol: Policy Press.

Hallett, S., Crowley, A., Deerfield, K., Staples, E. and Rees, A. 2017. *Review of the Wales Safeguarding Children and Young People from Sexual Exploitation (CSE) statutory guidance*. Available at: https://gov.wales/review-wales-safeguarding-children-and-young-people-sexual-exploitation-statutory-guidance-0 (accessed 31 May 2024).

Hammarberg, K., Kirkman, M. and de Lacey, S. 2016. Qualitative research methods: When to use them and how to judge them. *Human Reproduction*, 31(3): 498–501.

Hammersley, M. and Atkinson, P. 2007. *Ethnography: Principles and Practice*, 3rd edn. London: Routledge.

Harding, J. 2015. A discourse analysis approach to interview data: The guidance tutor role in higher education. *Sage Datasets*. https://doi.org/10.4135/9781473942172

Harper, D. 2002. Talking about pictures: A case for photo elicitation. *Visual Studies*, 17(1): 13–25.

Harrington, C. 2021. What is 'Toxic Masculinity' and Why does it Matter? *Men and Masculinities*, 24(2): 345–352.

Harrison, A.K. 2008. Racial authenticity in rap music and hip hop. *Sociology Compass*, 2(6): 1783–1800.

Harrison, G. 2014. Impact evaluation and welfare evaluation. *European Journal of Development Research*, 26: 39–45.

Harvey, W.S. 2011. Strategies for conducting elite interviews. *Qualitative Research*, 11(4): 431–441.

Head, E. 2009. The ethics and implications of paying participants in qualitative research. *International Journal of Social Research Methodology*, 12(4): 335–344.

Heath, S., Chapman, L. and the Morgan Centre Sketchers. 2018. Observational sketching as method. *International Journal of Social Research Methodology*, 21(6): 713–728.

Hedgecoe, A. 2020. *Trust in the System: Research Ethics Committee and the Regulation of Biomedical Research*. Manchester: Manchester University Press.

Henshaw, V. 2014. *Urban Smellscapes: Understanding and Designing City Smell Environments*. New York: Routledge.

Henwood, K. 2014. Qualitative research. In T. Teo (ed.), *Encyclopedia of Critical Psychology*. New York: Springer, pp. 1611–1614. https://doi.org/10.1007/978-1-4614-5583-7_256

Herbst-Debby, A. 2022. (De)legitimization of single mothers' welfare rights: United States, Britain, and Israel. *Journal of European Social Policy*, 32(3): 302–316.

Herrington, N. and Coogan, J. 2011. Q methodology: An overview. *Research in Teacher Education*, 1(2): 24–28.

Higher Education Statistical Agency. 2001. *Higher education statistics for the UK 2000/01*. Available at: www.hesa.ac.uk/data-and-analysis/publications/higher-education-2000-01 (accessed 26 March 2024).

Higher Education Statistical Agency. 2023. *What do HE students study?* Available at: www.hesa.ac.uk/data-and-analysis/students/what-study (accessed 26 March 2024).

Hirsch, D. 2011. *A minimum income standard for the UK in 2011*. Available at: www.bristol.ac.uk/poverty/ESRCJSPS/downloads/research/uk/1%20UK-Poverty,%20Inequality%20and%20Social%20Exclusion%20(General)/Report%20(UK%20general)/Hirsch%20et%20al.,%20A%20Minimum%20Income%20Standard%20for%20the%20UK%20in%202011.pdf (accessed 27 March 2024).

Hirsch, D.D. 2014. The Glass House effect: Big data, the new oil and the power of analogy. *Maine Law Review*, 66(2): 373–395.

Hochschild, A.R. 1983. *The Managed Heart: Commercialization of Human Feeling*. Berkeley, CA: University of California Press.

Hodgen, J., Pepper, D., Sturman, L. and Ruddock, G. 2010. *Is the UK an outlier? An international comparison of upper secondary mathematics education*. Available at: www.nuffieldfoundation.org/wp-content/uploads/2019/12/Is-the-UK-an-Outlier_Nuffield-Foundation_v_FINAL.pdf (accessed 3 June 2023).

Hoecker-Drysdale, S. 2011. Harriet Martineau. In G. Ritzer and J. Stepnisky (eds), *The Wiley-Blackwell Companion to Major Social Theorists*. London: Blackwell Publishing, pp. 61–95.

Holmes, H. and Hall, S.M. 2020. *Mundane Methods: Innovative Ways to Research the Everyday*. Manchester: Manchester University Press.

Holmes, R.M. 2021. Using narrative research to analyse the content and structure of young children's original stories. *Sage Datasets*. https://doi.org/10.4135/9781529762877

Hookway, N. 2008. 'Entering the blogosphere': Some strategies for using blogs in social research. *Qualitative Research*, 8(1): 91–113.

House of Lords. 2000. *Science and Society 3rd Report*. London: HMSO.

Housley, W. 2012. Ethnomethodology, conversation analysis and educational settings. In S. Delamont, (ed.), *Handbook of Qualitative Research in Education*. Cheltenham: Edward Elgar Publishing, pp. 446–449.

Howlett, M. 2022. Looking at the 'field' through a Zoom lens: Methodological reflections on conducting online research during a global pandemic. *Qualitative Research*, 22(3): 387–402.

Hudson, J. 2017. Identifying economics' place amongst academic disciplines: A science or a social science? *Scientometrics*, 113(2): 735–750.

Hughes, E.C. 1971. *The Sociological Eye*. Chicago: Aldine.

Humphreys, L. 1970. *Tearoom Trade: Impersonal Sex in Public Spaces*. London: Duckworth.

Hurdley, R. 2018. Drawing: Using participants' and researchers' drawings in social and cultural analysis. In J. Lewis (ed.), *Sage Datasets*. https://doi.org/10.4135/9781526439420

Hutchby, I. 2019. Conversation analysis. In P. Atkinson, S. Delamont, A. Cernat, J.W. Sakshaug and R.A. Williams (eds), *Sage Foundations*. Available at: https://methods.sagepub.com/foundations/conversation-analysis (accessed 7 October 2024).

Irwin, R. 2018. *Ibn Khaldun: An intellectual biography*. Princeton, NJ: Princeton University Press.

Israel, M. and Hay, I. 2006. *Research Ethics for Social Scientists*. London: Sage.

Jackson, E. 2020. Bowling together? Practices of belonging and becoming in a London ten-pin bowling league. *Sociology*, 54(3): 518–533.

Jackson, J. 1990. 'I am a fieldnote': Fieldnotes as a symbol of professional identity. In R. Sanjek (ed.), *Fieldnotes: The Makings of Anthropology*. Ithaca, NY: Cornell University Press, pp. 3–34.

Jagosh, J., Bush, P.L., Salsberg, J., Macaulay, A.C., Greenhalgh, T., Wong, G., Cargo, M., Green, L.W., Herbert, C.P. and Pluye, P. 2015. A realist evaluation of community-based participatory research: Partnership synergy, trust building and related ripple effects. *BMC Public Health*, 15(725). doi: 10.1186/s12889-015-1949-1

James, E., Robertshaw, T.L., Pascoe, M.J., Chapman, F.M., Westwell, A.D., Hoskins, M., Barrow, J., Sessa, B., Doblin, R., Rosky, R. and Smith, A. 2021. Online survey into developing a model for a legal cannabis market in the United Kingdom. *Drug Science, Policy and Law*, 7. doi:10.1177/20503245211034931

Jefferson, G. 1978. Sequential aspects of storytelling in conversation. In J. Schenkein (ed.), *Studies in the Organization of Conversational Interaction*. New York: Academic Press, pp. 219–248.

Jefferson, G. 2004. Glossary of transcript symbols with an introduction. In G.H. Lerner (ed.), *Conversation Analysis: Studies from the First Generation*. Philadelphia: John Benjamins, pp. 13–23.

Jeffreys, B. and Clarke, V. 2022. University students are far lonelier than other adults – study. *BBC*, 9 June. Available at: www.bbc.co.uk/news/education-61735272 (accessed 29 July 2022).

Jerolmack, C. and Khan, S. 2014. Talk is cheap: Ethnography and the attitudinal fallacy. *Sociological Methods & Research*, 43(2): 178–209.

Jimison, R. 2017. *Why we all need green in our lives*. Available at: https://edition.cnn.com/2017/06/05/health/colorscope-green-environment-calm/index.html (accessed 3 January 2023).

Johns Hopkins Coronavirus Resource Center. 2023. *Mortality analyses*. Available at: https://coronavirus.jhu.edu/data/mortality (accessed 12 December 2023).

Johnson, L.S. 2015. Using Sista circles to examine the professional experience of contemporary black women teachers in schools: A collective story about school culture and support, PhD dissertation, University of Georgia.

Jonathan-Zamir, T., Litmanovitz, Y. and Haviv, N. 2023. What works in police training? Applying an evidence-informed, general, ecological model of police training. *Police Quarterly*, 26(3): 279–306.

Kaiser, K. 2009. Protecting respondent confidentiality in qualitative research. *Qualitative Health Research*, 19(11): 1632–1641.

Kara, H. 2022. *How different are qualitative and quantitative research?* Available at: www.the-sra.org.uk/SRA/Blog/Howdifferentarequalitativeandquantitativeresearch.aspx (accessed 7 July 2022).

Kasperbauer, T.J. 2017. Should we bring back the passenger pigeon? The ethics of de-extinction. *Ethics, Policy & Environment*, 20(1): 1–14.

Kim, J. 2009. Public feeling for science: The Hwang affair and Hwang supporters. *Public Understanding of Science*, 18(6): 670–686.

King, A. 2011. The reverse sweep. *Sport in Society: Cultures, Commerce, Media, Politics*, 14(10): 1395–1406.

King, A. and de Rond, M. 2011. Boat race: Rhythm and the possibility of collective performance. *British Journal of Sociology*, 62(4): 565–585.

King, N. and Horrocks, C. 2010. *Interviews in Qualitative Research*. Thousand Oaks: Sage.

Kinkaid, E., Emard, K. and Senanyake, N. 2021. The podcast-as-method? Critical reflections on using podcasts to produce geographical knowledge. In K. McSweeney and A. WinklerPrins, *Geographical Fieldwork in the 21st Century*. London: Routledge.

Kitzinger, J. 1995. Qualitative research. Introducing focus groups. *British Medical Journal*, 311(7000): 299–302.

Knorr-Cetina, K. 1999. *Epistemic Cultures*. Cambridge, MA: Harvard University Press.

Kohler, U. and Kreuter, F. 2005. *Data Analysis Using STATA*. Texas: STATA Press.

Kootz, D. 1991. *The Eyes of Darkness*. New York: Pocket Books.

Kozinets, R. 2015. *Netnography: Redefined*. London: Sage.

Kress, K. and Van Leeuwen, T. 2006. *Reading Images: The Grammar of Visual Design*. London: Routledge.

Kusenbach, M. 2003. Street phenomenology: The go-along as ethnographic research tool. *Ethnography*, 4(3): 455–485.

Kyololo, O.M., Stevens, B.J. and Songok, J. 2023. Photo-elicitation technique: Utility and challenges in clinical research. *International Journal of Qualitative Methods*, 22. https://doi.org/10.1177/16094069231165714

L. I. 2022. *My experience with loneliness*. University of London Student Blog, 13 May. Available at: www.london.ac.uk/news-events/student-blog/experience-loneliness (accessed 26 March 2024).

Lamont, M. 2000. Comparing French and American sociology. *Tocqueville Review*, 21(1): 109–122.

Lasswell, H. 1927. The theory of political propaganda. *The American Political Science Review*, 21(3): 627–631.

Latour, B. 1996. On Actor-Network Theory: A few clarifications. *Soziale Welt*, 47(4): 369–381.

Latour, B. 1999. *Pandora's Hope: Essays on the Reality of Science Studies*. Cambridge, MA: Harvard University Press.

Latour, B. and Woolgar, S. 1986. *A Laboratory Life: The Social Construction of Scientific Facts*. London: Sage.

Leahy, C.P. 2022. The afterlife of interviews: Explicit ethics and subtle ethics in sensitive or distressing qualitative research. *Qualitative Research*, 22(5): 777–794.

Lefebvre, H. 2004. *Rhythmanalysis: Space, Time and Everyday*. Trans. by S. Elden and G. Moore. Bloomsbury: London

Leicester, M. and Taylor, D. 2017. *Get a Better Grade. Seven Steps to Excellent Essays and Assignments*. London: Sage.

Lewis, J. 2015. Dealing with qualitative questionnaire data: Studying an online irritable bowel syndrome (IBS) support group. *Sage Datasets*. https://doi.org/10.4135/9781473938045

Lewis, J. and Atkinson, P. In Press. Anonymity and pseudonyms in ethnographic work. In A. Ryen, *Research Agenda for Ethics and Qualitative Research*. Cheltenham: Edward Elgar Publishing.

Lewis, J. and Bartlett, A. 2024. The Shape of Bigfoot: transmuting absences into credible knowledge claims. *Cultural Sociology*.

Lewis, J., Bartlett, A., Riesch, H. and Stephens, N. 2023. Why we need a public understanding of social science. *Public Understanding of Social Science*, 32(5): 658–672.

Lewis, J. and Maisuria, A. 2023. *'Maths to 18' in England*. Available at: https://researchbriefings.files.parliament.uk/documents/CBP-9780/CBP-9780.pdf (accessed 5 April 2024).

Li, W., Schmidt, S. and Siedentop, S. 2023. Can polycentric urban development simultaneously achieve both economic growth and regional equity? A multi-scale analysis of German regions. *Environment and Planning A: Economy and Space*, 56(2). https://doi.org/10.1177/0308518X231191943

Lincoln, Y.S. and Guba, E.G. 1985. *Naturalistic Inquiry*. Newbury Park, CA: Sage.

Lindgren, S. 2017. *Digital Media and Society*. London: Sage.

Lindgren, S. and Krutrök, M.E. 2024. *Researching Digital Media and Society*. London: Sage.

Livingstone, D.M. 1995. The spaces of knowledge: Contributions towards a historical geography of science. *Environment and Planning D: Society and Space*, 13(1): 5–34.

London School of Economics (LSE) Impact Blog 2024. *LSE Blogs*. Available at: https://blogs.lse.ac.uk/ (accessed 9 January 2024).

Loseke, D.R. and Beahm, J. 2015. Narrative analysis of documents: Social policy hearings and welfare reform. *Sage Datasets*. https://doi.org/10.4135/9781473944374

Loxton, D. and Prothero, D.R. 2013. *Abominable Science! Origins of the Yeti, Nessie and Other Famous Cryptids*. New York: Columbia University Press.

Lupton, D. 2016. *The Quantified Self: A Sociology of Self-Tracking*. Cambridge: Polity.

Lupton, D. 2017. Self-tracking, health and medicine. *Health Sociology Review*, 26(1): 1–5.

Lydall, J. 1992. Filming the women who smile. In P.I. Crawford and J.K. Simonsen (eds), *Ethnographic Film Aesthetics and Narrative Traditions*. Aarhus: Intervention Press, pp. 141–158.

Lyon, D. 2019. Rhythmanalysis. In P. Atkinson, S Delamont, A. Cernat, J.W. Sakshaug and R.A. Williams (eds), *Sage Foundations*. Available at: https://methods.sagepub.com/foundations/rhythmanalysis (accessed 7 October 2024).

Lyon, D. and Carabelli, G. 2016. Researching young people's orientations to the future: The methodological challenges of using arts practice. *Qualitative Research*, 16(4): 430–445.

MacDougall, D. 2001. Renewing ethnographic film: Is digital video changing the genre? *Anthropology Today*, 17(3): 15–21.

MacInnes, J. 2016. *An Introduction to Secondary Data Analysis with IBM SPSS Statistics*. London: Sage.

MacKay, D. and Walker, R.L. 2021. Paying for fairness? Incentives and fair subject selection. *American Journal of Bioethics*, 21(3): 35–37.

Macquarie University. 2021. *World-leading research world-changing impact*. Available at: www.mq.edu.au/__data/assets/pdf_file/0004/1259554/MQ-ERA-2021-Brochure_Digital.pdf (accessed 5 April 2024).

Madill, A and Gough, B. 2008. Qualitative research and its place in psychological science. *Psychological Methods*, 13(3): 254–271.

Madill, A. and Todd, Z. 2002. *Proposal to the Council of the British Psychological Society for the formation of a new section of the society on 'Qualitative Methods in Psychology'*. Available at: https://eprints.whiterose.ac.uk/1492/1/madilla6_BPSQualSection.pdf (accessed 3 June 2024).

Maggio, L.A., Sewell, J.L. and Artino Jnr, A.R. 2016. The literature review: A foundation for high quality medical education research. *Journal of Graduate Medical Education*, 8(3): 297–303.

Maggio, R. 2021. Symbolic analysis of the (so-called) Shell money. *Sage Datasets*. https://doi.org/10.4135/9781529763263

Maguire, M. and Delahunt, D. 2017. Doing a thematic analysis: A practical, step-by-step guide for learning and teaching scholars. *All Ireland Journal of Higher Education*, 9(3): 3351–3354.

Malinowski, B. 1935. *Coral Gardens and their Magic, vol. II*. London: George Allen & Unwin Ltd.

Mandler, P. 2019. The language of science in everyday life. *History of the Human Sciences*, 32: 66–82.

Mannay, D. 2013. Who put that on there … why why why? Power games and participatory techniques of visual data production. *Visual Studies*, 28: 136–146.

Mannay, D., Fink, J. and Lomax, H. 2019. Visual ethnography. In P. Atkinson, S Delamont, A. Cernat, J.W. Sakshaug and R.A. Williams (eds), *Sage Foundations*. Available at: https://methods.sagepub.com/foundations/visual-ethnography (accessed 7 October 2024).

Mansourian, Y. 2021. Bonsai in the time of Covid: The miniature, the social and the solitary. *Cosmopolitan Civil Societies: An Interdisciplinary Journal*, 13(2): 12–27.

Markuksela, V. and Valtonen, A. 2018. Dance with a fish? Sensory human and non-human encounters in the waterscape of match fishing. *Leisure Studies*, 38(3): 353–366.

Martikainen, J. 2022. Membership categorization analysis as means of studying person perception. *Qualitative Research in Psychology*, 19(3): 703–721.

Marx, K. 1867. *Das Kapital. Kritik der politischen Oekonomie*. Hamburg: VSA Verlag.

Marzano, M. 2022. *Ethical Issues in Covert, Security and Surveillance Research*. Bingley: Emerald.

Mason, J. and Davies, K. 2009. Coming to our senses? A critical approach to sensory methodology. *Qualitative Research*, 9(5): 587–603.

May, T. and Perry, B. 2022. *Social Research: Issues, Methods and Process*, 5th edn. London: Open University Press.

Maynard, D. and Greenwood, M.A. 2014. Who cares about sarcastic tweets? Investigating the impact of sarcasm on sentiment analysis. *Proceedings of the Ninth International Conference on Language Resources and Evaluation*, 4238–4243.

McDrury, J. and Alterio, M. 2003. *Learning Through Storytelling in Higher Education*. Sterling, VA: Kogan Page Limited.

McLean, K. 2020. Sensory mapping. *International Encyclopaedia of Human Geography*, 12(2): 153–168.

Merton, R. and Kendall, P.L. 1946. The focussed interview. *American Journal of Sociology*, 51(6): 541–557.

Metzler, K. 2016. The Big Data rich and the Big Data poor: The new digital divide raises questions about future academic research. *The Impact Blog*, London School of Economics and Political Science. Available at: http://blogs.lse.ac.uk/impactofsocialsciences/2016/11/22/the-big-data-rich-and-the-big-data-poor-the-new-digital-divide-raises-questions-about-future-academic-research/ (accessed 28 November 2016).

Microsoft Support. 2024. *Insert a table of contents*. Available at: https://support.microsoft.com/en-us/office/insert-a-table-of-contents-882e8564-0edb-435e-84b5-1d8552ccf0c0 (accessed 5 April 2024).

Miczo, N. 2003. Beyond the 'Fetishism of Words': Consideration on the use of the interview to gather chronic illness narrative. *Qualitative Health Research*, 13(4): 469–490.

Mikecz, R. 2012. Interviewing elites: Addressing methodological issues. *Qualitative Inquiry*, 18(6): 482–493.

Milmo, D., Hern, A. and Ambrose, J. 2024. Can the climate survive the insatiable energy demands of the AI arms race?. *Guardian,* 4 July. Available at: https://www.theguardian.com/business/article/2024/jul/04/can-the-climate-survive-the-insatiable-energy-demands-of-the-ai-arms-race (accessed 7 October 2024)

Mind. 2022. *How to cope with student life*. Available at: www.mind.org.uk/information-support/tips-for-everyday-living/student-life/connecting-with-other-students/ (accessed 29 July 2022).

Mlynář, J. 2017. Analysing oral histories: Social roles and narrative self-regulation in holocaust survivors' testimonies. *Sage Datasets*. https://doi.org/10.4135/9781473999152

Mody, C.C.M. 2005. The sounds of science: Listening to laboratory practice. *Science, Technology, & Human Values*, 30(2): 175–198.

Moles, K. 2008. A walk in thirdspace: Place, methods and walking. *Sociological Research Online*, 13(4): 31–39.

Moles, K. 2021. The social world of outdoor swimming: Cultural practices, shared meanings, and bodily encounters. *Journal of Sport and Social Issues*, 45(1): 20–38.

Mollett, A., Williams, S., Gilson, C. and Brumley, C. 2017. *Communicating your Research with Social Media: A Practical Guide to Using Blogs, Podcasts, Data Visualisations and Video*. London: Sage.

Morgan, D.L. 2014. Pragmatism as a Paradigm for Social Research. Qualitative Inquiry 20(8): 1045-1053.

Myrdal, G. 1944. *An American Dilemma: The Negro Problem and Modern Democracy*. New York: Harper and Row.

Nobel Prize. 2019. *The Sveriges Riksbank Prize in Economic Sciences in memory of Alfred Nobel 2019*. Available at: www.nobelprize.org/prizes/economic-sciences/2019/summary/ (accessed 5 April 2024).

Noetzel, S., Mussalem Gentile, M.F., Lowery, G., Zemanova, S., Lecheler, S. and Peter, C. 2022. Social campaigns to social change? Sexual violence framing in US news before and after #metoo. *Journalism*, 24(6).

Nuffield Foundation. 2022. *Evaluation of the Q-Step Programme*. Available at: www.nuffieldfoundation.org/wp-content/uploads/2021/10/Q-Step-evaluation-report-August-2022-update.pdf (accessed 27 March 2024).

O'Connor, E. 2017. Touching tacit knowledge: Handwork as ethnographic method in a glassblowing studio. *Qualitative Research*, 17(2): 217–230.

O'Hara, L. and Higgins, K. 2019. Participant photography as a research tool: Ethical issues and practical implementation. *Sociological Methods & Research*, 48(2): 369–399.

O'Leary, Z. 2021. *The Essential Guide to Doing Your Research Project*, 4th edn. London: Sage.

Oakley, A. 1972. *Sex, Gender and Society*. London: Temple Smith.

Oakley, L. 2020. *Exploring Student Loneliness in Higher Education. A Discursive Approach.* London: Palgrave Macmillan.

Oliver, D.G, Serovich, J.M. and Mason, T.L. 2005. Constraints and opportunities with interview transcription: Towards reflection in qualitative research. *Social Forces*, 84(2): 1273–1289.

Orofino, E. 2021. Analysing non-violent extremism in the west using thematic analysis. *Sage Datasets*. https://doi.org/10.4135/9781529762761

Orr, E., Frederico, M. and Long, M. 2022. Messages for good practice: Aboriginal hospital liaison officers and hospital social workers. *Australian Social Work*, 75(3): 317–330.

Pallant, J. 2020. *SPSS Survival Manual: A Step-By-Step Guide to Data Analysis Using IBM SPSS*, 7th edn. London: Routledge.

Park, S.H. and Hepburn, A. 2022. The benefits of a Jeffersonian transcript. *Frontiers in Communication. Vol 7*. https://doi.org/10.3389/fcomm.2022.779434

Patton, M.Q. 2002. *Qualitative Research and Evaluation Methods*, 3rd edn. London: Sage.

Pavlidis, A. 2012. From Riot Grrrls to roller derby? Exploring the relations between gender, music and sport. *Leisure Studies*, 31(2): 165–176.

Payne, G. and Williams, M. 2005. Generalization in qualitative research. *Sociology*, 39(2): 295–314.

Peirce, C.S. 1883. *Studies in Logic, by Members of The Johns Hopkins University. Charles S. Peirce*. Boston: Little Brown.

Peirce, C.S. 1977. *Semiotics and significs* (ed. C. Hardwick). Bloomington, IN: Indiana University Press.

Pevalin, D. and Robson, K. 2009. *The STATA Survival Manual*. Maidenhead: McGraw-Hill Education.

Phellas, C.N., Block, A. and Seale, C. 2012. Structured methods: Interviews, questionnaires and observations. In C. Seale (ed.), *Researching Society and Culture*, 3rd edn. London: Sage, pp. 181–205.

Phillips, P. 2015. Narrative analysis: Institutional stories in prison. *Sage Datasets*. https://doi.org/10.4135/9781473937864

Phillips, R., Seaborne, K., Goldsmith, A., Curtis, N., Davies, A., Haynes, W., McEnroe, R., Murphy, N., O'Neill, L., Pacey, C., Walker, E. and Wordley, E. 2022. Student loneliness through the pandemic: How, why and where? *Geographical Journal*, 188(2): 277–293.

Picoult, J. 2004. *My Sister's Keeper*. New York City: Atria Books.

Pinch, T.J. 1992. Opening black boxes: Science, technology and society. *Social Studies of Science*, 22(3): 487–510.

Pink, S. 2009. *Doing Sensory Ethnography*. London: Sage.

Pink, S. 2011. Images, senses and applications: Engaging visual anthropology. *Visual Anthropology*, 24(5): 437–454.

Pink, S. 2021. *Doing Visual Ethnography*, 4th edn. London: Sage.

Pitts, M.J. and Miller-Day, M. 2007. Upward turning points and positive rapport development across time in researcher–participant relationships. *Qualitative Research*, 7(2): 177–201.

Ponzoni, E. 2016. Windows of understanding: Broadening access to knowledge production through participatory action research. *Qualitative Research*, 16(5): 557–574.

Popper, K. 1935. *The Logic of Scientific Discovery*. London: Hutchinson.

Popper, K. 1963. *Conjectures and Refutations*. London: Routledge.

Prior, L. 2003. *Using Documents in Social Research*. London: Sage.

Punch, S. and Snellgrove, M. 2023. Bridging time: Negotiating serious leisure in intimate couple relationships. *Annals of Leisure Research*, 1–21. https://doi.org/10.1080/11745398.2023.2197243

Quinn, K. 2023. Taking live methods slowly: Inhabiting the social world through dwelling, doodling and describing. *Qualitative Research*, 23(1): 3–20.

Rabe, M. 2003. Revisiting insiders and outsiders as social researchers. *African Sociological Review*, 7(2): 149–161.

Rafalovich, A. 2006. Making sociology relevant: The assignment and application of breaching experiments. *Teaching Sociology*, 34(2): 156–163.

Rantatalo, O., Lindberg, O., Kihlberg, R. and Hallgren, M. 2018. Negotiations and research bargains: Bending professional norms in the effort to gain field access. *International Journal of Qualitative Methods*, 17: 1–11.

Rathore, M. 2023. *Number of enrolled students in India as of 2018, by school type*. Available at: www.statista.com/statistics/1175285/india-number-of-enrolled-students-by-school-type/ (accessed 3 June 2024).

Regal, B. 2011 *Searching for Sasquatch: Crackpots, Eggheads and Cryptozoology*. New York: Palgrave MacMillan.

Renn, O. 2006. Risk communication: Consumers between information and irritation. *Journal of Risk Research*, 8: 883–849.

Resnik, D.B. 2009. International standards for research integrity: An idea whose time has come? *Accountability in Research*, 16: 218–228.

Resnik, D.B. and Shamoo, A.E. 2011. The Singapore Statement on Research Integrity. *Accountability in Research*, 18(2): 71–75.

Rettberg, J.W. 2014. *Blogging: Digital Media and Society Series*, 2nd edn. Bristol: Polity.

Revise Sociology. 2023. *A-Level sociology growing in popularity*. Available at: https://revisesociology.com/2023/03/10/a-level-sociology-growing-in-popularity/?utm_content=cmp-true (accessed 5 April 2024).

Rhys-Taylor, A. 2018. *Food and Multi-culture: A Sensory Ethnography of East London*. Abingdon-on-Thames: Routledge.

Riach, K. and Warren, S. 2015. Smell organization: Bodies and corporeal porosity in office work. *Human Relations*, 68(5): 789–809.

Rice, T. 2013. *Hearing and the Hospital: Sound, Listening, Knowledge and Experience*. Canon Pyon: Sean Kingston Publishing.

Richard, B., Sivo, S.A., Ford, R.C., Murphy, J., Boote, D.N., Witta, E. and Orlowski, M. 2021. A guide to conducting online focus groups via Reddit. *International Journal of Qualitative Methods*, 20. https://doi.org/10.1177/16094069211012217

Ridley, D. 2012. *The Literature Review: A Step-By-Step Guide for Students*, 2nd edn. London: Sage.

Riesman, D. 1950. *The Lonely Crowd: A Study of the Changing American Character*. New Haven, CT: Yale University Press.

Riessman, C.K. 2008. *Narrative Methods for the Human Sciences*. London: Sage.

Riley, A. 2006. The rebirth of tragedy out of the spirit of hip hop: A cultural sociology of gangsta rap music. *Journal of Youth Studies*, 8(3): 297–311.

Rintel, S. 2015. Conversation analysis of video-mediated communication: Interactional repair of distortion in long-distance couples' video calls. *Sage Datasets*. Available at: https://methods.sagepub.com/dataset/video-calling-couples (accessed 7 October 2024).

Roddy, D. and Castillo, M. 2020. Is Bigfoot racist? *Sh** Gets Weird* [Podcast].

Rogers, R. and Hammerstein, O. 1965. *The Sound of Music*. 20th Century Fox, Los Angeles.

Rogers-Hayden, T. and Pidgeon, N. 2007. Moving engagement 'upstream'? Nanotechnologies and the Royal Society and Royal Academy of Engineering's inquiry. *Public Understanding of Science*, 16(3): 345–364.

Rose, G. 2022. *Visual Methodologies: An Introduction to Researching With Visual Materials*. London: Sage.

Ross, N.J., Renold, E., Holland, S. and Hillman, A. 2009. Moving stories: Using mobile methods to explore the everyday lives of young people in public care. *Qualitative Research*, 9(5): 605–623.

Rossi, T., Slattery, F. and Richter, K. 2020. The evolution of the scientific poster: From eye-sore to eye-catcher. *Medical Writing*, 29(1): 36–40.

Rowe, N. and Ilic, D. 2011. Poster presentation: A visual medium for academic and scientific meetings. *Paediatric Respiratory Reviews*, 12(3): 208–213.

Rubin, H.J. and Rubin, I.S. 1995. *Qualitative Interviewing: The Art of Hearing*. London: Sage.

Rush, D. 2021. *Build Your Argument*. Super Skills Series. London: Sage.

Ryan, K., Gannon-Slater, N. and Culbertson, M.J. 2012. Improving survey methods with cognitive interviews in small-and medium-scale evaluations. *American Journal of Evaluation*, 33(3): 414–430.

Ryan, L. and Golden, A. 2006. 'Tick the box please': A reflexive approach to doing quantitative social research. *Sociology*, 40(6): 1191–1200.

Sacks, H., Schegloff, E.A. and Jefferson, G. 1974. A simplest systematics for the organization of turn-taking for conversation. *Language*, 50(4): 696–735.

Sage Ocean. 2019. *Top 10 Big Data and social science innovations*, 13 November. Available at: https://ocean.sagepub.com/blog/top-10-big-data-and-social-science-innovations (accessed 7 July 2022).

Sage Research Methods. *Top Tips: Ethics*. Available at: https://methods.sagepub.com/video/top-tips-ethics (accessed 5 April 2024).

Sage Students. 2020. *Give great presentations: A super quick skills video*. Available at: Py7Vzf J8&list=PLfW3Wp3x6cZRK7PA8gQ3PwJoFvU0kurZf&index=7 (accessed 5 April 2024).

Sataloff, R.T., Bush, M.L., Chandra, R., Chepeha, D., Rotenberg, B., Fisher, E.W., Goldenberg, D., Hanna, E.Y., Kerschner, E.J., Kraus, D.H., Krouse, J.H., Li, D., Link, M., Lustig, L.R., Selesnick, S.H., Sindwani, R., Smith, R.J., Tysome, J.R., Weber, P.C. and Welling, D.B. 2021. Systematic reviews: Complexities and other criteria. *World Journal of Otolaryngology – Head and Neck Surgery*, 7: 236–239.

Satwinder, R. 2022. The sportification and internationalization of Kabaddi: A sociological understanding. *The International Journal of Sport and Society*, 13(2): 49–64.

Saunders, B., Kitzinger, J. and Kitzinger, C. 2015. Anonymising interview data: Challenges and compromise in practice. *Qualitative Research*, 15(5): 616–632.

Savage, M. and Burrows, R. 2007. The coming crisis of empirical sociology. *Sociology: A Journal of the British Sociological Association*, 41(5): 885–899.

Scavarda, A. and Moretti, V. 2024. Health got graphic! The role of Graphic Medicine in unpacking autism. *Disability and Society*, 1–26. https://doi.org/10.1080/09687599.2023.2289361

Schneider, B. and Kayseas, B. 2018. Indigenous qualitative research. In C. Cassell, A.L. Cunliffe and G. Grandy (eds), *The SAGE Handbook of Qualitative Business and Management Research Methods: History and Traditions*. London: Sage, pp. 154–172.

Schreier, M. 2019. *Qualitative Content Analysis in Practice*. London: Sage.

Scott, J. 1990. *A Matter of Record*. Cambridge, UK: Polity Press.

Scott, S. 2009. Re-clothing the Emperor: The swimming pool as a negotiated order. *Symbolic Interaction*, 32(2): 123–145.

Scott, S., Hinton-Smith, T., Harma, V. and Broome, K. 2012. The reluctant researcher: Shyness in the field. *Qualitative Research*, 12(6): 715–734.

Seale, C. 2008. Mapping the field of medical sociology: A comparative analysis of journals. *Sociology of Health & Illness*, 30(5): 677–695.

Sellars, R.W. 1939. A statement of critical realism. *Revue Internationale de Philosophie*, 1(3): 472–497.

Shakespeare, W. 1623. All's Well that Ends Well. In W. Shakespeare (ed.), *The First Folio*. London: Edward Blount, and William and Isaac Jaggard.

Shirani, F.J. and Henwood, K.L. 2011. Continuity and change in a qualitative longitudinal study of fatherhood: Relevance without responsibility. *International Journal of Social Research Methodology*, 14(1): 17–29.

Silverman, D. 2021. *Doing Qualitative Research*, 6th edn. London: Sage.

Silverman, D. 2022. What you can (and can't) do with qualitative research. In D. Silverman (ed.), *Doing Qualitative Research*, 6th edn. London: Sage, Ch. 2.

Small, M.L. and Cook, J.M. 2023. Using interviews to understand why: Challenges and strategies in the study of motivated action. *Sociological Methods & Research*, 52(4): 1591–1631.

Smith, J.A. 1996. Beyond the divide between cognition and discourse: Using interpretative phenomenological analysis in health psychology. *Psychology & Health*, 11(2): 261–271.

Smith, J.A., Michie, S., Stephenson, M. and Quarrell, O. 2002. Risk perception and decision-making processes in candidates for genetic testing for Huntington's Disease: An interpretative phenomenological analysis. *Journal of Health Psychology*, 7(2): 131–144.

Smith, R. 2022. Membership categorisation analysis. In J. Turowetz and A.W. Rawls (eds), *Routledge International Handbook of Ethnomethodology and Conversation Analysis*. Abingdon and New York: Routledge.

Smith, R.J. and Delamont, S. 2023. *Leaving the Field: Methodological Insights from Ethnographic Exits*. Manchester: Manchester University Press.

Social Science Bites. Available at: www.socialsciencespace.com/about-socialsciencebites/ (accessed 5 April 2024).

Sociological Review Fiction. 2024. Available at: https://thesociologicalreview.org/publish-with-us/fiction/ (accessed 21 March 2024).

Sormani, P. 2019. Ethnomethodological analysis. In P. Atkinson, S Delamont, A. Cernat, J.W. Sakshaug and R.A. Williams (eds), *Sage Foundations*. Available at: https://methods.sagepub.com/foundations/ethnomethodological-analysis (accessed 7 October 2024).

Sousa, B.J. and Clark, A.M. 2019. Six insights to make better academic conference posters. *International Journal of Qualitative Methods*, 18. https://doi.org/10.1177/1609406919862370

Sousa, D. 2011. *How the Brain Learns*. London: Sage.

Spiers, J. and Smith, J. 2017. An interpretative phenomenological analysis of interview data: People on the renal waiting list consider deceased versus living donors. *Sage Datasets*. https://doi.org/10.4135/9781473999237

Spiers, J. and Smith, J. 2019. Interpretative phenomenological analysis. In P. Atkinson, S. Delamont, A. Cernat, J.W. Sakshaug and R.A. Williams (eds), *Sage Foundations*. https://doi.org/10.4135/9781526421036813346

Spivak, G.C. 1988. Can the subaltern speak? In C. Nelson and L. Grossberg (eds), *Marxism and the Interpretation of Culture*. Champaign: University of Illinois Press, pp. 271–313.

Springgay, S. and Truman, S. 2018. *Walking Methodologies in a More-than-human World*. London: Routledge.

Squire, C., Andrews, M. and Tamboukou, M. 2013. Introduction: What is narrative research? In M. Andrews, C. Squire and M. Tamboukou (eds), *Doing Narrative Research*. London: Sage.

Squire, C., Davis, M., Esin, C., Andrews, M., Harrison, B., Hydén, L-C. and Hydén, M. 2014. What is narrative research? In G. Crow, *Research Methods Series*. London: Bloomsbury.

Stanley, L. 2015. Documents of life: Analysing letters and other found data in researching 'Whites Writing Whiteness' in South Africa. *Sage Datasets*. https://doi.org/10.4135/9781473942974

Stanley, L. and Sereva, E. 2019. Documents of life. In P. Atkinson, S. Delamont, A. Cernat, J.W. Sakshaug and R.A. Williams (eds), *Sage Foundations*. Available at: https://methods.sagepub.com/foundations/download/documents-of-life (accessed 7 October 2024).

Stephens, N. 2007. Collecting data from elites and ultra elites: Telephone and face-to-face interviews with macroeconomists. *Qualitative Research*, 7(2): 203–216.

Stephens, N. and Lewis, J. 2017. Doing laboratory ethnography: Reflections on methods in scientific workplaces. *Qualitative Research*, 17(2): 202–216.

Stoller, P. 1989. *The Taste of Ethnographic Things*. Philadelphia: University of Pennsylvania Press.

Stoller, P. 1997. *Sensous Scholarship*. Philadelphia: University of Pennsylvania Press.

Strathern, M. 2000. *Audit Cultures: Anthropological Studies in Accountability, Ethics and the Academy*. London: Routledge.

Strong, P.M. 1988. Qualitative sociology in the UK. *Qualitative Sociology*, 11: 13–28.

Surmiak, A. 2020. Ethical concerns of paying cash to vulnerable participants: The qualitative researchers' views. *The Qualitative Report*, 25(12): 4461–4480.

Sweet, P. and Giffort, D. 2020. The bad expert. *Social Studies of Science*, 51(3): 313–338.

Taboada, M. 2016. Sentiment analysis: An overview from linguistics. *Annual Review of Linguistics*, 2: 325–347.

Tashakkori, A. and Teddlie, C. 1998. *Mixed Methodology: Combining Qualitative and Quantitative Approaches*. Thousand Oaks, CA: Sage.

Taussig, M. 1986. *Shamanism, Colonialism and the Wild Man: A Study in Terror and Healing*. Chicago: University of Chicago Press.

Taylor, J. 2023. Google says AI systems should be able to mine publishers' work unless companies opt out. *Guardian*. Available at: https://www.theguardian.com/

technology/2023/aug/09/google-says-ai-systems-should-be-able-to-mine-publishers-work-unless-companies-opt-out. (accessed 24 July, 2024).
Taylor, S.J.A. 2013. *What is Discourse Analysis?* London: Bloomsbury.
Taylor, S.J.A. 2019. Discourse analysis. In P. Atkinson, S. Delamont, A. Cernat, J.W. Sakshaug and R.A. Williams (eds), *Sage Foundations*. Available at: https://methods.sagepub.com/foundations/discourse-research (accessed 7 October 2024).
Testa, A., Turney, K., Jackson, D. and Jaynes, C.M. 2022. Police contact and future orientation from adolescence to young adulthood: Findings from the pathways to desistance study. *Criminology*, 60: 263–290.
The Age of Loneliness. 2016. BBC One, 19 October.
Thelwall, M. 2020. Sentiment analysis. P. Atkinson, S. Delamont, A. Cernat, J.W. Sakshaug and R.A. Willimas (eds), *Sage Foundations*. https://doi.org/10.4135/9781526421036754533
Thomas, D. 1964. *Under Milkwood*. New York: New Directions Paperbook.
Thomas, G. 2023a. *How to do your Research Project: A Guide for Students*, 4th edn. London: Sage.
Thomas, G. 2023b. Unfinished business: A reflection on leaving the field. In R.J. Smith and S. Delamont (eds), *Leaving the Field: Methodological Insights from Ethnographic Exits*. Manchester: Manchester University Press, pp. 74–85.
Thomas, G. and Thurnell-Read, T. 2024. Later-life masculinities: (Re)forming the gendered lives of older men. *Men and Masculinities*, 27(2). https://doi.org/10.1177/1097184X241231917
Thomas, G., Lupton, D. and Pedersen, S. 2018. 'The appy for a happy pappy': Expectant fatherhood and pregnancy apps. *Journal of Gender Studies*, 27(7): 759–770.
Thurnell-Read, T. 2020. Kindred spirits: Doing family through craft entrepreneurship. *The Sociological Review*, 69(1): 37–52.
Tinsley, B. 2020. *Coronavirus and the impact on students in higher education in England: September to December 2020*. Office of National Statistics. Available at: www.ons.gov.uk/peoplepopulationandcommunity/educationandchildcare/articles/coronavirusandtheimpactonstudentsinhighereducationinenglandseptembertodecember2020/2020-12-21 (accessed 29 July 2022).
Tom's Planner. 2024. *Gantt Charts made easy, quick and effortless*. Available at: www.tomsplanner.com (accessed 3 March 2023).
Tourangeau, R., Lance, J.R. and Rasinski, K. 2000. *The Psychology of Survey Response*, 1st edn. Cambridge: Cambridge University Press.
Turnbull, N. and Broad, R. 2022. Bringing the problem home: The anti-slavery and anti-trafficking rhetoric of UK non-government organisations. *Politics*, 42(2): 200–215.
United Kingdom Government. 2022. *Entries and results – A level and AS by subject and student characteristics (single academic year) from A level and other 16 to 18 results*. Available at: https://explore-education-statistics.service.gov.uk/data-tables/permalink/4000ba98-bbe6-4b65-b26c-508c06b578fb (accessed 27 March 2024).
United Kingdom Research Innovation (UKRI). 2024. *Framework for research ethics*. Available at: www.ukri.org/councils/esrc/guidance-for-applicants/research-ethics-guidance/framework-for-research-ethics/our-core-principles/#contents-list# (accessed 25 March 2024).

United States General Social Survey. 2022. *The General Social Survey*. Available at: https://gss.norc.org/getthedata/Pages/Home.aspx (accessed 27 March 2024).

University of Manchester, Cathie Marsh Institute for Social Research (CMIST), UK Data Service. 2021. *National Survey of Sexual Attitudes and Lifestyles, 2010–2012: Teaching Dataset* [data collection]. Available at: https://beta.ukdataservice.ac.uk/datacatalogue/doi/?id=8735#!#1 (accessed 3 June 2024).

University of Reading. 2024. *Reading and making notes*. Available at: https://libguides.reading.ac.uk/reading (accessed 26 March 2024).

Urquhart, C. 2019. Grounded theory's best kept secret: The ability to build theory. In A. Bryant and K. Charmaz (eds), *The SAGE Handbook of Current Developments in Grounded Theory*. London: Sage, Ch. 4.

Urry, J. 2010. Mobile sociology. *The British Journal of Sociology*, 61(s1): 347–366.

Vacchelli, E. 2018. Embodiment in qualitative research: Collage making with migrant, refugee and asylum seeking women. *Qualitative Research*, 18(2): 171–190.

Van Creveld, M. 2020. *Seeing into the Future: A Short History of Prediction*. London: Reaktion Books.

Van de Riet, M. 2008. Participatory research and the philosophy of social science: Beyond the moral imperative. *Qualitative Inquiry*, 14(4): 546–565.

van Dijk, T. A. 1993. Principles of critical discourse analysis. *Discourse & Society*, 4(2): 249–283.

van Dijk, T. A. 1995. Discourse analysis as ideology analysis. In C. Schäffne and A.L. Wendon (eds), *Language and Peace*. London: Routledge, Ch. 2.

Vannini, P. (ed.) 2023. *The Handbook of Sensory Ethnography*. London: Routledge.

Vannini, P., Waskul, D. and Gottschalk, S. 2011. *The Senses in Self, Society, and Culture: A Sociology of the Senses*. New York: Routledge.

Vasileiou, K., Barnett, J., Barreto, M., Vines, J., Atkinson, M., Long, K., Bakewell, L., Lawson, S. and Wilson, M. 2019. Coping with loneliness at university: A qualitative interview study with students in the UK. *Mental Health & Prevention*, 13: 21–30.

Vassallo, P. 2003. Executive summaries: Where less really is more. *ETC: A Review of General Semantics*, 60(1), 83–90.

Vigren, M. 2022. Rhythm analysis of the digital everyday life: Lefebvrian interpretations on self-tracking digital device use. *Sage Datasets*. https://doi.org/10.4135/9781529604290

Virilio, P. 1986. *Speed and Politics: An Essay on Dromology* (trans. Michael Polizzotti). New York: Semiotext(e).

Vygotsky, L. 1978. *Mind in Society*. London: Harvard University Press.

Walmsley, J. 1997. Life history interviews with people with learning difficulties. In R. Perks and A. Thomson (eds), *The Oral History Reader*. London: Routledge, pp. 126–140.

Warner, M. 2002. Publics and counter-publics. *Quarterly Journal of Speech*, 88(4): 413–425.

Watts, S. and Stenner, P. 2012. *Doing Q Methodological Research: Theory, Method and Interpretation*. London: Sage.

We Society Podcast. Available at: https://acss.org.uk/we-society-podcast/ (accessed 5 April 2024).

Weber, M. 1905[2001]. *The Protestant Ethic and the Spirit of Capitalism*. Abingdon-on-Thames: Routledge.

Weller, S., Davidson, E., Jamieson, L. and Edwards, R. 2023. *BigQual: A Guide to Breadth-and-Depth Analysis*. London: Palgrave MacMillan.

Wetherell, M. and Potter, J. 1992. *Mapping the Language of Racism: Discourse and the Legitimation of Exploitation*. New York: Columbia University Press.

Whiteman, N. 2018. Accounting for ethics: Towards a de-humanised comparative approach. *Qualitative Research*, 18(4): 383–399.

Whyte, W.F. 1955. *Street Corner Society: The Social Structure of an Italian Slum*. Chicago: University of Chicago Press.

Wilde, E.M. and Welch, G.F. 2022. Attention Deficit Hyperactivity Disorder (ADHD) and musical behaviour: The significance of context. *Psychology of Music*, 50(6): 1942–1960.

Wiles, R., Crow, G. and Pain, H. 2011. Innovation in qualitative research methods: A narrative review. *Qualitative Research*, 11(5): 587–604.

Williams, K. and Reid, M. 2023. *Planning Your Dissertation*, 3rd edn. London: Bloomsbury.

Williams, M. 2000. *Science and Social Science: An Introduction*. London: Routledge.

Williams, M., Burnap, P. and Sloan, L. 2017. Towards an ethical framework for publishing Twitter Data into social research: Taking into account users' views, online context and algorithmic estimation. *Sociology*, 51(6): 1149–1168.

Williams, M., Sloan, L. and Brookfield, C., 2017. A tale of two sociologies: Analyzing versus critique in UK sociology. *Sociological Research Online*, 22(4), pp.132–151.

Williams, M.L., Sutherland, A., Roy-Chowdhury, V., Loke, T., Cullen, A., Sloan, L., Burnap, P. and Giannasi, P. 2023. The effect of the Brexit vote on the variation in race and religious hate crimes in England, Wales, Scotland and Northern Ireland. *The British Journal of Criminology: An International Review of Crime and Society*, 63(4): 1003–1023.

Willis, G.B. 2004. *Cognitive Interviewing: A Tool for Improving Questionnaire Design*. London: Sage.

Wilson, C. 2019. *Manage Your Stress*. London: Sage.

Wohl, A.S. 1971. Octavia Hill and the homes of the London poor. *Journal of British Studies*, 10(2): 105–131.

Wong, B. 2023. *Top social media statistics and trends of 2024*. Available at: www.forbes.com/advisor/business/social-media-statistics/ (accessed 26 March 2024).

Woodman, D. and Threadgold, S. 2021. *This is Sociology: A Short Introduction*. London: Sage.

World Values Survey Association. 2020. *World values survey*. Available at: www.worldvaluessurvey.org/wvs.jsp (accessed 26 March 2024).

Wright, S. 2023. Mixed-methods content analysis with ATLAS.ti: Project setup, data preparation, and auto-coding. *Sage Datasets*. https://doi.org/10.4135/9781529629194

Wright Mills, C. 1959. *The Sociological Imagination*. Oxford: Oxford University Press.

Wynne, B. 1995. The public understanding of science. In S. Jasanoff, G.E. Markle, J.C. Petersen and T. Pinch (eds), *The Handbook of Science and Technology Studies*. Thousand Oaks, CA: Sage, pp. 361–388.

YouGov. 2023. *The most popular politicians and political figures*. Available at: https://yougov.co.uk/ratings/politics/popularity/politicians-political-figures/all (accessed 12 December 2023).

Younas, A., Fàbregues, S., Durante, A., Escalante, E.L., Inayat, S. and Ali, P. 2023. Proposing the 'Miracle' narrative framework for providing thick description in qualitative research. *International Journal of Qualitative Methods*, 22. https://doi.org/10.1177/16094069221147162

Yusupova, M. 2023. Coloniality of gender and knowledge: Rethinking Russian masculinities in light of postcolonial and decolonial critiques. *Sociology*, 57(3): 682–699.

Zhang, J. 2020. Influence of parenting costs on second-child fertility anxiety among adults of childbearing age in China: The moderating role of gender. *SAGE Open*, 10(2). https://doi.org/10.1177/2158244020920657

INDEX

Note: Page numbers in italics indicate figures and tables.

abstracts, 21, 39, 66, 218, 240–41
academic journals, 56–58, 62–63, 127, 132
   article structure, *14–15*
   literature reviews, *54*
   research questions, *18–19*
academic writing, 12–15
   back matter, 243–44
   collating chapters, 238–39
   conclusion chapter, 229–34, 235–36
   editing, 247–49
   ethics, 96–97
   findings and analysis chapters, 190–94, *195*
   front matter, 239–43
   introduction chapter, 221–29, 234, 235–36
   literature review chapter, 47–48, 67–70
   methods chapter, 132–44
   plagiarism check, 249–50
   proofreading, 245–47
   research plan, 38–43
acquiescence bias, 110
action research, 123; *see also* participatory action research (PAR)
active note taking, 64–67
Adorno, T., 199
advisors *see* supervisors
alternative hypothesis, 162, *163*
analysis chapter *see* findings and analysis chapters
anonymity, 79, 87–89, 91, 95, 96, 192, 216; *see also* confidentiality
ANOVA, 141, 170, *171*
anxiety, 202, 239, 250–51, 253
appendices, 14, 140, 243–44
argumentation, 194, *195*
artefacts, 112, 124, 174–78
Artificial Intelligence (AI), 58, 59, 171–72, 249
assessment criteria, 244–45, *246*, 251–53; *see also* module handbook/guide
Atkinson, P., 119
audience, 199–201
   blogposts, 214, 215
   executive summaries, 216–17
   oral presentations, 201–2, 203–4, 205–7, 208, *209*

podcasts, 215–16
posters, 211, *212*

back matter, 243–44
Baker, D., 213
Banerjee, A., 7
Becker, L., 204, 206
bias, 110, 162
Big Data, 5, 131–32
Bigfooting research project, 41
   ethics application form, 81, *82*, *83*, *84–85*, *86*, *87*, *88–89*
   interview transcripts, 176–78
   thematic analysis, 180–81
   methodological reflections, 143–44
   research plan, 42–43
biomedical ethics, 76
Blaxter, L., 48
blogs, 201, 214–15
Boolean search terms, 59–60
Bowen, G.A., 183
Braun, V., 179–80
breaching experiments, 115
Brewer, H.R., 131
British Psychology Society (BPS), 6
Brownlie, J., 12
Brumley, C., 216
Burawoy, M., 200
Burnap, P., 12
bystander theory, 7

Callegaro, M., 105
categorical variables, 151, *152*, 165
central tendency, measures of, 157, 158, *159*
ChatGPT, 58, 59, 171, 249
chi-square statistics, 141, 167, 171
child sexual exploitation (CSE), 8
Clarke, A., 187
clustered sampling, 137
co-construction, 127
coding manuals, 113, *114*, 115
cognitive interviewing, 111, 141
communication theory, 200
conclusion chapter, 229–34, 235–36, 252

confidentiality, 79, 85, 91, 192, 241; *see also* anonymity
consent, 11, 77, 86, 87, 95, 140
consent form, 92–93, 243, 244
content analysis, 112–15, 182–83, 241
contents page, 242
continuous variables, 151, 157, 170
control group, 115, 116
convenience sampling, 137
conversation analysis (CA), 176, 178, 184–85; *see also* discourse analysis (DA)
correlation, 168–69
covert observation, 112, 124
covert research, 95
crafted documents, 124
creative methods, 126–27
critical discourse analysis (CDA), 185–86
critical realism, 134
critiquing, 54–55
crosstabulations, 165–67

Darley, J., 7
data
  levels of, 151–52, *153*, 157
  missing, 155
  see also Big Data
data analysis, 10–11, 141
  findings and analysis chapters write up, 190–94, 195
  marking criteria, 252
  qualitative, 171–89
    conversation analysis (CA), 176, 178, 184–85
    discourse analysis (DA), 185–86
    documentary analysis, 183–84
    general qualitative analysis, 173–74
    interpretative phenomenological analysis (IPA), 188
    narrative analysis, 181–82
    qualitative content analysis (QCA), 182–83
    research artefact creation, 174–78
    rhythmanalysis, 187
    semiotic analysis, 186
    sentiment analysis, 188
    situational analysis, 187
    thematic analysis, 179–81
  quantitative, 150–71
    chi-square statistics, 167
    correlation, 168–69
    crosstabulations, 165–67
    data preparation, 152–56
    descriptive statistics, 157–62, *193*
    inferential statistics, 162–64
    levels of data, 151–52, *153*, 157
    multivariate analysis, 171
    T-tests, 169–70

see also secondary data analysis
data collection, 8–10, 11–12, 16–17
  ethics application form, 84–85
  hybrid methods, 130–32
  methods chapter write up, 132–44
  mixed methods, 9–10, 130, 145
  qualitative, 9–10, 16, 118–32
    amount of data, 129–30
    creative methods, 126–27
    documents, 124–25
    focus groups, 122–23, 128
    observational techniques, 123–24
    participatory research, 127
    qualitative interviews, 119–22, 128
    research settings, 128–29
    sensory methods, 127–28
    social media and online research, 125–26
    summary of approaches, *120–21*
  quantitative, 9–10, 17, 102–18
    content analysis, 112–15
    experiments, 115–16
    questionnaires, 103–11
    secondary data analysis, 116–18
    structured observations, 112
    summary of approaches, *103–4*
data extracts, 191–92
data preparation, 152–56
data security, 89
data visualisations, 192–93, 208
debrief sheets, 93
deductive reasoning, 102
deficit model of science communication, 200
degrees of freedom, 167
dependent variable, 162–63, 164, 167
descriptive statistics, 157–62, *193*
dichotomous variables, 155
discourse analysis (DA), 185–86; *see also* conversation analysis (CA)
discussion chapter *see* findings and analysis chapters
dissertation
  benefits, 21
  structure, xvi, 12–14
  submission, 250–51, 254
  see also social science research
documents, 124–25, 191
  content analysis, 112–15
  documentary analysis, 183–84
  qualitative content analysis (QCA), 182–83
  see also sources
Duflo, E., 7

Eales, J., 35
editing, 247–49
Edwards, R., 132
emic research, 127, 142
emotions, 188

INDEX

empirical research, 16, 134
epistemology, 134
ethical sensitivities, 86–87, 94, 141–42, 252
ethics, 76–78
   anonymity, 79, 87–89, 91, 95, 96, 192, 216
   confidentiality, 79, 85, 91, 192, 241
   content analysis, 114
   ethically challenging research, 95–96
   harmful research, 77, 78–79
   participant recruitment, 139
   personal, 77, 93–94
   procedural, 77, 80–93
      ethics application form, 80–89
      forward facing documents, 90–93
   secondary data, 97–98
   transcription, 175
   of writing up, 96–97
ethics application form, 80–89, *see also* consent form
ethics committees, 80
ethnography, 124
ethnomethodology, 184
etic research, 127, 142
executive summaries, 201, 216–18
experimental group, 115, 116
experiments, 115–16

Fernandez, F., 54
field experiments, 115
fieldnotes, 179, 191–92
findings and analysis chapters, 190–94, 195
Fleetwood-Smith, R., 126
focus groups, 17, 79, 122–23, 128, 175, 191
formal gatekeepers, 139–40
formatting, 246–47
foreshadowed problems, 44; *see also* research topic
forward facing documents, 90–93
found documents, 124–25
Frank, A., 182
freedom, degrees of, 167
front matter, 239–43

Gantt charts, 29–30, 37, 41
Gardiner, A., 214
gatekeepers, 11, 83, 139–40
gender, 96, 227–28, 241
gender-neutral language, 250
generative Artificial Intelligence (AI), 59, 172, 249
'golden thread', 56
Goode, E., 134
Google Scholar, 58, 59
governmental data sources, *117*
group interviews, 122

Hallett, S., 8
Hammersley, M., 123
harmful research, 77, 78–79
Hedgecoe, A., 80
Herbst-Debby, A., 54
hermeneutics, 188
Hirsch, D., 7
histograms, 160, 161
Horkheimer, M., 199
Hudson, J., 9
Humby, C., 131
Humphreys, L., 95
hybrid methods, 130–32; *see also* mixed methods
Hypodermic syringe model, 200
hypotheses, 162–63, 164

icons *see* semiotic analysis
in situ ethics *see* personal ethics
independent variables, 162–63, 164, 167
inductive reasoning, 103, 118
inferential statistics, 162–64
informal gatekeepers, 139–40
informed consent, 77, 95; *see also* consent
insiders, 142
Internet, 12, 105, 125–26
interpretative phenomenological analysis (IPA), 188
interpretivism, 118–19, 134
intertextuality, 125, 184
interval variables, 151–52
interviews, 119–22, 128, 176–78, 188, 191, 192; *see also* cognitive interviewing; transcription
introduction chapter, 221–29, 234, 235–36

Jefferson Transcription System, 176, 184
journal articles
   literature reviews, *54*
   peer-review, 56
   research questions, *18–19*
   structure, *14–15*
judgemental sampling, 137–38

Kanban boards, 30–31, 37, 41
Kinkaid, E., 216
Kremer, M., 7
Kruskal Wallis test, 170

Lasswell, H., 199
Latané, B., 7
Lefebvre, H., 187
Lennon, J., 229
Lewis, J., 187
literature reviews, 47–49, 223
   editing, 71–72
   note taking, 64–67

purpose, 50–52
sources, 56–64, 72
structure and selectivity, 52–56
types of, 49–50
writing up, 67–70
London School of Economics (LSE) blog, 214
Lyon, D., 127, 187

Magic Bullet model, 200
Manhattan Project, 76
Mann-Whitney U test, 170
marking criteria *see* assessment criteria
Marmot, M., 7
mathematics, 7
mathematics research project, 81–82, 83, 84, 85, 86, 88, 89
mean, 157, 158, 169
measures of central tendency, 157, 158, *159*
measures of spread, 157, 158
median, 157, 158
medical malpractice, 76
medical research, 116
meta-analysis literature reviews, 49
meta data, 153–54
meta-synthesis literature reviews, 49
metaphors *see* semiotic analysis
methodological divide, 3
methodological positioning, 133–34
methodological reflections, 142–44
methods chapter, 132–44
Metzler, K., 131
Microsoft Excel, 29, 103, 150, 158, *159*, 165, 169
Microsoft Word
  back matter, 243
  blogposts, 214
  creating research artefacts, 175
  front matter, 242
  note taking, 64, 66, 67
  oral presentations, 202, 205
  proofreading, 247
missing data, 155
mixed methods, 9–10, 130, 145, 158; *see also* hybrid methods
mode, 157, 158
module handbook/guide, 27, 36, 244–45; *see also* assessment criteria
Mollett, A., 215
Moss, K., 186
multi-method research, 130; *see also* hybrid methods; mixed methods
multimodality, 128
multivariate analysis, 171

narrative analysis, 181–82
narrative literature reviews, 50
national census surveys, 138

National Ethics Application Form (NEAF), Australia, 80
National Survey of Sexual Attitudes and Lifestyles, 2010-2012, 152, 153–56
  correlation, 168–69
  crosstabulations, 165–67
  descriptive statistics, 158, *160*, 161
  inferential statistics, 162–64
  T-tests, 169–70
nominal data, 152, 157
non-participant observation, 123
non-random sampling techniques, 137–38
normal distribution, 158, 160–62
normative research, 4
note taking, 64–67
null hypothesis, 162, 164, 167

observational techniques, 123–24
observations
  covert, 112, 124
  non-participant, 123
  overt, 112, 124
  participant, 123
  structured, 112
one-tailed tests, 163–64
online data archives, *117*
online data collection, 12
online interviews, 128
online journals, 127
online presentations, 205, 207; *see also* blogs
online questionnaires, 105
online research, 95–96, 125–26
online survey software, 12, 105, 150, 152
ontology, 134
Oppenheimer, R.J., 76
oral presentations, 201–10
  delivery, 204–7, 219
  slides, 202–4, 207–10
  structure, 202–4
ordinal data, 152, 157
originality, 33
orthogonal transcripts, 176
outsiders, 142
overt observations, 112, 124

p-values (probability values), 164
paraphrasing, 67–68, 70
participant information sheet (PIS), 90–92
participant observation, 123
participatory action research (PAR), 127
participatory research, 127
passive note taking, *65*
Pearson's Correlation Coefficient, 168, 169
peer-reviews, 56–58
personal ethics, 77, 93–94
phenomenology, 188
pilot studies, 36

piloting, 105, 111, 140–41
plagiarism, 69–70, 249–50
planning, 26
   module handbook/guide, 27, 36
   research plan, 38–43, 44–45
   research topic, 32–36 (*see also* foreshadowed problems)
   supervisory meetings, 36–37
   time-management tools, 29–31, 37
   timetabling, 27–28
podcasts, 201, 215–16
Popper, K., 102
population, 135
positivism, 134
posters, 201, 210–13
Powell, C., 26
pragmatism, 134
pre-testing, 115
presentation of research, 197–219
   and audience, 199–201
   blogs, 201, 214–15
   executive summaries, 201, 216–18
   formats, 198–99
   oral presentations, 201–10
     delivery, 204–7, 219
     slides, 202–4, 207–10
     structure, 202–4
   podcasts, 201, 215–16
   posters, 201, 210–13
primary data, 10
probability values (p-values), 164
procedural ethics, 77, 80–93
   ethics application form, 80–89
   forward facing documents, 90–93
professional ethics *see* procedural ethics
pronouns, 250
proofreading, 245–47
pseudonyms, 79, 88, 96, 192
psychology, 6, 9
Public Understanding of Science (PUS), 200
purposive sampling, 137–38

Q methodology, 10, 131
qualitative content analysis (QCA), 182–83
qualitative data analysis, 171–89
   conversation analysis (CA), 176, 178, 184–85
   discourse analysis (DA), 185–86
   documentary analysis, 183–84
   findings and analysis chapters, 190–92
   general qualitative analysis, 173–74
   interpretative phenomenological analysis (IPA), 188
   narrative analysis, 181–82
   qualitative content analysis (QCA), 182–83
   research artefact creation, 174–78
   rhythmanalysis, 187
   semiotic analysis, 186
   sentiment analysis, 188
   situational analysis, 187
   thematic analysis, 179–81
qualitative data collection, 9–10, 16, 118–32
   amount of data, 129–30
   creative methods, 126–27
   documents, 124–25
   focus groups, 122–23, 128
   observational techniques, 123–24
   participatory research, 127
   qualitative interviews, 119–22, 128
   research settings, 128–29
   sensory methods, 127–28
   social media and online research, 125–26
   summary of approaches, *120–21*
qualitative interviews, 119–22, 128
quantitative data analysis, 150–71
   chi-square statistics, 167
   correlation, 168–69
   crosstabulations, 165–67
   data preparation, 152–56
   descriptive statistics, 157–62, *193*
   findings and analysis chapters, 190–91, 192–93
   inferential statistics, 162–64
   levels of data, 151–52, *153*, 157
   multivariate analysis, 171
   T-tests, 169–70
quantitative data collection, 9–10, 17, 102–18
   content analysis, 112–15
   experiments, 115–16
   questionnaires, 103–11
   secondary data analysis, 116–18
   structured observations, 112
   summary of approaches, *103–4*
quasi experiments, 115
questionnaire distribution modes, *106–7*
questionnaires, 103–11
quota sampling, 138
quotes, verbatim, 70, 191

random sampling techniques, 136–37
range, 157
rapport building, 142–43
ratio variables, 151
realism, 134
recoding, 155
reference lists, 13, 14, 21, 35, 40–41, 43, 69–70, 243
Reissman, C.K., 182
representations, 176, 186, 228
research *see* social science research
research artefacts, 112, 124, 174–78
research bargains, 128, 140
research context, 39, 42
research ethics *see* ethics

research impact, 40, 43
research methods, 40, 43; *see also* data analysis; data collection
research overview, 39, 42
research participants
  anonymity, 79, 87–89, 91, 95, 96, 192
  confidentiality, 79, 91, 192
  ethics application form, 83, 87–89
  experimental group, 116
  harmful research, 78–79
  informed consent, 77
  participant information sheet (PIS), 90–92
  participatory research, 127
  payment, 94
  podcasts, 216
  sampling and recruitment, 135–39
  verbatim quotes, 191
research plan, 38–43, 44–45
research presentation, 197–219
  and audience, 199–201
  blogs, 201, 214–15
  executive summaries, 201, 216–18
  formats, 198–99
  oral presentations, 201–10
    delivery, 204–7, 219
    slides, 202–4, 207–10
    structure, 202–4
  podcasts, 201, 215–16
  posters, 201, 210–13
research project *see* dissertation
research questions, 15–20
  and conclusion chapter, 232
  and ethics application form, 82
  and literature reviews, 49
  and qualitative data analysis, 173
  and research plan, 39–40, 42, 45
  and submission, 244
research requirements, 244–45; *see also* assessment criteria; module handbook/guide
research settings, 11, 85, 96, 128–29, 227–28; *see also* research sites
research sites, 11, 85, 139; *see also* research settings
research topic, 32–36, 81–82; *see also* foreshadowed problems
results chapter *see* findings and analysis chapters
rhythmanalysis, 187
Ridley, D., 48
Rintel, S., 185
Rossi, T., 211
Rowe, N., 211
running frequencies, 154
Rush, D., 194

Sacks, H., 184
Sage Campus, 35

Sage Foundations, 35, 178, 185, 186, 187, 189
Sage Methods Datasets, 35, 178, 186, 188–89
sampling, 135–39
sampling frame, 135–36
SANDS, 34
Saunders, B., 79
Scott, J., 125
search terms, 59–61
secondary data, 10–11, 97–98
  governmental data sources, *117*
  international sources of, *10*
  online data archives, *117*
secondary data analysis, 10–11, 116–18, 153
secondary data collection, 11–12
secondary research artefacts, 174
selectivity, 50, 55, 173, 202, 204, 219
self-plagiarism, 69–70, 249
semi-structured interviews, 119, 122, 188
semiotic analysis, 186
sensory methods, 127–28
sentiment analysis, 188
settings, 11, 85, 96, 128–29, 227–28; *see also* sites
significance of research, 40, 43
signs *see* semiotic analysis
simple random sampling, 136
Singapore Statement on Research Integrity, 80
sites, 11, 85, 139; *see also* settings
situational analysis, 187
situational ethics *see* personal ethics
slides, 202–4, 207–10
smellwalks, 128
snowball sampling, 138
social media, 12, 43, 95–96, 114, 125–26, 131, 227; *see also* blogs
social science journal articles, structure, 14–15
social science research, 2–5
  benefits, 6–8, 21
  structure, 12–14
social science researchers, 5–6
social science students, 3–4
social scientific imagination, 4
sociological imagination, 4
sociology, 3
software packages, 35, 67, 172, 175, 243, 249; *see also* online survey software; statistical software packages
sources
  governmental data, *117*
  international sources of secondary data, *10*
  literature reviews, 56–64, 72
  online data archives, *117*
Spearman's Rho Correlation Coefficient, 168, 169
Spivak, G.C., 185

spread, measures of, 157, 158
SPSS, 8, 35, *159*, 161, 165, 166, 167, 168–69, 169–70
SQ3R, 66–67
standard deviation, 157–58
Stanley, L., 184
Stata, *159*, 161, 165, 166, 167, 168, 169, 170
statistical significance, 171
statistical software packages, 103, 150, 152, 157, *159*; *see also* Microsoft Excel; SPSS; Stata
statistics
  descriptive, 157–62, *193*
  inferential, 162–64
Stephenson, W., 131
storytelling, 181–82
stratified sampling, 137
structured observations, 112
student numbers, 3–4
subheadings, 190–91
submission, 250–51, 254
substantive significance, 171
supervisors, 245, 250–51
supervisory meetings, 36–37
survey weights, 154
symbols *see* semiotic analysis
systematic literature reviews, 49–50
systematic sampling, 137

T-tests, 169–70, 171
table of contents, 242
tables, 192–93
Taylor, S.J.A., 185
Tearoom Trade (Humphreys), 95
Testa, A., 54
thematic analysis, 179–81
thesis *see* dissertation
thick descriptions, 123–24
Thomas, G., 96
time-management tools, 29–31, 37, 41
timetabling, 27–28
title, 38–39, 42, 239–40
title page, 239
transcription, 174–78
transparency, 77
Twitter (now X), 12, 95, 132
two-tailed tests, 163

univariate analysis, *160*
unstructured interviews, 119, 122

Vacchelli, E., 126–27
Van Dijk, T.A., 185–86
variables, 116, 154, *156*
  categorical, 151, 152, 165
  continuous, 151, 157, 170
  dependent, 162–63, 164, 167
  dichotomous, 155
  independent, 162–63, 164, 167
  interval, 151–52
  ratio, 151
Vassollo, P., 218
verbatim quotes, 70, 191
videos, 209
Vigren, M., 187
visualisation of data, 192–93, 208
voice memos, 128
vulnerability, 78

X (formerly Twitter), 12, 95, 132

weighting variables, 154
Weller, S., 132
Whitehall studies, 7
Wikipedia, 58
Williams, M., 95
word counts, 247–49
Wright Mills, C., 4, 185, 230
Wright, S., 183
writing up, 12–15
  back matter, 243–44
  collating chapters, 238–39
  conclusion chapter, 229–34, 235–36
  editing, 247–49
  ethics of, 96–97
  findings and analysis chapters, 190–94, 195
  front matter, 239–43
  introduction chapter, 221–29, 234, 235–36
  literature reviews, 47–48, 67–70
  methods chapter, 132–44
  plagiarism check, 249–50
  proofreading, 245–47
  research plan, 38–43